Visual Basic for Students

Visit the *Visual Basic 2008* Companion Website at **www.pearsoned.co.uk/bell** to find valuable **student** learning material including:

- Programs from the book
- Instructions for how to run VB programs

We work with leading authors to develop the
strongest educational materials in computing,
bringing cutting-edge thinking and best
learning practice to a global market.

Under a range of well-known imprints, including
Addison-Wesley, we craft high-quality print and
electronic publications which help readers to understand
and apply their content, whether studying or at work.

To find out more about the complete range of our
publishing, please visit us on the World Wide Web at:
www.pearsoned.co.uk

Douglas Bell and Mike Parr

Visual Basic 2008
for Students

ADDISON-WESLEY

An imprint of Pearson Education

Harlow, England • London • New York • Boston • San Francisco • Toronto
Sydney • Tokyo • Singapore • Hong Kong • Seoul • Taipei • New Delhi
Cape Town • Madrid • Mexico City • Amsterdam • Munich • Paris • Milan

Pearson Education Limited
Edinburgh Gate
Harlow
Essex CM20 2JE
England

and Associated Companies throughout the world

Visit us on the World Wide Web at:
www.pearsoned.co.uk

First published as *Visual Basic .Net for Students* 2003
Second edition published as *Visual Basic 2005 for Students* 2008
Third edition published 2009

© Pearson Education Limited 2003, 2009

The rights of Douglas Bell and Michael Parr to be identified as authors of this work have been asserted by them in accordance with the Copyright, Designs and Patents Act 1988.

All rights reserved. No part of this publication may be reproduced, stored in a retrieval system, or transmitted in any form or by any means, electronic, mechanical, photocopying, recording or otherwise, without either the prior written permission of the publisher or a licence permitting restricted copying in the United Kingdom issued by the Copyright Licensing Agency Ltd, Saffron House, 6–10 Kirby Street, London EC1N 8TS.

All trademarks used herein are the property of their respective owners. The use of any trademark in this text does not vest in the author or publisher any trademark ownership rights in such trademarks, nor does the use of such trademarks imply any affiliation with or endorsement of this book by such owners.

Microsoft product screenshots reprinted with permission from Microsoft Corporation.

ISBN: 978-0-273-72402-5

British Library Cataloguing-in-Publication Data
A catalogue record for this book is available from the British Library

Library of Congress Cataloging-in-Publication Data
Bell, Doug, 1944–
  Visual Basic 2008 for students / Douglas Bell and Mike Parr. – 3rd ed.
      p. cm.
  Includes bibliographical references and index.
  ISBN 978-0-273-72402-5 (pbk. : alk. paper) 1. BASIC (Computer program language) 2. Microsoft Visual BASIC. I. Parr, Mike, 1949– II. Title.
  QA76.73.B3B4538 2009
  005.2'762—dc22
                                                                        2008052903

10 9 8 7 6 5 4 3 2
13 12 11 10

Typeset in 9.75/12pt Galliard by 35
Printed in Great Britain by Henry Ling Limited, at the Dorset Press, Dorchester, DT1 1HD

Contents

Detailed contents		*page* vii
Preface		xviii
1.	The background to Visual Basic	1
2.	The VB development environment	7
3.	Introductory graphics	25
4.	Variables and calculations	38
5.	Methods and arguments	60
6.	Using objects	90
7.	Selection – `If` and `Select`	109
8.	Repetition – `For`, `While` and `Do`	136
9.	Debugging	157
10.	Writing classes	168
11.	Inheritance	191
12.	Calculations	206
13.	Data structures – list boxes and lists	222
14.	Arrays	239
15.	Arrays – two-dimensional	261
16.	String manipulation	274
17.	Exceptions	290
18.	Files	305
19.	Console programs	328
20.	Object-oriented design	342
21.	Program style	363
22.	Testing	376
23.	Interfaces	390

24.	Polymorphism	396
25.	Databases	403

Appendices 421
Bibliography 428
Index 429

Detailed contents

	Preface	*page* xviii
1.	**The background to Visual Basic**	1
	The history of Visual Basic	1
	The Microsoft .NET framework	2
	What is a program?	2
	Programming principles	4
	Programming pitfalls	5
	Summary	5
	Exercises	5
	Answers to self-test questions	6
2.	**The VB development environment**	7
	Introduction	7
	Installation and configuration	7
	Creating a first program	8
	Controls at design-time	13
	Events and the `Button` control	15
	Opening an existing project	17
	Documenting property settings	17
	Program errors	18
	Editor facilities	18
	The message box	20
	Help	21
	Programming principles	21
	Programming pitfalls	21
	Grammar spot	22

	New language elements	22
	New IDE facilities	22
	Summary	22
	Exercises	22
	Answers to self-test questions	24
3.	**Introductory graphics**	**25**
	Introduction	25
	Objects, methods, properties, classes – an analogy	25
	A first drawing	26
	Creating the program	27
	The graphics coordinate system	28
	Explanation of the program	29
	Methods for drawing	30
	Colours	32
	The sequence concept and statements	34
	Adding meaning with comments	34
	Programming principles	35
	Programming pitfalls	35
	Grammar spot	35
	New language elements	35
	Summary	36
	Exercises	36
	Answers to self-test questions	37
4.	**Variables and calculations**	**38**
	Introduction	38
	The nature of `Integer`	39
	The nature of `Double`	39
	Declaring variables	40
	The assignment statement	43
	Calculations and operators	43
	The arithmetic operators	45
	The `Mod` operator	47
	Strings and numbers: the `&` operator	48
	Text boxes and labels	50
	The `InputBox`	53
	Converting between numbers	53
	The role of expressions	54
	Programming principles	55
	Programming pitfalls	55
	Grammar spot	55
	New language elements	56

	New IDE facilities	56
	Summary	56
	Exercises	56
	Answers to self-test questions	58
5.	**Methods and arguments**	**60**
	Introduction	60
	Writing your own methods	61
	A first method	61
	Calling a method	63
	Passing arguments	63
	Parameters and arguments	65
	A triangle method	66
	Local variables	69
	Name clashes	70
	Event-handling methods	71
	Function methods and results	71
	Building on methods	74
	Passing arguments by reference	77
	References – an example	78
	References: a `Swap` method	80
	`Me` and objects	81
	Overloading	82
	Passing objects to methods	83
	Programming principles	84
	Programming pitfalls	84
	Grammar spot	84
	New language elements	85
	New IDE facilities	85
	Summary	85
	Exercises	86
	Answers to self-test questions	88
6.	**Using objects**	**90**
	Introduction	90
	Instance variables	90
	The form constructor	93
	The `TrackBar` class	95
	`Imports` and namespaces	97
	Members, methods and properties	98
	The `Random` class	99
	The `Timer` class	102
	Programming principles	105

	Programming pitfalls	105
	Grammar spot	105
	New language elements	105
	New IDE facilities	106
	Summary	106
	Exercises	106
	Answers to self-test questions	108

7. Selection – `If` and `Select` — 109
- Introduction — 109
- The `If` statement — 110
- Comparison operators — 114
- `And, Or, Not` — 115
- Nested `If`s and `ElseIf` — 118
- `Select` — 122
- Boolean variables — 126
- Programming principles — 129
- Programming pitfalls — 129
- Grammar spot — 129
- New language elements — 130
- Summary — 131
- Exercises — 131
- Answers to self-test questions — 134

8. Repetition – `For`, `While` and `Do` — 136
- Introduction — 136
- `For` — 137
- `While` — 140
- `And, Or, Not` — 144
- `Do...Loop` — 145
- Nested loops — 146
- Combining control structures — 148
- Programming principles — 150
- Programming pitfalls — 151
- Grammar spot — 151
- New language elements — 152
- Summary — 152
- Exercises — 152
- Answers to self-test questions — 155

9. Debugging — 157
- Introduction — 157
- Using the debugger — 159
- Case study in debugging — 161

	Common errors	162
	Programming pitfalls	166
	New IDE facilities	166
	Summary	167
	Exercise	167
10.	**Writing classes**	**168**
	Introduction	168
	Designing a class	169
	Private variables	171
	Public methods	172
	Properties	174
	Method or property?	177
	Constructors	178
	Multiple constructors	178
	Private methods	179
	Operations on objects	180
	Object destruction	181
	`Shared` methods and properties	182
	Programming principles	183
	Programming pitfalls	185
	Grammar spot	186
	New language elements	186
	Summary	187
	Exercises	187
	Answers to self-test questions	189
11.	**Inheritance**	**191**
	Introduction	191
	Using inheritance	192
	`Protected`	193
	Additional items	194
	Overriding	195
	Class diagrams	196
	Inheritance at work	197
	`MyBase`	197
	Constructors	198
	Abstract classes	200
	Programming principles	201
	Programming pitfalls	203
	New language elements	203
	Summary	203
	Exercises	204
	Answers to self-test questions	205

12. Calculations — 206
- Introduction — 206
- Literals — 207
- Formatting numbers — 207
- Library mathematical functions and constants — 209
- Constants — 210
- Case study – money — 211
- Case study – iteration — 213
- Graphs — 213
- Exceptions — 216
- Programming principles — 218
- Programming pitfalls — 218
- Summary — 218
- Exercises — 218
- Answers to self-test questions — 221

13. Data structures – list boxes and lists — 222
- Introduction — 222
- Lists — 223
- Adding items to a list — 223
- The length of a list — 224
- Indices — 225
- Removing items from a list — 227
- Inserting items within a list — 227
- Lookup — 227
- Arithmetic on a list box — 229
- `For Each` — 230
- Searching — 231
- Using a list – generics — 232
- Methods and properties of lists — 233
- Lists of objects — 235
- Programming principles — 236
- Programming pitfalls — 237
- New language elements — 237
- Summary — 237
- Exercises — 238
- Answers to self-test questions — 238

14. Arrays — 239
- Introduction — 239
- Creating an array — 241
- Indices — 241
- The length of an array — 243
- Passing arrays as parameters — 244

	The `For Each` statement	245
	Using constants	246
	Initializing an array	247
	A sample program	248
	Lookup	250
	Searching	250
	Arrays of objects	252
	Programming principles	254
	Programming pitfalls	254
	Grammar spot	255
	Summary	255
	Exercises	255
	Answers to self-test questions	259
15.	**Arrays – two-dimensional**	**261**
	Introduction	261
	Declaring an array	262
	Indices	263
	The size of an array	264
	Passing arrays as parameters	265
	Constants	265
	Initializing an array	266
	A sample program	267
	`For Each` statement	269
	Programming principles	269
	Programming pitfalls	270
	Summary	270
	Exercises	270
	Answers to self-test questions	273
16.	**String manipulation**	**274**
	Introduction	274
	Using strings – a recap	274
	String indexing	276
	The characters within strings	276
	Comparing strings	276
	The `String` class methods and properties	277
	Amending strings	277
	Examining strings	279
	An example of string processing	283
	Case study – Ask Frasier	285
	Programming principles	287
	Programming pitfalls	287
	Grammar spot	287

	New language elements	288
	New IDE facilities	288
	Summary	288
	Exercises	288
	Answer to self-test question	289
17.	**Exceptions**	**290**
	Introduction	290
	The jargon of exceptions	292
	A `Try-Catch` example	292
	Using the exception object	295
	Classifying exceptions	295
	Multiple `Catch` blocks	297
	The search for a catcher	297
	Throwing – an introduction	299
	Handling – some possibilities	300
	`Finally`	301
	Programming principles	301
	Programming pitfalls	302
	Grammar spot	302
	New language elements	302
	New IDE facilities	302
	Summary	303
	Exercises	303
	Answers to self-test questions	304
18.	**Files**	**305**
	Introduction	305
	The essentials of streams	306
	The `StreamReader` and `StreamWriter` classes	306
	File output	307
	File input	308
	File searching	311
	Files and exceptions	313
	Message boxes and dialogs	315
	Using file dialogs	316
	Creating a menu	318
	The `Directory` class	321
	Programming principles	324
	Programming pitfalls	324
	Grammar spot	324
	New language elements	324
	New IDE facilities	325
	Summary	325

	Exercises	325
	Answers to self-test questions	326
19.	**Console programs**	**328**
	Introduction	328
	A first console program	329
	The command prompt: `cd` and `dir`	330
	The `dir` command	331
	The `cd` command	332
	Ways of running programs	332
	Classes in console applications	333
	Command-line arguments	334
	Scripting and output redirection	336
	Scripting and batch files	337
	Programming principles	338
	Programming pitfalls	338
	Grammar spot	338
	New language elements	339
	New IDE facilities	339
	Summary	339
	Exercises	339
	Answers to self-test questions	340
20.	**Object-oriented design**	**342**
	Introduction	342
	The design problem	343
	Identifying objects, methods and properties	343
	Case study in design	348
	Looking for reuse	353
	Composition or inheritance?	354
	Guidelines for class design	358
	Summary	360
	Exercises	360
	Answers to self-test questions	362
21.	**Program style**	**363**
	Introduction	363
	Program layout	364
	Comments	365
	Using constants	366
	Classes	367
	Nested `If`s	368
	Nested loops	370
	Complex conditions	372

Documentation 373
Programming pitfalls 374
Summary 374
Exercises 374

22. Testing 376
Introduction 376
Program specifications 377
Exhaustive testing 378
Black box (functional) testing 378
White box (structural) testing 381
Inspections and walkthroughs 383
Stepping through code 384
Formal verification 384
Incremental development 384
Programming principles 385
Summary 385
Exercises 386
Answers to self-test questions 387

23. Interfaces 390
Introduction 390
Interfaces for design 390
Interfaces and interoperability 393
Programming principles 394
Programming pitfalls 394
New language elements 394
Summary 394
Exercises 395

24. Polymorphism 396
Introduction 396
Polymorphism in action 397
Programming principles 400
Programming pitfalls 401
New language elements 401
Summary 401
Exercises 402

25. Databases 403
Introduction 403
The elements of a database 403
The SQL language – introduction 405
The VB database classes 406

Adding a data connection to Visual Basic	408
Example 1: creating a `BindingNavigator` program	409
Example 2: a `DataGridView` program	411
Example 3: SQL example	414
Programming principles	418
Programming pitfalls	419
Grammar spot	419
New language elements	419
New IDE facilities	419
Summary	419
Exercises	420
Answers to self-test questions	420

Appendices

A	Selected library components	421
B	Keywords	427

Bibliography   428

Index   429

Supporting resources
Visit **www.pearsoned.co.uk/bell** to find valuable online resources

Companion Website for students
- Programs from the book

For instructors
- Guidance on using this book for your course

For more information please contact your local Pearson Education sales representative or visit **www.pearsoned.co.uk/bell**

Preface

● This book is for novices

If you have never done any programming before – if you are a complete novice – this book is for you. This book assumes no prior knowledge of programming. It starts from scratch. It is written in a simple, direct style for maximum clarity. It is aimed at first level students at universities and colleges, but it is also suitable for novices studying alone.

● Why Visual Basic?

Visual Basic is arguably one of the best programming languages to learn and use in the 21st century because:

- Visual Basic is one of the most widely-used programming languages in the world today.
- Object-oriented languages are the latest and most successful approach to programming. Visual Basic 2008 is completely object-oriented from the ground up.
- Visual Basic 2008 is a completely general-purpose language. Anything that C++, Java, etc., can do, so can Visual Basic.
- Visual Basic 2008 is a simple language and most of its functionality is provided by pieces of program held in a comprehensive library.

● You will need

To learn to program you need a PC running a recent version of Windows and the software that allows you to prepare and run Visual Basic 2008 programs. There are two versions of the software:

- Visual Basic 2008 Express (for Visual Basic alone) provided with this book, and
- Visual Studio 2008 (a more fulsome package).

How is Visual Basic 2008 different from earlier versions of Visual Basic?

Visual Basic 2008 is a fully-fledged object-oriented language, supporting encapsulation, single inheritance and polymorphism. It is an elegant and consistent language. This makes it easier to learn, easier to use and programs more robust. In addition it encourages the use of good programming style.

Here is the recent history of Visual Basic:

- Visual Basic 6   not object oriented
- Visual Basic .Net   object oriented
                         incompatible with Visual Basic 6
- Visual Basic 2005   introduced generics (see chapter 13)
                         simpler development environment
- Visual Basic 2008   minor changes to the development environment
                         no other changes that affect this book

The approach of this book

We explain how to use objects early in this book. Our approach is to start with the ideas of variables, assignment and methods, then introduce using objects created from library classes. Next we explain how to use control structures for selection and looping. Then comes the treatment of how to write your own classes.

We wanted to make sure that the fun element of programming was paramount, so we use graphics right from the start. We think graphics is fun, interesting and clearly demonstrates all the important principles of programming. But we haven't ignored programs that input and output text – they are also included.

The programs we present use many of the features of graphical user interfaces (GUIs), such as buttons and text boxes. But we also explain how to write console programs.

We introduce new ideas carefully, one at a time rather than all at once. So, for example, there is a single chapter on writing methods. We introduce simple ideas early and more sophisticated ideas later on.

What's included?

This book explains the fundamental ideas of programming:

- variables;
- assignment;
- input and output using a GUI;

- calculation;
- repetition;
- selection between alternatives.

It explains how to use numbers and character strings. Arrays are also described. These are all topics that are fundamental, whatever kind of programming you do. This book also thoroughly explains the object-oriented aspects of programming – using objects, writing classes, methods and properties, and using library classes. We also look at some of the more sophisticated aspects of object-oriented programming including inheritance, polymorphism and interfaces.

What's not included?

This book confines itself to the essentials of Visual Basic 2008. It does not explain all the bits and pieces, the bells and whistles. Thus the reader is freed from unnecessary detail and can concentrate on mastering Visual Basic and programming in general.

UML

The Unified Modeling Language (UML) is the current mainstream notation for describing programs. We use elements of UML selectively, where appropriate, throughout this book.

Applications

Computers are used in many different applications and this book uses examples from all areas including:

- games;
- information processing;
- scientific calculations.

The reader can choose to concentrate on those application areas of interest and ignore other areas.

Exercises are good for you

If you were to read this book time and again until you could recite it backwards, you still wouldn't be able to write programs. The practical work of writing programs is vital to becoming fluent and confident at programming.

There are exercises for the reader at the end of each chapter. Please do some of them to enhance your ability to program.

There are also short self-test questions throughout the text, so that you can check you have understood things properly. The answers are given at the end of each chapter.

Have fun

Programming is creative and interesting, particularly in Visual Basic. Please have fun!

Visit our website

The website includes:

- the text of all the programs in this book;
- additional resources for instructors.

Our website can be reached via the Pearson Education website at: www.pearsoned.co.uk/bell

Changes for this edition

The latest version of Visual Basic is called Visual Basic 2008. This book uses the best of what is new in the 2008 version. We have not included every new feature, because our judgment is that some of them are not appropriate in a book aimed at novices.

The changes from the previous edition are mainly in Chapter 2, The VB Development Environment, which is changed to describe Visual Basic 2008.

The background to Visual Basic

This chapter explains:

- how and why Visual Basic came into being;
- what is novel about it;
- about Microsoft's .NET framework;
- about the introductory concepts of programming.

● The history of Visual Basic

A computer program is a series of instructions that are obeyed by a computer. The point of the instructions is to carry out a task – e.g. play a game, send an e-mail, etc. The instructions are written in a particular style: they must conform to the rules of the programming language we choose. There are hundreds of programming languages, but only a few have made an impact and become widely used.

In 1963 Kemeney and Kurtz introduced a language called BASIC. In a rather contrived way, this was said to stand for Beginner's All-purpose Symbolic Instruction Code, but the main point was that it was designed for beginners, not for programming experts.

Around 1975, the micro revolution happened, when the earlier invention of the microchip made it possible for an individual to afford a 'personal' computer. But the early ones were still hard to program – you had to be an expert. Then came the breakthrough: Bill Gates and Paul Allen produced a version of BASIC for the personal computer. They then went on to form Microsoft.

Of course, Microsoft's major product turned out to be their Windows operating system, supplied on most computers. Unfortunately, it was very difficult to write programs to run under Windows, until Microsoft introduced an updated BASIC, named Visual Basic, in 1991. It became possible for inexperienced programmers to write programs for Windows which manipulated buttons, scroll bars, etc. Versions of Visual Basic have progressed until version 6, which (at the time of writing) is still in use. It is one of the most popular languages in the world.

The Microsoft .NET framework

In 2002, Microsoft went beyond bringing out slightly enhanced versions of their software: there was no Visual Basic 7 following on from version 6. Instead, they introduced a major new product, named the .NET framework. This is pronounced 'dot net'.

Since the inception of the product, minor changes were made. This book uses the 2008 edition.

The main features are:

- It comes with the programming languages Visual Basic .NET, C# ('C sharp'), and C++ ('C plus-plus').
- It has facilities which help programmers to create interactive websites, such as those used for e-commerce. Microsoft sees the Internet as crucial, hence the name .NET.
- There is the possibility of .NET being available for other operating systems, not only Microsoft Windows.
- It lets us build software from components (*objects*) that can be spread over a network.

For our purposes, the main point is that it is a new version of Visual Basic. This is referred to as Visual Basic .NET, and we will refer to it as simply VB. It is a major change from VB6, and is fully in line with the modern programming trend of *object-oriented programming* (OOP), which is a major part of this book.

What of the other languages? Yes, you can use C# and C++ to write software, and many experienced programmers will choose this path. However, VB is considerably simpler for beginners, while still having powerful facilities.

So, when you learn VB you will learn not only the detail of the language but also the technique of OOP.

What is a program?

In this section we try to give the reader some impression of what a program is. One way to understand is by using analogies with recipes, musical scores and knitting patterns. Even the instructions on a bottle of hair shampoo are a simple program:

```
wet hair
apply shampoo
massage shampoo into hair
rinse
```

This program is a list of instructions for a human being, but it does demonstrate one important aspect of a computer program: a program is a sequence of instructions that is obeyed, starting at the first instruction and going on from one to the next until the sequence is complete. A recipe, musical score and a knitting pattern are similar; they constitute a list of instructions that are obeyed in sequence. In the case of a knitting pattern, knitting machines exist which are fed with a program of instructions, which they then carry out (or *execute*). This is what a computer is – it is a machine that automatically obeys a sequence of instructions, a *program*. (In fact, if we make an error in the instructions, the computer is likely to do the wrong task.) The set of instructions that are available for a computer to obey typically include:

- input a number;
- input some characters (letters and digits);
- output some characters;
- do a calculation;
- output a number;
- output some graphical image to the screen;
- respond to a button on the screen being clicked by the mouse.

The job of programming is one of selecting from this list those instructions that will carry out the required task. These instructions are written in a specialized language called a *programming language*. VB is one of many such languages. Learning to program means learning about the facilities of the programming language and how to combine them so as to do something you want. The example of musical scores illustrates another aspect of programs. It is common in music to repeat sections, for example a chorus section. Musical notation saves the composer duplicating those parts of the score that are repeated and, instead, provides a notation specifying that a section of music is repeated. The same is true in a program; it is often the case that some action has to be repeated: for example, in a word-processing program, searching through a passage of text for the occurrence of a word. Repetition (or iteration) is common in programs, and VB has special instructions to accomplish this.

Recipes sometimes say something like: 'if you haven't got fresh peas, use frozen'. This illustrates another aspect of programs – they often carry out a test and then do one of two things depending on the result of the test. This is called *selection* and, as with repetition, VB has special facilities to accomplish it.

If you have ever used a recipe to prepare a meal, you may well have got to a particular step in the recipe only to find that you have to refer to another recipe. For example, you might have to turn to another page to find out how to cook rice, before combining it with the rest of the meal: the rice preparation has been separated out as a sub-task. This way of writing instructions has an important analogue in programming, called methods in VB and other object-oriented languages. Methods are used in all programming languages, but sometimes go under other names, such as functions, procedures, subroutines or sub-programs.

Methods are sub-tasks, and are so called because they are a method for doing something. Using methods promotes simplicity where there might otherwise be complexity.

Now consider cooking a curry. A few years ago, the recipe would suggest that you buy fresh spices, grind them, and fry them. Nowadays though, you can buy ready-made sauces. Our task has become simpler. The analogy with programming is that the task becomes easier if we can select from a set of ready-made *objects* such as buttons, scroll bars, and databases. VB comes with a large set of objects that we can incorporate in our program, rather than creating the whole thing from scratch.

To sum up, a program is a list of instructions that can be obeyed automatically by a computer. A program consists of combinations of:

- sequences;
- repetitions;
- selections;
- methods;
- ready-made objects;
- objects you write yourself.

All modern programming languages share these features.

> **SELF-TEST QUESTIONS**
>
> **1.1** Here are some instructions for calculating an employee's pay:
>
>   obtain the number of hours worked
>   calculate pay
>   print pay slip
>   subtract deductions for illness
>
> Is there a major error?
>
> **1.2** Take the instruction:
>
>   massage shampoo into hair
>
> and express it in a more detailed way, incorporating the concept of repetition.
>
> **1.3** Here are some instructions displayed on a roller coaster ride:
>
>   Only take the ride if you are over 8 or younger than 70!
>
> Is there a problem with the notice? How would you rewrite it to improve it?

Programming principles

- Programs consist of instructions combined with the concepts of sequence, selection, repetition and sub-tasks.
- The programming task becomes simpler if we can make use of ready-made components.

Programming pitfalls

Human error can creep into programs – such as placing instructions in the wrong order.

Summary

- VB is derived from BASIC, which was designed to be easy for beginners.
- Microsoft's .NET framework is a major product, and has a new version of VB.
- A program is a list of instructions that are obeyed automatically by a computer.
- Object-oriented programming (OOP) is the main trend in current programming, and VB fully supports it.

EXERCISES

1.1 This question concerns the steps that a student goes through to wake up and get to college. Here is a suggestion for the first few steps:

```
wake up
dress
eat breakfast
brush teeth
...
```

- Complete the steps. Note that there is no ideal answer – the steps will vary between individuals.
- The 'brush teeth' step contains repetition – we do it again and again. Identify another step that contains repetition.
- Identify a step that contains a selection.
- Take one of the steps, and break it down into smaller steps.

1.2 You are provided with a huge pile of paper containing 10 000 numbers, in no particular order. Write down the process that you would go through to find the largest number. Ensure that your process is clear and unambiguous. Identify any selection and repetition in your process.

1.3 For the game of Tic Tac Toe (noughts and crosses), try to write down a set of precise instructions which enables a player to win. If this is not possible, try to ensure that a player does not lose.

ANSWERS TO SELF-TEST QUESTIONS

1.1 The major error is that the deductions part comes too late. It should precede the printing.

1.2 We might say:

```
keep massaging your hair until it is washed.
```

or

```
As long as your hair is not washed, keep massaging.
```

1.3 The problem is with the word 'or'. Someone who is 73 is also over 8, and could therefore ride.

We could replace 'or' with 'and' to make it technically correct, but the notice might still be misunderstood. We might also put:

```
only take this ride if you are between 8 and 70
```

but be prepared to modify the notice again when hordes of 8- and 70-year-olds ask if they can ride!

The VB development environment

This chapter explains:

- how to create a VB project;
- how to manipulate controls and their properties at design-time;
- how to run a program;
- how to handle a button-click event;
- how to display a message box;
- how to place text on a label at run-time;
- how to locate compilation errors.

● Introduction

Throughout this book, we use 'IDE' to stand for the VB Integrated Development Environment. In the same way that a word-processor is a program which provides facilities to create documents, an IDE provides facilities to create (develop) programs. All the facilities that we require have been integrated and we can work totally within the IDE, rather than having to use other programs. It provides a complete programming environment.

● Installation and configuration

This book provides a CD-ROM containing Microsoft's Visual Basic 2008 Express Edition. Follow its installation instructions, and register the product if you are asked to do so.

We now explain how to group your future VB programs in a convenient folder. When you make a program, VB creates a number of files and places them in a new folder. Such a collection of files is termed a 'project'. It is sensible to create a top-level folder to hold all your projects. The default folder that VB uses is called **Projects** in **My Documents\Visual Studio 2008** folder on the **C** drive. This will be fine for most users, but if you need to alter the folder, do the following:

1. Click on the **Tools** menu at the top of the screen. Select **Options...**
2. Click **Projects and Solutions** and click on ... to the right of **Visual Studio project location**
3. A **Project Location** window opens, allowing you to choose a folder or to create a new one. Click **OK** when finished.

From now on, VB will store all of your work in the default projects folder, or in your specially-selected one. However, the very first time you save a project, a **Browse** button (see figure 2.9) is provided, should you need to deviate from your selected folder.

Now we will set the **Strict** option.

In the same way that a spell checker is useful in word-processing, so the VB facilities for detecting typos and incorrect use of data are useful. They can prevent hours spent trying to find a mistake in the program. To configure VB for maximum checking, do the following:

1. Click on the **Tools** menu at the top of the screen. Select **Options** . . .
2. An options window opens. Open up **Projects and Solutions** by clicking the + alongside it. Select **VB Defaults**.
3. Set **Option Strict** to **On**, and ensure that **Option Explicit** is left at its **On** setting.
4. Click **OK** to confirm the settings.

VB will now perform its highest level of checking on your code.

Creating a first program

The program we create will display the message `Hello World` on the screen, but whatever the program, the steps are the same.

- Run the IDE. The Start Page appears, as in Figure 2.1
- Click the **Create Project** . . . link. Figure 2.2 shows the **New Project** window which appears.
- Ensure that **Windows Forms Application** is selected. Choose a project name. This will become a folder name. Stick to letters, digits and spaces. Here, we chose `First Hello`. Click **OK**. A design area opens up, similar (but not identical) to Figure 2.4.
- In your early days with VB, it will be useful to make the toolbox permanently visible. Click on the **View** menu and select **Toolbox**. Now click on the 'pin' symbol of the toolbox, as shown in Figure 2.3. The toolbox is now pinned permanently open, and your screen should now closely match Figure 2.4.

Creating a first program • 9

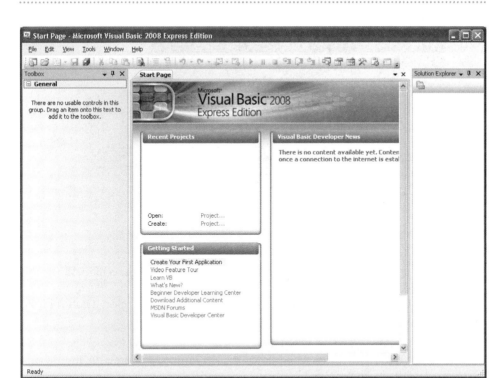

Figure 2.1 The Start Page.

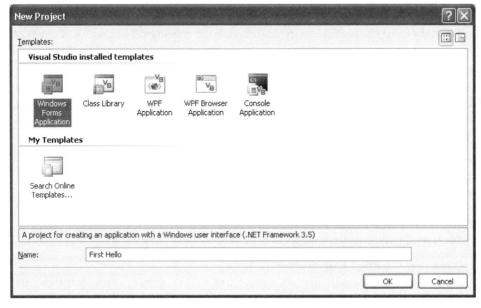

Figure 2.2 The **New Project** window.

10 ● Chapter 2/The VB development environment

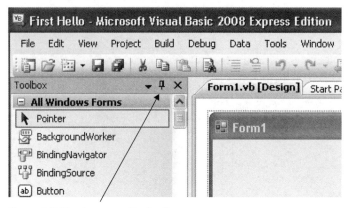

Figure 2.3 Pinning open the toolbox.

The above steps are typical for any project. Let us now do a specific task for this particular project.

Note the form and the toolbox in Figure 2.4. We are going to select a control from the toolbox and place it on the form. Here are the steps:

- Locate the toolbox. Click on **Label**.
- Move the mouse to the form. Hold down the left button, and drag the mouse to create a label as in Figure 2.5.
- We will now set some properties of the label: right-click on the label and select **Properties**. Move to the Properties list at the bottom right of the screen, as shown in Figure 2.6.
- Scroll down to the `Text` property, and replace the existing `Label1` with `Hello World`.
- Now, we run the program by clicking the arrow at the top of the IDE (Figure 2.7)

A new window appears, as in Figure 2.8. This is the program that you have created. It merely displays some text, but it is a proper window in the sense that you can move it, resize it and shut it down by clicking the `x` at the top right corner. Experiment with the window, then close it.

To save your program for future use:

- Go to the **File** menu, selecting the **Save All** option. (We use a shorthand for such actions, writing it as **File | Save All**.)
- The **Save Project** window appears, as in Figure 2.9. Ensure that **Create directory for solution** is checked. Leave its other settings unaltered, and click **Save**. When you do a save again, the same settings will be used automatically, and the **Save Project** window will not appear.

You can now use **File | Exit** to leave the IDE.

When you return to VB later, your project name will appear on the start page, and can be opened with a single click. The work we did on setting up the project does not need to be repeated.

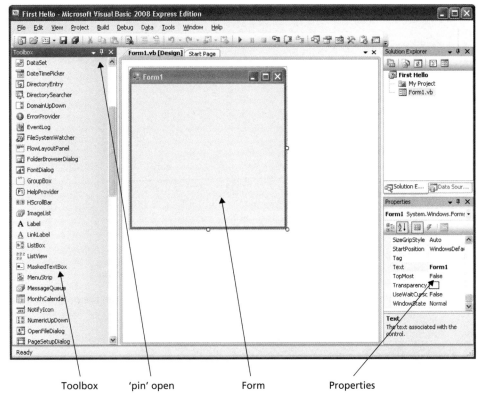

　　　　　Toolbox　　'pin' open　　　　Form　　　　Properties

Figure 2.4 The IDE at design-time.

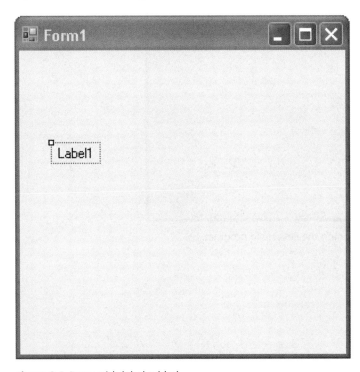

Figure 2.5 Form with label added.

12 ● Chapter 2/The VB development environment

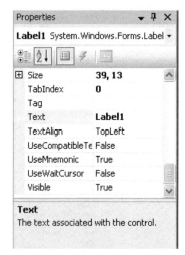

Figure 2.6 Properties of the label.

Figure 2.7 Click arrow to run the program.

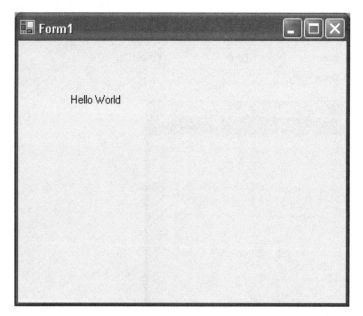

Figure 2.8 Screenshot of running the First Hello program.

Figure 2.9 The **Save Project** window, with **Create directory** checked.

● Controls at design-time

In our First Hello program, we placed a label on a form and altered the text that it displayed. The main point of the exercise was to go through the steps involved in creating a project. Now we will fill in some of the principles of controls and properties.

What *is* a control? A control is a 'gadget' that appears on the screen, to display information, to allow user interaction, or both of these. The VB IDE itself uses many controls. For example, you have made use of the drop-down menus to save projects, and the **OK** button to confirm actions. For Windows applications, the toolbox contains around 70 controls, and part of the programming task involves choosing appropriate controls, positioning them on a form, and setting their properties. This phase of using a control is termed *design-time* to distinguish it from *run-time*, when the program runs (executes) and the user interacts with the controls. We create a *graphical user interface (GUI)* for the user. Let us examine how controls can be manipulated at design-time.

- A control can be selected from the toolbox, and positioned on a form. The initial position is not crucial; it is easily changed.
- We can move the control. Hold the mouse within a control. A four-headed arrow will appear, as in Figure 2.10. The control can now be dragged with the mouse. Temporary lines appear, to help you align several controls.
- We can resize the control. Clicking on a control shows a number of small boxes (handles) on the edge of the control. Hold the mouse over one of them. A two-headed arrow appears, as in Figure 2.11. Drag the edge or corner to resize the rectangle.

In fact, the approach to resizing depends on the particular control. For example, the label control has an **AutoSize** property, which we set to **False** in Figure 2.11. If we left

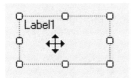

Figure 2.10 Moving a control.

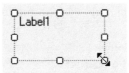

Figure 2.11 Resizing a control.

AutoSize set to **True**, the width of the label is determined by the width of the text it has to display, and its height is determined by the font size of the text. Some other controls allow the width to be dragged, but not the height. (We set the height via fonts.) Some controls – such as buttons – allow resizing in all directions. In general, resizing is intuitive, so explore. However, because labels are so common, don't forget about their **AutoSize** property.

Now we will examine *properties*. Here is an analogy: a television has properties, such as the colour of the case, the size of the screen, the current channel it is showing, its price, and its make.

Each control has a set of properties, which we can adjust at design-time to meet our requirements. Later, we will see a property being changed at run-time.

Once a control has been placed on a form, we can view its properties by right-clicking in it, and selecting **Properties**. A properties window for the selected control will be shown. The left column contains the property names, and the right column contains the current value. To change a property, we modify the value in the right-hand column. For some properties, this might involve further selections, as in the settings of colours and fonts. Sometimes this involves opening up a further window where the range of values is large.

Another vital aspect of a control is its name. This is not in fact a property, but is shown in the properties list for convenience, as **(Name)**. The brackets indicate that it is not really a property.

When you place several labels on a form, the IDE chooses names in this fashion:

```
Label1   Label2   Label3   ...
```

These are acceptable for now, but in future chapters we will suggest that you rename some controls, choosing meaningful names. A control is renamed by modifying the text to the right of **(Name)** in the properties list.

SELF-TEST QUESTIONS

2.1 Place two labels on a form. Make the following changes to their properties. After each change, run the program, note the effect, and stop the program by clicking on x at the top-right corner.

- Move the labels;
- set the **AutoSize** property of one of the labels to **True**;
- alter their **Text** properties to display your name and age;
- alter their fonts;
- alter their back colour.

2.2 Select the form itself. Perform the following tasks, running the program after each change.

- Resize the form;
- alter its text property;
- alter its back colour property.

● Events and the `Button` control

The program we created earlier was unrepresentative, in the sense that it always displayed the same words, and no user interaction was possible. Now we will extend this program, so that some text is displayed when the user clicks a button. This is an example of using an *event*.

Most events come from the user, and are generated when the user manipulates a control in some way at run-time. Each control has a number of events it can respond to, such as a single mouse-click, a double-click, or the mouse being held over the control. There are also other types of events that do not originate from a user – for example the notification that a web page has finished downloading.

In the program that follows, we will detect an event (the click of a button), and then cause some text to be displayed in a label. Here is how we create the user interface:

- create a new project named Hello Button;
- place a label and a button on the form. The positioning is not crucial;
- set the `Text` property of the button to `Click Me`;
- alter the `Text` property of the label so that it contains nothing.

The program is not yet complete, but run it. Note that you can click the button and it shifts slightly, to provide confirmation of the click; nothing else happens. Shut down the form.

Now we will detect the click event. On the design form, double-click on the button. A new pane of information will open up, as in Figure 2.12. Note the tabs at the top, showing:

```
Start Page
Form1.vb
Form1.vb [Design]
```

these can be clicked to switch panes. The **Form1.vb** pane shows a VB program. We call this *program text*, or VB *code*. We are going to modify this code using the editor within the IDE.

Locate the section:

```
Private Sub Button1_Click (ByVal sender As ... etc
End Sub
```

This section of code is termed a *method*. The name of the method is `Button1_Click`. When the user single-clicks on `Button1` at run-time, any instructions we place between the above two lines will be carried out, or 'executed'. This is because the line ends with `Handles Button1_Click`.

In this particular program, we will use an instruction to place `Hello World` into the text of `Label1`. The instruction to do this is:

```
Label1.Text = "Hello World"
```

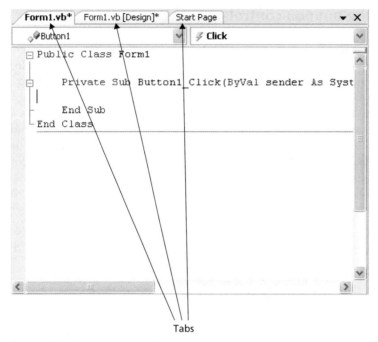

Figure 2.12 VB code in the editor pane.

Type it in exactly as shown, placing it between the `Private Sub` and the `End Sub` lines. Note carefully the last two characters of `Label1`. One of them is a lower-case L, and the other is the digit 1. The exact meaning of lines such as this (which involves an 'assignment statement') will be explained in later chapters.

The next step is to run the program. There are two possibilities:

- The program runs correctly. Click the button, and note that `Hello World` appears in the label.
- Alternatively, the program might not run, due to an error. In this case, VB displays a message as shown in Figure 2.13. Check the box, and choose **No**. The message will not appear again.

However, the error still needs fixing, so correct any errors in your typing, and run the program again. Errors are discussed in more detail below.

The new features in this program are:

- It has responded to the click on a button. Placing code so that it is obeyed when an event occurs is termed 'handling' the event.
- It has altered the value of a control's property at run-time. Previously, we only did this at design-time. This is a very important part of programming, because we often display results by placing them in a property of a control.

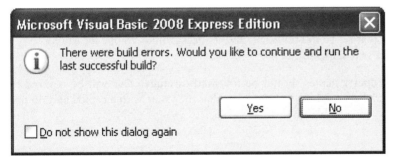

Figure 2.13 Error action. Check the box, and click **No**.

> **SELF-TEST QUESTION**
>
> **2.3** Place a second label on the form. Make it show your name when the button is clicked.

● Opening an existing project

To re-open a project that you created earlier, save and close any current project you are working on, and move to the Start Page. This displays your most recent projects. To open one, just click its name. If the project you want is not in the list, click the **Open Project . . .** link, and browse to the appropriate folder. Inside the folder, there is a file of type .sln (solution). Select this, and open the project. To view the form, move to the Project Explorer at the top right side, and click on the form name to open it.

● Documenting property settings

In this book, we need to provide you with the settings for controls. For a small number of properties, we can explain these in a few sentences of English, but for a larger number of properties, we will use a table. In general, we have a number of controls. Each control has a number of properties, and each property has a value. Note that there are a large number of properties for each control, but we only list the properties that you need to modify. The other properties keep their default setting. Here is an example:

Control	Property	Setting
Label1	Text	Hello World
Label1	BackColor	Red
Button1	Text	Click Me

It represents:

- `Label1` with its text set to `Hello World`, and its background colour set to red;
- `Button1` with its text set to `Click Me`.

The spelling of property names should be followed carefully. This will be covered in more detail in later chapters, but for now, note that they start with a capital and do not contain spaces.

Program errors

It is common for mistakes to occur in programs, and the IDE will spot some of them for you. Here is an example of a mistake:

```
Label1.Tixt = "Hello World"
```

When you enter this line, the IDE will underline it. If you hold the mouse over the underlined part, an explanation of the error pops up. You should note that the explanation might be hard to understand (even for experts) or it might be that the error is in another part of the program. However, your first step is always to inspect the underlined area for spelling errors. As you learn more of the VB language, your ability to spot mistakes will improve.

Once the underlined errors are corrected, we run the program. In fact, before the program runs, a program known as a compiler makes checks on it, and more errors might be detected. Only when all these compilation errors have been corrected will the program be allowed to run.

Compilation errors are listed in the **Error List** window, which opens below the code. Double-clicking on the error in the output window will take you to the point in the code where it can be corrected.

Everyone who begins to write programs will encounter lots of compilation errors. Do not be dismayed. It is part of the learning process.

Once the compilation errors have been fixed, the program will run. Then we might notice that it runs incorrectly – it has a 'bug'. Such run-time errors are much harder to fix, and debugging is needed. We cover this in Chapter 9.

Editor facilities

The editor does more than just display what you type in. Here are some of its facilities.

- It provides standard clipboard cut, copy and paste, letting you copy code from other Windows programs.

- The writing of bigger programs involves more controls and more events. The drop-down lists at the top of the editor allow you to select a control, and a particular event for that control. The editor positions itself to the appropriate method.
- As you type in VB code, the editor will lay it out according to certain rules. For example, spaces will automatically be inserted around the = symbol.
- Some lines will be indented – shifted to the right – by the insertion of extra spaces. Normally, this is in steps of four spaces. As you will see in later chapters, VB code consists of sections within sections, and indentation clarifies where a section begins and ends.
- Some of the letters you type will be converted to capitals, according to the conventions of the VB language.
- Each type of control has a different set of properties. If you type in a control name followed by a dot, as in:

    ```
    Label1.
    ```

    then wait, the editor will provide a list of the label's properties.
- Sections of code that we are not working on can be collapsed down to one line of code. This is done by clicking the small - at the left of the editor. Click + to expand a section. You will see these symbols alongside such lines as:

    ```
    Private Sub Button1_Click(...etc
    ```

You don't have to remember these features – they are there to help you.

One area of layout that is not done for you is the breaking up of long lines. To ensure that the whole of a line is visible on the screen, you can choose a suitable place to break the line, and type a space character followed by an underscore _ character, followed by a new line. Spaces can then be inserted at the left to provide a suitable indentation. The underscore character is available by using the **shift** and – combination. Here is an example, using this line:

```
Private Sub Button1_Click(ByVal Sender As System.Object   ...etc
```

We can set this out as:

```
Private Sub Button1_Click( _
             ByVal sender As System.Object, _
             ByVal e As System.EventArgs) _
             Handles Button1.Click
```

Note the space/underscore combination.

Often, the very long lines are created by the IDE and should not contain errors. Breaking them is not essential. However, when you progress in VB, some of the long lines will be your creation, and it is well worth breaking them so that the whole text can be seen at once. The readability of printed code (called a listing) is also improved.

> **SELF-TEST QUESTION**
>
> **2.4** Place a label and a button on a form, then do the following:
>
> (a) double-click on the button at design-time, and insert the line:
>
> ```
> Label1.Tixt = "Doug"
> ```
>
> Note the underlining, and the error message.
>
> (b) Run the program. Note the error in the Error List, then double-click on it. Fix the error.
>
> (c) Remove the spaces at the left of the line, and around the =. Click elsewhere in the code, and note the effect.
>
> (d) Alter `Text` to `text`. Note the effect.

● The message box

Earlier, we used the label control to display text on the screen. We can also use a message box. This does not occur in the toolbox, because it occupies no permanent space on a form. Instead, it pops up when required. Here is some code which displays `Hello World` in a message box, when a button is clicked:

```
    Private Sub Button1_Click( _
                    ByVal sender As System.Object, _
                    ByVal e As System.EventArgs) _
                    Handles Button1.Click
        MessageBox.Show("Hello World")
    End Sub
```

Figure 2.14 shows what happens when we run the program and click the button. The message box appears, and we must click the **OK** button to make it go away. This feature means that message boxes are used for vital messages that the user cannot ignore.

To use a message box, key in a line just like the above, putting your own message inside the double quotes. At this point we will not explain the purpose of the `Show`, or why the brackets are needed. This comes later, when we study methods in more detail.

Figure 2.14 A message box.

> **SELF-TEST QUESTION**
>
> **2.5** Write a program which has two buttons on a form. Clicking one button shows a message box containing `Hello World`. Clicking the other button shows a message box containing `Goodbye Cruel World`.

Help

The help system works from two possible sources: locally from your own computer, or from the Internet. The Internet one is updated frequently, but the local version will be sufficient when you are starting out. Should you not have an Internet connection, the local help will be used automatically.

If you wish to be specific about where your help comes from, you can reset it as follows:

1. On the main VB window, choose **Help | Search . . .**
2. On the new help window, choose **Tools | Options . . .** and choose **Online**. You are presented with choices about which help source takes precedence.

The VB help system is large but, if you are new to programming, the information it contains can be difficult. It is more useful when you have progressed in VB and you require precise technical detail.

The most useful options on the help menu are **Index** and **Search**. They allow you to enter some text, and will search to possible useful pages. The difference is that **Index** only looks in the titles of pages, whereas **Search** looks in the content of pages as well.

Programming principles

- Controls can be positioned on a form at design-time.
- The properties of controls can be set at design-time.
- Programs can change properties at run-time.
- When an event (such as a button-click) happens, the VB system uses the matching method. We place code within the method to handle the event.

Programming pitfalls

- Forgetting to terminate your running program before trying to modify the form or code.

Grammar spot

- In VB code, we refer to the property of a control by using the control's name, followed by a dot, followed by the property, as in:

    ```
    Label1.Text
    ```

- A section of code between:

    ```
    Private Sub ...
    End Sub
    ```

    is termed a method.

- A message box is not placed on a form. Instead, we cause one to be displayed by using:

    ```
    MessageBox.Show("Some text you choose")
    ```

New language elements

An introduction to properties, methods, events.

New IDE facilities

- A program is contained in a project.
- The IDE creates a folder to contain the files needed for a project.
- The setting of the project options **Strict** and **Explicit**.
- We can move and resize the controls on a form.
- The toolbox contains a range of controls.
- Right-clicking on a control allows us to select its properties.
- Double-clicking on a control at design-time will create event-handling methods.

Summary

Part of the programming task involves placing controls on a form and setting their initial properties. The VB IDE makes this task straightforward, but you need to practice with the IDE, as well as reading about it.

EXERCISES

2.1 Create a new project named Demo, and place three buttons on the form. Set their text to 1, 2, 3 respectively. Create three labels, and set their text to A, B and C. Now place suitable code in the appropriate button methods so that:

(a) clicking `Button1` sets the text of all the labels to `Yes`;
(b) clicking `Button2` sets the text of all the buttons to `No`;
(c) clicking `Button3` sets the text values back to `A`, `B`, `C`.

2.2 This involves the use of the `Visible` property of a control, which can be set to `True` or `False`. For example, the following code makes `Label1` invisible:

```
Label1.Visible = False
```

Write a program with two buttons and one label. Clicking one button makes the label invisible, and clicking the other button makes it visible again.

2.3 This program involves the use of the `Image` property of the label, which makes the label display an image. Setting this property involves browsing for an image file. Choose any image you encounter: there are many sample images on most computers, and their file name often ends in `.jpg` or `.bmp`. Write a program with two buttons, and an image on a label. Clicking one button makes the image disappear. Clicking the other button makes it reappear.

2.4 Write a program which firstly displays your name in a message box, and then your age in a message box, when a button is clicked.

2.5 This involves the creation of a simple text editor. Place a text box on the form, and resize it so that it fills most of the form. Set its `Multiline` property to `True`, and its `ScrollBars` property to `Both`. Run the program. Type some text into the text box. Note that a right-click on the mouse allows cut and paste. Run a word-processor, and paste text to and from your editor.

2.6 This involves using the `MouseHover` event, which happens when the user holds the mouse over a control for a few seconds. To create a method that handles this event, place a button on the form, and, at the top of the text editor panel, select `Button1` and `MouseHover`. The method to handle the event is created. Write a program which displays a message box containing `Over Button` when the mouse is held over the button.

ANSWERS TO SELF-TEST QUESTIONS

2.1 This question involves exploration; manipulating properties is a hands-on task. You will learn how to select controls and manipulate each one individually.

2.2 Note that the `Text` property affects the words that are shown in the title of the form.

2.3 At design-time, we clear the `Text` property of the label (which VB will have named as `Label2`). Then we add the following line:

```
Label2.Text = "Mike"
```

Place this line immediately below the line which displayed `Hello World`. Run the program.

2.4 (a) Hold the mouse over the underlined part to see the pop-up error.
(b) The cursor will be positioned at the incorrect line. Change `Tixt` to `Text`.
(c) The IDE puts the spaces back.
(d) The IDE replaces the `t` with `T`.

2.5 The following code is added to our message box example:

```
Private Sub Button2_Click( _
            ByVal sender As System.Object, _
            ByVal e As System.EventArgs) _
            Handles Button2.Click
    MessageBox.Show("Goodbye Cruel World")
End Sub
```

3

Introductory graphics

This chapter explains:

- how to use drawing facilities for simple shapes;
- how to call methods;
- how to pass arguments to methods;
- how to write programs as a sequence of instructions;
- how to add comments to a program.

● Introduction

The term 'computer graphics' conjures up a variety of possibilities. We could be discussing a computer-generated Hollywood movie, a sophisticated video game, a virtual reality environment, a static photographic-style image on a monitor or a more simple image built out of lines. Here we will restrict ourselves to the display of still images built from simple shapes. This simplicity is intentional, as we need to focus on the use of objects and methods, without being overwhelmed by graphics detail.

● Objects, methods, properties, classes – an analogy

Sometimes, you can approach object-oriented programming via an analogy. Here, we will look at the concept of a graphics drawing kit from a real-world point of view, and then from a computer object-oriented point of view. Please note that this is very much an introduction, and we will cover this material in more detail in following chapters.

In the real world, our drawing kit might consist of a pile of blank sheets of paper, some pens, and a set of shape-drawing tools (for example a ruler, and a template with shapes cut out). The pens must match the paper: if the sheets are transparencies, then we might use oil-based pens.

Note that the paper by itself, or the template by itself, is not enough – it is the *combination* of them that provides us with the drawing kit.

In the computer's object-oriented world, we request that VB supplies us with a drawing area (rather like selecting 'new' in a word-processor). This drawing area comes with a set of 'methods' (functions, operations) for shape-drawing. The idea of a sheet of paper that can do nothing goes against the object-oriented approach. To re-phrase: in VB's object style, we obtain a sheet of 'clever' paper, which comes with a set of facilities.

How many drawing kits can we create? There is no practical limit on a computer. For example, in a word-processor, you can create as many new document windows as you need, by clicking the 'new' button. In fact, in VB the word `New` is used to provide the programmer with newly created objects to work with. When we use `New`, we must also specify what type of new object we require. In other words, we choose the *class* of the object. VB has a large collection of existing classes (such as buttons, labels, forms, etc.).

Let us move slightly closer to actual coding. The approximate code for drawing a rectangle is:

```
paper.DrawRectangle(details of color, rectangle position, etc.)
```

For now, we will ignore the details of the rectangle colour and positioning. The main point is that `paper` is an object. We draw on it by using one of its methods. Here we chose `DrawRectangle`. Using a method is termed 'calling' or 'invoking' the method. To call a method of an object, we use the 'dot' notation, placing a '.' between the object and the method being called.

Objects can also have 'properties' as well as methods. We don't call properties – they don't do tasks for us. Rather, they let us access or change the current 'state' (settings) of an object. For example, the `Text` property of a button contains the message that the button shows. We can set this at design-time, and in fact at run-time if we wish.

In the following code, we will be calling methods of the `Graphics` class provided by VB. It comes with a list of methods (such as `DrawRectangle` etc.). Our drawing area – which we choose to name as `paper` – will in effect be a picture box control, available from the toolbox.

We will also be creating a new pen object and setting its colour.

● A first drawing

Now we will create a program which displays two rectangles on a picture box when the button is clicked, as in Figure 3.1. The instructions are all contained within one method. Here is the code listing:

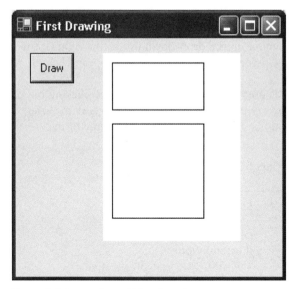

Figure 3.1 Screenshot of First Drawing program.

```
Private Sub Button1_Click( _
                ByVal sender As System.Object, _
                ByVal e As System.EventArgs) _
                Handles Button1.Click
    Dim paper As Graphics
    paper = PictureBox1.CreateGraphics()
    Dim myPen As Pen = New Pen(Color.Black)

    paper.DrawRectangle(myPen, 10, 10, 100, 50)
    paper.DrawRectangle(myPen, 10, 75, 100, 100)
End Sub
```

Creating the program

To create this program, we use the IDE as explained in Chapter 2. Basically, the steps are:

- enter the VB IDE;
- create a new Windows Application project, named (for example) First Drawing.

Next, we need to place controls on the screen, so:

- Place a button and a picture box on the form. The exact positioning is not crucial – use the screenshot of Figure 3.1 as a guide. Click on the button, and change its Text property to Draw.

- Click on the picture box, and change its size property to **150, 200**.
- Change the `BackColor` property of the picture box to a suitable colour. White is satisfactory. You can do this by opening up the drop-down list on the right of the `BackColor` property and choosing **Custom**. Examples of colours appear; click on the white one.
- If you wish, you can alter the words used for the title of the form by clicking on the form, then setting its `Text` property to a meaningful title, e.g. `First Drawing`. In fact you can choose any title you like – it need not match the name of the project.

Here is a summary of the control settings:

Control	Property	Setting
Button1	Text	Draw
PictureBox1	BackColor	(Custom) White
PictureBox1	Size	150, 200
Form1	Text	First Drawing

The final stage in creating the program is to double-click on the button and insert the drawing instructions. All of the instructions go within the `Button1_Click1` method, as shown in the above code.

Run the program, then click on the 'Draw' button to see the two rectangles. If you have compilation errors, correct any typing mistakes, and try again. Typing errors are quite normal, so don't panic.

Now we will examine the detail of drawing shapes.

● The graphics coordinate system

VB graphics are based on pixels. A pixel is a small dot on the screen which can be set to a particular colour. Each pixel is identified by a pair of numbers (its coordinates), starting from zero:

- the horizontal position, often referred to as x in mathematics, and also in the VB documentation. This value increases from left to right;
- the vertical position, often referred to as y – this value increases downwards.

When we place a visual object on the screen, effectively we set its x/y position. Figure 3.2 shows a form of size 400 by 200, with a `PictureBox` placed at 200, 100. However, when drawing on the picture box, we regard *its* top left corner as being the zero point of horizontal and vertical coordinates. In other words, we draw relative to the top left corner of the picture box, not relative to the top left corner of the form. This means that re-positioning the picture box has no effect on any drawing it contains. We use this system when we request VB to draw simple shapes.

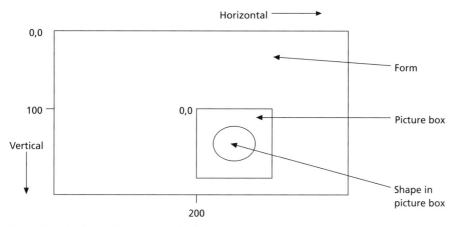

Figure 3.2 Pixel coordinate system in VB.

The size of the drawings depends on the quality of your screen, and on the graphics settings on your system. Higher-quality graphics have more (hence smaller) pixels, so your drawings will be smaller.

● Explanation of the program

We will not explain every detail of each line here. There are some big ideas. But trust us that subsequent chapters will deal with them.

Our drawing code is contained within one method, named `Button1_Click`. There are two phases here: firstly we set up the drawing facilities, and then we actually draw. Here is the first part:

```
Dim paper As Graphics
paper = PictureBox1.CreateGraphics()
Dim myPen As Pen = New Pen(Color.Black)
```

The good news is that the above lines will be the same for most of our drawing programs. We will provide a brief explanation of these lines, but it is not essential that you understand every detail at this stage.

- Line 1 is where we choose our name for the drawing area (we chose `paper`). The word `Dim` (short for 'dimension') allows us to choose a name for our object, and we must also choose its 'class' – i.e. its type. It is a `Graphics` item (rather than a `Button`, for example)
- In the second line, we link our drawing area to the picture box you placed on the form.
- In Line 3, we choose a name for our pen. The word `Pen` is already in use by VB – it is the name of a *class* of item – so we went for `myPen`. At the same time, we set it to the colour black.

This completes the preparation for drawing. You should use these three identical lines in all the programs in this chapter. We are now ready to put some shapes on our picture box.

To draw the shapes, we call (or invoke) VB's drawing methods. Here is the code:

```
paper.DrawRectangle(myPen, 10, 10, 100, 50)
paper.DrawRectangle(myPen, 10, 75, 100, 100)
```

The `DrawRectangle` method is one of the many methods provided by the VB system in a library. The statement shown is a call (also known as an invocation) of the method, asking it to carry out the task of displaying a rectangle. A method is so called because it is a method (or way) of doing something.

When we make use of the `DrawRectangle` method, we need to supply it with a pen, and with values to fix its position and size. We need to get these in the correct order, which is:

- a `Pen` object;
- the horizontal value of the top left corner of the rectangle;
- the vertical value of the top left corner of the rectangle;
- the width of the rectangle;
- the height of the rectangle.

These items are known as arguments in VB. Other languages also use the term 'parameter'. Here, the arguments are inputs to the `DrawRectangle` method. Arguments must be enclosed in round brackets and separated by commas. This particular method requires five arguments, and they must be a `Pen` object, followed by four integers (whole numbers). If we attempt to use the wrong number of arguments, or the wrong type, we get an error message from the compiler. We need to ensure that:

- we supply the correct number of arguments;
- we supply the correct type of arguments;
- we arrange them in the right order.

Some methods do not require any arguments. In this case, we must still use the brackets, as in:

```
PictureBox1.CreateGraphics()
```

Here, we have been calling pre-written methods, but with VB's help we have written our own method. VB has named it `Button1_Click`. We don't need to call it, because VB calls it for us when `Button1` is clicked. Its task is to call the `DrawRectangle` method twice. We shall cover the detail of writing our own methods in Chapter 5.

● Methods for drawing

As well as rectangles, VB provides us with facilities for drawing a range of shapes. Here, we have selected the simpler ones:

- lines;
- ellipses (i.e. ovals). These also include circles;
- filled rectangles and ellipses;
- images from files.

Additionally, we can change the colour of the pens we use for drawing, and use 'brushes' of a chosen colour to fill shapes.

Here we list the arguments for each method, and provide an example program (Some Shapes) which uses them.

DrawRectangle

- a pen object;
- the horizontal value of the top left corner of the rectangle;
- the vertical value of the top left corner of the rectangle;
- the width of the rectangle;
- the height of the rectangle.

DrawLine

Note that this method does not use the concept of an enclosing rectangle. The arguments are:

- a pen object;
- the horizontal value of the start of the line;
- the vertical value of the start of the line;
- the horizontal value of the end of the line;
- the vertical value of the end of the line.

DrawEllipse

Imagine the ellipse (an oval) squeezed inside a rectangle. We provide:

- a pen object;
- the horizontal value of the top left corner of the rectangle;
- the vertical value of the top left corner of the rectangle;
- the width of the rectangle;
- the height of the rectangle.

To produce filled shapes we have:

FillRectangle

Its coordinate arguments are mostly identical to those of the `Draw` equivalent. The main difference is that the first argument must be a `Brush` object rather than a pen. Brushes can use a range of colours and textures. Here we only show the simplest untextured version:

```
Dim myBrush As SolidBrush = New SolidBrush(Color.Black)
paper.FillRectangle(myBrush, 10, 10, 90, 90)
```

FillEllipse

This is used in a similar manner to `DrawEllipse`, but with a brush rather than a pen.

DrawImage

This method is rather different, as it does not use preset shapes. Instead, it can be used to display images that have been stored in files. These images might have originated from a paint program, or from a scanner or camera. To use `DrawImage`, we firstly create a `Bitmap` object by providing the name of a file containing an image. The bitmap is created with `Dim` in the same way as we created a `Pen` object earlier. We then use `DrawImage`, specifying the bitmap, the position of the image, and the size of its containing rectangle. The image is clipped (trimmed to fit) if it is too big for the rectangle. The Some Shapes program below shows how to create the bitmap object, which we chose to name as `pic`. Our image was created in a paint package, and saved as `imagedemo.jpeg`. We can also work with `gif` and `bmp` file types.

The order of arguments for `DrawImage` is:

- a bitmap object containing an image from a file.
- the horizontal value of the top left corner of the rectangle;
- the vertical value of the top left corner of the rectangle;
- the width of the rectangle;
- the height of the rectangle.

Colours

It is possible to create as many pens and brushes as you wish, with their own colours. In VB, there are around 150 named colours. Below, we name the main colours, but also list some more obscure ones:

Black	Violet	Blue
Indigo	Green	Yellow
Orange	Red	Gray
Purple	White	Firebrick
LemonChiffon	Maroon	OliveDrab

We use the colours when creating pens and brushes.

Here is a program (called Some Shapes) which draws a variety of shapes. Figure 3.3 shows the resulting output.

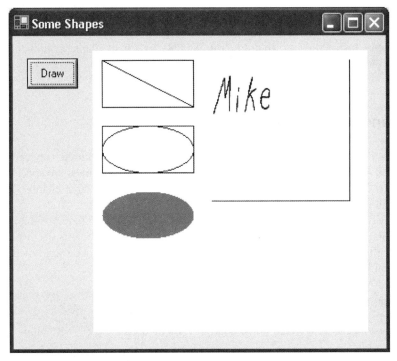

Figure 3.3 Screenshot of Some Shapes program.

```
Private Sub Button1_Click( _
                    ByVal sender As System.Object, _
                    ByVal e As System.EventArgs) _
                    Handles Button1.Click
    Dim paper As Graphics
    paper = PictureBox1.CreateGraphics()
    Dim pic As New Bitmap("c:\mike\vbbook\imagedemo.jpeg")
    Dim myPen As Pen = New Pen(Color.Black)
    Dim fillBrush As SolidBrush = New SolidBrush(Color.Gray)
    paper.DrawRectangle(myPen, 10, 10, 100, 50)
    paper.DrawLine(myPen, 10, 10, 110, 60)
    paper.DrawRectangle(myPen, 10, 80, 100, 50)
    paper.DrawEllipse(myPen, 10, 80, 100, 50)
    paper.FillEllipse(fillBrush, 10, 150, 100, 50)
    paper.DrawRectangle(myPen, 130, 10, 150, 150)
    paper.DrawImage(pic, 130, 10, 150, 150)
End Sub
```

Create the program in the same manner as the First Shapes one, but make the picture box larger: to **300, 300**.

SELF-TEST QUESTION

3.1 Write some VB instructions which produce a filled black circle of 50 pixels radius, 10 pixels in from the top left corner of a picture box.

The sequence concept and statements

When we have a number of instructions in a program, they are executed (obeyed, performed . . .) in sequence, from the top of screen to the bottom (unless we specify otherwise using the concepts of selection and repetition covered in later chapters). However, you will not observe this because of the speed of the computer.

In general, a VB program is composed of a series of 'statements'. There are many types of statements, such as a method call or an assignment. Some statements occupy a single line, but others (such as `If` and `While`, as we shall see) need to be written to spread over several lines.

SELF-TEST QUESTION

3.2 Write and run a program which draws a large 'T' shape on the screen, with blue lines.

Adding meaning with comments

What does the following do?

```
paper.DrawLine(myPen, 20, 80, 70, 10)
paper.DrawLine(myPen, 70, 10, 120, 80)
paper.DrawLine(myPen, 20, 80, 120, 80)
```

The meaning is not instantly obvious, and you probably tried to figure it out with pencil and paper. The answer is that it draws a triangle with a horizontal base, but this is not apparent from the three statements. In VB, we can add comments (a kind of annotation) to the instructions, by preceding them by with ′ (i.e. the single-quote key). For example, we might put:

```
' draw a triangle
paper.DrawLine(myPen, 20, 80, 70, 10)
paper.DrawLine(myPen, 70, 10, 120, 80)
paper.DrawLine(myPen, 20, 80, 120, 80)
```

A comment can contain anything – there are no rules. It is up to you to use them to convey meaning.

Comments can also be placed at the end of a line, as in:

```
' draw a triangle
paper.DrawLine(myPen, 20, 80, 70, 10)
paper.DrawLine(myPen, 70, 10, 120, 80)
paper.DrawLine(myPen, 20, 80, 120, 80)  ' draw base
```

Do not over-use comments. It is not normal to comment every line, as this often involves duplicating information. The following is a poor comment:

```
Dim aPen As Pen = New Pen(Color.Black)  ' create a black pen
```

Here, the statement says clearly what it does, without the need for a comment. Use comments to state the overall theme of a section of program, rather than restating the detail of each statement.

> **SELF-TEST QUESTION**
>
> **3.3** Provide a suitable comment for these lines:
>
> ```
> paper.DrawLine(myPen, 0, 0, 100, 100)
> paper.DrawLine(myPen, 100, 0, 100, 0)
> ```

Programming principles

- VB has a large collection of methods that we can call.
- The arguments we pass to graphics methods have the effect of controlling the shapes that are drawn.

Programming pitfalls

- Take care with punctuation and spelling. Commas and brackets must be exactly as in the examples.

Grammar spot

The order and type of arguments must be correct for each method.

New language elements

- () to enclose arguments.
- The use of Dim to declare items.

Chapter 3/Introductory graphics

- The use of New to create new objects.
- The use of the 'dot' notation to invoke methods of a class.
- ' to indicate comments.

Summary

- Statements are obeyed in sequence, top to bottom (unless we request otherwise).
- VB has a set of 'draw' methods which you can call up to display graphics.
- Graphics positioning is based on pixel coordinates.
- Argument values can be passed into methods.

EXERCISES

In the following, we recommend that you do rough sketches and calculations prior to writing the program. You can use the same project for each question, using a picture box for drawing, and a button event to initiate the drawing.

3.1 Write a program which draws a right-angled triangle. Choose an appropriate size.

3.2 Write a program which draws an empty tic-tac-toe (noughts and crosses) board, made out of lines.

3.3 Design a simple house, then write a program which draws it.

3.4 Here are some annual rainfall figures for the country of Xanadu, which we wish to display graphically:

```
1998    150 cm
1999    175 cm
2000    120 cm
2001    130 cm
```

- Display the data as a series of horizontal lines.
- Instead of lines, use filled rectangles.

3.5 Write a program which displays an archery-style target with concentric circles of different colours. The purchase of a rubber sucker gun to fire at the screen is optional.

3.6 Write a program which displays a simple face. The outline of the face, the eyes, ears, nose, and the mouth can be formed by ellipses.

ANSWERS TO SELF-TEST QUESTIONS

3.1 We imagine that the circle is fitted inside a square whose sides are 100 pixels long:

```
Dim fillBrush As SolidBrush = New SolidBrush(Color.Black)
paper.FillEllipse(fillBrush, 10, 10, 100, 100)
```

3.2
```
paper.DrawLine(myPen, 20, 20, 120, 20)
paper.DrawLine(myPen, 80, 20, 80, 120)
```

3.3 The instructions draw a large 'X' on the picture box, so a suitable comment might be:

```
'draw an 'X' at top left
```

Variables and calculations

This chapter explains:

- the types of numeric variables;
- how to declare variables;
- the assignment statement;
- arithmetic operators;
- the use of numbers with labels and text boxes;
- the essentials of strings.

● Introduction

Numbers of one type or another occur in most programs, for example, drawing pictures using screen coordinates, controlling spaceflight trajectories, calculating salaries and tax deductions.

Here we will introduce the two basic types of number:

- whole numbers, known as integers in maths and as the `Integer` type in VB;
- 'decimal-point' numbers, known as 'real' in maths, 'float' in C++ and Java, and as `Double` in VB. The general term for decimal-point numbers in computing is *floating-point*.

Previously we used values to produce screen graphics, but for more sophisticated programs we need to introduce the concept of a variable – a kind of storage box used to remember values, so that these values can be used or altered later in the program.

There are undeniably some `Integer` situations:

- the number of students in a class;
- the number of pixels on a screen;
- the number of copies of this book sold so far;

and there are some undeniable Double situations:

- my height in metres;
- the mass of an atom in grams;
- the average of the integers 3 and 4.

However, sometimes the type is not obvious; consider a variable for holding an exam mark – Double or Integer? The answer is that you don't know yet – you must seek further clarification, e.g. by asking the marker if they mark to the nearest whole number, or if they ever use decimal places. Thus, the choice of Integer or Double is determined by the problem.

The nature of Integer

When we use an Integer in VB, it can be a whole number in the range –2147483648 to +2147483647 or, approximately –2000000000 to +2000000000.

All Integer calculations are accurate, in the sense that all the information in the number is preserved correctly.

The nature of Double

When we use a Double number in VB, its value can be between -1.79×10^{308} to $+1.79 \times 10^{308}$. In less mathematical terms, the largest value is 179 followed by 306 zeroes – very large indeed! Numbers are held to an approximate accuracy of 15 digits.

The main point about Double quantities is that they are stored approximately in many cases. Try this on a calculator:

7 / 3

Using seven digits, for example, the answer is 2.333333, whereas we know that a closer answer is:

2.33333333333333333

Even this is not the exact answer!

In short, because Double quantities are stored in a limited number of digits, small errors can build up at the least significant end. For many calculations (e.g. exam marks) this is not important, but for calculations involving, say, the design of a space shuttle, it might be. However, Double has such a large range and digits of precision that calculations involving everyday quantities will be accurate enough.

Declaring variables

Once the type of our variables has been chosen, we need to name them. We can imagine them as storage boxes with a name on the outside and a number (value) inside. The value may change as the program works through its sequence of operations, but the name is fixed. The programmer is free to choose the names, and we recommend choosing meaningful ones rather than cryptic ones. But as in most programming languages, there are certain rules that must be followed. In VB, names:

- must start with a letter (A to Z, a to z);
- can contain any number of letters or digits (a digit is 0 to 9);
- can contain the underscore '_';
- can be up to 255 characters long.

Note that VB is not case-sensitive. If a programming language is case-sensitive, we can have two different variables with different capitalization, such as `width` and `Width`. In VB, once you have declared `width`, any attempt to declare a variable `Width` will result in a compilation error. Your variables must differ in spelling, not just capitalization.

Those are the VB rules – and we have to obey the rules. But there is also a VB style – a way of using the rules which is followed when a variable consists of several words. The rules do not allow spaces in names, so rather than use short names or the underscore, the accepted style for variables is to capitalize the start of each word.

There is another style guideline regarding whether or not the first letter of a name is capitalized. In this chapter we are dealing with variables that are only used within a method (rather than being shared between several methods). Variables such as these are known as *local* and can only be used between the `Sub` and the `End Sub` in which they are declared. Returning to style conventions, the VB approach is to *not* capitalize the first letter of local variables. Later, we will see that other types of name, such as method names, control names and class names are conventionally begun with a capital letter.

Thus, rather than:

```
Heightofbox
h
hob
height_of_box
```

we put:

```
heightOfBox
```

Here are some allowed names:

```
amount
x
pay2003
```

and here are some unallowable (illegal) names:

```
2001pay
_area
my age
```

Note that there are also some reserved names that VB uses and which can't be reused by the programmer. They are termed *keywords* in VB. You have seen some of them, e.g.:

```
Private
Dim
New
```

A full list is provided in Appendix B.

> **SELF-TEST QUESTION**
>
> **4.1** Which of the following local variable names are allowed in VB, and which have the correct style?
>
> ```
> volume
> AREA
> Length
> 3sides
> side1
> lenth
> Mysalary
> your salary
> screenSize
> Dim
> ```

Here is an example program, named 'Area Rectangle', which we will study in detail. It calculates the area of a rectangle. We have assumed that its sides are `Integer` quantities. There is only one control on the form – a button with its `Text` property set to 'Calculate'. All our added code will be inside the `Button1_Click` method.

```
Private Sub Button1_Click( _
              ByVal sender As System.Object, _
              ByVal e As System.EventArgs) _
              Handles Button1.Click
    Dim area As Integer
    Dim length As Integer
    Dim breadth As Integer
    length = 20
    breadth = 10
    area = length * breadth
    MessageBox.Show("Area is: " & CStr(area))
End Sub
```

42 ● Chapter 4/Variables and calculations

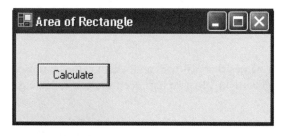

Figure 4.1 Screenshot of Area Rectangle.

Figure 4.1 shows what you will see on the screen.

In the program we have used three **Integer** variables, which eventually will hold our rectangle data. Recall that we can choose whatever names we like, but have opted for clear names rather than single-letter or funny names. (Funny names are only funny the first time you see them!)

Now that names are chosen, we must declare them to the VB system. Though this seems like tedious red tape at first, the point of introducing them is to enable the compiler to spot misspellings lower down the program. Here are the declarations:

```
Dim area As Integer
Dim length As Integer
Dim breadth As Integer
```

The word **Dim** is used to declare local variables that are only going to be used inside one method of the program, between **Private Sub**, and **End Sub**. Here our variables are used between **Sub Button1_Click** and its matching **End Sub**. **Dim** is not a very meaningful name, but it has been carried through from early versions of Basic, where it was short for 'dimension'.

Note the use of **Integer** to show that each variable will hold a whole number. Alternatively, we could have put:

```
Dim length, breadth, area As Integer
```

using commas to separate each name. The style is up to you, but we have a preference for the first style, which enables you to comment each name if you need to. If you use the second style, use it to group related names. For example, put:

```
Dim pictureHeight, pictureWidth As Integer
Dim myAge As Integer
```

rather than:

```
Dim pictureHeight, pictureWidth, myAge As Integer
```

In the majority of programs we will use several types, and in VB we are free to intermingle the declarations, as in:

```
Dim personHeight As Double
Dim examMark As Integer
Dim salary As Double
```

Additionally, we can choose to initialize the value of the variable as we declare it, as in:

```
Dim personHeight As Double = 1.68
Dim a As Integer = 3, b As Integer = 4
Dim examMark As Integer = 65
Dim betterMark As Integer = examMark + 10
```

This is good style, but only use it when you really know the initial value. If you don't supply an initial value, VB sets numeric variables to zero, and string variables to an empty string.

The assignment statement

Once we have declared our variables, we can place new values in them by means of the 'assignment statement', as in:

```
length = 20
```

Pictorially, we can imagine the process as in Figure 4.2. We say: 'the value 20 has been assigned to the variable `length`' or '`length` becomes 20'.

Note:

- The movement of data is from the right of the = to the left.
- Whatever value was in `length` before is now 'overwritten' by 20. Variables have only one value – the current one. And just to give you a flavour of the speed: an assignment takes less than one-millionth of a second.

Calculations and operators

Recall our rectangle program, which included the statement:

```
area = length * breadth
```

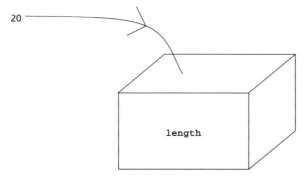

Figure 4.2 Assigning a value to a variable.

The general form of the assignment statement is:

```
variable = expression
```

An expression can take several forms: for example, a single number or a calculation. In our specific example, the sequence of events is:

1. '*' causes multiplication of the values stored in length and breadth, resulting in the value 200.
2. The equals symbol = causes the 200 to be assigned to (stored in) area.

The * is one of several 'operators' (so called because they operate on values) and, just as in maths, there are rules for their use.

An understanding of the movement of data is important, and enables us to understand the meaning of code such as:

```
Dim n As Integer = 10
n = n + 1
```

What happens is that the right-hand side of the = is calculated using the current value of n, resulting in 11. This value is then stored in n, replacing the old value of 10. In fact, years ago a large number of programs were studied, and statements of the form:

```
something = something + 1
```

were found to be the most common instructions!

The conclusion you can draw from the above is that = does not mean 'is equal to' in the algebra sense. You should imagine it as meaning 'becomes' or 'gets'.

The arithmetic operators

Here we present a basic set of operators – the arithmetic ones, akin to the buttons on your calculator. By the way, in this context, we pronounce the adjective 'arithmetic' as 'arithMETic'.

Operator	Meaning
^	exponent (power of)
*	multiply
/	division of doubles
\	division of integers
Mod	modulo
+	add
–	subtract

Note that we have split the operators into groups, to indicate their 'precedence' – the order in which they are obeyed. Thus, *, / and \ are carried out before + and -. We can also use parentheses (round brackets) to group calculations and force them to be calculated first. If a calculation involves operators of the same precedence, the calculation is performed from left to right. Here are some examples:

```
Dim i As Integer
Dim n As Integer = 3
Dim d As Double
i = n + 3              ' set to 6
i = n * 4              ' set to 12
i = 7 + 2 * 4          ' set to 15
n = n * (n + 2) * 4    ' set to 60
d = 3 * 2 ^ 4          ' set to 48.0
d = 3.5 / 2            ' set to 1.75
n = 6 \ 4              ' set to 1
```

Recall that the instructions form a sequence, executed from top to bottom of the page. Wherever brackets are used, the items within them are calculated first. Multiply and divide are performed before add and subtract, and the rarely used exponent ('to power of') operator is performed first. Thus:

```
3 * 2 ^ 4
```

is performed as if it had been written:

```
3 * (2 ^ 4)
```

We will explain the use of the Mod and \ operators below.

> **SELF-TEST QUESTION**
>
> **4.2** In the following, what are the values of the variables after each statement?
>
> ```
> Dim a, b, c, d As Integer
>     d = -8
>     a = 1 * 2 + 3
>     b = 1 + 2 * 3
>     c = (1 + 2) * 3
>     c = a + b
>     d = -d
> ```

Now we know the rules. But there are still pitfalls for the beginner. Let us look at some maths formulae, and their conversion into VB. We assume that all variables have been declared as doubles, and initialized.

Mathematics version	VB version
1 $y = mx + c$	$y = m * x + c$
2 $x = (a - b)(a + b)$	$x = (a - b) * (a + b)$
3 $y = 3[(a - b)(a + b)] - x$	$y = 3 * ((a - b) * (a + b)) - x$
4 $y = 1 - \dfrac{2a}{3b}$	$y = 1 - (2 * a) / (3 * b)$

In example 1, we insert the multiply symbol. In VB, `mx` would be treated as one variable name.

In example 2, we need an explicit multiply between the brackets.

In example 3, we replace the mathematics square brackets with parentheses.

In example 4, we might have gone for this incorrect version:

```
y = 1 - 2 * a / 3 * b
```

Recall the left-to-right rule for equal precedence operators. The problem is to do with `*` and `/`. The order of evaluation is as if we had put:

```
y = 1 - (2 * a / 3) * b
```

i.e. the `b` is now multiplying instead of dividing. The simplest way to handle potentially confusing calculations is to use extra brackets – there is no penalty in terms of program size or speed.

The use of `+`, `-` and `*` is reasonably intuitive, but division is slightly trickier, as we need to distinguish between `Integer` and `Double` types. The essential points are:

- division with `/` will convert the two items it is working on (whether integer or double) into doubles first. Then it divides, giving a double result. This is how dividing works on a calculator;

division with \ will only work with integers. A compilation error will result if we try to divide doubles. The integer values are divided, producing an integer result. The number is truncated, meaning that any 'decimal point' digits are erased. This is *not* how a calculator works.

Here are some examples:

```
' using /
Dim d As Double
d = 7.61 / 2.1         ' set to 3.7
d = 33 / 44            ' set to 0.75

'using \
Dim i As Integer
i = 10 \ 5             ' set to 2
i = 13 \ 5             ' set to 2
i = 33 \ 44            ' set to 0
```

In the first / case, the division takes place as you would expect.
In the second / case, the numbers are treated as 33.0 and 44.0. They are then divided.
In the first \ case, the division with integers is as expected. The exact answer of 2 is produced.
In the second \ case, the truncated answer is 2. Takes place.
In the third \ case, the 'proper' answer of 0.75 is truncated, giving 0.

> **SELF-TEST QUESTIONS**
>
> **4.3** My salary is $20 000, and I agree to give you half using the following calculation:
>
> ```
> Dim half As Integer = 20000 * (1 \ 2)
> ```
>
> How much do you get?
>
> **4.4** State the values that end up in a, b, c and d, after these calculations are performed:
>
> ```
> Dim a, b, c As Integer
> Dim d As Double
> a = 7 \ 3
> b = a * 4
> c = (a + 1) \ 2
> d = c / 3
> ```

The Mod operator

Our final operator is Mod. It is often used in conjunction with integer division, as it supplies the remainder part. Its name comes from the term 'modulo' used in a branch of mathematics known as modular arithmetic.

Earlier, we said that `Double` values are stored approximately, and integers are stored exactly. So how can it be that 33 \ 44 gives an integer result of 0? Surely losing the 0.75 means that the calculation is not accurate? The answer is that integers *do* operate exactly, but the exact answer is composed of two parts: the quotient (i.e. the main answer) and the remainder. Thus 4 divided by 3 gives an answer of 1, with remainder 3. This is more exact than 1.3333333 etc.

So, the `Mod` operator gives us the remainder, as if a division had taken place. Here are some examples:

```
Dim i As Integer
Dim d As Double
i = 12 Mod 4              ' set to 0
i = 13 Mod 4              ' set to 1
i = 15 Mod 4              ' set to 3
d = 14.9 Mod 3.9          ' set to 3.2 (divides 3 times)
```

By far the most frequent use of `Mod` is with `Integer` types, but, as a minor point of interest, note that it works with `Double` as well. Here is a problem involving `Mod`: convert a whole number of cents into two quantities – the number of dollars and the number of cents remaining. The solution is:

```
Dim cents As Integer = 234
Dim dollars, centsRemaining As Integer
dollars = cents \ 100              ' set to 2
centsRemaining = cents Mod 100     ' set to 34
```

> **SELF-TEST QUESTION**
>
> 4.5 Complete the following, adding assignment statements to split `totalSeconds` into two variables: `minutes` and `seconds`.
>
> ```
> Dim totalSeconds As Integer = 307
> ```

Strings and numbers: the & operator

So far we have looked at the use of numeric variables, but the processing of text data is also highly important. VB provides the `String` data type, and `string` variables can hold any characters. The maximum length of a string is around two billion – larger than the RAM size of current computers, in fact. This topic also introduces us to the area of 'type conversion'.

Here is an example of using strings:

```
Dim firstName As String = "Mike "
Dim lastName, wholeName As String
Dim greeting As String
```

Strings and numbers: the & operator

```
lastName = "Parr"
wholeName = firstName & lastName
greeting = "Hi from " & wholeName 'set to "Hi from Mike Parr"
```

In the above, we have declared some string variables, providing some initial values using double quotes. If we don't initialize a string, it contains no characters – a so-called 'empty string', as if it had been declared by:

```
Dim greeting As String = ""
```

We then used assignment, in which the value of the string to the right of the = is stored in the variable used on the left of the =, in a similar manner to numeric assignment.

The next lines illustrate the use of the & operator for string 'concatenation', or joining. After the statement:

```
wholeName = firstName & lastName
```

the value of `wholeName` is `Mike Parr`. When typing the & operator, you need to put a space before and after it, otherwise it will not be interpreted as we wish.

In addition, there is a wide range of string methods which provide such operations as searching and modifying strings. We consider these in Chapter 16.

One crucial use of the `string` data type is in input and output, where we process data entered by a user, and display results on the screen. Many of VB's GUI controls work with strings of characters rather than numbers, so we need to know how to convert between numbers and strings.

To convert a numeric variable or calculation (in general an expression) we can use the `CStr` (convert to string) function. We supply a numeric value in brackets, as in:

```
Dim s as String
Dim num As Integer
num = 44
s = CStr(num)
```

In our program which calculated the area of a rectangle, we made use of & and `CStr` when using a pop-up message box. Rather than just displaying the number, we joined it to a message:

```
MessageBox.Show("Area is: " & CStr(area))
```

Note that the following will not compile, as the `show` method expects a `String` as a parameter:

```
MessageBox.Show(area)      'NO - will not compile!
```

You must put:

```
MessageBox.Show(CStr(area))
```

To complement `CStr`, we have `CDbl` and `CInt`, which convert an item (often a string) to `Double` and `Integer` respectively. They can also be used to convert between `Double` and `Integer`, as shown later in this chapter. Here are some examples:

```
Dim d As Double
Dim i As Integer
Dim s As String = "12.3"
i = CInt("12")
d = CDbl(s)
```

Each of the functions has an argument in brackets, like the methods we studied in Chapter 3. Strictly, they are not part of a class, and we refer to them as functions rather than methods.

> **SELF-TEST QUESTION**
>
> **4.6** What are the final values of m, n and s after the following code executes?
>
> ```
> Dim m, n As Integer
> Dim s As String
> Dim v As String = "3"
> m = CInt(v & v & "4")
> n = CInt(v & v) + 4
> s = CStr(CInt(v) + CInt(v)) & "4"
> ```

Now we know about string conversion, we can begin to use some new controls.

Text boxes and labels

Our earlier programs made use of assignment statements to set up initial values for calculations, but in reality, we will not know these values when we write the program. Rather, the user will enter values as a program executes. Here we will introduce the `TextBox` control, which allows a user to key in some data, and the `Label` control, which is used to display data (e.g. results of calculations, instructions to the user) on a form.

Text boxes can be selected on the toolbox, and dropped on to a form. They have a large number of properties, but the main property is `Text`, which supplies us with the string that the user typed. We access it in this manner:

```
Dim s As String
s = TextBox1.Text
```

Often, we clear the `Text` property of the control at design time via the properties window, to give the user an empty area to type into.

Labels can also be selected on the toolbox, and positioned on a form. As with text boxes, the main property is `Text`, which allows us to set up the string that the label displays. We access it in this manner:

```
Dim s As String = "Stop"
Label1.Text = s
```

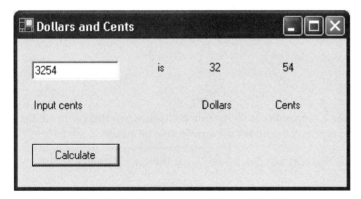

Figure 4.3 Screenshot of Dollars and Cents.

Some labels will display help for the user, and normally we set their `Text` property at design-time via the properties window. Their text need not change as the program runs. For labels that will display results, we set their `Text` property at run-time, as shown above. Text boxes can be overtyped by the user, but labels are protected from being overtyped.

We access properties with the familiar 'dot' notation: recall our use of graphics:

```
paper.DrawRectangle(myPen, 10, 10, 100, 100)
```

In general, classes have both methods and properties. Methods make objects do things, whereas properties let us access the current state of an object.

Here is an example program (Dollars And Cents) – which breaks down a number of cents into dollars and cents. We looked at the use of \ and `Mod` earlier in this chapter. A screenshot of its execution is shown in Figure 4.3. The program uses a text box and several labels.

```
    Private Sub Button1_Click( _
                    ByVal sender As System.Object, _
                    ByVal e As System.EventArgs) _
                    Handles Button1.Click
        Dim cents As Integer
        cents = CInt(TextBox1.Text)
        DollarsLabel.Text = CStr(cents \ 100)
        CentsLabel.Text = CStr(cents Mod 100)
    End Sub
```

The main controls we use are:

- a button to initiate the conversion;
- a text box where the user enters a number of cents;
- two labels for the display of the number of dollars and number of cents.

52 ● Chapter 4/Variables and calculations

In addition, there are three labels alongside the input text box and the two output labels, to improve the user's understanding of the form. Their text values are:

```
Input Cents
Dollars
Cents
```

As we explained in Chapter 2, our policy is to rename controls when there is more than once instance of the same type of control on a form. In this program:

- there is one button and one text box, so we can leave these with the name that VB provides;
- there are two labels which display results, so we choose to rename them;
- the remaining labels have their text set at design-time, and are never manipulated by the program. We can safely leave these unaltered.

Here is a summary of the main properties.

Control	Property	Setting
Button1	Text	Calculate
TextBox1	Text	(empty)
DollarsLabel	Text	(empty)
CentsLabel	Text	(empty)

Remember that renaming should be done as soon as you place a control on the form, before double-clicking to create any event code.

When the program runs, the user enters a number in the text box. Clicking the button causes the calculation to take place, and causes results to be placed in the two labels. However, note that we must convert from strings to numbers and vice versa. Here is an extract:

```
cents = CInt(TextBox1.Text)
DollarsLabel.Text = CStr(cents \ 100)
```

The program illustrates the use of a text box, and the use of labels to display changing results and unchanging messages.

> **SELF-TEST QUESTION**
>
> **4.7** Both message boxes and labels can be used to display results. What is the main difference?

Figure 4.4 An `InputBox`.

The `InputBox`

The input box is rather like a message box, in that it occupies no permanent screen space – it pops up when needed. Like the message box it must be acknowledged, and we can use it to force the user to enter data. You will have encountered this type of input when you log on to a computer. However, the over-use of input boxes can slow down the user interaction. Use them with care. Figure 4.4 shows the input box created from the first line of code below, where we input a string. The second line shows the input of a number:

```
Dim n As Integer
Dim s As String
s = InputBox("Enter your name")
n = CInt(InputBox("Enter your age"))
```

The string in brackets provides a prompt for the user. The input box sends the string that the user enters into our program, where typically we assign it to a variable. In the case of numeric input, we use one of the conversion functions before assigning it. For our introductory programs, we assume that the user will not make a typing error, and will not cancel the input box.

Converting between numbers

Sometimes, we need to convert numeric values from one type to another. The most common cases are converting an `Integer` to a `Double`, and a `Double` to an `Integer`. Here are some examples:

```
Dim i As Integer = 33
Dim d As Double = 3.9
Dim d1 As Double
```

```
d1 = i                  ' set to 33
' or, explicitly:
d1 = CDbl(i)            ' set to 33
i = CInt(d)             ' set to 4
```

The main points are:

- assigning an `Integer` to a `Double` works without any additional programming. This is safe, as no information can be lost – there are no decimal places to worry about;
- assigning a `Double` to an `Integer` requires that something be done with the decimal places, which will not fit into the integer. Because of this potential loss of information, VB requires that we explicitly use type conversion (e.g. by using `CInt`). The double value is rounded to the nearest integer as it is converted.

> **SELF-TEST QUESTION**
>
> **4.8** What are the values of a, b, c, i, j, k after the following code is executed?
>
> ```
> Dim i, j, k As Integer
> Dim a, b, c As Double
> Dim x As Integer = 3
> Dim y As Double = 2.7
>
> i = CInt(y)
> j = CInt(y + 0.6)
> k = CInt(CDbl(x) + 0.2)
>
> a = x
> b = CInt(y)
> c = CDbl(y)
> ```

The role of expressions

Though we have emphasized that expressions (calculations) can form the right-hand side of assignment statements, they can occur in other places. In fact, we can place an `Integer` expression anywhere we can place a single `Integer`. Recall our use of the `DrawLine` method, which has four integers specifying the start and end of the line. We could (if it was useful) replace the numbers with variables, or with expressions:

```
Dim x As Integer = 100
Dim y As Integer = 200
paper.DrawLine(myPen, 100, 100, 110, 110)
paper.DrawLine(myPen, x, y, x + 50, y + 50)
paper.DrawLine(myPen, x * 2, y - 8, x * 30 - 1, y * 3 + 6)
```

The expressions are calculated, and the resulting values are passed into `DrawLine` for it to make use of.

Programming principles

- A variable has a name, which the programmer chooses.
- Variables are declared with `Dim`.
- A variable holds a value.
- The value of a variable can be changed with an assignment statement.

Programming pitfalls

- Take care with the spelling of variable names. For example, in:

    ```
    Dim circ1e As Integer  ' misspelling
    circle = 20
    ```

    there is a misspelling of a variable, using a '1' (one) instead of a lower-case 'L'. The VB compiler will complain about the second spelling being undeclared. Another favourite error is using a zero instead of a capital 'O'.
- Compilation errors are tricky to spot at the beginning. Though the VB compiler gives an indication of where it thinks the error is, the actual error could be in a previous line.
- Brackets must balance – there must be the same number of '(' as ')'.
- When using numbers with the text property of labels and text boxes, remember to use the string conversion facilities.
- When multiplying items, you must place * between them, whereas in maths it is omitted.

Grammar spot

- Use `Dim` to declare all variables, as in:

    ```
    Dim myVariable As Integer
    Dim yourVariable As String = "Hello there!"
    ```

- The most useful types are `Integer`, `Double`, and `String`.
- The arithmetic operators are ^, *, /, \, Mod, +, -.
- The `&` operator is used to join strings.
- We can convert numbers to strings with `CStr`.
- We can convert strings to numbers with `CInt` and `CDbl`.
- We can obtain a string from the user with an input box, as in:

    ```
    someString = InputBox("message")
    ```

New language elements

- `Dim Double Integer String`.
- The operators `+ - * / \ ^ Mod &`.
- `=` for assignment.
- Type conversion: `CStr CInt CDbl`.

New IDE facilities

- The `TextBox` and `Label` controls, with their `Text` properties.
- The renaming of controls.
- The `InputBox`.

Summary

- Variables are used to hold (store) values. They keep their value until explicitly changed (e.g. by another assignment statement).
- Operators operate on values.
- An expression is a calculation which produces a value. It can be used in a variety of situations, including the right-hand side of an assignment, and as an argument of a method call.

EXERCISES

4.1 Extend the rectangle program provided in this chapter to compute the volume of a box, given its three dimensions.

4.2 (a) Using the following value:

```
Dim radius As Double = 7.5
```

use assignment statements to calculate the circumference of a circle, the area of a circle, and the volume of a sphere, based on the same radius. Display the results with messages boxes. The message should state what the result is, rather than merely displaying a number. These calculations involve the use of Pi, which is 3.14 approximately. However, VB provides us with this value to more digits of precision. It is part of the `Math` class, as the following formulae show its use:

```
circumference = 2* Math.PI * radius
area = Math.PI * radius ^ 2
volume = (4 / 3) * Math.PI * radius ^ 3
```

(b) Modify part (a) so that the value of the radius is obtained from an input box.

(c) Modify part (a) to use a text box for the input of the radius, and labels for results. Use additional labels to clarify the presentation of the results.

4.3 Two students take a VB exam, and their results are assigned to two variables:

```
Dim mark1 As Integer = 44
Dim mark2 As Integer = 51
```

Write a program which calculates and displays the average mark as a Double value. Check your answer with a calculator.

4.4 Two students take a VB exam, and their results – as produced by a very discriminating examiner – are Double values. Write a program which calculates and displays the average mark as a Double value. Check your answer with a calculator.

4.5 Assume that individuals are taxed at 20% of their income. Obtain an income value from a text box, then calculate and display the initial amount, the amount after deductions, and the deducted amount. Use labels to make the results understandable.

4.6 Using Double types, write a program which converts a Fahrenheit temperature to its Celsius (centigrade) equivalent. The formula is:

```
c = (f - 32) * 5 / 9
```

4.7 We are provided with an initial number of seconds:

```
Dim totalSeconds As Integer = 2549
```

Write a program to convert this to hours, minutes and seconds. Do an example with pen and paper before you write the program. Use one message box to display the result, is the form:

```
H:1 M:24 S:9
```

4.8 This problem is to do with electrical resistors, which 'resist' the flow of electrical current through them. An analogy is a hosepipe – a thin one has a high resistance, and a thick one has a low resistance to water. We can imagine connecting two hosepipes in series, resulting in a higher resistance, or in parallel, reducing the resistance (effectively, a fatter pipe). Starting with:

```
Dim r1 as Double = 4.7
Dim r2 As Double = 6.8
```

calculate and display the series resistance, given by:

```
series = r1 + r2
```

and the parallel resistance, given by:

$$parallel = \frac{r1 * r2}{r1 + r2}$$

4.9 We require some software for installation in a European drink-dispensing machine. Here are the details: all items cost less than 1 euro (100 euro cents), and a 1 euro coin is the highest value that can be inserted. Given the amount inserted and the cost of the item, your program should give change, using the lowest number of coins. For example, if we had:

```
Dim amountGiven As Integer = 100
Dim itemCost As Integer = 45
```

the result should be a series of message boxes (one for each coin) of the form:

```
Number of 50 cent coins is 1
Number of 20 cent coins is 0
Number of 10 cent coins is 0
Number of 5 cent coins is 1
Number of 2 cent coins is 0
Number of 1 cent coins is 0
```

Hint: work in cents, and make extensive use of the Mod operator. The euro coins are: 100, 50, 20, 10, 5, 2, 1

4.10 Write a program which calculates the final amount (*f*) left in a bank account. The initial amount (*i*), number of years (*n*), and compound interest rate (*r*) per year can vary. Use the formula:

$$f = i\left[1 + \frac{r}{100}\right]^n$$

ANSWERS TO SELF-TEST QUESTIONS

4.1 volume – allowed, correct style;
AREA – allowed, but area preferred;
Length – allowed, but lower-case l preferred;
3sides – not allowed, starts with a digit;
side1 – allowed, correct style;
lenth – allowed, even with incorrect spelling of length;
mysalary – allowed, but capital S is preferred;
your salary – not allowed (no spaces allowed in middle of a name);
screenSize – allowed, correct style;
Dim – not allowed – it is a keyword.

4.2 The final values of a, b, c, d are 5, 7, 12, 8.

4.3 Unfortunately, you get zero, as (1 \ 2) is calculated first, resulting in 0. Use / instead.

4.4 The final values of a, b, c, d are 2, 8, 1, 0.333333 etc.

4.5
```
Dim totalSeconds As Integer = 307
Dim seconds, minutes As Integer
minutes = totalSeconds \ 60
seconds = totalSeconds Mod 60
```

4.6 The final values of `m`, `n` and `s` are 334, 37 and 64.

4.7 A label displays its results on the form, and requires no further user interaction. A message box pops up, and the user must click 'OK' to remove it. Thus, the message box forces the user to acknowledge its presence.

4.8 The values of the `Integer` variables `i, j, k` are 3, 3, 3, and the values of the `Double` variables `a, b, c` are 3.0, 3.0, 2.7.

Methods and arguments

This chapter explains:

- how to write methods and functions;
- how arguments and parameters are used;
- passing arguments by value and by reference;
- using `Return` in functions.

● Introduction

Large programs can be complex, with the result that they can be difficult to understand and debug. The most significant technique for reducing complexity is to split a program into (relatively) isolated sections. This allows us to focus on an isolated section without the distractions of the complete program. Furthermore, if the section has a name, we can 'call' or 'invoke' it (cause it to be used) merely by using this name. In a way, it enables us to think at a higher level. In VB, such sections are known as methods. We made extensive use of pre-written graphics methods to draw shapes on the screen in Chapter 3.

Recall the `DrawRectangle` method, which we call with five arguments in this manner:

```
paper.DrawRectangle(myPen, 10, 20, 60, 60)
```

First, the use of arguments – the items in brackets – allows us to control the size and position of the rectangle. This ensures that `DrawRectangle` is flexible enough for a variety of circumstances. The arguments modify its actions.

Second, note that we could produce a rectangle by using four calls of `DrawLine`. However, bundling up the four `DrawLine` instructions inside a method known as `DrawRectangle` is a sensible idea – it enables the programmer to think at a higher level.

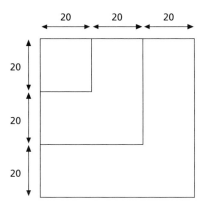

Figure 5.1 The company logo.

Writing your own methods

Here, we will introduce the concept of creating our own methods. Initially, we will choose a toy example for simplicity, then move on to a more practical example.

The Worldwide Cardboard Box Corporation has a logo, which consists of three squares within one another, as in Figure 5.1.

They wish to use this logo in several positions in a picture box, as in Figure 5.2. Here is the code to draw two identical logos at positions (10, 20) and (100, 100).

```
' Draw logo at top left
paper.DrawRectangle(myPen, 10, 20, 60, 60)
paper.DrawRectangle(myPen, 10, 20, 40, 40)
paper.DrawRectangle(myPen, 10, 20, 20, 20)

' Draw logo at bottom right
paper.DrawRectangle(myPen, 100, 100, 60, 60)
paper.DrawRectangle(myPen, 100, 100, 40, 40)
paper.DrawRectangle(myPen, 100, 100, 20, 20)
```

Note that the squares are of size 20, 40 and 60 pixels, with all their top left corners at the same point. Look at the code, and note that the three instructions to draw one logo are basically repeated, apart from the position of the top left of the logo. We will bundle up these three instructions as a method, so that a logo can be drawn with one instruction.

A first method

Here is a complete program, named Logo Method. It shows the creation and use of a method, which we chose to name `DrawLogo`. The VB style convention is to begin method names with a capital letter.

62 ● Chapter 5/Methods and arguments

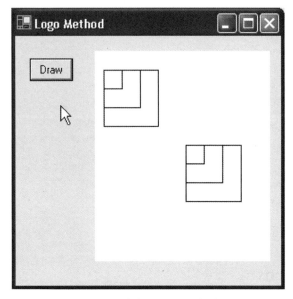

Figure 5.2 Screenshot of the Logo Method program.

```
    Private Sub Button1_Click( _
                    ByVal sender As System.Object, _
                    ByVal e As System.EventArgs) _
                    Handles Button1.Click
        Dim paper As Graphics
        paper = PictureBox1.CreateGraphics()
        Dim myPen As Pen = New Pen(Color.Black)
        DrawLogo(paper, myPen, 10, 20)
        DrawLogo(paper, myPen, 100, 100)

    End Sub
    Private Sub DrawLogo(ByVal drawingArea As Graphics, _
                    ByVal penToUse As Pen, _
                    ByVal xPos As Integer, _
                    ByVal yPos As Integer)
        drawingArea.DrawRectangle(penToUse, xPos, yPos, 60, 60)
        drawingArea.DrawRectangle(penToUse, xPos, yPos, 40, 40)
        drawingArea.DrawRectangle(penToUse, xPos, yPos, 20, 20)
    End Sub
```

The program has a picture box and a button. Clicking on the button causes two logos to be drawn, as in Figure 5.2.

The concept of methods and arguments is a major skill that all programmers need to master. We will now discuss the program in detail.

Look at the extract:

```
Private Sub DrawLogo(ByVal drawingArea As Graphics, _
                    ByVal penToUse As Pen, _
                    ByVal xPos As Integer, _
                    ByVal yPos As Integer)
```

This declares (introduces) the method, and is known as the method header. The word `Sub` is short for subroutine (another name for a method). The header states the name of the method (which we had the freedom to choose), and the items that must be supplied to control its operation. VB uses the terms *arguments* and *parameters* in this area – we shall examine them below. The rest of the method, ended by an `End Sub`, is known as the body, and is where the work gets done. Often the header is a long line, and we may choose to split it up at suitable points using space and underscore.

Calling a method

In VB, we call a private method by stating its name, together with a list of arguments in brackets. In our program, the first call is:

```
DrawLogo(paper, myPen, 10, 20)
```

This statement has two effects:

- The argument values are automatically transferred into the method. We cover this in more detail below.
- The program jumps to the body of the method (the statements after the header), and executes the statements. When it runs out of statements and reaches the `End Sub`, execution is continued back at the point where the method was called from.

The second call then takes place:

```
DrawLogo(paper, myPen, 100, 100)
```

Figure 5.3 illustrates this. There are two calls, producing two logos.

Passing arguments

It is essential to have an understanding of how arguments are transferred (i.e. passed) into methods. In our example, the concept is shown in the following lines:

```
DrawLogo(paper, myPen, 10, 20)

Private Sub DrawLogo(ByVal drawingArea As Graphics, _
                    ByVal penToUse As Pen, _
                    ByVal xPos As Integer, _
                    ByVal yPos As Integer)
```

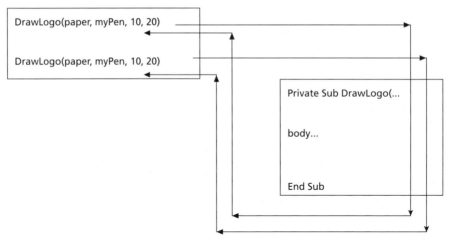

Figure 5.3 Execution path of two calls.

The area to focus on is the two lists of items in brackets. In a call, the items are termed *arguments*. In the header of the method, the items are termed *parameters*. To clarify the situation, we will extract the parameters and arguments:

```
arguments:    paper         myPen        10      20
parameters:   drawingArea   penToUse     xPos    yPos
```

Recall our likening of a variable to a box. Inside the method, a set of empty boxes (the parameters) awaits the transfer of argument values. After the transfer, we have the situation shown in Figure 5.4. We don't have any numeric values to use for the passing of the drawing area and pen, so focus on the passing of the coordinates.

The transfer takes place in a left-to-right order. The call must provide the correct number and type of arguments. If the caller (the user) accidentally gets arguments in the wrong order, the transfer process won't re-order them! When the DrawLogo method executes, the above values control the drawing process. Though we have called the method with numbers, we can use expressions (i.e. involving variables and calculations), as in:

```
Dim x As Integer = 6
DrawLogo(paper, myPen, 20 + 3, 3 * 2 + 1)  ' 23 and 7
DrawLogo(paper, myPen, x * 4, 20)  ' 24 and 20
```

Figure 5.4 Transferring arguments into parameters.

In VB there are two ways to pass items to a method – by reference and by value. We cover passing by reference later in this chapter.

> **SELF-TEST QUESTION**
>
> 5.1 Whereabouts will the logos be drawn in the following code?
>
> ```
> Dim a As Integer = 10
> Dim b As Integer = 20
> DrawLogo(paper, myPen, a, b)
> DrawLogo(paper, myPen, b + a, b - a)
> DrawLogo(paper, myPen, b + a - 3, b + a - 4)
> ```

Parameters and arguments

There are two bracketed lists that we are discussing, and it is important to be clear about the purpose of each list:

- The writer of the method must choose which items the method will request via parameters. Thus, in `DrawLogo`, the dimensions of the nested squares are always set to 20, 40 and 60, so the caller need not supply this data. However, the caller might wish to vary the position of the logo, to use a different pen, or even to draw the logo on a different component (such as a button). These items have been made into parameters.
- The writer of the method must choose names for each parameter. If similar names are used in other methods, no problem arises – each method has its own copy of its parameters. In other words, the writer is free to choose any name.
- The writer of the method must choose how the argument will be passed into the parameter: the choice is between `ByVal` or `ByRef`. We will use `ByVal` in all our introductory examples.
- The type of each parameter must be provided by using the `As` keyword, rather like its use in `Dim`. The types depend on the particular method. A comma is used to separate one parameter from another. Look at the `DrawLogo` header to see the arrangement.
- The caller must supply a list of arguments in brackets. The arguments must be in the correct order for the method, and must be of the correct type.

The two benefits of using a method for the logo drawing are that we remove the duplication of the three `DrawRectangle` statements when several logos are needed, and giving the task a name enables us to think at a higher level.

Finally, we recognize that you might wish to transfer the programming skills that you learn here into other languages. The concepts are similar, but the terminology is different: in many languages, the caller supplies 'actual parameters', and the method declaration has 'formal parameters'.

> **SELF-TEST QUESTIONS**
>
> **5.2** Explain what is wrong with these calls:
>
> ```
> DrawLogo(paper, myPen, 50, "10")
> DrawLogo(myPen, paper, 50, 10)
> DrawLogo(paper, myPen, 10)
> ```
>
> **5.3** Here is the call of a method:
>
> ```
> JustDoIt("Oranges")
> ```
>
> and here is the method itself:
>
> ```
> Private Sub JustDoIt(ByVal fruit As String)
>     MessageBox.Show(fruit)
> End Sub
> ```
>
> What happens when the method is called?

● A triangle method

In order to introduce more features of methods, we shall create a more useful method, which we shall name `DrawTriangle`. Because *we* are writing the method (rather than making use of a pre-written one) we can choose what kind of triangle, and can choose the arguments that we want the caller to supply. We will choose to draw a right-angled triangle, pointing to the right, as in Figure 5.5.

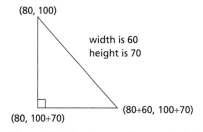

Figure 5.5 Triangle coordinate calculations.

In choosing arguments, there are a number of possibilities – for example we might demand that the caller gives us the coordinates of the three corners. However, we have chosen the arguments to be:

- the drawing area and pen, as before;
- the coordinates of the top point of the triangle;

- the width of the triangle;
- the height of the triangle.

Another way to regard these coordinates is that they specify the position of an enclosing rectangle for our right-angled triangle.

We can draw the lines in any order. Let us examine the drawing process with numbers at first. As an example, we will draw a triangle with the top corner at (80, 100) and with a width of 60 and a height of 70. Figure 5.5 shows the calculations. The process is:

- Draw from (80, 100) down to (80, 100+70). Remember that the *y* coordinate increases as we move down.
- Draw from (80, 100+70) across to (80+60, 100+70).
- Draw from the top corner (80, 100) diagonally to (80+60, 100+70).

Ensure that you can follow the above – maybe sketch it out on paper.

Note that in our explanation, we did not simplify the calculations: we left 100+70 as it is, rather than as 170. When we come to the coding, the position of the triangle and the size of the triangle will be passed in as separate arguments.

Here is a complete program which is named Triangle Method. It contains a `DrawTriangle` method. It also contains the `DrawLogo` method, to illustrate that a program can contain many methods.

```
    Private Sub Button1_Click( _
                    ByVal sender As System.Object, _
                    ByVal e As System.EventArgs) _
                    Handles Button1.Click
        Dim paper As Graphics
        paper = PictureBox1.CreateGraphics()
        Dim myPen As Pen = New Pen(Color.Black)
        DrawLogo(paper, myPen, 10, 20)
        DrawLogo(paper, myPen, 100, 100)
        DrawTriangle(paper, myPen, 100, 10, 40, 40)
        DrawTriangle(paper, myPen, 10, 100, 20, 60)
    End Sub

    Private Sub DrawLogo(ByVal drawingArea As Graphics, _
                    ByVal penToUse As Pen, _
                    ByVal xPos As Integer, _
                    ByVal yPos As Integer)
        drawingArea.DrawRectangle(penToUse, xPos, yPos, 60, 60)
        drawingArea.DrawRectangle(penToUse, xPos, yPos, 40, 40)
        drawingArea.DrawRectangle(penToUse, xPos, yPos, 20, 20)
    End Sub
```

68 ● Chapter 5/Methods and arguments

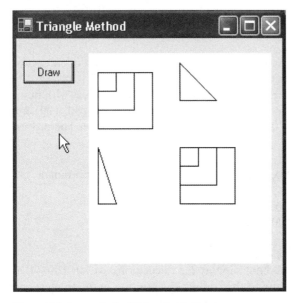

Figure 5.6 Screenshot of Triangle Method program.

```
Private Sub DrawTriangle(ByVal drawingArea As Graphics, _
                        ByVal penToUse As Pen, _
                        ByVal xPlace As Integer, _
                        ByVal yPlace As Integer, _
                        ByVal width As Integer, _
                        ByVal height As Integer)
    drawingArea.DrawLine(penToUse, xPlace, yPlace, _
                         xPlace, yPlace + height)
    drawingArea.DrawLine(penToUse, xPlace, _
                         yPlace + height, _
                         xPlace + width, yPlace + height)
    drawingArea.DrawLine(penToUse, xPlace, yPlace, _
                         xPlace + width, yPlace + height)
End Sub
```

It has a button and a picture box. Click on the button to draw two logos and two triangles. Figure 5.6 shows the output.

Here are some points about the coding of the `DrawTriangle` method:

- We chose to name it `DrawTriangle`, but it is up to us. We could have chosen `Triangle`, or even `DrawThing`, but `DrawTriangle` fits with the names of the library methods.
- The names for the parameters: `drawingArea`, `penToUse`, `xPlace`, `yPlace`, `width`, and `height` were our choice.

- The order of the parameters was also under our control. We could re-code the method to require the height before the width if we wanted to. (We put the width first because many of VB's library methods use this order.)

So – we have our triangle. We will use it to look at local variables, and also show how it can be a 'building brick' for more powerful methods.

Local variables

In Chapter 4, we saw the use of `Dim` to declare variables, but we did not look at the relationship between variables and methods. Here we will do this.

Look at this modified version of `DrawTriangle`, which we have named `DrawTriangle2`:

```
Private Sub DrawTriangle2(ByVal drawingArea As Graphics, _
                  ByVal penToUse As Pen, _
                  ByVal xPlace As Integer, _
                  ByVal yPlace As Integer, _
                  ByVal width As Integer, _
                  ByVal height As Integer)
    Dim rightCornerX, rightCornerY As Integer
    rightCornerX = xPlace + width
    rightCornerY = yPlace + height

    drawingArea.DrawLine(penToUse, xPlace, yPlace, _
                    xPlace, rightCornerY)
    drawingArea.DrawLine(penToUse, xPlace, rightCornerY, _
                    rightCornerX, rightCornerY)
    drawingArea.DrawLine(penToUse, xPlace, yPlace, _
                    rightCornerX, rightCornerY)
End Sub
```

It is called in just the same way as `DrawTriangle`, but internally it uses two variables, named `rightCornerX` and `rightCornerY`, which have been introduced to simplify the calculations. Look at how they are used to refer to the rightmost point of the triangle. These variables exist only within `DrawTriangle2`. They are local to the method (the terminology is that they have local *scope*). If variables of the same name exist within other methods, then there is no conflict, in that each method uses its own copy. Another way to look at this is that when other programmers are creating methods they can invent local variables without cross-checking with everyone.

The role of local variables is to assist in the work of the method, whatever it is doing. The variables have a limited scope, restricted to their own method. Their existence is temporary – they are created when a method is called, and destroyed when it exits.

Name clashes

In VB, the creator of a method is free to choose appropriate names for local variables and parameters – but what happens if names are chosen which clash with other variables? We could have:

```
Private Sub MethodOne(ByVal x As Integer, _
                     ByVal y As Integer)
    Dim z As Integer = 0
    ' code ...
End Sub

Private Sub MethodTwo(ByVal z As Integer, _
                     ByVal x As Integer)
        Dim w As Integer = 1
        ' code ...
End Sub
```

Let us assume that the methods have been written by two people. `MethodOne` has `x` and `y` as parameters, and declares an integer `z`. These three items are all local to `MethodOne`. In `MethodTwo`, the programmer exercises the right of freedom to name local items, and opts for `z`, `x`, and `w`. The name clash of `x` (and of `z`) does not give a problem, as VB treats the `x` of `MethodOne` as different from the `x` of `MethodTwo`.

> **SELF-TEST QUESTION**
>
> **5.4** Here is the call of a method:
>
> ```
> Dim a As Integer = 3
> Dim b As Integer = 8
> DoStuff(a, b)
> MessageBox.Show(CStr(a))
> ```
>
> and here is the method itself:
>
> ```
> Private Sub DoStuff(ByVal x As Integer, _
>                    ByVal y As Integer)
>     Dim a As Integer = 0
>     a = x + y
> End Sub
> ```
>
> What is shown in the message box?

Let us summarize the method facilities we have discussed so far. Later we will include the `Return` statement, and the use of `ByRef`.

- The general form of a `Sub` declaration is:

```
Private Sub SomeName(parameter list)
    body
End Sub
```

The programmer chooses the method name.
- The parameter list is a list of types and names, with the type of passing required (`ByVal` in our examples so far). If a method doesn't need arguments, we use empty brackets for the parameter list when we declare it, and empty brackets for the argument list when we call it.

```
Private Sub MyMethod()
    body
End Sub
```

and the method call is:

```
MyMethod()
```

- A class can contain any number of methods, in any order. In this chapter, our programs only consist of one class. The essence of the layout is:

```
Public Class Form1

    Private Sub SomeName(parameter list ...)
        body
    End Sub

    Private Sub AnotherName(parameter list ...)
        body
    End Sub
End Class
```

We will make use of the `Class` and `End Class` keywords in Chapter 10. For now, merely note that a class can group together a series of methods.

Event-handling methods

A class contains a set of methods. We write some of them ourselves (such as `DrawLogo`) and we explicitly call them. However there are other methods which VB creates for us, such as:

```
Private Sub Button1_Click
```

When is this method called? The answer is that the VB system routes all events (such as button-clicks, mouse-clicks, etc.) to their appropriate event method, provided that a matching method exists. Normally, we never call these methods ourselves.

Function methods and results

In our previous examples of arguments and parameters, values were passed *into* methods, which the method made use of. However, often we need to code methods which perform a calculation and send a result back to the rest of the program, so that the result can be used in subsequent calculations. In this case we must use a `Function` method, rather than a `Sub` method. Let us look at a function method which calculates the area of a rectangle, given its two sides as input arguments. Here is the complete program, named Area Function:

```
Private Sub Button1_Click(ByVal sender As System.Object, _
                          ByVal e As System.EventArgs) _
                          Handles Button1.Click
    Dim a As Integer
    a = AreaRectangle(10, 20)
End Sub

Private Function AreaRectangle( _
                ByVal length As Integer, _
                ByVal width As Integer) As Integer
    Dim area As Integer
    area = length * width
    Return area
End Function
```

There are a number of new features in this example, which go hand in hand.

Examine the function header:

```
Private Function AreaRectangle( _
                ByVal length As Integer, _
                ByVal width As Integer) As Integer
```

Instead of `Sub`, we have used `Function`. Also, we need to specify the type of item that the function will return to the caller. In this case, because we are multiplying two `Integer` values, the type of the answer will also be an `Integer`. The final `As Integer` in the function header states that `AreaRectangle` will return an `Integer` to us.

The choice of this type depends on the problem. For example, it might be an integer or a string, but it could also be a more complicated object such as a picture box or button. The writer of the function chooses what type of value is returned.

To return a value from the function, we make use of the `Return` statement. We put:

```
Return expression
```

The expression (as usual) could be a number, a variable or a calculation (or even a function call), but it must be of the correct type, as specified in the declaration of the method – i.e. its header. Additionally, the `Return` statement causes the current method to stop executing, and returns immediately to where it left off in the calling method. Now we will look at how a function can be called.

Here is how *not* to call a function. They cannot be used as complete statements, as in:

```
AreaRectangle(10, 20)      'wrong
```

Instead, the caller must arrange to 'consume' the returned value. Here is an approach to understanding the returning of values: imagine that the method call (the name and argument list) is erased, and is replaced by the returned result. If the resulting code makes sense, then VB will allow you to make such a call. Look at this example:

```
answer = AreaRectangle(30, 40)
```

The result is 1200, which we imagine as replacing the call, effectively giving:

```
answer = 1200
```

This is valid VB. But if we put:

```
AreaRectangle(30, 40)
```

the substitution would produce a VB statement consisting only of a number:

```
1200
```

which is meaningless. Here are some more ways that we might consume the result:

```
Private Sub Button2_Click(ByVal sender As System.Object, _
                          ByVal e As System.EventArgs) _
                          Handles Button2.Click
    Dim n As Integer
    n = AreaRectangle(10, 20)
    MessageBox.Show("area is " & CStr(AreaRectangle(3, 4)))
    n = AreaRectangle(10, 20) * AreaRectangle(7, 8)
End Sub
```

> **SELF-TEST QUESTION**
>
> **5.5** Work through the above statements with pencil and paper, substituting results for calls.

To complete the discussion of `Return`, note that it can be used with `Sub` methods. In this case, we must use `Return` without specifying a result, as in:

```
Private Sub Demo(ByVal n As Integer)
    ' do something
    Return
    ' do something else
End Sub
```

This can be used when we want the method to terminate at a statement other than the last one.

Let us look at an alternative way of coding our area example:

```
Private Function AreaRectangle2(ByVal length As Integer, _
                                ByVal width As Integer) _
                                As Integer
    Return length * width
End Function
```

Because we can use `Return` with expressions, we have omitted the variable `area` in `AreaRectangle2`.

Such reductions in program size are not always beneficial, because the reduction in meaningful names can reduce clarity, hence leading to more debugging and testing time.

> **SELF-TEST QUESTION**
>
> **5.6** Here is a function named `Twice`, which returns the doubled value of its `Integer` argument.
>
> ```
> Private Function Twice(ByVal n As Integer) As Integer
>     Return 2 * n
> End Function
> ```
>
> Here are some calls:
>
> ```
> Dim n As Integer = 3
> Dim r As Integer
> r = Twice(n)
> r = Twice(n + 1)
> r = Twice(n) + 1
> r = Twice(3 + 2 * n)
> r = Twice(Twice(n))
> r = Twice(Twice(n + 1))
> r = Twice(Twice(n) + 1)
> r = Twice(Twice(Twice(n)))
> ```
>
> For each call, state the returned value.

● Building on methods

As an example of methods which make use of other methods, let us create a method which draws a primitive 'lean-to' house with a cross-section shown in Figure 5.7. The height of the roof is the same as the height of the walls, and the width of the wall is the same as the width of the roof. We will choose the `Integer` arguments to be:

- the horizontal position of the top right point of the roof;
- the vertical position of the top right point of the roof;
- the height of the roof (excluding the wall);
- the width of the house. The triangle for the roof and the rectangle for the walls have the same width.

We will use `DrawRectangle` from the VB library, and use our own `DrawTriangle`.

Here is the program, with the resulting images shown in Figure 5.8.

Building on methods ● 75

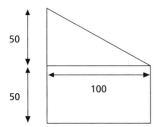

Figure 5.7 House with width of 100 and roof height of 50.

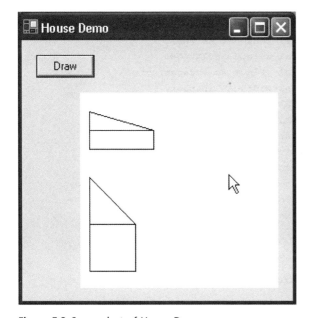

Figure 5.8 Screenshot of House Demo program.

```
Private Sub Button1_Click( _
                ByVal sender As System.Object, _
                ByVal e As System.EventArgs) _
                Handles Button1.Click
    Dim paper As Graphics
    paper = PictureBox1.CreateGraphics
    Dim myPen As Pen = New Pen(Color.Black)
    DrawHouse(paper, myPen, 10, 20, 70, 20)
    DrawHouse(paper, myPen, 10, 90, 50, 50)
End Sub
```

```
    Private Sub DrawHouse(ByVal drawingArea As Graphics, _
                         ByVal penToUse As Pen, _
                         ByVal topRoofX As Integer, _
                         ByVal topRoofY As Integer, _
                         ByVal width As Integer, _
                         ByVal height As Integer)
        DrawTriangle(drawingArea, penToUse, topRoofX, _
                     topRoofY, width, height)
        drawingArea.DrawRectangle(penToUse, topRoofX, _
                          topRoofY + height, width, height)
    End Sub

    Private Sub DrawTriangle(ByVal drawingArea As Graphics, _
                             ByVal penToUse As Pen, _
                             ByVal xPlace As Integer, _
                             ByVal yPlace As Integer, _
                             ByVal width As Integer, _
                             ByVal height As Integer)
        drawingArea.DrawLine(penToUse, xPlace, yPlace, _
                     xPlace, yPlace + height)
        drawingArea.DrawLine(penToUse, xPlace, _
                     yPlace + height, _
                     xPlace + width, yPlace + height)
        drawingArea.DrawLine(penToUse, xPlace, yPlace, _
                     xPlace + width, yPlace + height)
    End Sub
```

The program is straightforward if you recall that:

- Methods return to where they were called from, so:
  - `Button1_Click` calls `DrawHouse`;
  - `DrawHouse` calls `DrawRectangle`;
  - `DrawHouse` calls `DrawTriangle`;
  - `DrawTriangle` calls `DrawLine` (three times).
- Arguments can be expressions, so `yPlace + height` is evaluated, then passed into `DrawLine`.
- The `width` and `height` of `DrawHouse` and the `width` and `height` of `DrawTriangle` are totally separate. Their values are stored in different places.

You will see that what might have been a longer program has been written as a short program, split into methods with meaningful names. This illustrates the power of using methods.

Passing arguments by reference

So far, we have used the concept of passing arguments by value, either with a sub or a function. We use a function when a single value needs passing back to the caller. This seems fine initially, but there is another situation not yet covered – what if our method needs to pass back more than one result? Here is such a situation:

> Given a number of cents, write a method to calculate the equivalent whole number of dollars, and the number of cents remaining. We have one input and two results.

Before we look at the VB approach to returning several results, we need to look more deeply into the nature of passing arguments. Previously, we stated that we pass *values* of arguments. This seems obvious – what else could we do? In fact, VB also allows us to pass arguments *by reference* as well as by value and we can use this facility to pass back any number of results from a method.

Here is an analogy to illustrate passing by reference: imagine that you are working on a written report, with some friends. Your friend asks you for the report. There are two ways you could pass this document to them:

- You could photocopy the document.
- You could tell your colleague 'Oh yes that one. Just look on the fourth shelf down. There it is'.

The analogy:

- The document is an argument.
- Your colleague is a method who is being called by you, to whom an argument is to be passed.
- Passing a photocopy of the document is passing 'by value'
- Telling your colleague where the original copy is stored at is termed 'passing by reference'.

There are two important points about these ways of passing arguments:

- Passing a copy of the data (by value) is safer. You keep hold of the original item. Any changes your colleague makes will *not* affect your copy.
- Passing the whereabouts of the data (passing by reference) is fast. In fact, no data is physically moved, and your colleague can make changes without removing the document from your room. But remember that there is only a single copy of the item. Your colleague has the same power as you have to change this single copy. Sometimes you will want this, but sometimes you won't.

Bearing in mind the concepts of passing by value and passing by reference, let us look at how your computer's random access memory (RAM) is organized. The precise organization is rather complicated but, approximately, RAM consists of millions of storage boxes, known as memory locations. Each location has an address, rather like numbered houses on a street. Each variable we create is stored at a particular place in memory. In other words, each variable is associated with an address.

Chapter 5/Methods and arguments

Now we reach the point about passing by reference: if we wish to pass a variable to a method, there are two choices:

- Either we pass a copy of the current value.
- Or we pass the address. In VB jargon we pass a reference to the variable. When the method knows the whereabouts of a variable, it knows which memory location to look in. In other languages, a reference is known as a *pointer*.

> **SELF-TEST QUESTION**
>
> **5.7** Imagine that we have a large number of variables stored in RAM. If we know the value of a variable, is it possible to find out where the variable is stored?

Let us move closer to VB. The way we can obtain *several* results from a method is as follows:

Before calling a method, the caller declares some variables, to be regarded as places for holding results calculated by the method. When the method is called, the addresses of the variables (the references) are passed into the method. The method can make use of the original values of the variables if it needs to, and it can also assign new values to them.

Though this sounds rather complicated, the manipulation of references is done behind the scenes in VB, as we will see.

● References – an example

Let us tackle the problem posed earlier: a method which converts a number of cents into a whole number of dollars, and the cents left over. This will involve coding a method which has one input and two results. Figure 5.9 shows a screenshot of the Dollars Method program, and here is the code, which uses a text box to obtain the

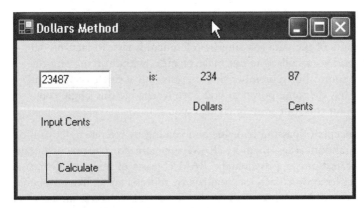

Figure 5.9 Screenshot of Dollars Method program.

number of cents, and labels to display the results. We used a similar GUI in Chapter 4, when we did this task without using a function.

```
Private Sub Button1_Click(ByVal sender As System.Object, _
                         ByVal e As System.EventArgs) _
                         Handles Button1.Click
    Dim originalCents, wholeDollars, centsLeft As Integer
    originalCents = CInt(TextBox1.Text)
    DollarsAndCents(originalCents, wholeDollars, centsLeft)
    DollarsLabel.Text = CStr(wholeDollars)
    CentsLabel.Text = CStr(centsLeft)
End Sub

Private Sub DollarsAndCents(ByVal totalCents As Integer, _
                            ByRef dollars As Integer, _
                            ByRef centsLeft As Integer)
    dollars = totalCents \ 100
    centsLeft = totalCents Mod 100
End Sub
```

The property settings are as follows:

Control	Property	Setting
Button1	Text	Calculate
TextBox1	Text	(empty)
DollarsLabel	Text	(empty)
CentsLabel	Text	(empty)

Here are some points about the above program:

- We chose the name `DollarsAndCents` for the method.
- The method has two results, so we could not use the `Return` statement.
- We use `ByRef` to pass references.
- The `totalCents` parameter is passed by value. We *could* have passed it by reference, but the method does not place a new value in this variable. Passing by value ensures that the method cannot change the original value, hence is safer.
- `dollars` and `centsLeft` are passed by reference. In effect, they are empty boxes and we are informing `DollarsAndCents` of their whereabouts.
- When the method assigns a new value to `centsRemaining`, it is actually using the variable `centsLeft`, declared in `Button1_Click`. In other words, `centsRemaining` stands for `centsLeft`.
- As usual, the writer of a method has free choice of argument names. In this example, one name was the same as the caller chose (`dollars`) and the other pairs were different (`originalCents`, `cents`, and `centsLeft`, `centsRemaining`). Perhaps `Dollars` was used twice because the same person both wrote the method and called it. For large programs, this will not be the case, and in general, the names differ.

Chapter 5/Methods and arguments

SELF-TEST QUESTIONS

5.8 Would `DollarsAndCents` work correctly if we re-coded it as:

```
Private Sub DollarsAndCents2(ByVal a As Integer, _
                            ByRef b As Integer, _
                            ByRef c As Integer)
    b = a \ 100
    c = a Mod 100
End Sub
```

5.9 Here is the call of a method:

```
Dim x As Integer = 4
Dim y As Integer = 9
DoWork(x, y)
```

and here is the method:

```
Private Sub DoWork(ByVal a As Integer, _
                  ByRef b As Integer)
    a = a + 1
    b = b + 1
End Sub
```

What are the resulting values of `x` and `y`?

References: a `Swap` method

A classic example of the use of arguments is to code a method which swaps over the values of two variables. First, here is the code without making use of a method:

```
aCopy = a
a = b
b = aCopy
```

Note that if we put:

```
a = b
b = a
```

then both `a` and `b` end up set to the original value of `b`.

So, rather than some code which only works for the variables `a` and `b`, we want to bundle the code up as a method which works for any names. There are two arguments, and the method changes their value. Here is the code:

```
Private Sub Swap(ByRef a As Integer, ByRef b As Integer)
    Dim aCopy As Integer
    aCopy = a
    a = b
    b = aCopy
End Sub
```

Note that the method needs the references of the variables *and* their values. But we don't need to pass four arguments, because once a method has the reference, it can also use the value. Here are some examples of calling the `Swap` method:

```
Dim a As Integer = 6
Dim b As Integer = 8
Dim c As Integer = 20
Dim d As Integer = 30

Swap(c, d)
Swap(a, b)
Swap(a, c)
```

Here are some incorrect calls of `Swap`:

```
Dim a As Integer = 3
Swap(a, 6)
```

In VB, numbers (and the results of calculations) have a value, but *not* a reference. In other words, they are not stored at a known place in RAM. So, when supplying arguments, we *must* use variable names where `ByRef` has been used. In the above example, because 6 doesn't have a reference, there is no place to accept the value of a. The program will compile and run, but the only effect of the method is to set a to 6. However, where a method stipulates `ByVal`, we can supply a variable *or* a calculation.

● Me and objects

You are probably reading this book because VB is an object-oriented language, but you might be wondering why this chapter has not mentioned objects. The truth is that methods and objects are vitally connected. When you run small VB programs, you are running an instance of a class, i.e. an object. This object contains methods (e.g. `Swap`) and properties (which we have not yet covered).

When an object calls a method which is declared within itself, we can simply put

```
Swap(a, b)
```

or we can use the full object notation, as in

```
Me.Swap(a, b)
```

`Me` is a VB keyword, and stands for the currently running object. So you have been doing object-oriented programming without realizing it. Here are some examples:

```
Swap(a, b)

'works as above
Me.Swap(a, b)

'compilation error
Me.DrawLine(myPen, 10, 10, 100, 50)
```

In the above, an error is detected because we are asking VB to locate the `DrawLine` method within the current object. In fact, `DrawLine` exists outside the program in the `Graphics` class, and must be called in this way:

```
Dim paper As Graphics
paper = PictureBox1.CreateGraphics()
paper.DrawLine(myPen, 10, 10, 100, 50)
```

Overloading

Our `Swap` method is useful, in the sense that it can work on arguments with any name. The drawback is that they must be integers. Recall the code:

```
Private Sub Swap(ByRef a As Integer, ByRef b As Integer)
    Dim aCopy As Integer
    aCopy = a
    a = b
    b = aCopy
End Sub
```

But what if we wanted to swap two `Double` variables? We will code *another* `Swap` method, intentionally coding it differently:

```
Private Sub Swap2(ByRef a As Double, ByRef b As Double)
    Dim aCopy As Double
    aCopy = a
    a = b
    b = aCopy
End Sub
```

However, it would be convenient to use the same name for both methods, and in VB we can. Here is how we code the method declarations:

```
Private Sub Swap(ByRef a As Integer, ByRef b As Integer)
    Dim aCopy As Integer
    aCopy = a
    a = b
    b = aCopy
End Sub

Private Sub Swap(ByRef a As Double, ByRef b As Double)
    Dim aSafe As Double = a
    Dim bSafe As Double = b
    a = bSafe
    b = aSafe
End Sub
```

Now we call the methods:

```
Dim c As Integer = 3
Dim d As Integer = 4
Dim g As Double = 1.2
Dim h As Double = 4.5
Swap(c, d)
Swap(g, h)
```

How does VB decide which method to use? There are two methods named `Swap`, so VB additionally looks at the number of parameters and at their types. In our example, if `a` and `b` had been declared as `Double` variables, VB would call the method which swaps doubles. The code contained by the methods can be different – it is the number of parameters and their types that determine which method is called.

If the method is a function, the return type plays no part in overloading, i.e. it is the parameter types of the function which must be different.

What we have done is termed *overloading*. The `Swap` method has been overloaded with several possibilities.

So if you are writing methods which perform similar tasks, but differ in the number of arguments and/or types, it is sensible make use of overloading by choosing the *same* name rather than invent an artificially different name.

There are hundreds of examples of overloading used in the VB libraries. For example, there are four versions of `DrawLine`.

● Passing objects to methods

In our examples we have concentrated on passing numbers, but we also need to pass more complicated objects, such as pens and picture boxes. Here is an example, in which we pass two numbers to be added, and also pass the label where the result is to be displayed:

```
Private Sub ShowSum(ByVal display As Label, _
                  ByVal a As Integer, ByVal b as Integer)
    display.Text = CStr(a + b)
End Sub
```

Here is how we might call the method:

```
ShowSum(Label1, 3, 4)
ShowSum(Label2, 5, 456)
```

Passing an object by value allows us to manipulate its properties and call its methods.

Programming principles

- A method is a section of code which has a name. We call the method by using its name.
- We can use subroutine methods and function methods.
- We can pass arguments to a method. They can be passed by value or by reference.
- Passing by value is the safer of the two approaches. Passing by reference allows the method to change the original item.
- When a method returns only one value, use a function.
- If you can identify a well-defined task in your code, consider separating it out and writing it as a method.

Programming pitfalls

- The method header must include type names. The following is wrong:

    ```
    Private Sub MethodOne(x)    ' wrong
    ```

    Instead we must put, for example:

    ```
    Private Sub MethodOne(ByVal x As Integer)
    ```

- A method call must not include type names. For example, rather than:

    ```
    MethodOne(ByVal y As Integer)
    ```

    we put:

    ```
    MethodOne(y)
    ```

- When calling a method, you must supply the correct number of arguments and the correct types of arguments.
- You must arrange to consume the result of a function in some way. The following style of call does not consume a return value:

    ```
    SomeFunction(e, f)
    ```

Grammar spot

- The general pattern for methods takes two forms. First, for a `Sub` method (that does not return a result), we declare the method by:

    ```
    Private Sub MethodName(parameter list)
        body
    End Sub
    ```

    and we call the method by a statement, as in:

    ```
    MethodName(argument list)
    ```

- For a `Function` method, the form is:

   ```
   Private Function FunctionName(parameter list) As some type
       body
   End Function
   ```

   Any type or class can be specified as the returned type.
- We call the function as part of an expression, e.g.:

   ```
   n = FunctionName(a, b)
   ```

- The body of the function method must include a `Return` statement featuring the correct type of value.
- When a method has no arguments, we use empty brackets ( ) in both the declaration and the call.
- The parameter list is created by the writer of the method. Each parameter needs `ByVal` or `ByRef`, a name, and a type.
- The argument list is written by the caller of the method. It consists of a series of items in the correct (matching) order, and of the correct types. Unlike parameters within a method, the type names are not used.

New language elements

- The declaration of private `Sub` and `Function` methods.
- The call of a method, consisting of the method name and arguments.
- The use of `Return` to simultaneously exit and pass a value back from a function method.
- The use of `Return` to exit from a `Sub` method.
- The use of overloading.
- The use of `Me` to stand for the current object.

New IDE facilities

There are no new IDE facilities introduced in this chapter.

Summary

- Methods contain subtasks of a program.
- We can pass arguments into methods.
- Using a method is termed *calling* the method.
- Function methods return a result.

Chapter 5/Methods and arguments

EXERCISES

To try out the methods you write, build a simple GUI with text boxes, labels and message boxes, as required. Use a button click to execute your code.

The first problems involve `Sub` methods, and passing by value:

5.1 Write a method named `ShowName`, with one `String` parameter. It should display the supplied name in a message box.

5.2 Write a method named `ShowNames`, with two string parameters representing your first name and your last name. It should display your first name in a message box, and then display your last name in another message box.

5.3 Write a method named `DisplayEarnings`, with two integer parameters representing an employee's salary, and the number of years they have worked. The method should display their total earnings in a message box, assuming that they earned the same amount every year.

5.4 Code a method which draws a circle, given the coordinates of the centre and the radius. Its header should be:

```
Private Sub Circle( _
        ByVal drawingArea As Graphics, _
        ByVal penToUse As Pen, ByVal xCentre As Integer, _
        ByVal yCentre As Integer, ByVal radius As Integer)
```

5.5 Code a method named `DrawStreet`, which draws a street of houses, using the provided `DrawHouse` method. For the purposes of this question, a street consists of four houses, and there should be a 20-pixel gap between each house. The arguments provide the location and size of the leftmost house, and are identical to `DrawHouse`.

5.6 Code a method (to be known as `DrawStreetInPerspective`), which has the same arguments as Exercise 5.5. However, each house is to be 20 per cent smaller than the house to its left.

The following programs involve function methods with arguments passed by value:

5.7 Write a function method which returns the inch equivalent of its centimetre argument. An example call is:

```
Dim inches As Integer = InchEquivalent(10.5)
```

Multiply centimetres by 0.394 to calculate inches.

5.8 Write a method which returns the volume of a cube, given the length of one side. A sample call is:

```
Dim vol As Double = CubeVolume(1.2)
```

5.9 Write a method which returns the area of a circle, given its radius as an argument. A sample call is:

    Dim a As Double = AreaCircle(1.25)

The area of a circle is given by the formula `Math.PI * r * r`. Though we could use a number such as `3.14`, a more accurate value is provided by `Math.PI`.

5.10 Write a function method named `SecsIn`, which accepts three integers, representing a time in hours, minutes, and seconds. It should return the total time in seconds. A sample call is:

    Dim totalSecs As Integer = SecsIn(1, 1, 2)   'returns 3662

5.11 Write a function method which returns the area of a solid cylinder. Decide one of its parameters. You should call `AreaCircle` from above, to assist in calculating the area of the top and bottom. (The circumference of a circle is given by `2 * Math.PI * r`).

5.12 Write a function method called `Increment`, which adds 1 to its integer argument. An example of a call is:

    Dim n As Integer = 3
    Dim a As Integer = Increment(n)   'returns 4

The following problems involve `Sub` and `Function` methods, and passing arguments by reference and value:

5.13 Write a sub method named `SumAndDifference`, which calculates the sum and the difference of any two integer values (i.e. if the input arguments are 3 and n, it passes back 3+n, and 3−n.)

5.14 Write a sub method named `SecsToHMS`, which takes in a number of seconds, and converts it into hours, minutes and seconds. Make use of the `Mod` and `\` operators. (For example, 3662 seconds is 1 hour, 1 minute, and 2 seconds.)

5.15 Write a sub method named `Input3`, which has three integer arguments, passed by reference. It should use three input boxes to input three integers from the user. Here is how we might call it:

    Dim a, b, c As Integer
    Input3(a, b, c)

5.16 Write a function method named `TimeDifferenceInSecs`, with six `ByVal` arguments and an integer result. It takes in two times, in hours, minutes and seconds, and returns the difference between them in seconds. Use the `Input3` method from Exercise 5.15, and `SecsIn` from Exercise 5.10.

5.17 Write a sub method named `HMSBetween`, which accepts two times in seconds, and passes back the hours, minutes and seconds between them. Your method should make use of `SecsToHMS`.

5.18 Write a sub method named `Increment`, which increments its integer argument. An example of a call is:

```
Dim v as Integer = 4
Increment(v)      'v is now 5
```

The following problems involve overloading:

5.19 Use any program which contains `SecsIn`. Add an additional function method also named `SecsIn`, which has two arguments, for minutes and seconds.

5.20 Use your program from Exercise 5.18, with `Increment` in use. Write two other versions of `Increment`: one with a `Double` argument, and one with a `String` argument. The latter should use the `&` operator to join a space on to the end of the string.

ANSWERS TO SELF-TEST QUESTIONS

5.1 At (10, 20), (30, 10), (27, 26).

5.2 In the first call, the quotes should not be used. They indicate a string, not an integer.
In the second call, the paper and the pen are in the wrong order.
In the third call, an argument is missing

5.3 A message box displaying `Oranges` will appear.

5.4 The message box displays the original value of `a`, which is 3. The `a` that is set to 11 inside the method is a local variable.

5.5 Here are the stages in replacing a call by its result. For

```
n = AreaRectangle(10, 20)
```

we have:

```
n = 200
```

For the line

```
MessageBox.Show("area is " & CStr(AreaRectangle(3, 4)))
```

we have the stages:

```
MessageBox.Show("area is " & CStr(12))
MessageBox.Show("area is 12")
```

For the line

```
n = AreaRectangle(10, 20) * AreaRectangle(7, 8)
```

we have the stages:

```
n = 200 * 56
n = 11200
```

5.6 The values that `r` takes are:

6
8
7
18
12
16
14
24

5.7 No. Several variables might hold the same value, so values are not unique. To use a house number analogy: houses have an address and a value (e.g. the number of people currently in a house). We could not track down the address of the house containing three people, because there are many such houses.

5.8 It would work correctly – though the names are not very meaningful. The writer of a method has free choice of parameter names; they need not match names used by the caller of the method. It is, however, the responsibility of the caller to supply arguments in the correct left-to-right order.

5.9 The value of `x` is left at 4, and the value of `y` changes to 10. Within the method, changing `a` to 5 only has a local effect. `ByVal` prevents the original variable `x` from being altered.

Using objects

This chapter explains:
- the use of instance variables and `Private`;
- the form constructor;
- the use of library classes;
- the use of `New`;
- using methods and properties;
- the `Random` class;
- the `TrackBar` and `Timer`.

● Introduction

In this chapter, we will deepen our understanding of objects. In particular, we will look at the use of different types of objects from the VB library of classes. Note that, though there are many hundreds of these, the principles of using them are similar.

Here is an analogy: reading a book – whatever the book – involves opening it at the front, reading a page, then moving to the next page. We know what to do with a book. It is the same with objects. When you have used a few of them, you know what to look for when presented with a new one.

In general, the objects we will make use of are termed controls or components. The terms are really interchangeable, but VB uses 'control' for items which can be manipulated on a form.

● Instance variables

In order to tackle more advanced problems, we need to introduce a new place to declare variables. So far, we have used `Dim` to declare local variables within methods. But local variables alone are insufficient to tackle most problems.

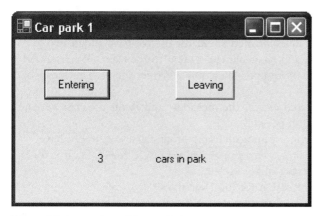

Figure 6.1 Screenshot of Car park 1.

Here we introduce a simple program (Car park 1) to assist in the running of a car park (or parking lot). It has two buttons: 'entering' and 'leaving'. The attendant clicks the appropriate button as a car enters or leaves. The program keeps a count of the number of cars in the park, and displays it in a label.

Note that the count is changed by two methods, so it cannot be declared locally within only one of them. It is tempting to think that the variable can be declared within *each* method, but this would result in two separate variables.

The screenshot is shown in Figure 6.1, and here is the code:

```
Public Class Form1
    Private carCount As Integer = 0

    Private Sub EnterButton_Click( _
                        ByVal sender As System.Object, _
                        ByVal e As System.EventArgs) _
                        Handles EnterButton.Click
        carCount = carCount + 1
        CountLabel.Text = CStr(carCount)
    End Sub

    Private Sub LeaveButton_Click( _
                        ByVal sender As System.Object, _
                        ByVal e As System.EventArgs) _
                        Handles LeaveButton.Click
        carCount = carCount - 1
        CountLabel.Text = CStr(carCount)
    End Sub
End Class
```

There are a number of points to note:

- VB has automatically created a class named `Form1` for us. We have added two methods, `EnterButton_Click` and `LeaveButton_Click`, to the class. (We renamed the buttons to make the code more understandable.) We set the `Text` property of `Label1` to `0` at design-time.
- The variable `carCount` is declared *outside* the methods, and *inside* the class `Form1`. It can be used by any method in `Form1`.
- It has been declared as `Private`, meaning that any other classes we might have cannot use it. The variable is *encapsulated* or sealed up inside `Form1`, i.e. it is for the use of the methods and properties of `Form1` only.
- `Dim` has not been used. We only use it for local variables.
- `carCount` is an example of an *instance variable*. It belongs to an instance of a class, rather than to one method. Another term is 'class-level' variable.
- `carCount` is said to have *module scope*. (A class is a type of module in VB.) The scope of an item is the area of the program in which it can be used. The other type of scope we have seen is local scope used with local variables.
- The word `Private` means that other classes (outside of our `Form1` class) cannot access the item. This is the preferred style for instance variables.
- The VB convention is not to capitalize the first letter of an instance variable.

Note that the programmer has free choice of names for instance variables. But what if a name coincides with a local variable name, as in:

```
Public Class Form1

    Private n As Integer = 8
    Private Sub MyMethod()
        Dim n As Integer
        n = 3            'which n?
    End Sub
End Class
```

Although both variables are accessible (in scope) within `MyMethod`, the rule is that the local variable is chosen. The instance variable (module-level) `n` remains set to `8`.

> **SELF-TEST QUESTION**
>
> 6.1 In the above `Form1` class, what are the consequences of deleting the `Dim` statement?

Instance variables are essential, but you should not ignore locals. For example, if a variable is used inside one method only, and need not keep its value between method calls, make it local.

The form constructor

Let us re-visit the car park program. We used a variable `carCount` to count with, and we used a label to display the `carCount` value. We set the value of `carCount` to 0 within the program, and we set the `Text` property of `Label1` to 0 at design-time. In fact, these are not separate. Consider the possibility that five cars are left in the car park for an extended period. We have to alter the initial value of `carCount` as well as the initial value of the `Text` property of `Label1`. In reality, there is only one item holding the number of cars. This is `carCount`. Rather than separately setting the initial text value of `Label1` at design-time, it would be better to arrange that the value of `carCount` – whatever it is – is placed in the label as the program starts running.

It is common for the initial values of controls to depend on variables and on other controls. We could attempt to set up this situation at design-time, but for several controls this is error-prone, and does not express the dependencies. It is better if we set up related initial values in code. Fortunately VB provides a special area of the program for such once-only initialization. Look at the second version: Car park 2.

```
Public Class Form1
    Private carCount As Integer = 0

    Public Sub New()

        ' This call is required by the Windows Form Designer.
        InitializeComponent()

        ' Add any initialization after the InitializeComponent() call.
        CountLabel.Text = CStr(carCount)
    End Sub

    Private Sub LeaveButton_Click( _
                    ByVal sender As System.Object, _
                    ByVal e As System.EventArgs) _
                    Handles LeaveButton.Click
        carCount = carCount - 1
        CountLabel.Text = CStr(carCount)
    End Sub

    Private Sub EnterButton_Click( _
                    ByVal sender As System.Object, _
                    ByVal e As System.EventArgs) _
                    Handles EnterButton.Click
        carCount = carCount + 1
        CountLabel.Text = CStr(carCount)
    End Sub
End Class
```

To create this code, we need to use the editor to open up an area of code that has not been explored before. Use your Car park 1 example, and view the code in the editor.

- In the left drop-down list at the top of the editor, select **Form1**.
- In the right drop-down list, select **New**.

Figure 6.2 Showing the **New** method.

Figure 6.2 shows the choice.

You will see that another method has appeared in your code, headed:

```
Public Sub New()
```

When the VB system runs your program, it creates a new instance of `Form1`, and it calls its `New` method first. This method is known as a *constructor* – it does some initial 'building' of the object. First, it creates your form and its controls by calling the `InitializeComponent` method. After the controls are created, you can write code to modify their initial values.

You can imagine that the `New` method is always there, but does not need modifying in some introductory programs. For this reason, it is not shown. However, in this chapter, we will edit it.

Look at the above code. You will see that it is composed of three methods: `New`, `LeaveButton_Click` and `EnterButton_Click`. In fact, the order of the methods does not matter. It is a convention in object-oriented programming to show the constructor method at the top, and we follow the convention here. However, the VB IDE places the methods in order of addition, so if you add `New` after creating the event code, `New` goes at the bottom. If you want to follow the convention, select **View Code** then add `New` first, or cut and paste it to the appropriate position. Programs run fine even if the `New` method is not at the top of the code.

In this improved version of the program, we have no need to set the `Text` of the label at design-time – instead, we insert code to do it towards the end of `New`, and the value is guaranteed to be the same as `carCount`. The comment:

```
'Add any initialization...
```

in the code shows you where it is safe to put your initialization. Do not put it anywhere else.

SELF-TEST QUESTION

6.2 What is wrong with:

```
Public Sub New()
    ... etc
    Label1.Text = "38"
    InitializeComponent()
End Sub
```

The `TrackBar` class

In the above example, we modified the `New` constructor, but did not call it ourselves. Later in this chapter, we will create new objects by explicitly calling the constructor of their class.

● **The `TrackBar` class**

Here is another example of component initialization. The track bar is a GUI control from the toolbox. Open up **All Windows Forms** to make it visible. It is similar in nature to the scroll bar at the side of a word-processor window, but the track bar can be placed anywhere on a form. The user can drag the 'thumb' to the required position, and the minimum and maximum values can be set via properties – at design-time and run-time.

The track bar is not used for precise settings such as entering your age, where the range might be large, i.e. 10 to 100. It is used for more informal settings, such as setting the volume of a loudspeaker.

Here we look at a program (Oval Shape) which allows the user to modify the width and the height of an ellipse. The current dimensions are displayed on the form in labels. Figure 6.3 shows a screenshot, and the code is shown overleaf:

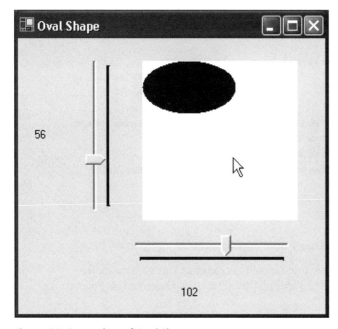

Figure 6.3 Screenshot of Oval Shape.

```
Public Class Form1
    Private paper As Graphics

    Public Sub New()

        ' This call is required by the Windows Form Designer.
        InitializeComponent()

        ' Add any initialization after the InitializeComponent() call.
        paper = PictureBox1.CreateGraphics()
        VertTrackBar.Minimum = 0
        VertTrackBar.Maximum = PictureBox1.Height
        VertLabel.Text = CStr(VertTrackBar.Value)

        HorizTrackBar.Minimum = 0
        HorizTrackBar.Maximum = PictureBox1.Width
        HorizLabel.Text = CStr(HorizTrackBar.Value)
    End Sub

    Private Sub VertTrackBar_Scroll( _
                        ByVal sender As System.Object, _
                        ByVal e As System.EventArgs) _
                        Handles VertTrackBar.Scroll
        Dim myBrush As SolidBrush = New SolidBrush(Color.Black)
        VertLabel.Text = CStr(VertTrackBar.Value)
        paper.Clear(Color.White)
        paper.FillEllipse(myBrush, 0, 0, HorizTrackBar.Value, _
                        VertTrackBar.Value)
    End Sub

    Private Sub HorizTrackBar_Scroll( _
                        ByVal sender As System.Object, _
                        ByVal e As System.EventArgs) _
                        Handles HorizTrackBar.Scroll
        Dim myBrush As SolidBrush = New SolidBrush(Color.Black)
        HorizLabel.Text = CStr(HorizTrackBar.Value)
        paper.Clear(Color.White)
        paper.FillEllipse(myBrush, 0, 0, HorizTrackBar.Value, _
                        VertTrackBar.Value)
    End Sub

End Class
```

Here are some points on design-time initialization:

- The track bars have been renamed as `HorizTrackBar` and `VertTrackBar`.
- A track bar can be positioned vertically, by setting its **Orientation** property to **Vertical**.
- The labels have been renamed as `HorizLabel` and `VertLabel`.
- We set the picture box to a size of `100, 100`.

At run-time, we used the constructor to initialize some components:

- We set the **Minimum** property of the track bars to **0**, and the **Maximum** properties to the height and width of the picture box.
- The initial value of the **Text** property of **HorizLabel** – which displays the current track bar value – is set to **HorizTrackBar.Value**. **VertTrackbar** is initialized in a similar way.

Note that:

- The track bar's event method (**Scroll**) is called when we move it to a new position.
- The track bar's **Value** property gives us the current setting. We use this to control the size of an imaginary rectangle enclosing the oval.
- The drawing area is used by two methods, so it must be declared as an instance variable at class-level, above the methods.

This program illustrates the benefits of initializing components in the form's constructor.

> **SELF-TEST QUESTION**
>
> 6.3 In the track bar example, what are the consequences of altering the size of the track bar at design-time?

Imports and namespaces

VB comes with a huge library (or collection) of classes which we can use. A very important aspect of VB programming is to make use of these, rather than write our own code. This is termed 'software reuse'.

Because there are thousands of classes, they are subdivided into groups known as *namespaces*. To use a class, we must ensure that it has been imported into our program. However, there are two possibilities, because some of the most frequently used namespaces are automatically imported into any Windows application. These namespaces are:

```
System
System.Data
System.Drawing
System.Windows.Forms
System.XML
```

There is a decision:

- if the class we require is in one of the above namespaces, we can use it with no further action;
- if the class we require is not in one of the above namespaces, we should put an **Imports** at the top of our program.

Here is an example. When we use files in Chapter 18, we will see the use of `StreamReader`, as in:

```
Dim myStream As StreamReader
```

The `StreamReader` class is in the `System.IO` namespace, so we must place the line:

```
Imports System.IO
```

at the very top of our code.

There are two points to note:

- The importing does not work in a hierarchical way. Importing the `System` namespace does not automatically import every namespace which starts with `System`. Every namespace must be imported explicitly.
- The use of `Imports` merely provides us with a shorthand. For example, we could use the `StreamReader` class without importing, but we would have to put:

```
Dim myStream As System.IO.StreamReader
```

To summarize, the vast library of VB classes is organized into namespaces, which can be imported into any program. When you have imported your class, you need to know how to create a new instance, and how to use its properties and methods. We shall look at these areas in a range of classes.

Members, methods and properties

The members of a class are its properties and its methods. Properties contain values which represent the current state of an instance of a class (such as the text contained in a label), whereas methods cause an instance to do a task – such as drawing a circle.

Properties can be used in a similar manner to variables: we can place a new value in them, and access their current value. As an example, here is how the `Width` and `Height` properties of a label might be manipulated:

```
'set a new value in a property:
Label1.Height = 30
Label1.Height = CStr(TextBox1.Text)

'get current value of property:
Dim a As Integer
a = Label1.Height
a = label1.Height * Label1.Width
```

In VB terminology, we can *set* a property to a new value and *get* the current value of a property. Each one also has a type. For example, the `Width` property of the label holds an integer, whereas the `Text` property holds a string. The names and types of properties are available from the Help system.

> **SELF-TEST QUESTIONS**
>
> **6.4** Imagine a CD player; list some methods and properties that it has. Which of these are members?
>
> **6.5** In geometrical terms, what do the following statements accomplish?
>
> ```
> Dim a As Integer
> a = Label1.Width * Label1.Height
> Label1.Height = Label1.Width
> ```

● The Random class

Here we will look at a class (`Random`) which needs explicit declaration and initialization. Random numbers are very useful in simulations and in games; for example we can give the game-player a different initial situation every time. Instances of the `Random` class provide us with a 'stream' of random numbers, which we can obtain one-at-a-time via the `Next` method. Here is a program (Guesser) which attempts to guess your age (in a rather inefficient way) by displaying a sequence of random numbers. When you click on 'correct', the program displays the number of guesses it took. The screenshot is in Figure 6.4, and here is the code:

```
Public Class Form1
    Private ageGuesser As Random = New Random()
    Private tries As Integer = 0

    Public Sub New()

        ' This call is required by the Windows Form Designer.
        InitializeComponent()
```

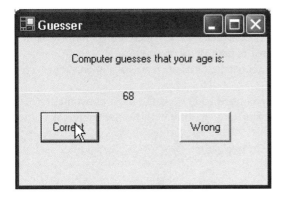

Figure 6.4 Screenshot of Guesser.

```
        ' Add any initialization after the InitializeComponent() call.
        GuessLabel.Text = CStr(ageGuesser.Next(5, 110))
    End Sub

    Private Sub CorrectButton_Click( _
                    ByVal sender As System.Object, _
                    ByVal e As System.EventArgs) _
                    Handles CorrectButton.Click
        tries = tries + 1
        MessageBox.Show("Number of tries was: " & CStr(tries))
        tries = 0
        GuessLabel.Text = CStr(ageGuesser.Next(5, 110))
    End Sub

    Private Sub WrongButton_Click( _
                    ByVal sender As System.Object, _
                    ByVal e As System.EventArgs) _
                    Handles WrongButton.Click
        GuessLabel.Text = CStr(ageGuesser.Next(5, 110))
        tries = tries + 1
    End Sub
End Class
```

To use a new class, we use the Help system to find its namespace, and we put the appropriate `Imports` at the top of our program. The `Random` class turns out to be in the `System` namespace, which is imported automatically. No imports are needed in this program.

We must then declare and initialize an instance of our class. This can be done in two ways. First we can use one statement, as in

```
Private ageGuesser As Random = New Random()
```

Note that:

- We chose the name `ageGuesser` for our instance.
- The statement calls the constructor of the `Random` class, which always has the same name as the class itself. The constructor is basically a method.
- The word `New` precedes the use of the constructor. `New` creates a new instance of a class in RAM.
- Constructors may be overloaded, so you need to choose the most convenient constructor. `Random` has two constructors, and the one with no parameters is suitable here.
- You can consider the statement to be in two parts:

```
Private ageGuesser As Random...
```

and

```
... = New Random()
```

The first part declares `ageGuesser` as a variable of class `Random`, but it does not yet have a concrete instance (containing methods and property values) associated with it. The second part calls the constructor of the `Random` class to complete the task of declaring and initialization.

The second way to declare and initialize instances is with declaration and initialization in different areas of the program, as in

```
Public Class Form1
    Private ageGuesser As Random

...

    ageGuesser = New Random()
```

Whichever approach we choose, there are a number of points:

- The declaration establishes the class of the instance. Here it is an instance of `Random`.
- The declaration establishes the scope of the object. `AgeGuesser` has module scope – it can be used by any method of the `Form1` class, rather than being local to a method.
- `ageGuesser` is private. It cannot be used by other classes outside our `Form1` class. Normally we make all such variables private.
- The initialization must be within the form's constructor or within another method.
- When it is possible to use the single-statement form of declaration and initialization, do so.

Why would we need to separate declaration and initialization? The situation often exists where we need an instance variable (as opposed to a local variable). It must be declared outside of the methods. But sometimes we cannot initialize the object until the program starts running – maybe the user enters a data value to be passed as a parameter to the constructor.

In this case, we would put the initialization code inside a method (or perhaps the constructor). We cannot put the declaration within the method, as this would declare the item as local to the method.

Let us return to the `Random` program. So far, we have created an instance of the `Random` class, named `ageGuesser`. We have yet to create any actual random numbers.

Once an object has been created with `New`, we can use its properties and methods. The documentation tells us that there are several methods which provide us with a random number, and we chose to use the method which lets us specify the range of the numbers. The method is named `Next` (in the sense of fetching the next random number from a sequence of numbers). In our program, we put:

```
GuessLabel.Text = CStr(ageGuesser.Next(5, 110))
```

We could have coded it less concisely as:

```
Dim guess As Integer
guess = ageGuesser.Next(5, 110)
GuessLabel.Text = CStr(guess)
```

The range of random numbers was chosen to be 5 to 109 inclusive. The second parameter of `Next` is one greater than the largest number we require.

To summarize, we declare an instance of the appropriate class (`Random` here), and use `New` to create and initialize it. These two stages can be combined, or separated; it depends on the particular program you are working on. Then we use properties and methods of the instance. The documentation provides us with details of their names and the types of data/parameters they require.

> **SELF-TEST QUESTION**
>
> **6.6** I went to my car sales showroom and, after browsing through the brochure, I ordered a specially built 5-litre Netster in blue. When it arrived, I drove it away. Does the `Car` class have a constructor? Does the constructor have any parameters? Which is the instance – the photo of the car or the real car?

The `Timer` class

So far, the classes we have used have fallen into two groups:

- Those from the toolbox, such as the button. They have a design-time representation on the form (e.g. they can be re-sized). They bring event-handling code templates with them, and code to call their constructors will automatically be placed in your code. Their initial properties can be set at design-time.
- Those from the libraries, without a visual representation – such as `Random`. They do not appear at design-time, and we have to explicitly code up a call to its constructor. Properties can only be set at run-time.

The timer is slightly different: it is in the toolbox (open **All Windows Forms**), but when it is dropped on to a form, the IDE opens up a new **Component Tray** window below the design form, and puts a timer icon (a clock) on it. We can set properties at design-time, and double-clicking on the icon takes us to the timer's event-handling code. When we run the program, the timer does not appear on the form.

Here are the main timer facilities:

- The timer creates ticks at regular intervals. Each tick is an event which calls the `Tick` method.
- The `Interval` property can be set to an integer value, representing the time between ticks in milliseconds.
- We can start and stop a timer with `Start` and `Stop` methods.
- We can put any number of timers in a program, each with a different interval.

Here is a program (Raindrops) which simulates a sheet of paper left out in the rain. It shows random-sized drops falling, at random intervals. The random intervals can be changed via a track bar. Figure 6.5 shows a screenshot, and here is the code:

The Timer class

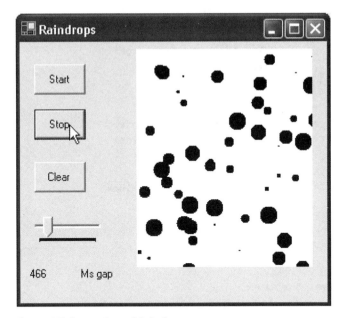

Figure 6.5 Screenshot of Raindrops.

```
Public Class Form1
    Private randomNumber As Random = New Random()
    Private paper As Graphics
    Public Sub New()
        'This call is required by the Windows Form Designer.
        InitializeComponent()
        'Add any initialization after the InitializeComponent() call
        paper = PictureBox1.CreateGraphics()
        GapLabel.Text = CStr(TrackBar1.Value)
    End Sub
    Private Sub StartButton_Click( _
                        ByVal sender As System.Object, _
                        ByVal e As System.EventArgs) _
                        Handles StartButton.Click
        Timer1.Start()
    End Sub
    Private Sub StopButton_Click( _
                        ByVal sender As System.Object, _
                        ByVal e As System.EventArgs) _
                        Handles StopButton.Click
        Timer1.Stop()
    End Sub
```

Chapter 6/Using objects

```
            Private Sub ClearButton_Click( _
                            ByVal sender As System.Object, _
                            ByVal e As System.EventArgs) _
                            Handles ClearButton.Click
                paper.Clear(Color.White)
            End Sub

            Private Sub Timer1_Tick(ByVal sender As System.Object, _
                            ByVal e As System.EventArgs) _
                            Handles Timer1.Tick
                Dim x, y, size As Integer
                Dim myBrush As Brush = New SolidBrush(Color.Black)

                x = randomNumber.Next(0, PictureBox1.Width)
                y = randomNumber.Next(0, PictureBox1.Height)
                size = randomNumber.Next(1, 20)
                paper.FillEllipse(myBrush, x, y, size, size)

                'set new interval for timer
                Timer1.Stop()
                Timer1.Interval = _
                        randomNumber.Next(1, TrackBar1.Value)
                Timer1.Start()
            End Sub

            Private Sub TrackBar1_Scroll( _
                            ByVal sender As System.Object, _
                            ByVal e As System.EventArgs) _
                            Handles TrackBar1.Scroll
                Dim timeGap As Integer = TrackBar1.Value
                GapLabel.Text = CStr(timeGap)
            End Sub
```

The program works by drawing a randomly sized filled circle at a random position at every tick. We also reset the timer interval to a random value controlled by the track bar. (This necessitates stopping and starting the timer.) Each time the track bar is moved, we display its current value in a label. The `Minimum` and `Maximum` track bar values were chosen by experimentation, and are 200 and 2000, set at design-time. We also made use of the `Clear` method of the picture box, which sets all the box to a specified colour.

> **SELF-TEST QUESTION**
>
> **6.7** We have a timer with an interval set to `1000`, i.e. one second. Explain how we can get a display of minutes on the form.

Programming principles

For many years it has been the dream of programmers to be able to build programs in the same way that hi-fi systems are built – i.e. from 'off-the-shelf' components, such as speakers, amplifiers, volume controls, etc. The rise in object-oriented programming has made this more possible, and it is used to some extent in the C++ and Java languages. However, the largest example of software reuse is that shown by earlier versions of VB, and this is likely to continue as VB becomes more widespread. Thousands of pre-packaged VB controls are available, to do such tasks as speech recognition and Internet access. In VB, it is possible to write new controls for use by other programmers.

Such controls are simple to incorporate: they are added to a project by a menu action. From then on, they appear on the toolbox like any other control, and provide event-handling method headers and properties that can be set at design-time. In practical terms, it is well worth searching for an existing control which meets your requirements, rather than reinventing the wheel by coding from scratch.

Programming pitfalls

If an instance is declared but its initialization with `New` is omitted, a run-time error is produced, of type `System.NullReferenceException`. Run-time errors (i.e. bugs) are more problematic than compile-time errors; they are harder to find, and they are more serious, because the program's execution is halted. We guarantee that you will meet this error!

Grammar spot

- Instance variables are declared outside methods, using `Private`, as in:

    ```
    Private yourVariable As Integer
    Private myVariable As Random = New Random()
    ```
- Instance variables can be initialized at declaration time, or inside a constructor or method.
- Properties can be manipulated in a similar manner to variables: we can get and set their values.

New language elements

- Private instance (class-level) variables.
- Using `New` for initialization.
- `Imports` for namespaces.
- The `TrackBar`, `Random` and `Timer` classes.

New IDE facilities

The component tray, for controls that do not have a visual representation on a form.

Summary

The VB system has a vast number of classes which you can (and ought to) use. As well as the control classes which are in the toolbox, there are classes which can be incorporated into your programs by using `Imports` and the appropriate constructor.

EXERCISES

6.1 Place a track bar on a form, together with two text boxes and a button. When the button is clicked, the track bar's `Minimum` and `Maximum` properties should be set from numbers entered in the text boxes. When the track bar is scrolled, display its `Minimum` and `Maximum` properties in message boxes.

6.2 Write a program which initially displays the number 1 in a label. Clicking a button should increment the value. Make use of a private variable initialized to 1, and set up the label in the constructor.

6.3 Write a program which produces a random number between 200 and 400 each time a button is clicked. The program should display this number, and the sum and average of all the numbers so far. As you click again and again, the average should converge on 300. If it doesn't, we would suspect the random number generator – just as we would be suspicious of a coin that came out heads 100 times in a row!

6.4 (a) Write a program which converts degrees Celsius to degrees Fahrenheit. The Celsius value should be entered in a text box. Clicking a button should cause the Fahrenheit value to be displayed in a label. The conversion formula is:

```
f = c * 9 / 5 + 32
```

(b) Modify the program so that the Celsius value is entered via a track bar, with its minimum set to 0, and its maximum set to 100.

(c) Represent both the temperatures as long thin rectangles in a picture box.

6.5 Write a program which calculates the volume of a swimming pool, and which also displays its cross-section in a picture box. The width of the pool is fixed at 5 metres and the length is fixed at 20 metres. The program should have two track bars – one to adjust the depth of the deep end, and one to adjust the depth of the shallow end. The minimum depth of each end is 1 metre. Choose suitable values for the maximum and minimum track bar values at design time. The volume formula is:

```
v = averageDepth * width * length
```

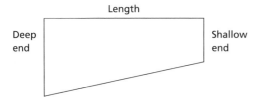

Figure 6.6 Swimming pool cross-section.

Figure 6.6 shows the cross-section.

6.6 Write a program which displays changing minutes and seconds, representing them by two long rectangles: make the maximum width of the rectangles equal to 600 pixels to simplify the arithmetic (10 pixels for each minute and each second). Redraw the two rectangles every second. Figure 6.7 shows a representation of 30 minutes and 15 seconds.

600 pixels wide

Figure 6.7 Time display – for 30 mins, 15 secs.

The program should count up in seconds with a timer, and display the total seconds, and the time in minutes and seconds. Recall that, given a total number of seconds, we can use the Mod operator to break it down into whole hours and seconds remaining. In order to speed up testing the program, you should reduce the timer interval from 1000 milliseconds to, say, 200.

6.7 This question guides you through the writing of a geometry game:
   (a) Write a program with two track bars which control the horizontal and vertical position of a circle of 200 pixels diameter.
   (b) Add a third track bar to control the diameter of the circle.
   (c) What follows is a game based on the mathematical fact that a circle can be drawn through any three points. The program should display 3 points (each is a small filled circle) when a 'Next Game' button is clicked. Good initial positions are (100,100), (200,200), (200,100) but you can add a small random number to them for variety. The player has to manipulate the circle until they judge that the circle goes through each point; they then click a 'Done' Button.
   (d) Add a timer to display how long the task takes.

ANSWERS TO SELF-TEST QUESTIONS

6.1 The program will still compile and run – but will probably produce wrong results. It now modifies the value of a variable that is shared between methods. Before, it modified a local variable.

6.2 The program accesses a label before that label has been created (in `InitializeComponent`). This produces a run-time error.

6.3 There are no serious consequences. The track bars alter their maximum value to the size of the picture box as the program runs.

6.4 Typical methods are: move to next track, stop, start. Properties are not as universal, but many players display the current track number. They are all members.

6.5 a becomes the area of the label, in pixels.
  The height of the label becomes the same as the width: the label becomes square.

6.6 There is a constructor, to which we pass a colour. The instance is the real car which you drive away. (The photo in the catalogue is really nothing more than documentation, showing you what your car will look like.)

6.7 We introduce a variable, which might be named `secondCount`. It is incremented in the `Tick` method for the timer. This variable cannot be local, as it would lose its value when the method ends. Instead, it must be declared as an instance variable, at the top of the program. To display the minute value, we use \ to convert the seconds into minutes.

```
Public Class Form1
    Inherits...
    Private secondCount As Integer = 0

    Private Sub Timer1_Tick(etc...)
        secondCount = secondCount + 1
        Label1.Text = CStr(secondCount \ 60)
    End Sub
End Class
```

Selection – If and Select

This chapter explains:

- how to use If and Select statements to carry out tests;
- how to use operators such as >;
- how to use And, Or and Not;
- how to declare and use Boolean data.

● Introduction

We all make selections in daily life. We wear a coat if it is raining. We buy a CD if we have enough money. Selections are also used a lot in programs. The computer tests a value and, according to the result, takes one course of action or another. Whenever the program has a choice of actions and decides to take one action or the other, an If or a Select statement is used to describe the situation.

We have seen that a computer program is a series of instructions to a computer. The computer obeys the instructions one after another in sequence. But sometimes we want the computer to carry out a test on some data and then take one of a choice of actions depending on the result of the test. For example, we might want the computer to test someone's age and then tell them either that they may vote or that they are too young. This is called selection. It uses a statement (or instruction) called the If statement, the central subject of this chapter.

If statements are so important that they are used in every programming language that has ever been invented.

110 ● Chapter 7/Selection – If and Select

Figure 7.1 Screen for the safe program.

● The If statement

Our first example is a program that simulates the digital lock on a safe. The screen is as shown in Figure 7.1. The safe is locked unless the user enters the correct code into a text box. The text box is initially emptied when the form is designed. The program compares the text that is entered with the correct code. If the code is correct, a message is displayed.

```
Private Sub Button1_Click(ByVal sender As System.Object, _
                          ByVal e As System.EventArgs) _
                          Handles Button1.Click
    Dim code As String

    Label2.Text = ""
    code = TextBox1.Text
    If code = "bill" Then
        Label2.Text = "unlocked"
    End If
End Sub
```

The If statement tests the value of the string. If the string equals the value 'bill', the statement sandwiched between the If and the End If is carried out. Next, any statement after the End If is executed. On the other hand, if the string is not equal to 'bill', the sandwiched statement is ignored and any statement after the End If is executed.

The If statement ● 111

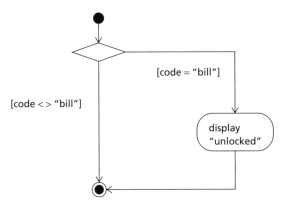

Figure 7.2 Activity diagram for an If statement.

One way of visualizing an If statement is as an activity diagram (Figure 7.2). This shows the above If statement in graphical form. To use this diagram, start at the blob at the top and follow the arrows. A decision is shown as a diamond, with the two possible conditions shown in square brackets. Actions are shown in rounded boxes and the end of the sequence is a specially shaped blob at the bottom of the diagram.

There are two parts to the If statement:

- the condition being tested;
- the statement or sequence of statements to be executed if the condition is true.

All programs consist of a sequence of actions, and the sequence evident here is:

1. A piece of text is input from the text box.
2. Next a test is done.
3. If appropriate, a message is displayed to say that the safe is unlocked.

Very often we want not just one, but a complete sequence of actions carried out if the result of the test is true, and these are sandwiched between the If statement and the End If statement.

Indentation

Notice that the lines are indented to reflect the structure of this piece of program. (Indentation means using spaces to push the text over to the right.) The VB development system does this automatically when you type in an If statement. Although indentation is not essential, it is highly desirable so that the (human) reader of a program can understand it easily. All good programs (whatever the language) have indentation and all good programmers use it.

Figure 7.3 The voting checker program screen.

If . . . Else

Sometimes we want to specify *two* sequences of actions – those that are carried out if the condition is true and those that are carried out if the condition is false.

The user of the voting checker program enters their age into a text box and the program decides whether they can vote or not. The screen is shown in Figure 7.3. When the user clicks on the button, the program extracts the information that the user has entered into the text box, converts the string into an integer and places the number in the variable called `age`. Next we want the program to take different actions depending on whether the value is:

- greater than 17, or
- less than or equal to 17.

Then the results of the test are displayed in a number of labels.

```
Private Sub Button1_Click(ByVal sender As System.Object, _
                ByVal e As System.EventArgs) _
                Handles Button1.Click
    Dim age As Integer

    age = CInt(TextBox1.Text)
    If age > 17 Then
        DecisionLabel.Text = "you may vote"
        CommentaryLabel.Text = "congratulations"
```

```
    Else
         DecisionLabel.Text = "you may not vote"
         CommentaryLabel.Text = "sorry"
    End If
    SignOffLabel.Text = "Best Wishes"
End Sub
```

There are three parts to this If statement:

- the condition being tested – in this case whether the age is greater than 17;
- the statement or sequence of statements to be executed if the condition is true;
- the statement or statements to be executed if the condition is false.

The new element here is the word Else, which introduces the second part of the If statement. Notice again how the indentation helps to emphasize the intention of the program.

We can visualize an If...Else statement as an activity diagram, as shown in Figure 7.4. The diagram shows the condition being tested and the two separate actions.

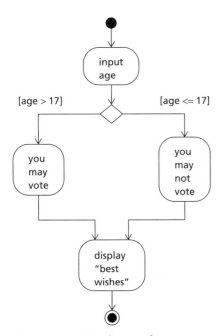

Figure 7.4 Activity diagram for an If...Else statement.

Comparison operators

The programs above used some of the comparison operators. Here is a complete list:

Symbol	Means
>	greater than
<	less than
=	equals
<>	not equal to
<=	less than or equal to
>=	greater than or equal to

Notice that VB uses the equals sign (=) to test whether two things are equal. This same symbol is also used to assign a value to a variable.

Choosing the appropriate operator often has to be done with great care. In the program to test whether someone can vote, the appropriate test should probably be:

```
If age >= 18 Then
    DecisionLabel.Text = "you can vote"
End If
```

Note that it is usually possible to write conditions in either of two ways. The following two program fragments achieve exactly the same result, but use different conditions:

```
If age >= 18 Then
    DecisionLabel.Text = "you may vote"
Else
    DecisionLabel.Text = "sorry"
End If
```

achieves the same end as:

```
If age < 18 Then
    DecisionLabel.Text = "sorry"
Else
    DecisionLabel.Text = "you may vote"
End If
```

Although these two fragments achieve the same end result, the first is probably better, because it spells out more clearly the condition for eligibility to vote.

> **SELF-TEST QUESTION**
>
> 7.1 Do these two pieces of VB achieve the same end or not?
>
> ```
> If age > 18 Then
>     Label2.Text = "you may vote"
> End If
> If age < 18 Then
>     Label2.Text = "you may not vote"
> End If
> ```

And, Or, Not

Often in programming we need to test two things at once. Suppose, for example, we want to test whether someone should pay a junior rate for a ticket:

```
If age > 6 And age < 16 Then
    Label1.Text = "junior rate"
End If
```

The word `And` is one of the VB logical operators and simply means 'and' as we would use it normal language.

Brackets can be used to improve the readability of these more complex conditions. For example we can rewrite the above statement as:

```
If (age > 6) And (age < 16) Then
    Label1.Text = "junior rate"
End If
```

Although the brackets are not essential, they serve to distinguish the two conditions being tested.

It might be very tempting to write:

```
If age > 6 And < 18 Then       ' error!
```

but this is incorrect because the conditions have to be spelled out in full as follows:

```
If age > 6 And age < 18 Then       ' OK
```

We would use the `Or` operator in an `If` statement like this:

```
If age < 6 Or age > 60 Then
    Label1.Text = "reduced rate"
End If
```

in which the reduced rate is applicable for people who are younger than 6 or older than 60.

The Not operator, with the same meaning as in English, gets a lot of use in programming, even though in English the use of a negative can suffer from lack of clarity. Here is an example of the use of not:

```
If Not (age > 18) Then
    Label1.Text = "too young"
End If
```

This means: test to see if the age is greater than 18. If this result is true, make it false. If it is false, make it true. Then, if the outcome is true, display the message. This can, of course, be written more simply without the Not operator.

> **SELF-TEST QUESTION**
>
> **7.2** Rewrite the above If statement without using the Not operator.

This next program illustrates a more complex series of tests. Two dice are thrown in a betting game and the program has to decide what the result is. We will create two track bars, each with a range of 1 to 6 to specify the values of each of the two dice (Figure 7.5). To start with, we make the rule that only a total score of six wins anything.

The program code is given below. Whenever either of the two track bars is moved, the method is called to display the total value and decide whether a win has occurred.

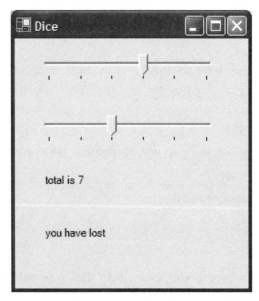

Figure 7.5 The dice program, version 1.

```
Private Sub TrackBar1_Scroll(ByVal sender As Object, _
                    ByVal e As System.EventArgs) _
                    Handles TrackBar1.Scroll
    CheckValues()
End Sub

Private Sub TrackBar2_Scroll(ByVal sender As Object, _
                    ByVal e As System.EventArgs) _
                    Handles TrackBar2.Scroll
    CheckValues()
End Sub

Private Sub CheckValues()
    Dim die1, die2, total As Integer

    die1 = TrackBar1.Value
    die2 = TrackBar2.Value
    total = die1 + die2
    Label1.Text = "total is " & total
    If total = 6 Then
        Label2.Text = "you have won"
    Else
        Label2.Text = "you have lost"
    End If
End Sub
```

Now we will alter the rules and see how to rewrite the program. Suppose that any pair of identical values wins, i.e. two ones, two twos, etc. Then the `If` statement is:

```
If die1 = die2 Then
    Label2.Text = "you have won"
End If
```

Now let's suppose that you only win if you get a total of either 2 or 7:

```
If (total = 2) Or (total = 7) Then
    Label2.Text = "you have won"
End If
```

Notice that we have enclosed each of the conditions with brackets. These brackets aren't strictly necessary in VB, but they help a lot to clarify the meaning of the condition to be tested.

> **SELF-TEST QUESTIONS**
>
> 7.3 Alter the program so that a win is a total value of 2, 5 or 7.
>
> 7.4 Write `If` statements to test whether someone is eligible for full-time employment. The rule is that you must be 16 or above and younger than 65.

Nested `If`s and `ElseIf`

Look at the following program fragment:

```
If age > 6 Then
    If age < 16 Then
        Label1.Text = "junior rate"
    Else
        Label1.Text = "adult rate"
    End If
Else
    Label1.Text = "child rate"
End If
```

You will see that the second `If` statement is completely contained within the first. (The indentation helps to make this clear.) This is called *nesting*. Nesting is not the same as indentation – it is just that the indentation makes the nesting very apparent. The meaning of this nested code is as follows:

- If the age is greater than 6, then the second `If` is carried out.
- If the age is not greater than 6, then the `Else` part is carried out.

The overall effect of this piece of program is:

- If the age is greater than 6 and less than 16, the rate is the junior rate.
- If the age is greater than 6 but not less than 16, the rate is the adult rate.
- If the age is not greater than 6, the rate is the child rate.

It is common to see nesting in programs, but a program like this has a complexity which makes it slightly difficult to understand. Often it is possible to write a program more simply using the logical operators and/or a variation of the `If` statement that uses `ElseIf`. Here, for example, the same result as above is achieved without nesting:

```
If (age > 6) And (age < 16) Then
    Label1.Text = "junior rate"
ElseIf age >= 16 Then
    Label1.Text = "adult rate"
Else
    Label1.Text = "child rate"
End If
```

The `If...ElseIf` statement describes a series of mutually exclusive choices. The first condition follows the initial `If`. Subsequent conditions follow any number of `ElseIf` keywords. Optionally there is a final `Else` to address any condition that has not already been met. There is a single `End If` at the end of the complete statement.

We now have two pieces of program that achieve the same end result, one with nesting and one without. Some people argue that it is hard to understand nesting, such a

Nested Ifs and ElseIf • 119

program is prone to errors and that therefore nesting should be avoided. Nesting can always be avoided using either logical operators or ElseIf or both.

> **SELF-TEST QUESTION**
>
> **7.5** Write a program to input a salary from a track bar and determine how much tax someone should pay according to the following rules:
>
> People pay no tax if they earn up to $10 000. They pay tax at the rate of 20% on the amount they earn over $10 000 but up to $50 000. They pay tax at 90% on any money they earn over $50 000. The track bar should have a range from 0 to 100 000.

In the next program we create two track bars, labelled as Tom and Jerry. The program compares the values and reports on which one is set to the larger value. The screen is shown in Figure 7.6. The library method FillRectangle is used to draw a solid rectangle whose width across the screen is equal to the value obtained from the corresponding track bar.

```
Private Sub TrackBar1_Scroll(ByVal sender As Object, _
                             ByVal e As System.EventArgs) _
                             Handles TrackBar1.Scroll

    CompareValues()
End Sub

Private Sub TrackBar2_Scroll(ByVal sender As Object, _
                             ByVal e As System.EventArgs) _
                             Handles TrackBar2.Scroll

    CompareValues()
End Sub
```

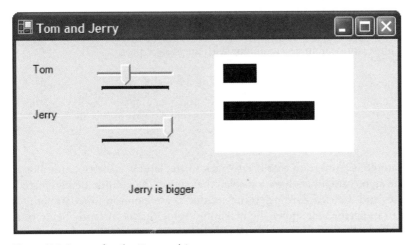

Figure 7.6 Screen for the Tom and Jerry program.

```
Private Sub CompareValues()
    Dim paper As Graphics
    paper = PictureBox1.CreateGraphics()
    Dim myBrush As New SolidBrush(Color.Black)

    Dim tomValue, jerryValue As Integer
    tomValue = TrackBar1.Value
    jerryValue = TrackBar2.Value

    paper.Clear(Color.White)
    paper.FillRectangle(myBrush, 10, 10, tomValue, 20)
    paper.FillRectangle(myBrush, 10, 50, jerryValue, 20)

    If tomValue > jerryValue Then
        Label1.Text = "Tom is bigger"
    Else
        Label1.Text = "Jerry is bigger"
    End If

End Sub
```

This program works fine, but again illustrates the importance of care when you use `If` statements. In this program, what happens when the two values are equal? The answer is that the program finds that Jerry is bigger – which is clearly not the case. We could enhance the program to spell things out more clearly by changing the `If` statement to:

```
If jerryValue > tomValue Then
    Label1.Text = "Jerry is bigger"
ElseIf tomValue > jerryValue Then
    Label1.Text = "Tom is bigger"
Else
    Label1.Text = "They are equal"
End If
```

This is another illustration of an `If` statement with an `ElseIf` part.

> **SELF-TEST QUESTION**
>
> **7.6** Write a program that creates three track bars and displays the largest of the three values.

This next example is a program that keeps track of the largest value of a number as it changes. Some stereo amplifiers have a display that shows the volume being created. The display waxes and wanes according to the volume at any point in time. Sometimes the display has an indicator that shows the maximum value that is currently being output. This program displays the numerical value of the maximum value that the track bar is set to (see Figure 7.7). It uses a single `If` statement that compares the current value

Nested Ifs and ElseIf ● 121

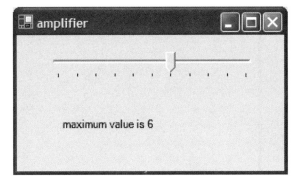

Figure 7.7 Screen for the amplifier display.

of the track bar with the value of a variable named `max`, a class-level variable that holds the value of the largest value achieved so far. `max` is declared like this:

```
Private max As Integer = 0
```

and the method to handle track bar events is:

```
Private Sub TrackBar1_Scroll(ByVal sender As Object, _
                             ByVal e As System.EventArgs) _
                             Handles TrackBar1.Scroll
    Dim volume As Integer

    volume = TrackBar1.Value
    If volume > max Then
        max = volume
    End If
    Label1.Text = "maximum value is " & CStr(max)
End Sub
```

> **SELF-TEST QUESTIONS**
>
> **7.7** Write a program that displays the numerical value of the minimum value that the track bar is set to.
>
> **7.8** The Young and Beautiful holiday company restricts its clients to ages between 18 and 30. (Below 18 you have no money; after 30 you have too many wrinkles.) Write a program to test whether you are eligible to go on holiday with this company.

We now return to the dice-throwing program discussed earlier. Instead of inputting the dice values via the track bars, we change the program so that the computer decides the die values randomly. We will create a button, labelled 'throw'. When it is clicked, the program will obtain two random numbers and use them as the die values (Figure 7.8).

Figure 7.8 The dice program, version 2.

To get a random number in VB, we create an object from the library class `Random` and then use its method `Next`. This method returns a random number, an `Integer` in any range we choose, specified by the parameters. We met this class back in Chapter 6.

The program to throw two dice is given below. At class level we declare:

```
Private randomNumber As Random = New Random()
```

and then the event-handling method is:

```
Private Sub Button1_Click(ByVal sender As Object, _
                    ByVal e As System.EventArgs) _
                    Handles Button1.Click
    Dim die1, die2 As Integer

    die1 = randomNumber.Next(1, 6)
    die2 = randomNumber.Next(1, 6)

    Label1.Text = "the die values are " _
            & CStr(die1) & " and " & CStr(die2)
    If die1 = die2 Then
        Label2.Text = "dice equal - a win"
    Else
        Label2.Text = "dice not equal - lose"
    End If
End Sub
```

● Select

The `Select` statement is another way of doing a lot of `If` statements. You can always accomplish everything you need with the aid of `If` statements but `Select` can be useful in appropriate circumstances. For example, suppose we need a piece of program to display the day of the week as a string. Suppose that the program represents the day of the week as an `Integer` variable called `dayNumber`, which has one of the values 1 to 7, representing the days Monday to Sunday. We want to convert the integer version of the day into a string version called `dayName`. We could write the following series of `If` statements:

```
If dayNumber = 1 Then
    dayName = "Monday"
ElseIf dayNumber = 2 Then
    dayName = "Tuesday"
ElseIf dayNumber = 3 Then
    dayName = "Wednesday"
ElseIf dayNumber = 4 Then
    dayName = "Thursday"
ElseIf dayNumber = 5 Then
    dayName = "Friday"
ElseIf dayNumber = 6 Then
    dayName = "Saturday"
ElseIf dayNumber = 7 Then
    dayName = "Sunday"
End If
```

Now although this piece of coding is neat, clear and well-structured, there is an alternative that has the same effect using the `Select` statement:

```
Select Case dayNumber
    Case 1
        dayName = "Monday"
    Case 2
        dayName = "Tuesday"
    Case 3
        dayName = "Wednesday"
    Case 4
        dayName = "Thursday"
    Case 5
        dayName = "Friday"
    Case 6
        dayName = "Saturday"
    Case 7
        dayname = "Sunday"
End Select
```

This now exploits the symmetry of what needs to happen more clearly than the equivalent series of `ElseIf`s. Notice that the complete `Select` statement ends with a `End Select` statement.

A `Select` statement like this can be visualized as an activity diagram in Figure 7.9.

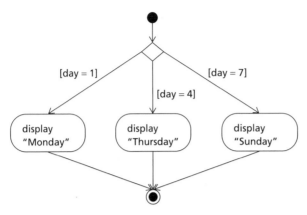

Figure 7.9 Activity diagram showing part of a `Select` statement.

> **SELF-TEST QUESTION**
>
> **7.9** Write a method that converts the integers 1, 2, 3 and 4 into the words diamonds, hearts, clubs and spades respectively.

Several statements can follow one of the options in a `Select` statement. For example, one of the options could be:

```
Case 6
    MessageBox.Show("hurray")
    dayName = "Saturday"
```

Another feature of the `Select` statement is grouping several options together, like this:

```
Select Case dayNumber
Case 1, 2, 3, 4, 5
    dayName = "weekday"
Case 6, 7
    dayName = "weekend"
End Select
```

Another, sometimes useful, part of the `Select` statement is the `Else` option. Suppose in the above example that the value of the integer denoting the day of the week is input from a text box. Then there is the distinct possibility that the user will erroneously enter a number that is not in the range 1 to 7. Any decent program needs to take account of this, in order to prevent something odd happening or the program crashing. The `Select` statement is very good at dealing with this situation, because we can supply a 'catch-all' or default option that will be used if none of the others are valid:

```
Select Case dayNumber
    Case 1
        dayName = "Monday"
    Case 2
        dayName = "Tuesday"
    Case 3
        dayName = "Wednesday"
    Case 4
        dayName = "Thursday"
    Case 5
        dayName = "Friday"
    Case 6
        dayName = "Saturday"
    Case 7
        dayName = "Sunday"
    Case Else
        dayName = "illegal day"
End Select
```

If an `Else` option is not written as part of a `Select` statement and if none of the cases provided corresponds to the actual value of the variable, then all the options are ignored.

The `Select` statement is very useful, but unfortunately it is not as flexible as it could be. Suppose, for example, we want to write a piece of program to display two numbers, with the larger first, followed by the smaller. Using `If` statements, we would write:

```
If a > b Then
    Label1.Text = CStr(a) & " is greater than " & CStr(b)
ElseIf b > a Then
    Label1.Text = CStr(b) & " is greater than " & CStr(a)
Else
    Label1.Text = "they are equal"
End If
```

We may be tempted to rewrite this using a `Select` statement as follows:

```
Select Case ?  ' beware! illegal VB
    Case a > b
        Label1.Text = CStr(a) & " is greater than" & CStr(b)
    Case b > a
        Label1.Text = CStr(b) & " is greater than" & CStr(a)
    Case a = b
        Label1.Text = "they are equal"
End Select
```

but this is not allowed because, as indicated by the question mark, `Select` only works with a single integer or string variable as its subject, and `Case` cannot use >, <, etc.

126 ● Chapter 7/Selection – `If` and `Select`

Figure 7.10 The fast food sign.

● Boolean variables

All of the types of variable that we have met so far are designed to hold numbers or strings. Now we meet a new kind of variable called a `Boolean`, that can only hold either the value `True` or the value `False`. The words `Boolean`, `True` and `False` are reserved keywords in VB and cannot be used for any other purpose. This type of variable is named after the 19th-century British mathematician George Boole who made a large contribution towards the development of mathematical logic, in which the ideas of true and false play a central role.

We will introduce `Boolean` variables by looking at the properties of the labels that are available from the toolbox. Figure 7.10 shows a display that can either be switched on or switched off using buttons. When the user clicks on the buttons the `visible` property of the label is changed:

```
Private Sub OffButton_Click(ByVal sender As Object, _
                    ByVal e As System.EventArgs) _
                    Handles OffButton.Click
    Label1.Visible = False
End Sub

Private Sub OnButton_Click(ByVal sender As Object, _
                    ByVal e As System.EventArgs) _
                    Handles OnButton.Click
    Label1.Visible = True
End Sub
```

The `visible` property is a `Boolean` and we can change the value as shown above. We can also test its value using `If` statements. So we could rewrite the program so that it has a single button that switches the display from visible to invisible, or vice versa, using the statements:

```
Private Sub Button1_Click(ByVal sender As Object, _
                         ByVal e As System.EventArgs) _
                         Handles Button1.Click
    If Label1.Visible = True Then
        Label1.Visible = False
    Else
        Label1.Visible = True
    End If
End Sub
```

Now that we have seen how to use a `Boolean` property, we next look at declaring our own `Boolean` variables. We can declare a variable of type `Boolean` like this:

```
Dim finished As Boolean
```

and we can assign either of the values `True` and `False`, as in:

```
finished = True
```

Equally importantly, we can test the value of a `Boolean` in an `If` statement, for example:

```
If finished Then
    MessageBox.Show("Good bye")
End If
```

The value of `finished` is tested, and if it is `True` the accompanying statement is executed. An equivalent, but slightly more cumbersome, way of writing the same test is:

```
If finished = True Then
    MessageBox.Show("Good bye")
End If
```

`Boolean` variables are used in programming to remember something, perhaps for a short time, perhaps for the whole time that the program is running. As an example, we look at a program, Figure 7.11, that draws a rectangle in a picture box when a button is clicked. Sometimes we want the rectangle to be drawn in outline and sometimes we want it drawn filled in. We provide two buttons allowing the user to specify their option. Once a button has been clicked, the program remembers the option until the user clicks again on a button.

The class-level declaration of the `Boolean` variable is:

```
Private filled As Boolean = True
```

This is the variable that remembers what the user has specified. It either has the value `True` (to denote that rectangles should be filled in) or it has the value `False`.

The methods to handle button-clicks simply make the `Boolean` `True` or `False` as appropriate:

128 ● Chapter 7/Selection – If and Select

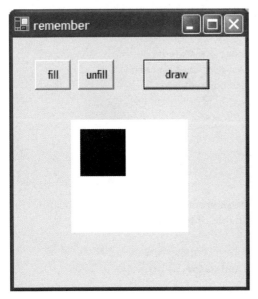

Figure 7.11 The display from the remember program.

```
Private Sub FillButton_Click(ByVal sender As Object, _
                             ByVal e As System.EventArgs) _
                             Handles FillButton.Click
    filled = True
End Sub

Private Sub UnFillButton_Click(ByVal sender As Object, _
                               ByVal e As System.EventArgs) _
                               Handles UnFillButton.Click
    filled = False
End Sub
```

When the user clicks on the **draw** button, the program first tests the value of the Boolean value `filled` using an If statement and then either draws a filled or an unfilled rectangle.

```
Private Sub DrawButton_Click(ByVal sender As Object, _
                             ByVal e As System.EventArgs) _
                             Handles DrawButton.Click
    Dim paper As Graphics = PictureBox1.CreateGraphics()
    Dim myPen As Pen = New Pen(Color.Black)
    Dim myBrush As SolidBrush = New SolidBrush(Color.Black)
    paper.Clear(Color.White)
    If filled = True Then
```

```
            paper.FillRectangle(myBrush, 10, 10, 50, 50)
        Else
            paper.DrawRectangle(myPen, 10, 10, 50, 50)
        End If
    End Sub
```

Methods can use `Boolean` values as parameters and as return values. For example, here is a method that checks whether three numbers are in numerical order:

```
    Private Function InOrder(ByVal a as Integer, _
                             ByVal b As Integer, _
                             ByVal c As Integer) As Boolean
        If (a <= b) And (b <= c) Then
            Return True
        Else
            Return False
        End If
    End Sub
```

Programming principles

The computer normally obeys instructions one-by-one in a sequence. An `If` statement instructs the computer to test the value of some data and then take one of a choice of actions depending on the result of the test. This choice is sometimes called *selection*. The test of the data is called a *condition*. After an `If` statement is completed, the computer continues obeying the instructions in sequence.

Programming pitfalls

You might find that you have written an `If` statement like this:

```
    If a > 18 And < 25 Then
```

which is wrong. Instead, the `And` must link two complete conditions, preferably in brackets for clarity, like this:

```
    If (a > 18) And (a < 25) Then
```

Grammar spot

The first kind of `If` statement has the structure:

```
    If condition Then
        statements
    End If
```

The second type of If statement has the structure:

```
If condition Then
    statements
Else
    statements
End If
```

The third type of If statement has the structure that follows this pattern:

```
If condition Then
    statements
ElseIf condition Then
    statements
ElseIf condition Then
    statements
Else
    statements
End If
```

The final Else is optional.

The Select statement has the structure:

```
Select Case variable
    Case value1
        statements
    Case value2
        statements
    Case Else
        statements
End Select
```

The final Case Else is optional.

New language elements

- Control structures for decisions:

    ```
    If, Then, ElseIf, Else, End If
    Select, Case, Else, End Select
    ```

- The comparison operators >, <, =, <>, <= and >=
- The logical operators And Or Not
- Variables declared as Boolean, which can take either the value True or the value False.

Summary

- `If` statements allow the programmer to control the sequence of actions by making the program carry out a test. Following the test, the computer carries out one of a choice of actions.
- There are three varieties of `If` statement:

  ```
  If ... Then ... End If
  If ... Then ... Else ... End If
  If ... Then ... ElseIf ... End If
  ```

- A `Boolean` variable can be assigned the value `True` or the value `False`. A `Boolean` variable can be tested with an `If` statement.
- The `Select` statement provides a convenient way of carrying out a number of tests. However, the `Select` statement is restricted to tests on integers or on strings.

EXERCISES

7.1 Deal a card Write a program with a single button on it which, when clicked, randomly selects a single playing card. First use the random number generator in the library to create a number in the range 1 to 4. Then convert the number to a suit (heart, diamond, club, spade). Next use the random number generator to create a random number in the range 1 to 13. Convert the number to an ace, 2, 3, etc. and finally display the value of the chosen card. (Hint: use `Select` as appropriate.)

7.2 Sorting Write a program to input numbers from three track bars, or three text boxes, and display them in increasing numerical size.

7.3 Cinema (movie theatre) price Write a program to work out how much a person pays to go to the cinema. The program should input an age from a track bar or a text box and then decide on the following basis:

- under 5, free;
- aged 5 to 12, half price;
- aged 13 to 54, full price;
- aged 55, or over, free.

7.4 Betting A group of people are betting on the outcome of three throws of the dice. A person bets $1 on predicting the outcome of the three throws. Write a program that uses the random number method to simulate three throws of a die and displays the winnings according to the following rules:

- all three throws are sixes: win $20;
- all three throws are the same (but not sixes): win $10;
- any two of the three throws are the same: win $5.

7.5 Digital combination safe Write a program to act as the digital combination lock for a safe. Create three buttons, representing the numbers 1, 2 and 3. The user clicks on the buttons, attempting to guess the correct numbers (say 331121). The program remains unhelpfully quiet until the correct buttons are pressed. Then it congratulates the user with a suitable message. A button is provided to allow users to restart.

Enhance the program so that it has another button which allows the user to change the safe's combination.

7.6 Rock, scissors, paper game In its original form, each of the two players simultaneously chooses one of rock, scissors or paper. Rock beats scissors, paper beats rock and scissors beats paper. If both players choose the same, it is a draw. Write a program to play the game. The player selects one of three buttons, marked rock, scissors or paper. The computer makes its choice randomly using the random number generator. The computer also decides and displays who has won.

7.7 The calculator Write a program which simulates a simple desk calculator (Figure 7.12) that acts on integer numbers. It has one button for each of the 10 digits, 0 to 9. It has a button to add and a button to subtract. It has a clear button, to clear the display, and an equals (=) button to get the answer.

When the clear button is pressed, the display is set to zero and the (hidden) total is set to zero.

When a digit button is pressed, the digit is added to the right of those already in the display (if any).

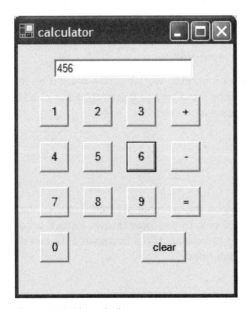

Figure 7.12 The calculator.

When the + button is pressed, the number in the display is added to the total (and similarly for the – button).

When the = button is pressed, the value of the total is displayed.

7.8 **The elevator** Write a program to simulate a very primitive elevator. The elevator is represented as a filled rectangle. There are two buttons – one to make it move up the screen and one to make it move down.

7.9 **Nim** is a game played with matchsticks (unused or used, it does not matter). It doesn't matter how many matches there are. The matches are put into three piles. Again, it doesn't matter how many matches there are in each pile. Each player goes in turn. A player can remove any number of matches from any one pile, but only one pile. A player must remove at least one match. The winner is the person who causes the other player to take the last match.

Write a program to play the game. Initially the computer deals three piles, with a random number (in the range 1 to 200) of matches in each pile. One player is the computer, which chooses a pile and an amount randomly. The other player is the human user, who specifies the pile number and quantity using text boxes, before clicking on a 'go' button.

7.10 **Turtle graphics** Turtle graphics is a way of making programming easy for young children. Imagine a pen fixed to the belly of a turtle. As the turtle crawls around a floor, the pen draws on the floor. The turtle can be issued with commands as follows:

- pen up
- pen down
- turn left 90°
- turn right 90°
- go forward *n* pixels

Initially the turtle is at coordinates 0, 0 and facing to the right.

So, for example, we can draw a rectangle using the sequence:

1. pen down
2. go forward 20 pixels
3. turn right 90°
4. go forward 20 pixels
5. turn right 90°
6. go forward 20 pixels
7. turn right 90°
8. go forward 20 pixels

Write a program that behaves as the turtle, with one button for each of the commands. The number of pixels, *n*, to be moved is input via a track bar or a text box.

ANSWERS TO SELF-TEST QUESTIONS

7.1 No, because they treat the particular age of 18 differently.

7.2
```
If age <= 18 Then
    Label1.Text = "too young"
End If
```

7.3
```
If (total = 2) Or (total = 5) Or (total = 7) Then
    Label2.Text = "you have won"
End If
```

7.4
```
If age >= 16 And age < 65 Then
    MessageBox.Show("you are eligible")
End If
```

7.5
```
Dim salary, tax As Integer
salary = TrackBar1.Value
If (salary > 10000) And (salary <= 50000) Then
    tax = (salary - 10000)/5
ElseIf salary > 50000 Then
    tax = 8000 + ((salary - 50000) * 9 / 10)
Else
    tax = 0
End If
```

7.6
```
Dim a, b, c As Integer
a = TrackBar1.Value
b = TrackBar2.Value
c = TrackBar3.Value
If a > b And a > c Then
    largest = a
ElseIf b > a And b > c Then
    largest = b
ElseIf c > a And c > b Then
    largest = c
End If
MessageBox.Show("largest value is " & CStr(largest))
```

7.7 The essential part of this program is:
```
If volume < min Then
    min = volume
End If
Label2.text = "Minimum value is " & CStr(min)
```

7.8
```
Dim age As Integer
age = CInt(TextBox1.Text)
If age >= 18 And age <= 30 Then
    TextBox2.Text = "you are eligible"
End If
```

7.9
```
Function Convert(ByVal s As Integer) As String
    Dim suit As String
    Select Case s
        Case 1
            suit = "diamonds"
        Case 2
            suit = "hearts"
        Case 3
            suit = "clubs"
        Case 4
            suit = "spades"
    End Select
    Return suit
End Function
```

Repetition – For, While and Do

This chapter explains:

- how to perform repetitions (loops) using `For` statements;
- how to perform repetitions using `While` statements;
- how to perform repetitions using `Do` statements;
- how to choose which kind of loop to use;
- how to use `And`, `Or` and `Not` in loops;
- how to combine repetitions with selections.

● Introduction

We humans are used to doing things again and again – eating, sleeping and working. Computers similarly routinely perform repetition. Examples are:

- adding up a list of numbers;
- searching files for some desired information;
- solving a mathematical equation iteratively, by repeatedly obtaining better and better approximations;
- making a graphical image move on the screen (animation).

We have already seen that a computer obeys a *sequence* of instructions. Now we shall see how to repeat a sequence of instructions a number of times. Part of the power of computers arises from their ability to perform repetitions extremely quickly. In the language of programming, a repetition is called a *loop*.

There are three ways in which the VB programmer can instruct the computer to perform repetition: `For`, `While` and `Do`. Any of these can be used to carry out repetition, but there are differences between them, as we shall see.

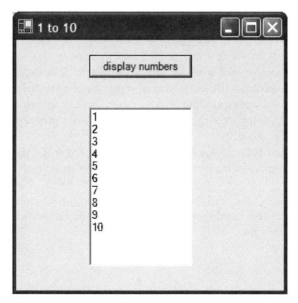

Figure 8.1 Display of the numbers 1 to 10.

For

We begin by using a loop to display the integers 1 to 10 (Figure 8.1) in a multiline text box.

```
Private Sub Button1_Click(ByVal sender As System.Object, _
                         ByVal e As System.EventArgs) _
                         Handles Button1.Click
    Dim number As Integer
    Textbox1.Clear()
    For number = 1 To 10
        Textbox1.AppendText(CStr(number) & NewLine)
    Next
End Sub
```

The word `For` signifies that a repetition is required. The statements enclosed between `For` and `Next` are repeated; this is called the *body* of the loop. The repetition starts with the value of `number` equal to 1, then 2, etc., up to and including `number` equal to 10. The indentation of the statements within the loop (displayed automatically by the VB development environment) assists us in seeing the structure of the loop.

The text box is initially emptied using the method `Clear`. Each time the loop repeats, a number is added to the text box using the method `AppendText`.

This program uses the `NewLine` property from the VB library. There is also a similar `Tab` property. To use these, you need an `Imports` statement like this at the head of the program:

```
Imports Microsoft.VisualBasic.ControlChars
```

You will see that this text box allows multiple lines of text to be displayed. In order to accomplish this the `Multiline` property of the text box must be set to `True`.

A good way to understand how loops work is to use the debugger to follow the execution of this loop. Instead of clicking on the start button, select `Step Into` from the `Debug` menu or alternatively hit the corresponding shortcut key. Repeat to single step through the program. Place the cursor over the text `number` within the program and watch its value change as the loop proceeds.

This example of a `For` loop is typical because `For` loops are normally used when the number of repetitions is known in advance. In the above case we know how many numbers are to be displayed.

This program displays the value of the variable `number` controlling the loop. Although it is fine to use the value of the variable in this way, it is highly dangerous (and not recommended) to change the value.

SELF-TEST QUESTION

8.1 What does this program fragment do?

```
Dim number As Integer
For number = 0 to 5
    TextBox1.AppendText(CStr(number * number) & NewLine))
Next
```

The next program adds up (calculates the sum of) the numbers 1 to 100. When a button is clicked, the following method calculates and displays the result in a text box.

```
Private Sub Button1_Click(ByVal sender As Object, _
                         ByVal e As System.EventArgs) _
                         Handles Button1.Click

    Dim number As Integer
    Dim sum As Integer

    sum = 0
    For number = 1 To 100
        sum = sum + number
    Next
    Textbox1.Text = "The sum is " & CStr(sum)

End Sub
```

This program makes use of a common programming technique – a running total. The value of the variable `sum` is initially equal to zero. Each time the loop is repeated, the value of `number` is added to the value of `sum` and the result placed back in `sum`.

The next program uses a `For` loop to display a row of boxes. The number of boxes is determined by the value selected on a track bar. Whenever the pointer is changed, an event is created and the program displays the matching number of boxes. To do this, we will need a counter. The counter, initially equal to 1, is incremented by one each time a single box is output. We need to repeat the addition of a box until the counter reaches the desired total using a `For` loop as follows:

```
Private Sub TrackBar1_Scroll(ByVal sender As System.Object, _
                             ByVal e As System.EventArgs) _
                             Handles TrackBar1.Scroll

    Dim x, numberOfBoxes, counter As Integer
    Dim paper As Graphics
    Dim myPen As Pen = New Pen(Color.Black)

    numberOfBoxes = TrackBar1.Value
    paper = PictureBox1.CreateGraphics()
    paper.Clear(Color.White)
    x = 10
    For counter = 1 To numberOfBoxes
        paper.DrawRectangle(myPen, x, 10, 10, 10)
        x = x + 15
    Next
End Sub
```

The output from this piece of program is shown in Figure 8.2.

This program will draw as many boxes as we like. Imagine how many instructions we would have to write in order to display 100 boxes – if we were not able to use a `For` statement.

One way to visualize a `For` loop is using an activity diagram, as shown in Figure 8.3. The computer normally obeys instructions in sequence from top to bottom as shown

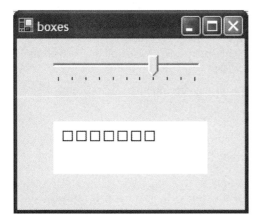

Figure 8.2 Screen showing the display of boxes using `For`.

140 ● Chapter 8/Repetition – For, While and Do

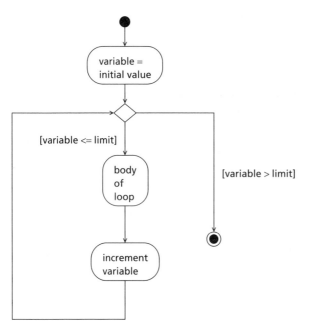

Figure 8.3 Activity diagram of a For loop.

by the arrows. A For loop means that the variable is tested before the loop is executed and again before any repetition of the loop. If the value is less than or equal to the final value the loop is executed. When, finally, the value of the variable exceeds the final value, the body of the loop ceases to be executed and the repetition ends.

> **SELF-TEST QUESTIONS**
>
> **8.2 Prison bars** Write a program to draw five vertical parallel lines.
>
> **8.3 Chessboard** Write a program to draw a chessboard with 9 vertical lines, 10 pixels apart, and 9 horizontal lines, 10 pixels apart.
>
> **8.4 Squaring numbers** Write a program to display the numbers 1 to 5 and their squares.

● While

The While loop is more flexible than the For loop, but with power comes responsibility.

We have seen how to use loops to repeat something when we knew in advance how many repetitions were needed. But in some situations, we don't know how many

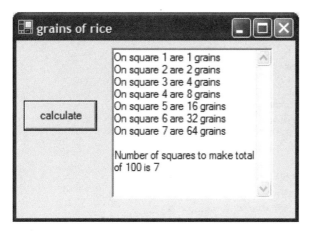

Figure 8.4 Screen for the grains of rice program.

repetitions will be needed. As an example illustrating how to use `While`, we use an old fable about a ruler of India. In the fable someone is asked what he wants as a reward for inventing the game of chess. The response is that he would like as many grains of rice as you would get if you put one on the first square of a chess board, two on the second, four on the third, and so on, doubling the amount on the previous square. Let us write a program to find out how many squares would be needed to get 100 grains of rice. The screen looks like Figure 8.4.

We need a loop, but in this situation the significant feature is that we don't know in advance how many repetitions will be needed – this is what we want to find out. Initially the number of grains is 1 and the number of squares is 1. Each time we move to a new square, we add one to the square number and double the number of grains on the new square. We calculate the total amount of rice using a running total, initially equal to zero. We use a multiline text box, set as a property of the text box when the form is designed. We also use a vertical scroll bar with the text box because we do not know in advance how much output will be created by the program. The code is:

```
Private Sub Button1_Click(ByVal sender As Object, _
                ByVal e As System.EventArgs) _
                Handles Button1.Click
    Dim square, rice, total As Integer
    square = 1
    rice = 1
    total = 1
    DisplayCounts(square, rice)

    While total < 100
```

```
            square = square + 1
            rice = rice * 2
            DisplayCounts(square, rice)
            total = total + rice
    End While
    TextBox1.AppendText(Newline & _
            "Number of squares to make total of 100 is " & _
            square)
End Sub

Private Sub DisplayCounts(ByVal square As Integer, _
                          ByVal rice As Integer)
    TextBox1.AppendText("On square " & square & _
            " are " & rice & " grains" & NewLine)
End Sub
```

The `While` loop works like this. Initially the value of `total` is equal to 1. This is less than 100, so the loop is carried out and the output created. Then `total` is increased by the amount of rice on the new square. This is still less than 100, so the loop is repeated again. This continues until `total` becomes 100 or more and the loop is over. Initially the text box is empty. Each time the loop repeats, a new line of text is appended to the multiline text box using the method `AppendText`.

The condition determines whether a `While` loop is executed or completed as follows:

- If the condition is true, the body of the loop is executed.
- If the condition is false, the loop ends and the statements after the `End While` are executed.

`While` loops tend to have the following components:

- some initialization before the loop (e.g. `total = 1`);
- a condition controlling the repetition (e.g. `total < 100`);
- something inside the loop that affects the condition (e.g. `total = total + rice`).

The above program fragment used the less than (`<`) operator. This is one of a number of available comparison operators, which are the same as those used in `If` statements. Here, again, is the complete list of the comparison operators:

Symbol	Means
>	greater than
<	less than
=	equals
<>	not equal to
<=	less than or equal to
>=	greater than or equal to

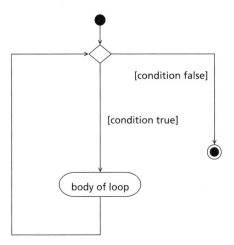

Figure 8.5 Activity diagram of a While statement.

One way to visualize how a While statement works is to study an activity diagram, as shown in Figure 8.5. Notice that, as in the For statement, the test on the condition is made at the start of the loop.

It is wise to exercise great care when you write a While loop to make sure that the counting is done properly. A common error is to make the loop repeat one too many times or one too few times. This is sometimes known as an 'off by one' error. Sometimes a loop is written so as to start with a count of 0 and the test is to see whether it is less than the number required, as follows:

```
count = 0
While count < numberRequired
    ' loop
    count = count + 1
End While
```

Alternatively the loop is written to start with a count of 1 and the test is to see whether it is less than or equal to the number required, as follows:

```
count = 1
While count <= numberRequired
    ' loop
    count = count + 1
End While
```

Both of these styles are used in this book.

Chapter 8/Repetition – For, While and Do

And, Or, Not

On occasions, the condition that controls a loop is more complex and we need the **And**, **Or** and **Not** logical operators. You would use these in everyday life if you wanted to say 'I'm going for a walk until it starts raining or it is 5 o'clock.' (We've already met these operators in Chapter 7 on decisions using the **If** statement.)

If we wanted to describe how long we are going walking for using a **While** statement, we would say 'While it is not raining and it is not 5 o'clock, I am going walking.' Notice that each of the two conditions (raining, 5 o'clock) is preceded by a 'not' and that the two conditions are linked by an 'and'. This is what tends to happen when you write a loop with a **While** statement – and you have to be very careful to write the condition very clearly.

We will revisit the grains of rice program. Suppose we want to add up the number of grains as before, but this time we want to stop either when we have got to 64 squares (the number of squares on a chessboard) or when the total is 10 000 grains. So we want the loop to continue while the total is less than 10 000 and the number of squares is less than 64. The program is:

```
Private Sub Button1_Click(ByVal sender As Object, _
                    ByVal e As System.EventArgs)
    Dim square, rice, total As Integer

    square = 1
    rice = 1
    total = 1
    DisplayCounts(square, rice)

    While total < 10000 And square < 64

        square = square + 1
        rice = rice * 2
        total = total + rice
        DisplayCounts(square, rice)

    End While
    TextBox1.AppendText(Newline & "Total is " & total)
    TextBox1.AppendText(NewLine & "on " & square & " squares")
End Sub

Private Sub DisplayCounts(ByVal square As Integer, _
                    ByVal rice As Integer)
    TextBox1.AppendText("On square " & square & _
             " are " & rice & " grains" & NewLine)
End Sub
```

SELF-TEST QUESTION

8.5 What is displayed when the following code is executed? Is it $n = 0$ and $m = 5$ or is it $n = 0$ and $m = -5$?

```
Dim n, m As Integer
n = 10
m = 5
While (n > 0) Or (m > 0)
    n = n - 1
    m = m - 1
End While
MessageBox.Show("n = " & CStr(n) & " m = " & CStr(m))
```

Do...Loop

If you use `While`, the test is always carried out at the beginning of the repetition. The `Do` loop comes in four varieties and in two of the varieties the test is carried out at the end of the loop. You also have the choice of making the test using either `While` or `Until`. The best choice is determined by the particular programming situation. We illustrate the different varieties of `Do` loop by writing pieces of program to display the numbers 0 to 9 in a text box using all the available loop structures.

Using `For`:

```
Dim count As Integer
TextBox1.Clear()
For count = 0 To 9
    TextBox1.AppendText(CStr(count))
Next
```

Using `While`:

```
Dim count As Integer
TextBox1.Clear()
count = 0
While count <= 9
    TextBox1.AppendText(CStr(count))
    count = count + 1
End While
```

Using `Do` with the test at the start of the loop:

```
Dim count As Integer
TextBox1.Clear()
```

```
count = 0
Do While count <= 9
    TextBox1.AppendText(CStr(count))
    count = count + 1
Loop
```

Using Do with a different test at the start of the loop:

```
Dim count As Integer
TextBox1.Clear()
count = 0
Do Until count = 10
    TextBox1.AppendText(CStr(count))
    count = count + 1
Loop
```

Using Do with the test at the end of the loop:

```
Dim count As Integer
TextBox1.Clear()
count = 0
Do
    TextBox1.AppendText(CStr(count))
    count = count + 1
Loop While count < 10
```

Using Do with a different test at the end of the loop:

```
Dim count As Integer
TextBox1.Clear()
count = 0
Do
    TextBox1.AppendText(CStr(count))
    count = count + 1
Loop Until count = 10
```

You can see that the choices provided by a Do loop are:

- testing at either the start or the end of the repetition;
- testing using either While or Until.

● Nested loops

A nested loop is a loop within a loop. Suppose, for example, we want to display the output shown in Figure 8.6, which is a crudely drawn block of apartments. Suppose that

Nested loops • 147

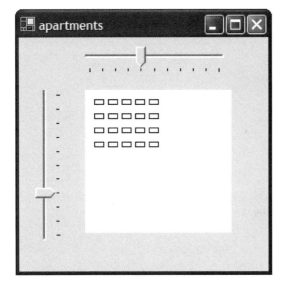

Figure 8.6 Display of apartment block.

there are four floors, each with five apartments, shown as rectangles. The loop that draws an individual floor has this structure:

```
For apartment = 1 To 5
    ' code to draw one apartment
Next
```

and the loop that draws a number of floors has this structure:

```
For floor = 1 To 3
    ' code to draw one floor
Next
```

What we need is to enclose the first loop within the second loop so that the loops are nested. We make the number of apartments per floor and the number of floors both set by track bars. Whenever either track bar is changed, an event is caused and we will call this method:

```
Private Sub DrawFlats(ByVal floors As Integer, _
                     ByVal flats As Integer)
    Dim x, y As Integer
    Dim floor, flat As Integer

    Dim paper As Graphics
    paper = PictureBox1.CreateGraphics()
    paper.Clear(Color.White)
    Dim myPen As Pen = New Pen(Color.Black)
```

```
        y = 10
        For floor = 0 To floors
            x = 10
            For flat = 0 To flats
                paper.DrawRectangle(myPen, x, y, 10, 5)
                x = x + 15
            Next
            y = y + 15
        Next
    End Sub
```

and you will see that the indentation helps considerably in understanding the program. It is always possible to rewrite nested loops using methods, and this code is sometimes clearer. We explore this further in Chapter 21 on style.

> **SELF-TEST QUESTION**
>
> **8.6** A music score is written on paper printed with staves. Each stave consists of five horizontal lines across the page, approximately 2 mm (1/10 inch) apart. Each page holds eight of these staves. Write a program to draw a page of musical score.

● Combining control structures

In the last chapter we looked at selection using the `If` statement and in this chapter we have looked at repetition using `For`, `While` and `Do`. Most programs consist of combinations of these control structures. In fact most programs consist of:

- sequences;
- loops;
- selections;
- calls of library methods;
- calls of methods that we, the programmer, write.

We will now look at an example program where both repetition and selection are used. In this program a ball bounces around the screen, leaving a trace as shown in Figure 8.7. Its position at any time is specified by its *x*- and *y*-coordinates. Initially it starts at the top left-hand corner of the window. It moves in increments of 7 pixels in the *x* direction, and 2 in the *y* direction, and leaves a series of images as it moves. The library method `DrawEllipse` is used to draw the ball, with diameter 10 pixels. When the ball strikes any of the four walls, its direction is reversed. The ball appears to bounce randomly around the picture box, because of the values chosen for the increments.

A `For` loop causes the ball to move through 200 repetitions. `If` statements check whether the boundary has been encountered.

Combining control structures • 149

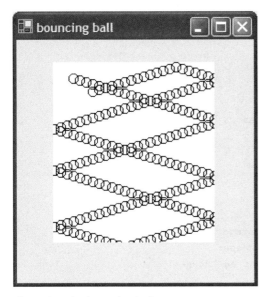

Figure 8.7 The bouncing ball.

```
Private Sub PictureBox1_Click(ByVal sender As Object, _
                              ByVal e As System.EventArgs) _
                              Handles PictureBox1.Click
    Dim x, y, diameter, count As Integer
    Dim xChange As Integer = 7
    Dim yChange As Integer = 2

    x = 10
    y = 10
    diameter = 10

    For count = 1 To 200
        MoveBall(x, y, xChange, yChange)
        DrawBall(x, y, diameter)
    Next
End Sub

Private Sub MoveBall(ByRef x As Integer, _
                     ByRef y As Integer, _
                     ByRef xChange As Integer, _
                     ByRef yChange As Integer)

    If x <= 0 Then
        xChange = -xChange
    End If
```

```
            If x >= PictureBox1.Width Then
                xChange = -xChange
            End If

            If y <= 0 Then
                yChange = -yChange
            End If
            If y >= PictureBox1.Height Then
                yChange = -yChange
            End If

            x = x + xChange
            y = y + yChange
    End Sub

    Private Sub DrawBall(ByVal x As Integer, _
                        ByVal y As Integer, _
                        ByVal diameter As Integer)
        Dim paper As Graphics
        paper = PictureBox1.CreateGraphics()
        Dim myPen As Pen = New Pen(Color.Black)
        paper.DrawEllipse(myPen, x, y, diameter, diameter)
    End Sub
```

This is a typical example of a program in which loops and selection are used together.

Programming principles

There are three varieties of looping statement – `For`, `While` and `Do`. So which one do you choose to use? The guidelines are:

- The `For` loop is used when the number of repetitions is known in advance. A `For` loop repeats zero or more times.
- The `While` loop is generally used when the number of repetitions that will be needed is not known in advance. A `While` loop can be used for zero or more repetitions.
- The `Do` loop is used as a style alternative, or when the test for the end of the repetition needs to be made at the end of the loop.

Thus the most widely applicable facility is the `While` loop, but it isn't necessarily the most appropriate choice in all circumstances. If `For` and `Do` were abolished from VB, we would manage without them by using `While`, but on the right occasion they are simply the best thing to use.

Loops come into their own in programs that process collections of data. We will meet various collections later in this book. They include strings, files, arrays and databases.

Programming pitfalls

- In `While` statements, be very careful with the condition. It is a very common error to make a loop finish one repetition too early or else repeat once too many times.
- Be careful with complex conditions in `While` loops. Do you need `Or` or do you need `And`?
- Within a `For` loop, do not alter the value of the controlling variable.
- To use `Tab` and `NewLine`, you need an `Imports` statement like this at the head of the program:

    ```
    Imports Microsoft.VisualBasic.ControlChars
    ```

Grammar spot

- The `For` loop has the structure:

    ```
    For variable = startValue To endValue
        statement(s)
    Next
    ```

    where `variable` is an `Integer` variable, `startValue` and `endValue` are `Integer` values. Notice that all other statements have an `End` statement to match, but because of a historical legacy VB breaks its grammatical rules with the `For`.

- The `While` loop has the structure:

    ```
    While condition
        statement(s)
    End While
    ```

    where the condition is tested before any repetition of the loop. If it is true, the loop continues. If it is false, the loop ends.

- The `Do` loop has four alternative structures:

    ```
    Do While condition
        statement(s)
    Loop

    Do Until condition
        statement(s)
    Loop

    Do
        statement(s)
    Loop While condition

    Do
        statement(s)
    Loop Until condition
    ```

In the first two varieties, the test is performed before each repetition and in the last two varieties, the test is performed after each repetition.

New language elements

- The control structures for repetition:

    `For` and `Next`
    `While` and `End While`
    `Do` and `Loop`

Summary

- A repetition in programming is called a loop.
- There are three ways in VB of instructing the computer to loop – `For`, `While` and `Do`.
- Use `For` when you know in advance how many repetitions will have to be performed.
- Use `While` when you do not know in advance how many repetitions will have to be performed.
- `Do` is used as an alternative style or when a condition needs to be tested at the end of a loop.

EXERCISES

8.1 **Display integers** Write a program to display the integer numbers 1 to 10 and the cubes of each of their values using a loop.

8.2 **Random numbers** Write a program to display 10 random numbers using a loop. Use the library class `Random` to obtain random numbers in the range 1 to 100. Display the numbers in a text box.

8.3 **The milky way** Write a program that draws 100 circles in a picture box at random positions and with random diameters up to 100 pixels.

8.4 **Steps** Write a program to draw a set of steps made from bricks, as shown in Figure 8.8. Use the library method `DrawRectangle` to draw each brick.

8.6 **Sum of the integers** Write a program that adds up the numbers 0 to 39 using a loop. Check that it has obtained the right answer by using the formula for the sum of the numbers 0 to n:

$$\text{sum} = n \times (n + 1)/2$$

Exercises ● 153

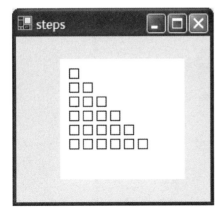

Figure 8.8 Steps.

8.7 Saw-tooth pattern Write a program to display a saw-tooth pattern, as shown in Figure 8.9, in a text box.

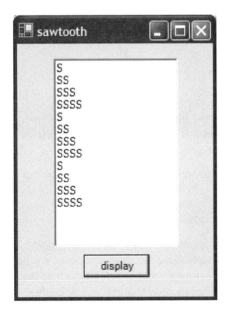

Figure 8.9 Saw-tooth pattern.

8.8 Multiplication table Write a program to display a multiplication table, such as young children use. For example, the table for numbers up to 6 is shown in Figure 8.10. The program should be capable of displaying a table of any size, specified by an integer entered into a text box. Use the library `Tab` property.

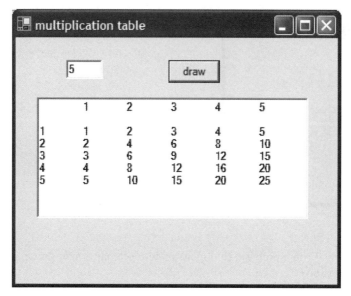

Figure 8.10 Multiplication table.

8.9 Fibonacci The Fibonacci series is the series of numbers:

1   1   2   3   5   8   13 . . .

Each number (except for the first two), is the sum of the previous two numbers. The first two numbers are 1 and 1. The series is supposed to govern growth in plants. Write a program to calculate and display the first 20 Fibonacci numbers.

8.10 Sum of series Write a program to calculate and display the sum of the series:

1 − 1/2 + 1/3 − 1/4 + . . .

until a term is reached that is less than 0.0001.

8.11 Bouncing ball The bouncing ball program could do with some improvements. First, it doesn't bounce properly when it hits a wall. Alter it so that whenever any part of the ball hits a wall it bounces. Provide a feature to alter the direction that the ball moves in, using text boxes to specify the *x* and *y* pixel changes. Provide a feature so that the picture box looks like a pool table with a single pocket right in the middle of the table down which the ball will vanish.

8.12 Nursery rhyme Write a program to display all the verses of a nursery rhyme in a text box with a vertical scrollbar. The first verse is:

10 green bottles, hanging on a wall,
10 green bottles, hanging on a wall,

If 1 green bottle were to accidentally fall
There'd be 9 green bottles, hanging on the wall.

In successive verses there are reduced numbers of bottles, as they fall off the wall.

ANSWERS TO SELF-TEST QUESTIONS

8.1 It displays the numbers 0 1 4 9 16 25 on separate lines.

8.2
```
Dim x, numberOfBars, counter As Integer
Dim paper As Graphics
Dim myPen As Pen = New Pen(Color.Black)

numberOfBars = 5
paper = PictureBox1.CreateGraphics()
paper.Clear(Color.White)

x = 10
For counter = 1 To numberOfBars
    paper.DrawLine(myPen, x, 10, x, 100)
    x = x + 15
Next
```

8.3
```
Dim x, y, counter As Integer
Dim paper As Graphics
Dim myPen As Pen = New Pen(Color.Black)

paper = PictureBox1.CreateGraphics()
paper.Clear(Color.White)

x = 10
For counter = 1 To 9
    paper.DrawLine(myPen, x, 10, x, 90)
    x = x + 10
Next

y = 10
For counter = 1 To 9
    paper.DrawLine(myPen, 10, y, 90, y)
    y = y + 10
Next
```

8.4
```
Dim number As Integer
For number = 1 To 5
    TextBox1.AppendText(CStr(number) & _
                        CStr(number * number) & _
                        NewLine)
Next
```

8.5 $n = 0$ and $m = -5$.

8.6
```
Dim y, staves, lines As Integer
Dim paper As Graphics
Dim myPen As Pen = New Pen(Color.Black)
paper = PictureBox1.CreateGraphics()
paper.Clear(Color.White)
y = 10
For staves = 1 To 8
    For lines = 1 To 5
        paper.DrawLine(myPen, 10, y, 90, y)
        y = y + 2
    Next
    y = y + 5
Next
```

Debugging

This chapter explains:

- different types of bugs;
- how to use the debugger;
- how to use breakpoints and single stepping;
- common errors.

● Introduction

Debugging is the name given to the job of finding out where the bugs are in a program and then fixing the problem. A bug is an error in a program and, because we are all human, all programs tend to have bugs in them – especially when they are first written. The VB integrated development environment provides a debugger to assist in finding bugs.

The VB debugger is also a useful tool in helping to understand how variables, assignments, `If` statements and loops work, because (as we shall see) the debugger can be used to visualize program execution.

As part of the story of where bugs come from, let us trace what happens to a program. There are three stages:

1. compilation;
2. linking;
3. running.

We now consider these in turn.

Compilation

As you type in a program, the VB development environment carries out comprehensive checks, exposing many errors that might otherwise persist. These errors are shown underlined as soon as you type the program statements. These errors are termed compilation errors. A common example is an undeclared variable.

It is important to ensure that the options **Explicit** and **Strict** are switched on. Go to **Tools | Options | Project and Solutions | VB defaults** and switch these options **On**. These ensure that the greatest possible error checking is brought into action. The first option ensures that the compiler checks that all variables are declared. The second option makes the compiler check that all data conversions are carried out explicitly. For example, in the following code extract:

```
Dim age As Integer
age = CInt(TextBox1.Text)
```

the string in the text box is explicitly converted into an integer value.

When all the errors have been corrected, the program will compile 'cleanly' and it will execute, even though it may not do exactly what you want.

Linking

All programs make use of library methods and some make use of programmer-written classes. These classes are linked only when the class is called, when the program is running. But the integrated development environment checks a program as soon as it is typed in, to ensure that all the methods that are called do exist and that the parameters match in number and type. Again, any errors are shown underlined as soon as you type the program statements.

Running

A program runs, but it is most unusual for it to work first time as expected. In fact it is usual for the program to fail in some way or behave in a way other than was intended. Some errors are detected automatically and the programmer is notified – like an attempt to divide `Integer` quantities by zero. Others are subtler and simply give rise to unexpected behaviour. You have a bug in the program – or more likely many bugs! So you have to carry out some debugging.

Later on in this chapter we give examples of common errors that arise in VB programming.

The term 'bug' originated in the days of valve computers, when (the story goes) a large insect became lodged in the circuitry of an early computer, causing it to malfunction. Hence the term 'bug' and the term 'debugging'.

The problem with debugging is that the symptoms of a bug are usually rather uninformative. So we have to resort to detective work to find the cause. It's like being a doctor: there is a symptom, you have find the cause, then you have to fix the problem.

Once the more obvious faults in a program have been eliminated, it is usual to start carrying out some systematic testing. Testing is the repeated running of a program with a variety of data as input and is discussed in Chapter 22. The aim of testing is to convince the world that the program works properly. But normally testing reveals the existence of more bugs. Then it is time to do some debugging. So testing and debugging go hand-in-hand.

Many programmers like debugging; they see it as exciting – like watching a mystery thriller in which the villain is revealed only at the last moment. Certainly, along with testing, debugging often takes a long time. Do not be worried that debugging takes you some time – this is normal!

Using the debugger

A program runs but behaves unexpectedly. How do we find the source of the problem? Most programs display something on the screen, but otherwise what they do is invisible. We need something like X-ray specs to gain some insight into how the program is behaving. This is the key to successful debugging – getting additional information about the running program.

The VB integrated development environment provides a *debugger*. A debugger is a program that helps you debug your program. It runs alongside your program, allowing the progress of the program to be inspected. It provides several facilities, including single stepping and breakpoints.

Breakpoints

Using the debugger, the programmer can place a *breakpoint* in the program. A breakpoint is a place in the program where execution stops. A breakpoint is inserted as follows:

1. Click on the grey bar to the left side of a line in the text of the program (Figure 9.1) (the line is highlighted in brown and a brown circle is shown onthe grey bar).
2. Start the program as usual.

When the breakpoint is reached, the program pauses as it is just about to execute the line highlighted in yellow. A yellow pointer is shown superimposed on the brown

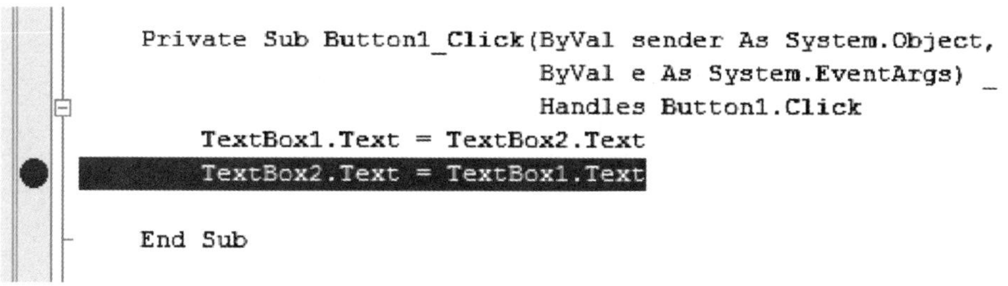

```
        Private Sub Button1_Click(ByVal sender As System.Object, _
                                  ByVal e As System.EventArgs) _
                                  Handles Button1.Click
            TextBox1.Text = TextBox2.Text
            TextBox2.Text = TextBox1.Text
        End Sub
```

Figure 9.1 Placing a breakpoint.

Figure 9.2 Menu obtained by right-clicking on a variable name.

Watch		
Name	Value	Type
TextBox1	{Text = "Romeo"}	System.Windows.Forms.TextBox
TextBox2	{Text = "Romeo"}	System.Windows.Forms.TextBox

Figure 9.3 A Watch window.

circle. You can then position the cursor over the name of a variable or a property and see its value displayed. Any discrepancy between what the value actually is and what it should be provides valuable information for debugging.

Instead of displaying values by placing the cursor over the name, a watch window can be created. This is a separate window that displays the values of selected variables. Right-clicking on a variable name displays a menu, part of which is shown in Figure 9.2.

Selecting **Add Watch** creates the watch window, showing the variable name and its value (Figure 9.3). Any number of variables can be added to this watch window, so that their values can be continuously monitored.

Once information has been obtained, an individual breakpoint can be removed by clicking on the brown dot to the left of the line.

Multiple breakpoints can be inserted into a program. Once a breakpoint is reached, clicking on **Continue** on the **Debug** menu resumes execution of the program until it either ends or reaches the next breakpoint. The **Clear All Breakpoints** option from the **Debug** menu removes them all at once.

To find bugs quickly, the trick is to choose the best points in the program for breakpoints. Generally, good points to choose are:

- At the start of a method, to check that the parameters are OK.
- Immediately after a method has been called (to check that the method has done its work correctly) or right at the end of the method (for the same reason).

Single stepping

The debugger also allows us to execute a program one line at a time; this is called *single stepping*. This is achieved by selecting **Step Into** from the **Debug** menu, or more conveniently using a function key. (The number of this function key depends on your setup. Look at the **Debug** menu, Figure 9.4, to see which it is.) The program executes

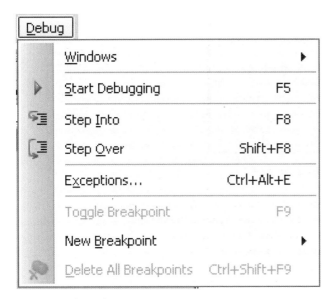

Figure 9.4 The **Debug** menu.

a line and pauses before the line that is highlighted. Any difference between the expected path and the actual path of execution gives useful information about the cause of the bug. At any time we can place the cursor over a variable name and observe its value. Alternatively, we can set up a watch window as explained above. Again, any difference between the expected value and the actual value gives useful information.

It is easy to have a lot of fun with a debugger, but the downside can be using a lot of time. A productive way to use a debugger is as follows:

1. From the symptoms of the bug, make a hypothesis about where the bug lies. You may be able to predict that the error lies within any of two or three methods.
2. Place breakpoints at the entry and exit of the methods under suspicion.
3. Run the program. When the program stops at the entry to a method, inspect the values of the parameters. At the exit, inspect the value of the return value and the values of significant instance variables. Thus identify the method within which the bug lies.
4. Run the program again, stopping at the entry to the erroneous method. Single step through this method until you see the discrepancy between expectation and reality. You have found the bug.

● Case study in debugging

The program (Figure 9.5) illustrates the love between Romeo and Juliet. A button is provided to swap the names in the two text boxes. But the code, as written, simply displays the same name in each box. The erroneous code is:

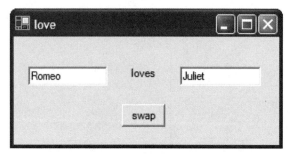

Figure 9.5 The Romeo and Juliet program.

```
Private Sub Button1_Click(ByVal sender As System.Object, _
                ByVal e As System.EventArgs) _
                Handles Button1.Click
    LeftTextBox.Text = RightTextBox.Text
    RightTextBox.Text = LeftTextBox.Text

End Sub
```

There is only one method in this program, so the source of the problem must be within this method. We place a breakpoint at the beginning of the method and then single step through the statements, placing the cursor over the two variables (the text box values) to display their values. Alternatively we create a watch window, as described above. It becomes immediately clear that the value of `LeftTextBox.Text` has been overwritten and therefore lost. We have made a classic mistake – which we can rectify by storing this value in a temporary variable as follows:

```
Private Sub Button1_Click(ByVal sender As System.Object, _
                ByVal e As System.EventArgs) _
                Handles Button1.Click
    Dim temp As String
    temp = LeftTextBox.Text
    LeftTextBox.Text = RightTextBox.Text
    RightTextBox.Text = temp
End Sub
```

● Common errors

Certain errors are commonly made by VB programmers. We list some of them below. It's worthwhile checking any suspect program for these errors.

Compilation errors

The VB development environment carries out a lot of checking on a program as you type in the program and displays a curvy blue line underneath anything it finds that is a problem. These are termed compilation or syntax errors. You can get a brief explanation of the error by positioning the cursor over the curvy line. This is part of trying to ensure that VB programs are robust. An error caught at compile-time is easily fixed, but any errors left undetected until run-time may take a lot of debugging. So although compile-time errors can be annoying, they are good value.

Here are some areas which often cause compilation errors:

Variable names

All variables should be declared and then spelled consistently. It is tempting on occasion to use a keyword as a variable name (for example, the word `Error` is a keyword).

Method and property names

It is not unusual to:

- omit an `Imports` statement;
- misspell a method or property name;
- get the parameters for a method wrong.

Conversions

If you write:

```
TextBox1.Text = 23
```

you will get an error message (code underlined with a wiggly blue line) to say that an implicit conversion from string to number is not allowed. This needs to be done like this:

```
TextBox1.Text = CStr(23)
```

A similar error can occur when a number is input via a text box:

```
Dim number As Integer
number = TextBox1.Text
```

This causes a compilation error message saying that the text needs to be explicitly converted to a number. To remedy this problem, the conversion can be accomplished as follows:

```
number = CInt(TextBox1.Text)
```

Run-time errors

Run-time errors are errors that occur as the program is running, but are detected by the run-time system. Again this is part of the measures designed to ensure that programs are robust – preventing a program that has gone wrong acting like a bull in a china shop. Run-time errors lead to an error message being displayed and the program being stopped.

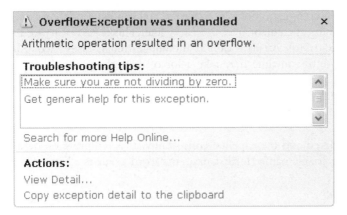

Figure 9.6 Division by zero.

Arithmetic exceptions

If a program attempts to divide by zero, the program will stop and an error message is displayed. It is fairly easy to let this happen inadvertently, for example in a program that contains this fragment:

```
Dim a, b, c As Integer
b = 1
c = CInt(TextBox1.Text)
a = b / c
```

If the user enters the number zero into the text box, an attempt is made to divide by zero, the program is stopped and a message box is displayed (Figure 9.6). The line of VB that caused the error is highlighted in yellow.

The message box tells us fairly clearly what has happened – a calculation was attempted, but overflow occurred. Clicking on **Continue** causes the program to continue execution. Clicking on **Break** allows us to inspect the values of variables.

A remedy for this situation is to write code to check the value of c before the division takes place.

Array indices

The topic of arrays is something that we will not explain until Chapter 14. However, we have included here for completeness a common error that arises when arrays are used. If an array is declared as:

```
Dim table(10) As Integer
Dim index As Integer

For index = 0 To 11 'warning, erroneous
    table(index) = 0
Next
```

Common errors

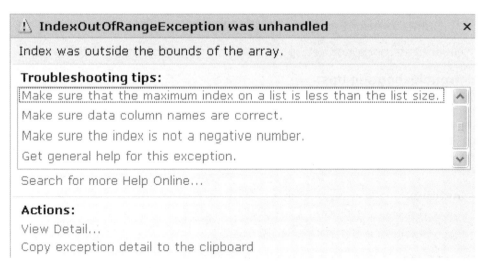

Figure 9.7 Array index out of range.

This places a zero in all of the elements of the array `table`, but then goes on to try to place a zero in index value 11. This is beyond the end of the array, so the program fails and a message box (Figure 9.7) is displayed. The VB statement that caused the error is highlighted. The message is fairly clear in telling us that the index was out of range.

The remedy for this situation is to correct the design flaw in the code.

Using a non-existent object

In earlier chapters we saw how to declare an object as an instance of a class. For example we can declare a variable `ageGuesser` as a variable of the class `Random`:

```
Dim ageGuesser As Random
```

If we now try to use the variable `ageGuesser` by calling the method `Next` as follows:

```
Dim age As Integer
age = ageGuesser.Next(5, 110)
```

the program will fail and a message box (Figure 9.8) is displayed.

We have attempted to use an object that has not been created. What was missing was an instruction to create an instance of the `Random` class, such as:

```
ageGuesser = New Random()
```

Logic errors

Logic errors are the hardest to find, because they depend on the way that the individual program works. Therefore there is no automatic way of detecting such errors. Two types of error are, however, common.

166 ● Chapter 9/Debugging

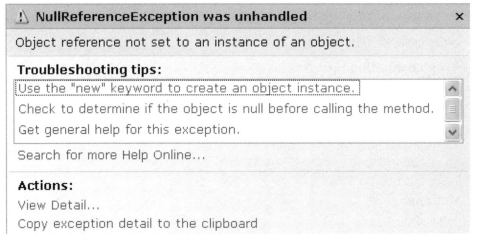

Figure 9.8 Attempt to use a non-existent object.

Initialization means giving a variable an initial value, and it is easy to fail to initialize a variable appropriately. In VB, all variables are automatically initialized to some definite value – for example, `Integer` values are initialized to zero automatically – but this may not be the required value.

It is all too easy to fail to provide handling for an event (a click on a button, for example). This can happen when you change the name of a component such as a button, but forget to match the change of name in the `Handles` part of the event handler method.

Programming pitfalls

Ensure that the **Explicit** and **Strict** options are always switched on. This reduces errors by ensuring that the compiler does its utmost to check the program.

New IDE facilities

To insert or remove a breakpoint, click on the grey bar at the left of the line. The **Debug** menu provides options to remove all breakpoints and to single step through a program.

Summary

- Debugging is finding errors (bugs) in a program and fixing them.
- The VB integrated development environment provides a 'debugger' program.
- A breakpoint is a place where the program temporarily stops.
- Single stepping is watching the execution flow through the program.
- The values of variables can be displayed at breakpoints or during single stepping.

EXERCISE

9.1 Using a program that you have already written, practise using the debugger. Place breakpoints within the program and run it. Then single step through the program, placing the cursor over variable names so as to display their values.

Writing classes

This chapter explains:

- how to write a class;
- how to write constructor methods;
- how to write `Public` methods;
- how to use variables within an object;
- how to write properties.

● Introduction

In earlier chapters we have seen how to make use of library classes – either by selection from the toolbox or by explicit coding. In this chapter we see how to write our own classes. A class describes any number of objects that can be manufactured from it using the keyword `New`.

We shall see that a class consists of:

- `Private` data (variables) that hold information about the object;
- a constructor method, named `New`, used when an object is created. It is used to carry out any initialization, for example assigning initial values to the variables within the object;
- `Public` methods that can be called by the user of the object to carry out useful functions;
- `Property`s that allow the properties of an object to be accessed or changed;
- `Private` methods that are used purely within the object and are inaccessible from outside the object.

Designing a class • 169

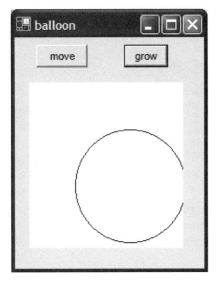

Figure 10.1 Screen layout for the balloon program.

● Designing a class

When the programmer is thinking about a new program, he or she may see the need for an object that is not already available in the VB library of classes. As our first illustration we will use a program to display and manipulate a simplified balloon and we will represent the balloon as an object. The program simply displays a balloon as a circle in a picture box, as shown in Figure 10.1. Buttons are provided to change the position and size of the balloon.

We will construct this program from two objects and therefore two classes:

- Class `Balloon` represents the balloon. We can foresee that it will provide methods named `Move` and `ChangeSize` – with obvious meanings.
- Class `Form1` handles the GUI for the program. It uses class `Balloon` as necessary.

These are shown in the class diagram (Figure 10.2). A class diagram shows each class represented by a rectangle. Any connections between classes are shown as a line joining the two. In this case the relationship is shown as an annotation above the line.

We will complete class `Form1` and then we will write class `Balloon`.

Figure 10.2 Class diagram showing the two classes in the balloon program.

At the head of the class `Form1`, we declare instance variables as usual, including a variable named `myBalloon`:

```
Private myBalloon As Balloon
Private drawArea As Graphics
```

Within `Sub New` we perform any necessary initialization, including creating a new instance of the class `Balloon`. This is the crucial step where we create an object from our own class.

```
myBalloon = New Balloon()
drawArea = PictureBox1.CreateGraphics()
```

Now the code to respond to button-click events:

```
Private Sub MoveButton_Click(ByVal sender As System.Object, _
                    ByVal e As System.EventArgs) _
                    Handles MoveButton.Click
    myBalloon.MoveRight(20)
    drawArea.Clear(Color.White)
    myBalloon.Display(drawArea)
End Sub

Private Sub GrowButton_Click(ByVal sender As System.Object, _
                    ByVal e As System.EventArgs) _
                    Handles GrowButton.Click
    myBalloon.ChangeSize(20)
    drawArea.Clear(Color.White)
    myBalloon.Display(drawArea)
End Sub
```

This concludes the coding for the class `Form1`. Writing this code helps us to clarify how a balloon object will be used, enabling us to see what methods and properties need to be provided by class `Balloon`, as well as the nature of any parameters. This leads us to write the code for class `Balloon`:

```
Public Class Balloon

    Private x As Integer = 50
    Private y As Integer = 50
    Private diameter As Integer = 20
    Dim myPen As Pen = New Pen(Color.Black)

    Public Sub MoveRight(ByVal xStep As Integer)
        x = x + xStep
    End Sub

    Public Sub ChangeSize(ByVal change As Integer)
        diameter = diameter + change
    End Sub
```

```
    Public Sub Display(ByVal drawArea As Graphics)
        drawArea.DrawEllipse(myPen, x, y, diameter, diameter)
    End Sub

End Class
```

The heading of a class description starts with the keywords `Public` and `Class`, and gives the class name. The complete description is terminated with an `End Class` statement. The VB convention is that names of classes start with a capital letter. The body of a class consists of declarations of variables, methods and properties. Note how the readability of the class is enhanced using blank lines and indentation. In the next few sections of this chapter we will go on to look in detail at each of the ingredients in the above class description for balloons.

The overall structure of a class is:

```
Public Class Balloon
' variables
' methods
' properties
End Class
```

Where are classes held? One approach is to write all the classes and place them in a single file, but a better approach is to place different classes in different files. The IDE helps by providing a facility to do this. The steps are:

1. Choose **Add Class** from the **Project** menu. A window appears.
2. Select **Class** from the list of templates.
3. Type in the name of the file to hold the class (usually the name of the class with the extension `.vb`).
4. Click on **Add**.

This creates a distinct file to hold the code for the class. The file is part of the project for the program and it is automatically compiled and linked when the program is run.

● Private variables

A balloon has data associated with it – its size (diameter) and its position (as *x* and *y* coordinates). A balloon object must remember these values. This data is held in variables that are described like this:

```
Private diameter As Integer
Private x, y As Integer
```

The variables `diameter`, `x` and `y` are declared at the top of the class. They can be accessed by any of the statements in the class. They are called *class-level variables* or *instance variables*.

As we saw in Chapter 6, you will see that the word normally used to introduce variables – `Dim` – has been replaced by the word `Private`. Class-level variables are almost always declared as `Private`. Although we *could* describe these variables as `Public`, this is regarded as bad practice. Instead we keep them as `Private`, and use properties or methods to access their values, as we shall see.

> **SELF-TEST QUESTION**
>
> 10.1 Extend the balloon object so that it has a variable that describes the colour of the balloon.

Public methods

Some features of an object need to be publicly available to other pieces of program. This includes those methods which, after all, have been designed for the use of others. As we have seen, a balloon has actions associated with it – for example, to change its size. These actions are written as methods. Changing the size is accomplished by:

```
Public Sub ChangeSize(ByVal change As Integer)
    diameter = diameter + change
End Sub
```

To signify that it is publicly available, we precede the method header with the VB word `Public`. Next we write the method to move a balloon:

```
Public Sub MoveRight(ByVal xStep As Integer)
    x = x + xStep
End Sub
```

To complete the class we provide an additional method for a balloon to display itself when requested to do so.

We have now distinguished clearly between those items that we are making publicly available and those that are private. This is an important ingredient of the philosophy of OOP. Data (variables) and actions (methods) are bundled up together, but in such a way as to hide some of the information from the outside world. Normally it is the data that is hidden away from the rest of the world. This is termed *encapsulation* or *information hiding*.

> **SELF-TEST QUESTIONS**
>
> 10.2 Write a method that moves a balloon upwards by an amount given as the parameter. Name the method `MoveUp`.
>
> 10.3 Write a method that an enables the colour of a balloon to be changed.
>
> 10.4 Rewrite method `Display` so that it displays a coloured balloon.

Public methods 173

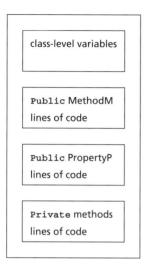

Figure 10.3 Structure of an object or class as seen by the programmer who writes it.

Figure 10.4 Structure of an object or class as seen by its users.

A class or object has the general structure shown in Figure 10.3. This is the view as seen by the programmer who writes it – it consists of variables, properties and methods. The view of an object as seen by its users is shown in Figure 10.4. The view to its users, to whom it is providing a service, is very different. Only the public items (usually methods and properties) are visible – everything else is hidden within an impenetrable box.

Properties

We have seen that it is very bad practice to make `Public` any of the instance variables of a class. The way to give users convenient but controlled access to the data associated with an object is to use properties. We have already used properties of components of the toolkit. For example, we can write statements to access the values of the properties of a text box:

```
name = TextBox1.Text
TextBox1.Visible = False
```

These are examples of accessing data that is part of an object. Notice that there are two distinct kinds of access:

- Reading a value – this is called *get* access (for example extracting the text from a text box using the `Text` property).
- Writing the value – this is called *set* access (for example changing the `Visible` property of a text box).

We will now explore how to provide these kinds of access to data. For example, suppose we want to allow a user of a balloon object to refer to (get) the *x* coordinate of the balloon. This is held in the variable named `x` at the top of the class. As a user of a balloon object, `myBalloon`, we want to be able to extract and use the value, as in:

```
TextBox1.Text = CStr(myBalloon.XCoord)
```

Suppose also that we want the user to be able to change (set) the value of the *x* coordinate with a statement such as:

```
myBalloon.XCoord = 56
```

The way to provide these facilities is to write a property. Here is the revised class that includes the property code:

```
Public Class BalloonWithProperties

    Private x As Integer = 50
    Private y As Integer = 50
    Private diameter As Integer = 20
    Private myPen As Pen = New Pen(Color.Black)

    Public Sub MoveRight(ByVal xStep As Integer)
        x = x + xStep
    End Sub

    Public Sub ChangeSize(ByVal change As Integer)
        diameter = diameter + change
    End Sub
```

```
Public Sub Display(ByVal drawArea As Graphics)
    drawArea.DrawEllipse(myPen, x, y, diameter, diameter)
End Sub

Public Property XCoord() As Integer

    Get
        Return x
    End Get

    Set(ByVal value As Integer)
        x = value
    End Set

End Property

End Class
```

The name of the property (xCoord in this example) follows the key word Property in the header. The complete declaration ends with the End Property statement.

The description consists of two complementary components – one has Get as the heading and the other has Set as the heading. Each component ends with its respective End Get or End Set. The Get part is just like a function – it returns the desired value. The Set part is just like a method – it assigns the value of the parameter (named value in this example) as shown.

We can now use these properties in the program that uses this class. We enhance it to provide a button to display the value of the *x* coordinate in a text box. Figure 10.5 shows the screen.

The code that responds to a click on the button to display the *x* coordinate is given below. It uses the Get property that we have just seen:

```
Private Sub DisplayXButton_Click( _
                    ByVal sender As System.Object, _
                    ByVal e As System.EventArgs) _
                    Handles DisplayXButton.Click
    TextBox1.Text = CStr(myBalloon.XCoord)
End Sub
```

The program also provides a button to change the *x* coordinate (entered in the text box). It uses the Set property that we have just seen. The code that responds to a click on this button is:

```
Private Sub ChangeXButton_Click( _
                    ByVal sender As System.Object, _
                    ByVal e As System.EventArgs) _
                    Handles ChangeXButton.Click
    myBalloon.XCoord = CInt(TextBox1.Text)
    myBalloon.Display(drawArea)
End Sub
```

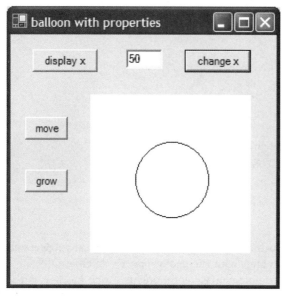

Figure 10.5 Balloon program using properties.

If we only need a way of viewing a property (but not changing its value), we write the property declaration with the prefix `ReadOnly` like this:

```
Public ReadOnly Property XCoord() As Integer

    Get
        Return x
    End Get

End Property
```

If, on the other hand, we need to change a value, but do not need the facility to view it, we write:

```
Public WriteOnly Property XCoord() As Integer

    Set(ByVal value As Integer)
        x = value
    End Set

End Property
```

When you see properties for the first time, you may be tempted to wonder why such a long-winded mechanism is needed. Surely it would be easier simply to declare the value x as `Public`? Then the user of the object could simply refer to the value as `myBalloon.x`. There are several reasons:

- The class can hide the internal representation of the data from the users, while still maintaining the external interface. For example, the author of the balloon class might choose to hold the coordinates of the centre point of a balloon, but provide users with the coordinates of the top left of an enclosing square.
- The author of the class can decide to restrict access to data. For example restrict the *x* coordinate to read-only (`Get`) access, while disallowing write (`Set`) access.
- The class can validate or screen the values used. For example, ignore negative values for a coordinate.

> **SELF-TEST QUESTION**
>
> 10.5 Write properties to allow a user `Set` and `Get` access to the *y* coordinate of a balloon.

Method or property?

Methods and properties both provide mechanisms for accessing an object. So how do we choose which to use? The answer is that we use methods when we want an object to carry out some action. (A method usually has a name that is a verb.) We use properties when we want to refer to some information associated with an object. (A property usually has a name that is a noun.)

We can see this in the library classes. For example, a text box has methods `Clear` and `AppendText` to carry out actions. It has properties `Text` and `Visible` to refer to the state of the object.

Examples of methods associated with a balloon, discussed above, are: `Display`, `MoveUp`, `MoveDown`, `MoveLeft`, `MoveRight`, `Shrink` and `Grow`.

Examples of balloon properties are: `XCoord`, `YCoord`, `Diameter`, `Color` and `Visible`.

Sometimes there is a choice over whether to make something a property or a method, and the choice is a matter of style. For example, to change the colour of a component we could have a method `ChangeColor`; alternatively we could have a property `Color`.

> **SELF-TEST QUESTION**
>
> 10.6 In designing a class `Account` to represent a bank account, which of the following should be methods and which should be properties?
>
>   CreditAccount, DebitAccount, CurrentBalance,
>   CalculateInterest, Name

Constructors

When a balloon object is created, the position and size of the balloon need to be given some values. This is called initializing the variables. There are two ways to do the initialization of variables. One way is to do the initialization as part of the declaration of the class-level variables:

```
Private x As Integer = 50
Private y As Integer = 50
Private diameter As Integer = 20
```

Another way to initialize an object is to write a special method to do the initialization. This method is named a *constructor method* or simply a *constructor* (because it is involved in the construction of the object). This method always has the special name `New`. It has no return value, but it can have parameters. Here is a constructor method for the `Balloon` class:

```
Public Sub New(ByVal initialX As Integer, _
               ByVal initialY As Integer, _
               ByVal initialDiameter As Integer)
    x = initialX
    y = initialY
    diameter = initialDiameter
End Sub
```

This method assigns the values of the parameters (the size and position) to the appropriate variables within the object. A constructor method such as this is written at the top of the class, after the declarations of the class-level variables.

The above constructor method would be used as shown by this example:

```
Dim myBalloon As Balloon = New Balloon(10, 10, 50)
```

If a variable is not explicitly initialized by the programmer, the VB system gives every variable a default value. This is zero for any numbers, `False` for a `Boolean`, " " (an empty string) for a `String` and the value `Nothing` for any object. It is regarded as bad practice to rely on this method of initialization of variables. Instead, it is better to do it explicitly either when the item is declared or by a statement in a constructor.

Other actions that a constructor method might take include creating any objects that the object uses or opening a file that the object uses.

If a class does not have an explicit constructor, then it is assumed to have a single constructor with zero parameters, known as the default constructor.

Multiple constructors

A class can have none, one or several constructor methods. If a class has one or more constructors, they will normally involve parameters and must be called with the appropriate parameters. For example, in the `Balloon` class, we can write the two constructors:

```
Public Sub New(ByVal initialX As Integer, _
               ByVal initialY As Integer, _
               ByVal initialDiameter As Integer)
    x = initialX
    y = initialY
    diameter = initialDiameter
End Sub

Public Sub New(ByVal initialX As Integer, _
               ByVal initialY As Integer)
    x = initialX
    y = initialY
    diameter = 20
End Sub
```

which would allow us to create balloon objects in either of the following ways:

```
Dim balloon1 As Balloon = New Balloon(10, 10, 50)
Dim balloon2 As Balloon = New Balloon(10, 10)
```

but not allow:

```
Dim balloon3 As Balloon = New Balloon()
```

So if you write several constructors, but you still need a constructor with zero parameters, you must explicitly write it, for example:

```
Public Sub New()
End Sub
```

We have now written three constructors for the class `Balloon`, and here is how they might be used to create three different objects from the same class:

```
Dim balloon1 As Balloon = New Balloon()
Dim balloon2 As Balloon = New Balloon(10, 10, 50)
Dim balloon3 As Balloon = New Balloon(10, 10)
```

> **SELF-TEST QUESTION**
>
> **10.7** Write a constructor method to create a new balloon, specifying only the diameter.

Private methods

The whole purpose of writing a class is to allow the creation of objects that present useful facilities to other objects. These facilities are the `Public` methods and properties that the object offers. But often a class has methods that do not need to be made public and, indeed, all the methods in the programs given earlier in this book are `Private`. In the `Balloon` class, suppose we wanted to supply a method that allowed another object to find out the area of a balloon. This would be provided as a `Public` method and let us name this method `Area`. However, we might decide that the detailed calculation of the area is a little complicated and therefore should be packaged up within another `Private` method named `CalcArea` that `Area` calls when it needs to. We have created a `Private` method that acts in support of the public methods in the class:

```
Private Function CalcArea() As Double
    Dim radius As Double
    radius = diameter / 2.0
    Return 3.142 * radius * radius
End Function
```

To call a method from within the object, you do it like this:

```
Dim area As Double
area = CalcArea()
```

giving the name of the method and any parameters as usual. If this method was called by another object, it would need to be prefixed by the name of an object. But because it is called by a method within the same object, the object is implicit. If we really want to emphasize which object is being used, we could write the following equivalent code:

```
area = Me.CalcArea()
```

using the keyword `Me` that means the current object.

Depending on its size and complexity a class might have a number of private methods. Their purpose is to clarify and simplify the class.

● Operations on objects

Many of the variables that are used in VB programs are true objects, but some variables are not. Variables declared as `Integer`, `Boolean` and `Double` are not objects, but are called *primitive types*. When you declare a primitive variable, it is immediately usable. For example:

```
Dim number As Integer
```

both declares the variable `number` and creates it. By contrast, the creation of an object has to be done explicitly either using `New` (or graphically by dragging the class from the toolbox). For example:

```
Dim balloon1 As Balloon = New Balloon(10, 20, 50)
```

So variables in VB are either:

- primitive types such as `Integer`, `Boolean` and `Double`; these are not objects, or
- objects created from classes, either visually or by using `New`.

Primitive variables come ready-made with a whole collection of things you can do with them. For example, with variables of type `Integer` you can:

- declare variables;
- assign values using =;
- carry out arithmetic;
- compare using =, <, etc.;
- use as a parameter or as a return value.

You cannot necessarily do all these things with objects. Many things that a VB program uses are objects but, as we have seen, not everything is an object. And it is tempting to assume that it is possible to use all these operations with any object but this is not so. What can you do with an object? The answer is that when you write a class, you define the collection of operations that can be performed on objects of that type. With the `Balloon` class, for example, we have defined the operations `ChangeSize`, `Move` and `Display`. The programmer should not assume that you can do anything else to a balloon. However, you can confidently assume that for every object you can:

- create it;
- use it as a parameter and as a return value;
- assign it to a variable of the same class using =;
- use the methods and properties that are provided as part of its class.

> **SELF-TEST QUESTION**
>
> **10.8** Write down a list of operations that are possible with an object of the class `Balloon` and give examples of using them.

Object destruction

We have seen how objects are created, using the powerful word `New`. How do they die? One obvious and certain situation is when the program ceases to run. They can also die when they cease to be used by the program. For example, if we do this to create a new object:

```
Dim myBalloon As Balloon
myBalloon = New Balloon(20, 100, 100)
```

and then:

```
myBalloon = New Balloon(40, 200, 200)
```

what happens is that the first object created with `New` lived a brief life. It died when the program no longer had any knowledge of it and its value was usurped by the newer object. When an object is destroyed, the memory that was used to store the values of its variables and any other resources is reclaimed for other uses by the run-time system.

This is termed *garbage collection*. In VB, garbage collection is automatic. (In some other languages it is not and the programmer has to keep track of objects that are no longer needed.)

Finally, we can destroy an object by assigning the value `Nothing` to it, for example:

```
myBalloon = Nothing
```

The word `Nothing` is a special VB word that describes a non-existent (un-instantiated) object.

`Shared` methods and properties

Some methods do not need an object to work on. An example is the mathematical square root function. Mathematical methods such as square root (`Sqrt`) and sine of an angle (`Sin`) are provided within a library class named `Math`. In a program we write statements such as:

```
Dim x, y As Double
x = Math.Sqrt(y)
```

In this statement there are two `Double` variables, `x` and `y`, but no objects. Note that `Math` is the name of a class, not an object. The square root method `Sqrt` acts on its parameter, `y`. The question is: if `Sqrt` is not a method of some object, what is it? The answer is that methods like this are part of a class, but they are described as `Shared`. When you use one of these methods, its name must be preceded with the name of its class.

The class `Math` has the following structure, in which the methods are labelled as `Shared`:

```
Public Class Math

    Public Shared Function Sqrt(ByVal x As Double) As Double
        ' body of Sqrt
    End Function

    Public Shared Function Sin(ByVal x As Double) As Double
        ' body of Sin
    End Function

End Class
```

Other examples of `Shared` methods are `CInt` and `CStr`. An example of a `Shared` property is to be seen in the library class `Color`. The various colours are available for use by other classes as `Color.White`, `Color.Black`, etc. Other `Shared` properties are `NewLine` and `Tab`.

What is the point of `Shared` methods? In OOP, everything is written as a part of a class; nothing exists other than classes. If we think about the `Balloon` class, it contains `Private` variables such as `x` and `y` that record the state of an object. But some methods, such as `Sqrt`, do not involve a state. So free-standing methods such as `Sqrt` which are not obviously part of some class, have to obey the central rule of OOP – they have to be a part of some class. Hence the reason for `Shared` methods. It is common for programmers to make use of the library `Shared` methods and properties but it is rare for novice programmers to write them.

Incidentally, there is a more concise way of calling a shared method such as `Sqrt`, provided that a suitable `Imports` statement appears at the head of the program. So, once we have written this at the top of the program:

```
Imports System.Math
```

We can subsequently write the more concise:

```
x = Sqrt(y)
```

> **SELF-TEST QUESTION**
>
> 10.9 The `Shared` method `Max` within the class `Math` finds the maximum of its two `Integer` parameters. Write a sample call on `Max`.

Programming principles

Object-oriented programming is about constructing programs from objects. An *object* is a combination of some data (variables) and some actions (methods) that performs some useful role in a program. The programmer designs an object so that the data and the actions are closely related, rather than being randomly collected together.

In VB, as in most OOP languages, it is not possible to write instructions that describe an object directly. Instead the language makes the programmer define all objects of the same class. For example, if we need a button object, we go to the tool bar and select the `Button` class. We drag an instance of this class and place it on the form. If we need a second button, we create a second instance of this same class. The description of the structure of all possible buttons is called a *class*. A class is the template or the master plan to make any number of them; a class is a generalization of an object.

The idea of classes is a common idea in most design activity. It is usual before actually constructing anything to create a design for the object. This is true in automobile design, architecture, construction – even in fine art. Some kind of a plan is drafted, often on paper, sometimes on a computer. Sometimes it is called a blueprint. Such a design specifies the desired object completely, so that if the designer gets run over by a bus, someone else can carry out the construction of the object. Once designed, any number of identical objects can be constructed – think of cars, books or computers. So the design specifies the composition of one or any number of objects. The same is true in OOP – a class is the plan for any number of identical objects. Once we have specified a class, we can construct any number of objects with the same behaviour.

Looking at the button again, what we have is the description of what each and every button object will look like. Buttons only differ in their individual properties, such as their positions on the form. So in OOP, a class is the specification for any number of objects that are the same. Once a class has been described, a particular object is constructed by creating an *instance* of the class. It's a bit like saying we have had an instance of flu in the house. Or, this Model T Ford is an instance of the Model T Ford design. Your own bank account is an instance of the bank account class.

An object is a logical bundling together of variables, methods and properties. It forms a self-contained module that can be easily used and understood. The principle of information hiding or encapsulation means that users of an object have a restricted view of an object. An object provides a set of services as `Public` methods and properties that others can use. The remainder of the object, its variables and the instructions that implement the methods are hidden from view. This enhances abstraction and modularity.

In programming, the term *accessibility* (sometimes called *scope rules* or *visibility*) means the rules for accessing variables and methods. For humans, accessibility rules are like the rule that in Australia you must drive on the left, or the rule that you should only enter someone's home via the front door. In a program, rules like these are rigidly enforced by the compiler, to prevent deliberate or erroneous access to protected information. Accessibility rules constrain the programmer, but help the programmer to organize a program in a clear and logical manner. The accessibility rules associated with classes and methods allow the programmer to encapsulate variables and methods in a convenient manner.

The programmer can describe each variable, method and property as either `Public` or `Private`. Within a class, any instruction anywhere in the class can call any method, `Public` or `Private`. Also any instruction can refer to any variable. The exception is that local variables, those declared within a method, are only accessible by instructions within the method.

When one class refers to another, only those methods, properties and variables labelled as `Public` are accessible from outside a class. All others are inaccessible. It is good design practice to minimize the number of methods and properties that are `Public`, restricting them so as to offer only the services of the class. It is also good practice never (or very rarely) to make variables `Public`. If a variable needs to be inspected or changed, a method or property should be provided to do the job.

In summary, a variable, method or property within a class can be described as either:

- `Public` – accessible from anywhere (from within the class or from any other class);

or
- `Private` – accessible only from within the class.

In computer science a class is sometimes called an *abstract data type* (ADT). A data type is a kind of variable, like an `Integer`, a `Double` or a `Boolean`. These primitive types are types built into the VB language and are immediately available for use. Associated with each of these types is a set of operations. For example, with an `Integer` we can do assignment, addition, subtraction and so on. The `Balloon` class described above is an example of an ADT. It defines some data (variables), together with a collection of operations (methods) and properties that can carry out operations on the data. The class presents an abstraction of a balloon; the concrete details of the implementation are hidden.

Look at the code that is created when you open a new VB windows application within the Integrated Development Environment. You will see the following code is automatically created:

```
Public Class Form1
```

As you can see this is a description of a class called `Form1`, because like everything else a form is a class. When the run-time system starts this program it implicitly carries out a

```
Dim myForm As Form1 = New Form1()
```

statement to create an object from this class. You will not see this instruction in any program because it is hidden within the run-time system. Thus the run-time system acts as a god, creating the first object in the world. This object itself goes on to create other objects, such as buttons.

Programming pitfalls

- Novices sometimes want to code an object straight away. You can't – instead you have to declare a class and then create an instance of the class.
- `New` is used for two purposes – the word used to create an object and the name of a constructor method.
- Do not forget to initialize instance variables. Explicitly initialize them by means of a constructor method or as a part of the declaration itself and do not rely on VB's default initialization.

If you declare:

```
Dim redBalloon As Balloon
```

and then perform:

```
redBalloon.Display()
```

your program will terminate with an error message that says there is a `Nothing` pointer exception. This is because you have declared an object but not created it (with `New`). The object `redBalloon` does not exist. More accurately, it has the value `Nothing` – which amounts to the same thing. In most elementary programming you do not make use of `Nothing` – except if you inadvertently forget to use `New`.

Grammar spot

- A class has the structure:

    ```
    Public Class ClassName
        ' declarations of variables
        ' declarations of methods and properties
    End Class
    ```

- Variables, methods and properties can be either described as `Public` or `Private`.
- One or more of the methods in a class can have the name `New`. One of these constructor methods may be called (with appropriate parameters) to initialize the object when it is created.
- The declaration of a public method has the structure:

    ```
    Public Sub MethodName(parameters)
        ' body
    End Sub
    ```

- The declaration of a property has the structure:

    ```
    Public Property Name() As Integer
        Get
            ' statements to return a value
        End Get
        Set (ByVal value As Integer)
            ' statements to assign value to some variable
        End Set
    End Property
    ```

- A `Property` can be declared `ReadOnly` (with no `Set` part) or `WriteOnly` (with no `Get` part).
- A shared method or property is prefixed by the word `Shared` in its header:
- To call a shared method of a class:

    ```
    ClassName.MethodName(parameters)
    ```

New language elements

- `Class`: appears in the heading of the description of a class.
- `Public`: the description of a variable, method or property that is accessible from anywhere.
- `Private`: the description of a variable, method or property that is only accessible from within the class.
- `New`: used to create a new instance of a class (a new object).

- `New`: the name of a constructor method of a class.
- `Property`: introduces a property declaration.
- `Set`: introduces the part of a property declaration that changes the value of the property.
- `Get`: introduces the part of a property declaration that returns a value.
- `ReadOnly`: prefaces a property that can only access (but not change) the value of the property.
- `WriteOnly`: prefaces a property that can only change the value of the property.
- `Me`: the name of the current object.
- `Nothing`: the name of an object that does not exist.
- `Shared`: the description attached to a variable, property or method that belongs to a class as a whole, not to any instance created as an object from the class.

Summary

- An object is a collection of data and the associated actions, methods and properties, that can act upon the data. VB programs are constructed as a collection of objects.
- One particular method, named `New`, carries out the initialization of a newly created object. This is termed the constructor method.
- Items in a class can be declared to be `Private` or `Public`. A `Private` item can only be referred to from within the class. A `Public` item can be referred to by anything (inside or outside the class). In designing a VB program, `Public` items are normally kept to a minimum so as to enhance information hiding. In particular, data items are usually kept private.
- The description `Shared` means that the variable, property or method belongs to the class and not to particular objects. A `Shared` method can be called directly, without any need for instantiating an instance of the class with `New`. A `Shared` method or property is useful when a method does not need to be associated with a particular object, or for carrying out actions for the class as a whole.

EXERCISES

10.1 Balloons Add to the class `Balloon` some additional data, a `String` that holds the name of the balloon and a variable that describes its colour. Add code to initialize these values using a constructor method and add the code to display them.

Enhance the balloon program with buttons that move the balloon left, right, up and down.

10.2 Amplifier display Some stereo amplifiers have a display that shows the volume being output. The display waxes and wanes according to the volume at any point in time. Some displays have indicators that show the maximum and minimum values that have been reached since the amplifier was switched on.

Write a program that displays in text boxes the values of the maximum and minimum values that a track bar has been set to.

Write the piece of program that remembers the values and compares them as a class. This class has a method `NewValue` and properties `LowestValue` and `HighestValue`.

10.3 Bank account Write a program that simulates a bank account. A text box allows deposits (a positive number) to be made into the account and withdrawals (a negative number) to be made. The state of the account is continually displayed and, if the account goes into the red (negative balance), a suitable message is displayed. Create a class named `Account` to represent bank accounts. It has methods `Deposit` and `Withdraw`, and a property `CurrentBalance`.

10.4 Scorekeeper Design and write a class that acts as a scorekeeper for a computer game. It maintains a single integer, the score. It provides a method to initialize the score to zero, a method to increase the score, a method to decrease the score, and a method to return the score. Write instructions to create a single object and use it.

10.5 Dice Design and write a class that acts as a die, which may be thrown to give a value 1 to 6. Initially write it so that it always gives the value 6. Write a program that creates a die object and uses it. The screen displays a button, which when pressed causes the die to be thrown and its value displayed.

Then alter the die class so that it gives the value one higher than when it was last thrown, for example 4 when it was 3.

Then alter it so that it uses the library random number generator.

Some games like backgammon and Monopoly need two dice. Write VB statements to create two instances of the dice object, throw them and display the outcomes.

10.6 Random number generator Write your own random number generator as a class that uses a formula to obtain the next pseudo-random number from the previous one. A random number program works by starting with some 'seed' value. Thereafter the current random number is used as a basis for the next by performing some calculation on it which makes it into some other (apparently random) number. A good formula to use for integers is:

```
nextR = ((oldR * 25173) + 13849) Mod 65536
```

which produces numbers in the range 0 to 65535. The particular numbers in this formula have been shown to give good, random-like, results.

10.7 Complex numbers Write a class called `Complex` to represent complex numbers (together with their operations). A complex number consists of two parts – a real part (a `Double`) and an imaginary part (a `Double`). The constructor method should create a new complex number, using the `Double` values provided as parameters, like this:

```
Dim c As Complex = New Complex(1.0, 2.0)
```

Write methods `GetReal` and `GetImaginary` to get the real part and the imaginary part of a complex number and which is used like this:

```
Dim x As Double = c.GetReal()
```

Write a method to add two complex numbers and return their sum. The real part is the sum of the two real parts. The imaginary part is the sum of the two imaginary parts. A call of the method looks like:

```
Dim c As Complex = c1.Sum(c2)
```

Write a method to calculate the product of two complex numbers. If one number has components x_1 and y_1 and the second number has components x_2 and y_2:

- the real part of the product is the product $= x_1 \times x_2 - y_1 \times y_2$
- the imaginary part of the product $= x_1 \times y_2 + x_2 \times y_1$

ANSWERS TO SELF-TEST QUESTIONS

10.1
```
Private myColor As Color
```

10.2
```
Public Sub MoveUp(ByVal amount As Integer)
    yCoord = yCoord - amount
End Sub
```

10.3
```
Public Sub ChangeColor(ByVal newColor As Color)
    myColor = newColor
End Sub
```

10.4
```
Public Sub Display(ByVal drawArea As Graphics)
    Dim myPen As Pen = New Pen(myColor)
    drawArea.DrawEllipse(myPen, x, y, diameter, diameter)
End Sub
```

10.5
```
Public Property YCoord() As Integer
    Get
        Return y
    End Get

    Set(ByVal value As Integer)
        y = value
    End Set
End Property
```

10.6 Methods: `CreditAccount`, `DebitAccount`, `CalculateInterest`
Properties: `CurrentBalance`, `Name`

10.7
```
Public Sub New(ByVal initialDiameter As Integer)
    diameter = initialDiameter
End Sub
```

10.8 Methods are: `ChangeColor`, `MoveUp`, `MoveRight`, `ChangeSize`, `Display`.
Examples:

```
myBalloon.ChangeColor(Color.Red)
myBalloon.MoveUp(20)
myBalloon.MoveRight(50)
myBalloon.ChangeSize(10)
myBalloon.Display(drawArea)
```

Properties are: `XCoord`, `YCoord`, `Diameter`
Examples:

```
myBalloon.XCoord = 20
Dim y = myBalloon.YCoord
myBalloon.Diameter = 50
```

10.9
```
Dim x as Integer
x = Math.Max(7, 8)
```

Inheritance

This chapter explains:

- how to create a new class from an existing class using inheritance;
- when and how to declare variables as `Protected`;
- when and how to use overriding;
- how to draw a class diagram that describes inheritance;
- how to use the `MyBase` keyword;
- how to use abstract classes and `MustInherit`.

Introduction

Programs are built from objects, which are instances of classes. Some classes are in the VB library and some classes the programmer writes. When you start to write a new program you look for useful classes in the library and you look at any classes you have written in the past. This OO approach to programming means that instead of starting programs from scratch, you build on earlier work. It's not uncommon to find a class that looks useful, and does nearly what you want, but not exactly what you want. Inheritance is a way of resolving this problem. With inheritance, you use an existing class as the basis for creating a modified class.

Here is an analogy. Suppose you want to buy a new car and you go to a showroom and see a range of mass-produced cars. You like one in particular – but it doesn't have that special feature that you like. Like the description of a class, the car has been manufactured from plans that describe many identical cars. If inheritance was available, you could specify a car that had all the features of the mass-produced car, but with the added extras or changes that you require.

Using inheritance

We start with a class similar to one used already several times in this book. It is a class to represent a sphere. A sphere has a radius and a position in space. When we display a sphere on the screen, it will be shown as a circle. (The method to display a sphere simply calls the library method `DrawEllipse`.) The diameter of the sphere is fixed at 20 pixels. We have only modelled the *x*- and *y*-coordinates of a sphere (and not the *z*-coordinate) because we are displaying a two-dimensional representation on the screen.

Here is the class description for a sphere. This class is normally placed in its own file, as we saw in Chapter 10.

```
Public Class Sphere

    Protected xCoord As Integer = 100, yCoord As Integer = 100
    Protected myPen As Pen = New Pen(Color.Black)

    Public WriteOnly Property X() As Integer
        Set(ByVal value As Integer)
            xCoord = value
        End Set
    End Property

    Public WriteOnly Property Y() As Integer
        Set(ByVal value As Integer)
            yCoord = value
        End Set
    End Property

    Public Overridable Sub Display(ByVal drawArea As Graphics)
        drawArea.DrawEllipse(myPen, xCoord, yCoord, 20, 20)
    End Sub
End Class
```

You will notice that there are a number of new elements to this program, including the words `Protected` and `Overridable`. This is because the class has been written in such a way that it can be used for inheritance. We shall see during the course of this chapter what these new elements mean.

Let us suppose that someone has written and tested this class, and made it available for use. But now we come to write a new program and find that we need a class very like this, but one that describes bubbles. This new class, called `Bubble`, will allow us to do additional things – to change the size of a bubble and move it vertically. The limitation of class `Sphere` is that it describes objects that do not move and whose size cannot change. We need an additional property that will allow us to set a new value for the radius of the bubble. We can do this without altering the existing class, instead writing a different class that uses the code that is already in `Sphere`. We say that the new class inherits variables, properties and methods from the old class. The new class is a subclass of the old. The old class is called the superclass of the new class. This is how we write the new class:

```
Public Class Bubble
    Inherits Sphere

    Protected radius As Integer = 10

    Public WriteOnly Property Size() As Integer
        Set(ByVal value As Integer)
            radius = value
        End Set
    End Property

    Public Overrides Sub Display(ByVal drawArea As Graphics)
        drawArea.DrawEllipse(myPen, xCoord, yCoord, _
                             2 * radius, 2 * radius)
    End Sub

End Class
```

This new class has the name `Bubble`. On the next line it says that it `Inherits Sphere`. This means that it inherits all the items not described as `Private` within class `Sphere`. We will explore the other features of this class in the following sections.

Protected

When you use inheritance, `Private` is just too private and `Public` is just too public. If a class needs to give its subclasses access to particular variables, properties or methods, but prevent access from any other classes, it can label them as `Protected`. In the family analogy, a mother allows her descendants to use her car keys but not anyone else.

Looking at the class `Sphere`, we need variables to describe the coordinates:

```
Private xCoord, yCoord As Integer
```

This is a sound decision, but there may be a better idea. It might be that someone later writes a class that inherits this class and provides an additional method to move a sphere. This method will need access to the variables `xCoord` and `yCoord` – which are unfortunately inaccessible because they have been labeled `Private`. So to anticipate this possible future use, we might instead decide to label them as `Protected`:

```
Protected xCoord, yCoord As Integer
```

This declaration now protects these variables against possible misuse by any arbitrary classes, but permits access by certain privileged classes – the subclasses.

Suppose we had declared these variables as `Private`, as originally planned. The consequence is that it would have been impossible to reuse the class as described. The only option would be to edit the class, replacing the description `Private` by `Protected` for these particular items. But this violates one of the principles of object-oriented programming, which is never to alter an existing class that is tried and tested. So when we write a class we strive to think ahead about possible future users of the class. The programmer who writes a class always writes it in the hope that someone will reuse the class by extending it. This is another of the principles of object-oriented programming. Careful use of `Protected` instead of `Public` or `Private` can help make a class more attractive for inheritance.

In summary, the four levels of accessibility of a variable, property or method in a class are:

1. `Public` – accessible from anywhere. As a rule, any properties or methods offering a service to users of a class should be labelled as `Public`.
2. `Protected` – accessible from this class and from any subclass.
3. `Private` – accessible only from this class. As a rule, all instance variables should be declared as `Private`.
4. Local variables, those declared within a method, are never accessible from outside the particular method.

So a class can have good, but controlled, access to its immediate superclass and the superclasses above it in the class hierarchy, just as if the classes are part of the class itself. If we make the family analogy, it is like being able to freely spend your mother's money or that of any of her ancestors – provided that they have put their money in an account labelled `Public` or `Protected`. People outside the family can only access `Public` money.

● Additional items

An important way of constructing a new class from another is to include additional variables, properties and methods.

You can see that the new class `Bubble` declares an additional variable and an additional property:

```
Protected radius As Integer = 10

Public WriteOnly Property Size() As Integer
    Set(ByVal value As Integer)
        radius = value
    End Set
End Property
```

The new variable is `radius`, which is additional to the existing variables (`xCoord` and `yCoord`) in `Sphere`. The number of variables is thereby extended.

The new class also has the property `size` in addition to those in `Sphere`.

> **SELF-TEST QUESTION**
>
> **11.1** A ball object is like a `Sphere` object, but it has the additional features of being able to move left and move right. Write a class called `Ball` which inherits the class `Sphere` but provides additional methods `MoveLeft` and `MoveRight`.

Overriding

Another feature of the new class `Bubble` is a new version of the method `Display`.

```
Public Overrides Sub Display(ByVal drawArea As Graphics)
    drawArea.DrawEllipse(myPen, xCoord, yCoord, _
                         2 * radius, 2 * radius)
End Sub
```

This is needed because the new class has a radius that can be changed, whereas in class `Sphere`, the radius was fixed. This new version of `Display` in `Bubble` supersedes the version in the class `Sphere`. We say that the new version overrides the old version. The old version has the description `Overridable` and the new version has the description `Overrides`.

Do not confuse overriding with overloading, which we met in Chapter 5 on methods:

- Overloading means writing a method (in the same class) that has the same name, but different parameters.
- Overriding means writing a method in a subclass that has the same name and parameters.

In summary, in the inheriting class we have:

- created an additional variable;
- created an additional property;
- overridden a method (provided a method which is to be used instead of the method that is already provided).

Let us sum up what we have accomplished. We had an existing class called `Sphere`. We had a requirement for a new class, `Bubble`, that was similar to `Sphere`, but needed additional facilities. So we created the new class by extending the facilities of the old class. We have made maximum use of the commonality between the two classes, and we have avoided rewriting pieces of program that already exist. Both of the classes we have written, `Sphere` and `Bubble`, are of course still available to use.

Making an analogy with human families, inheritance means you can spend your own money and also that of your mother.

As a detail we note that it is possible to override variables – to declare variables in a subclass that override variables in the superclass. We will not discuss this further for two reasons: one, there is never any need to do this, and two, it is very bad practice. When you subclass a class (inherit from it) you only ever:

- add additional methods and/or properties;
- add additional variables;
- override methods and/or properties.

Class diagrams

A good way to visualize inheritance is by using a *class diagram*, as shown in Figure 11.1. This shows that `Bubble` is a subclass of `Sphere`, which is in turn a subclass of `Object`. Each class is shown as a rectangle. A line between classes shows an inheritance relationship. The arrow points from the subclass to the superclass.

Every class in the library or written by the programmer fits within a class hierarchy. If you write a class beginning with the heading:

```
Public Class Sphere
```

which has no explicit superclass, it is implicitly a subclass of the class `Object`.

Figure 11.2 shows another class diagram in which another class, called `Ball`, is also a subclass of `Sphere`. The diagram is now a tree structure, with the root of the tree, `Object`, at the top. In general a class diagram is a tree, like a family tree, except that it only shows one parent.

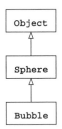

Figure 11.1 Class diagram for classes `Sphere` and `Bubble`.

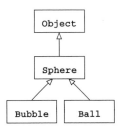

Figure 11.2 Class diagram showing a tree structure.

Inheritance at work

As the class `Bubble` shows, a class often has a superclass, which in turn has a superclass, and so on up the inheritance tree. It is not only the `Public` and `Protected` items in the immediate superclass that are inherited, but all the `Public` and `Protected` variables, properties and methods in all of the superclasses up the inheritance tree. So you inherit from your mother, your grandmother and so on.

The VB language allows a class to inherit from only one immediate superclass. This is called single inheritance. In the family analogy it means that you can inherit from your mother but not from your father.

Suppose we create an object `bubble1` from the class `Bubble`:

```
Dim bubble1 As Bubble = new Bubble()
```

What happens if we make use of the property x as follows?

```
bubble1.X = 200
```

Now `bubble1` is an object of the class `Bubble` but the property x is a property of a different class `Sphere`. The answer is that all the methods and properties labelled `Public` (and `Protected`) within the immediate superclass (and all the superclasses in the class hierarchy) are available to a subclass. And since `Bubble` is a subclass of `Sphere`, x is available to objects of class `Bubble`.

The rule is that when a method or property is used, the VB system first looks in the class description of the object to find the method. If it cannot find it there, it looks in the class description of the immediate superclass. If it cannot find it there, it looks at the class description for the superclass of the superclass, and so on up the class hierarchy until it finds a method or property with the required name. In the family analogy, you implicitly inherit from your grandmother, your great grandmother and so on.

MyBase

A class will sometimes need to call a method in its immediate superclass or one of the classes up the tree. There is no problem with this – the methods in all the classes up the inheritance tree are freely available, provided that they are labelled as `Public` or `Protected`. The only problem that can arise is when the desired method in the superclass has the same name as a method in the current class. To fix this problem, prefix the method name with the keyword `MyBase`. For example, to call the method `Display` in a superclass:

```
MyBase.Display(drawArea)
```

Generally this is neater and shorter than duplicating instructions and can help make a program more concise by making the maximum use of existing methods.

Constructors

Constructors were explained in Chapter 10 on writing classes. They allow us to pass parameters to an object when we create it using `New`. A constructor is a method with the name `New`. Remember that:

- if you write a class without constructors, VB assumes that there is a single constructor (with zero parameters);
- if you write a class with one or more constructors with parameters, and a zero-parameter constructor is also needed, you must explicitly write it.

Constructor methods are not inherited. This means that if you need one or more explicit constructors – as you often will – in a subclass, you need to write them explicitly. Suppose, for example, we have an existing class, with two constructors:

```
Public Class Balloon

    Protected xCoord, yCoord, radius As Integer

    Public Sub New()
        xCoord = 10
        yCoord = 10
        radius = 20
    End Sub

    Public Sub New(ByVal initialX As Integer, _
                   ByVal initialY As Integer, _
                   ByVal initialRadius As Integer)
        xCoord = initialX
        yCoord = initialY
        radius = initialRadius
    End Sub

    ' remainder of class
End Class
```

If we now write a new class that inherits from class `Balloon`, the options are:

1. Do not write a constructor. VB assumes that there is a zero-parameter constructor.
2. Write one or more explicit constructors.
3. Write one or more explicit constructors that call a constructor in the superclass, using `MyBase`.

However, VB forces us to call a constructor in the superclass, in the following way. If the first instruction in the constructor is not a call on a constructor in the superclass, then VB automatically calls the zero-parameter constructor in the superclass.

For novice programmers it is probably wise to make things clear and therefore to explicitly write a call to a superclass constructor as the first instruction of every constructor, as shown in the following examples.

Here is a subclass of `Balloon` with a constructor that calls the zero-parameter constructor in the superclass, using `MyBase`:

```
Public Class DifferentBalloon
    Inherits Balloon

    Public Sub New(ByVal initialX As Integer, _
                   ByVal initialY As Integer)
        MyBase.New()
        xCoord = initialX
        yCoord = initialY
        radius = 20
    End Sub

    ' remainder of class

End Class
```

and here is a subclass with a constructor that explicitly calls the second constructor in the superclass, again using `MyBase`:

```
Public Class ModifiedBalloon
    Inherits Balloon

    Public Sub New(ByVal initialX As Integer, _
                   ByVal initialY As Integer, _
                   ByVal initialRadius As Integer)

        MyBase.New(initialX, initialY, initialRadius)
    End Sub

    ' remainder of class

End Class
```

SELF-TEST QUESTIONS

11.2 A coloured sphere is like a sphere, but with some colour. Write a new class named `ColoredSphere` that inherits `Sphere` to provide a colour that can be set when the balloon is created. This is accomplished using a constructor method, so that your class should enable the following to be written:

```
Dim coloredSphere1 As ColoredSphere = _
    New ColoredSphere(Color.Red)
```

▶

> **11.3** What is wrong with the subclass in the following?
>
> ```
> Public Class BankAccount
>     Protected deposit As Integer
>     Public Sub New(ByVal initialDeposit As Integer)
>         ' remainder of constructor
>     End Sub
>     ' remainder of class
> End Class
>
> Public Class BetterAccount
>     Inherits BankAccount
>     Public Sub New()
>         deposit = 1000
>     End Sub
>     ' remainder of class
> End Class
> ```

● Abstract classes

Consider a program that maintains graphical shapes of all types and sizes – circles, rectangles, squares, triangles, etc. These different shapes, similar to the classes we have already met in this chapter, have information in common – their position, colour and size. So we will declare a superclass, named `Shape`, that describes this common data. Each individual class inherits this common information. Here is the way to describe this common superclass:

```
MustInherit Class Shape

    Protected xCoord, yCoord As Integer
    Protected size As Integer
    Protected myPen As Pen = New Pen(Color.Black)

    Public Sub MoveRight()
        xCoord = xCoord + 10
    End Sub

    Public MustOverride Sub Display(ByVal drawArea As Graphics)

End Class
```

The class to describe circles inherits from the class `Shape` as follows:

```
Public Class Circle
    Inherits Shape
```

```
Public Overrides Sub Display(ByVal drawArea As Graphics)
    drawArea.DrawEllipse(myPen, xCoord, yCoord, size, size)
End Sub

End Class
```

It is meaningless to try to create an object from the class `Shape`, because it is incomplete. This is why the keyword `MustInherit` is attached to the header of the class, and the compiler will prevent any attempt to create an instance of this class. The method `MoveRight` is provided and is complete, and is inherited by any subclass. But the method `Display` is simply a header (without a body or an `End Sub` statement). It is described with the keyword `MustOverride` to say that any class must provide an implementation of the method. The class `Shape` is termed an abstract class because it does not exist as a full class but is provided simply to be used for inheritance.

There is a reasonable rule that if a class contains any methods or properties that are `Overridable`, the class itself must be labelled as `MustInherit`.

Abstract classes enable us to exploit the common features of classes. Declaring a class as abstract forces the programmer who is using the class (by inheritance) to provide the missing methods. This is a way, therefore, by which the designer of a class can encourage a particular design. The term abstract is used because as we look higher and higher up a class hierarchy, the classes become more and more general or abstract. In the example above, the class `Shape` is more abstract and less concrete than a `Circle`. The superclass abstracts features, such as the position and size in this example, that are common between its subclasses. It is common in large OO programs to find that the top few levels of the class hierarchies consist of abstract methods. Similarly in biology, abstraction is used with classes like mammals, which do not exist (in themselves), but serve as abstract superclasses to a diverse set of subclasses. Thus we have never seen a mammal object, but we have seen a cow, which is an instance of a subclass of mammal.

> **SELF-TEST QUESTION**
>
> **11.4** Write a class `Square` that uses the abstract class `Shape` given above.

Programming principles

Writing programs as a collection of classes means that programs are modular. Another bonus is that the parts of a program can be reused in other programs. Inheritance is another way in which OO programming provides potential for reusability. Very often programmers reinvent the wheel – they write new software when they could simply make use of existing software. One of the reasons for writing new software is that it is fun. But software is increasingly becoming more complex, so there simply is not enough time to rewrite. Imagine having to write the software to create the GUI components provided by the VB libraries. Imagine having to write a mathematical function like `sqrt` every time you needed it. It would just take too long. So a good reason for reusing software is to save time. It is not just the time to write the software that you save, it is the time to test it thoroughly – and this can take even longer than actually writing the software. So reusing classes makes sense.

One reason why programmers sometimes don't reuse software is that the existing software doesn't do exactly what they need it to do. Maybe it does 90% of what they want, but some crucial bits are missing or some bits do things differently. One approach would be to modify the existing software to match the new needs. This, however, is a dangerous strategy because modifying software is a minefield. Software is not so much soft as brittle – when you try to change it, it breaks. When you change software it is very easy to introduce new and subtle bugs into it, which necessitate extensive debugging and correction. This is a common experience, so much so that programmers are very reluctant to modify software. This is where OO programming comes to the rescue. In an OO program, you can inherit the behaviour of those parts of some software that you need, override those (few) methods and/or properties that you want to behave differently, and add new methods and/or properties to do additional things. Often you can inherit most of a class, making only the few changes that are needed using inheritance. You only have to test the new bits, sure in the knowledge that all the rest has been tested before. So the problem of reuse is solved. You can make use of existing software in a safe way. Meanwhile, the original class remains intact, reliable and usable.

OO programming means building on the work of others. The OO programmer proceeds like this:

1. Clarify the requirements of the program.
2. Browse the library for classes that perform the required functions and use them to achieve the desired results.
3. Review the classes within other programs you have written and use them as appropriate.
4. Extend library classes or your own classes using inheritance when useful.
5. Write your own new classes.

This is why OO programs are often very short – they simply use the library classes or they create new classes that inherit from library classes. This approach requires an investment in time – the programmer needs a very good knowledge of the libraries. This idea of reusing OO software is so powerful that some people think of OO programming entirely in this way. In this view, OO programming is the process of extending the library classes so as to meet the requirements of a particular application.

Nearly every program in this book uses inheritance. Every program starts with these lines created automatically by the development environment:

```
Public Class Form1
    Inherits Form
```

This says that the class `Form1` inherits features from the library class `Form`. The features in `Form` include methods for creating a graphical user interface (GUI) window with icons to resize and close the window. Extending the class `Form` is the main way in which the programs in this book extend the library classes.

Beware: sometimes inheritance is not the appropriate technique. Instead, composition – using existing classes unchanged – is very often better. This issue is discussed in Chapter 20 on design.

Programming pitfalls

- Novice programmers use inheritance of a library class, the class `Form`, from their very first program. But learning to use inheritance within your own classes takes time and experience. It usually only becomes worthwhile in larger programs. Don't worry if you don't use inheritance for quite some time.
- It is common to confuse overloading and overriding:
  - *Overloading* means writing two or more methods in the same class with the same name (but different parameters).
  - *Overriding* means writing a method in a subclass to be used instead of the method in the superclass (or one of the superclasses above it in the inheritance tree).

New language elements

- `Inherits` – means that this class inherits from another named class.
- `Protected` – the description of a variable, property or method that is accessible from within the class or any subclass (but not from elsewhere).
- `Overridable` – describes a method or property that can be overridden in a subclass.
- `Overrides` – describes a property or method that overrides an item in the superclass.
- `MustInherit` – the description of an abstract class that cannot be created but is provided only to be used in inheritance.
- `MustOverride` – the description of a property or method that is simply given as a header and must be provided by an implementation of the class.
- `MyBase` – the name of the superclass of a class, the class it inherits from.

Summary

- Extending (inheriting) the facilities of a class is a good way to make use of existing parts of programs (classes).
- A subclass inherits the facilities of its immediate superclass and all the superclasses above it in the inheritance tree.
- A class has only one immediate superclass (it can only inherit from one class). This is called *single inheritance* in the jargon of OOP.

- A class can extend the facilities of an existing class by providing one or more of:
  - additional methods and/or properties;
  - additional variables;
  - methods and/or properties that override (act instead of) methods in the superclass.

- A variable, method or property can be described as having one of three types of access:
  - `Public` – accessible from any class;
  - `Private` – accessible only from within this class;
  - `Protected` – accessible only from within this class and any subclass.

- A class diagram is a tree showing the inheritance relationships.
- The name of the superclass of a class is referred to by the word `MyBase`.
- An abstract class is described as `MustInherit`. It cannot be instantiated to give an object, because it is incomplete. Such a class provides useful variables, properties and methods that can be inherited by subclasses.

EXERCISES

11.1 Spaceship Write a class `SpaceShip` that describes a spaceship. A spaceship is oval, but otherwise it behaves exactly like a `Balloon` object. Make maximum use of inheriting from the classes shown in the text.

Draw a class diagram to show how the different classes are related.

11.2 Pool Write a class `PoolBall` which restricts the movements of a ball to a rectangle, corresponding to the cushions bordering a pool table. Make maximum use of inheriting from the classes shown in the text.

11.3 The bank A class describes bank accounts and provides methods `CreditAccount`, `DebitAccount`, `CalculateInterest` and a `ReadOnly` property, `CurrentBalance`. There are two types of account – a regular account and a gold account. The gold account gives interest at 10%, while the regular account gives interest at 1% on credits above $100. Write classes that describe the two types of account, making use of an abstract class to describe the common features. (Assume for simplicity that amounts of money are held as `Integer`.)

11.4 Write an abstract class to describe two-dimensional graphical objects (square, circle, rectangle, triangle, etc.) that have the following features. All such objects share `Integer` variables that specify the *x*- and *y*-coordinates of the top left of a bounding rectangle, and `Integer` variables that describe the height and the width of the rectangle. All the objects share the same properties `X` and `Y` to set the values of these coordinates. All the objects share properties `Width` and `Height` to set the values of the width and height of the object. All the objects have a property `Area` which returns the area of the object and a method `Display` which displays it but these methods are different depending on the particular object.

11.5 A three-dimensional drawing package supports three kinds of objects – cube, sphere and cone. All have a position in space, defined by x-, y- and z-coordinates. Each has a size, defined by a height, width and depth. Every object provides a method to move the object from the origin to a position in space. Every object provides a method to rotate it around the x-, y- and then z-axes. All the objects provide a method to display themselves. Write an abstract class to describe these three-dimensional objects.

ANSWERS TO SELF-TEST QUESTIONS

11.1
```
Public Class Ball
    Inherits Sphere

    Public Sub MoveLeft(ByVal amount As Integer)
        xCoord = xCoord - amount
    End Sub

    Public Sub MoveRight(ByVal amount As Integer)
        xCoord = xCoord + amount
    End Sub
End Class
```

11.2
```
Public Class ColoredSphere
    Inherits Sphere

    Private theColor As Color

    Sub New(ByVal initialcolor As Color)
        theColor = initialColor
    End Sub
End Class
```

11.3 The compiler will find fault with the subclass. There is no explicit call to a constructor in the superclass. So VB will try to call a zero-parameter constructor in the superclass and no such method has been written.

11.4
```
Public Class Square
    Inherits Shape

    Public Overrides Sub Display(ByVal drawArea As Graphics)
        drawArea.DrawRectangle(myPen, xCoord, yCoord, _
                                size, size)
    End Sub
End Class
```

Calculations

This chapter explains:

- how to format numbers for convenient display;
- how to use the mathematical library functions;
- how to carry out both business and scientific calculations.

● Introduction

We have already seen in Chapter 4 how to carry out simple calculations. This chapter is about more serious calculations. It enhances the earlier explanation and brings together all the information needed to write programs that carry out calculations. If you are not interested in programs that do numerical calculations, skip this chapter.

Calculations arise in many programs – not just programs that carry out mathematical, scientific or engineering calculations. In information systems, calculations arise in payrolls, accountancy and forecasting. In graphics, calculations are necessary to scale and move images on the screen.

Chapter 4 explained several important ideas about numbers and calculations. The reader might like to review that chapter before continuing. The ideas were:

- input and output using text boxes and labels;
- conversion between the string representations of numbers and their internal representations;
- precedence rules in expressions;
- conversions in expressions that mix `Integer` and `Double` data.

Literals

A value like 10 000 or 12.34 is named a *literal* in the jargon of programming languages. If the programmer uses a literal such as 10 000, the compiler assumes that the number is an `Integer`. If a value like 12.34 is used in a VB program, it is assumed by the compiler to be a `Double` value.

Very large or very small `Double` literals can be written using exponent notation:

- `0.0001` is the same as `1.0E-4`
- `12300000.0` is the same as `1.23E7`

where for example `E4` means $\times\ 10^4$.

> **SELF-TEST QUESTION**
>
> **12.1** Write these quantities as literals in exponent form:
>
> 5000
>
> -0.00000056

Formatting numbers

Formatting is the setting out of text in a convenient way. The display of numbers is especially important, as we do not want them to be misinterpreted. Also we don't always need the detail of unnecessary decimal places. For example, if the value `33.198765` represents the area of a room in square metres, then all the decimal places are probably not necessary.

VB has a large range of facilities for formatting values, but here we restrict ourselves to the most common cases of formatting `Integer` and `Double` values. Each data type has a `Format` method, to which we can pass two parameters:

- a value to be formatted, and
- a string containing format information.

The method returns a string containing the formatted value, which is ready to be displayed.

We will start out with `Integer` values. Suppose we have an integer value:

```
Dim i as Integer = 123
```

We have already widely used the `CStr` method to convert a number:

```
Label1.Text = CStr(i)
```

which gives the string:

```
123
```

But now we will use the formatting method `Format`. For example:

```
Dim formattedValue as String
Dim i as Integer = 123

formattedValue = Format(i, "0000")
Label1.Text = formattedValue
```

This causes the label to be given the value:

```
0123
```

because a zero in a format string means that a digit will always be produced at the position indicated. We would use this format string when we know that the integer may be up to four digits long, and we want to align the numbers in a tabular form.

Another formatting character is the `#` character. This stipulates that a digit will only appear when needed. For example:

```
Label1.Text = Format(123, "#####")
```

gives the string:

```
123
```

For large integer numbers, commas can make the number more readable. This is illustrated by the following code:

```
Label1.Text = Format(123456, "#,###,###")
```

which gives the string:

```
123,456
```

Formatting tends to be more useful when `Double` values are to be displayed. The same formatting characters (#, 0 and comma) are used, with the addition of the period character to specify where the decimal point is to be placed. In this example:

```
Dim formattedValue as String
Dim d as Double = 123.456

FormattedValue = Format(d, "0.00")
Label2.Text = formattedValue
```

the label is assigned the value:

```
123.46
```

On the left of the decimal point, digits are displayed as needed to present all of the number. But at least one digit is displayed. On the right of the decimal point, the number is rounded in order to fit into the two digits specified.

The following table gives a summary of the special characters in format strings.

.	Place the decimal point here.
0	Place a digit here. If the data value is too small and does not fill the format, a 0 is inserted.
#	Place a digit here, but if the value does not fill the format, nothing is displayed – not even a space.
,	Place a comma here.

> **SELF-TEST QUESTION**
>
> **12.2** What do these give:
>
> ```
> Label1.Text = Format(0.123, "0.00")
> Label1.Text = Format(123456.7, "#,###,###.00")
> ```

● Library mathematical functions and constants

It is common in mathematical, scientific or engineering programs to use functions like sine, cosine and log. In VB, these are provided in one of the libraries – the `Math` library. To use one of the functions, you can write, for example:

```
x = Math.Sqrt(y)
```

Alternatively you can use an `Imports` statement at the top of the program like this:

```
Imports System.Math
```

and then write the more concise:

```
x = Sqrt(y)
```

Some of the more widely used functions in the `Math` library are given in alphabetical order below. Where the parameter is an angle, it must be expressed in radians.

`Abs(x)`	the absolute value of x, sometimes written |x| in mathematics
`Ceil(x)`	rounds x up to the smallest `Integer` greater than or equal to x
`Cos(x)`	cosine of the angle x, where x is expressed in radians
`Exp(x)`	e^x
`Floor(x)`	rounds x down to the smallest `Integer` less than or equal to x
`Log(x)`	natural logarithm of x (to the base e)
`Log10(x)`	logarithm to base 10 of x
`Max(x, y)`	the larger of x and y
`Min(x, y)`	the smaller of x and y
`Pow(x, y)`	x raised to the power of y, or x^y
`Round(x)`	rounds a `Double` value to the nearest `Integer` value; for example `Math.Round(3.4)` is 3.0 – with a decimal point
`Sin(x)`	sine of the angle x, expressed in radians

```
Sqrt(x)        the positive square root of x
Tan(x)         tangent of the angle x, expressed in radians
```

When you use these methods, you sometimes have to be careful about the type of the variables or literals used as parameters. For example, the method `Abs` can be passed any numeric values but the method `Cos` can only be passed a `Double` number.

The mathematical constants pi (π) and e are also available as properties within the Math library, so that we can write, for example:

```
Dim x, y As Double
x = Math.PI
y = Math.E
```

or you can use an `Import` statement:

```
Imports System.Math
```

and then write:

```
x = PI
z = E
```

Constants

Constants are values that don't change while the program is running. We have already met two, `E` and `PI`, that are already provided for use in the `Math` class. But it is often the case that there are other values in a program that will not change. Examples could be the factor for converting inches to centimetres, or the velocity of light. One approach is to write the values for these quantities directly into the program, like this:

```
cm = inches * 2.54
```

Another, better, approach is to declare such numbers as variables that have a constant value and give them a name, for example:

```
Const inchesToCm As Double = 2.54
```

A variable declared like this cannot be changed (by an assignment, for example) when the program runs. In fact the compiler will reject any attempt made to give such a variable a new value. We can then use the name in the calculation:

```
cm = inches * inchesToCm
```

This is clearer because we are using the programming language to explain what we are doing, rather than using unexplained numbers.

> **SELF-TEST QUESTION**
>
> **12.3** The velocity of light is 299 792 458 metres per second. Write this as a `Double` constant.

● Case study – money

We will now trace the development of a program to carry out calculations with money. In most countries, money comes in two parts – dollars and cents, euros and cents, pounds and pence. We have a choice – we can represent an amount of money either as a `Double` quantity (like 20.25 dollars) or as an `Integer` (2025 cents). If we use cents, we will need to convert amounts into dollars and cents and vice versa. We will opt to use `Double` variables to represent values.

We will construct a program that calculates compound interest. An amount is invested at a particular annual interest rate and accumulates in value. The user enters the initial amount (as a whole number) and an interest rate (a number that may have a decimal point) into text boxes. The user then clicks on a button to see the amount accumulated each year, as shown in Figure 12.1. We start by declaring the main quantities:

```
Dim rate, newAmount As Double
Dim oldAmount As Double
```

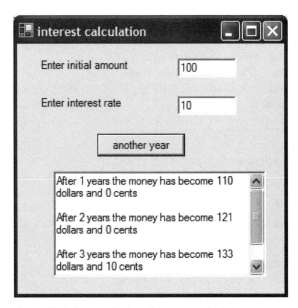

Figure 12.1 Screen display of interest calculation.

When the button is clicked to move on to the next year, the program must calculate:

```
newAmount = oldAmount + (oldAmount * rate / 100)
```

When we display an amount of money, we need to display a whole number of dollars and a whole number of cents, so that if the value is 127.2341 dollars for example, we need to display it as 127 dollars and 23 cents.

First the dollar part. Simple use of the cast operator CInt converts the Double number to an Integer, truncating the fractional part:

```
dollars = CInt(newAmount)
```

Next the cents part. We need to get rid of the dollars part of the number. We can do this by subtracting the whole number of dollars so that a number like 127.2341 will become 0.2341. Now multiply by 100.0 to convert to cents, so that 0.2341 becomes 23.41. Next use Math.Round to convert to the nearest whole number (23.0). Then finally we convert the Double value to an Integer value using CInt.

```
cents = CInt(Math.Round(100 * (newAmount - dollars)))
```

We can now display the values properly converted. Finally,

```
oldAmount = newAmount
```

which is what investment is all about.

The complete program follows and the form is shown in Figure 12.1. At the class level, the instance declarations are:

```
Private year As Integer = 1
Private oldAmount As Double
```

The response to a button-click is:

```
Private Sub Button1_Click(ByVal sender As System.Object, _
                    ByVal e As System.EventArgs) _
                    Handles Button1.Click
    Dim rate, newAmount As Double
    Dim dollars, cents As Integer

    If year = 1 Then
        oldAmount = CDbl(TextBox1.Text)
    End If

    rate = CDbl(TextBox2.Text)

    newAmount = oldAmount + (oldAmount * rate / 100)

    dollars = CInt(newAmount)
    cents = CInt(Math.Round(100 * (newAmount - dollars)))
    TextBox3.AppendText("After " & CStr(year) & " years " _
                    & "the money has become " _
                    & CStr(dollars) & " dollars and " _
```

```
                          & CStr(cents) & " cents" _
                          & NewLine & NewLine)
        oldAmount = newAmount
        year = year + 1
    End Sub
```

Case study – iteration

It is quite common in numerical programming to write iterations – loops that continue searching for a solution to an equation until the solution is found to sufficient accuracy.

As an example of using iteration, here is a formula for the sine of an angle:

$$\sin(x) = x - x^3/3! + x^5/5! - x^7/7! + \ldots$$

(Please note that if we need the sine of an angle in a program, we don't need to use this formula, because it is available as a library function.)

We can see that each term is derived from the previous term by multiplying by:

$$-x^2/(n + 1) \times (n + 2)$$

so we can construct a loop that iterates until the new term is less than some acceptable figure, say 0.0001.

```
Private Function Sin(ByVal x As Double) As Double

    Dim term, result As Double
    Dim n As Integer

    result = 0.0
    term = x
    n = 1
    While Math.Abs(term) >= 0.0001
        result = result + term
        term = - term * x * x / ((n + 1) * (n + 2))
        n = n + 2
    End While
    Return result

End Function
```

in which the library method **Abs** calculates the absolute value of its parameter.

Graphs

It is common to present mathematical, engineering and financial information graphically. We will now look at a program to draw mathematical functions. Suppose we want to draw the function:

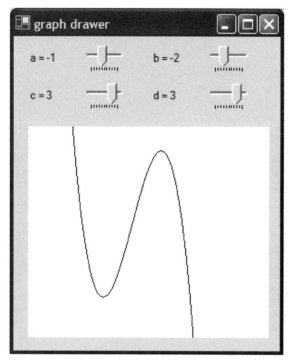

Figure 12.2 Screen of the graph drawer program, with cubic function displayed.

$$y = ax^3 + bx^2 + cx + d$$

with values for *a*, *b*, *c*, and *d* input via track bars as in Figure 12.2.

We must resolve several design issues. First we want to see the graph with the *y*-coordinate going up the screen, whereas *y* pixel coordinates measure downwards. We will distinguish between *x* and its equivalent pixel coordinate `xPixel`, and between *y* and `yPixel`.

Next we have to ensure that the graph will fit conveniently within the picture box, that it is not too small to see or too big to fit. Solving this problem is called scaling. We will assume that the available area in a picture box is 200 pixels in the *x* direction and 200 pixels in the *y* direction. We will design the program to display *x* and *y* values in the range –5.0 to +5.0. So 1 unit of *x* (or *y*) is 20 pixels.

Finally, since we will be using `DrawLine` to draw the graph, we will have to draw a curved shape as a large number of small lines. We will move along the *x* direction, one pixel at a time, drawing a line from the equivalent *y*-coordinate to the next. For each *x* pixel, the program:

1. calculates the *x* value from the *x* pixel value,
2. calculates the *y* value, the value of the function,
3. calculates the *y* pixel value from the *y* value,

using the following statements:

```
x = ScaleX(xPixel)
y = TheFunction(x)
yPixel = ScaleY(y)
```

The program then goes on to the next *x* pixel and again calculates the equivalent *y* pixel:

```
nextXPixel = xPixel + 1
nextX = ScaleX(nextXPixel)
nextY = TheFunction(nextX)
nextYPixel = ScaleY(nextY)
```

Finally the small section of the curve is drawn:

```
paper.DrawLine(myPen, xPixel, yPixel, nextXPixel, nextYPixel)
```

You will see that the program uses several private methods to help simplify the logic. Also just one method is used to handle the events from all the four track bars. Here is the complete code for this graph-drawing program.

At class level are the variables:

```
Private a, b, c, d As Double
Private paper As Graphics
Private myPen As Pen = New Pen(Color.Black)
```

Then the methods:

```
Private Sub TrackBar_Scroll(ByVal sender As System.Object, _
                            ByVal e As System.EventArgs) _
                            Handles TrackBarA.Scroll, _
                                    TrackBarB.Scroll, _
                                    TrackBarC.Scroll, _
                                    TrackBarD.Scroll
    DrawGraph()
End Sub

Private Sub DrawGraph()
    a = TrackBarA.Value
    LabelA.Text = "a = " & CStr(a)
    b = TrackBarB.Value
    LabelB.Text = "b = " & CStr(b)
    c = TrackBarC.Value
    LabelC.Text = "c = " & CStr(c)
    d = TrackBarD.Value
    LabelD.Text = "d = " & CStr(d)
    paper.Clear(Color.White)
    Draw()
End Sub
```

```
Private Sub Draw()
    Dim x, y, nextX, nextY As Double
    Dim xPixel, yPixel, nextXPixel, nextYPixel As Integer
    For xPixel = 0 To PictureBox1.Width
        x = ScaleX(xPixel)
        y = TheFunction(x)
        yPixel = ScaleY(y)
        nextXPixel = xPixel + 1
        nextX = ScaleX(nextXPixel)
        nextY = TheFunction(nextX)
        nextYPixel = ScaleY(nextY)
        paper.DrawLine(myPen, xPixel, _
                        yPixel, nextXPixel, nextYPixel)
    Next
End Sub

Private Function TheFunction(ByVal x As Double) As Double
    Return a * x * x * x + b * x * x + c * x + d
End Function

Private Function ScaleX(ByVal xPixel As Integer) As Double
    Dim xStart As Double = -5, xEnd As Double = 5
    Dim xScale As Double = PictureBox1.Width / (xEnd - xStart)
    Return (xPixel - (PictureBox1.Width / 2)) / xScale
End Function

Private Function ScaleY(ByVal y As Double) As Integer
    Dim yStart As Double = -5, yEnd As Double = 5
    Dim pixelCoord As Integer
    Dim yScale As Double = PictureBox1.Height / (yEnd - yStart)
    pixelCoord = CInt(-y * yScale) + _
                 CInt(PictureBox1.Height / 2)
    Return pixelCoord
End Function
```

If you run this program you can alter the track bar values to see the effect of changing the parameters. You can also draw quadratics (by making the value of coefficient a equal to zero) and straight lines, of course.

● Exceptions

If you are reading this chapter for the first time, you should probably skip this section, because it deals with things that don't happen very often.

When you write a program that does calculations, you have to watch out that you don't exceed the size of numbers that are allowed. It is not like doing a calculation on a piece of paper, where numbers can get as big as you like – it is more like using a calculator, which has a definite upper limit on the size of numbers that it will hold.

So for example if you declare an `Integer`:

```
Dim number As Integer
```

you must be aware that the biggest number that can be held in an `Integer` is 2147483647. So if you write this:

```
number = 2147483647
number = number + 2147483647
```

the result of the addition cannot be accommodated as an `Integer` value. The program terminates and an error message is displayed. This is called *overflow* and is one of a number of possible *exceptions* that can arise as a program executes.

Overflow can happen more subtly than this, particularly when a user enters data into a text box and its size is therefore unpredictable. For example, here is a simple program to calculate the area of a room in which overflow could occur:

```
Dim length, area As Integer
length = CInt(Textbox1.Text)
area = length * length
```

Situations that can lead to overflow are:

- adding two large numbers;
- subtracting a large positive number from a large negative number;
- dividing by a very small number;
- multiplying two large numbers.

You can see that even with a simple calculation that looks harmless, vigilance is required. There are several ways to deal with an exception:

- Ignore it, hope it will not happen, and be prepared for the program to crash and/or give strange results when it does. This is OK for novice programs, but may be less than ideal for real programs designed to be robust.
- Allow the exception to arise but handle the exception by writing an exception handler as described later in Chapter 17.
- Avoid it by writing in checks to ensure that such a situation is prevented. For example, in a program to calculate the area of a room, avoid overflow by checking the size of the data:

    ```
    If length > 10000 Then
        ' take some action here
    End If
    ```

We have seen how overflow can happen when a program uses `Integer` values. We might expect the same thing to happen if `Double` values get too large – but it doesn't. Instead, if a value gets too large, the program keeps on going, and the value takes on a special value, one of NAN (Not A Number), positive infinity or minus infinity.

Programming principles

- Many programs in science, engineering, mathematics and statistics employ lots of calculations. But even small programs that might not obviously need to do computations often use some arithmetic.
- The first and key step is deciding what types of variable to use to represent the data. The main choice is between `Integer` and `Double`.
- It is common to use iteration in numerical computation as the solution converges towards the answer. This involves a loop.
- The library of mathematical functions is invaluable in programs of this type.
- Exceptional situations, like overflow, can arise during calculations and should be anticipated if the program is to work robustly in all circumstances.

Programming pitfalls

- Exceptional situations such as trying to divide by zero can lead to strange results or else the program terminating. Make your programs robust.

Summary

- Numbers can be represented as either `Integer` or `Double`. These provide different ranges and precision.
- A variable can be declared as `Const`. The value of such a variable cannot be changed when the program executes.
- Library functions provide the common mathematical functions, e.g. the sine of an angle.
- The programmer should be aware of exceptions that might arise during calculations.

EXERCISES

12.1 Cost of phone call A phone call costs 10 cents per minute. Write a program that inputs via text boxes the duration of a phone call, expressed in hours, minutes and seconds, and displays the cost of the phone call in cents.

12.2 Measurement conversion Write a program to input a measurement via two text boxes expressed in feet and inches and convert the measurement to centimetres. There are 12 inches in a foot. One inch is 2.54 centimetres.

12.3 Cash register Write a program that represents a cash register. Amounts of money can be entered into a text box and are automatically added to the running total. The running total is displayed in another text box. A button allows the sum to be cleared (made zero).

12.4 **Sum of integers** The sum of the integers from 1 to n is given by the formula:

sum = $n(n + 1)/2$

Write a program that inputs a value for n from a text box and calculates the sum two ways – first by using the formula and second by adding up the numbers using a loop.

12.5 **Random numbers** Random numbers are often used in computational and simulation programs, called Monte Carlo methods. The library class Random enables us to create a random number generator as follows:

```
Dim generator As Random = New Random()
```

This class has a method named Next, which returns a random number, an Integer in any range we choose (specified by the parameters). For example:

```
Dim number As Integer
number = generator.Next(1, 6)
```

Write a program to check out the random number generator method by asking it for 100 random numbers that have the value either 1 or 2. Count the number of values equal to 1 and those equal to 2. Provide a button that enables a further set of 100 values to be created.

12.6 **Series for e** The value of e^x can be calculated by summing the series:

$e^x = 1 + x + x^2/2! + x^3/3! + \ldots$

Write a program to input a value of x from a text box and calculate e^x to a desired degree of accuracy. Check the value against the value obtained by referring to the constant E in the Math library.

12.7 **Tax calculation** Write a program that carries out a tax calculation. The tax is zero on the first $10 000, but is 33% on any amount over that amount. Write the program to input a salary in dollars from a text box and calculate the tax payable. Watch out for errors when you perform the calculation – the answer needs to be accurate to the nearest cent!

12.8 **Area of triangle** The area of a triangle with sides of length a, b, c is:

area = $\sqrt{s(s - a)(s - b)(s - c)}$

where

$s = (a + b + c)/2$

Write a program that inputs the three values for the sides of a triangle from text boxes and uses this formula to calculate the area. Your program should first check that the three lengths specified do indeed form a triangle. So, for example, $a + b$ must be greater than c.

12.9 Square root
The square root of a number can be calculated iteratively as shown below. Write a program to do this for a number input using a text box.

- The first approximation to the square root of x is x/2.
- Then successive approximations are given by the formula:

nextApproximation = (lastApproximation^2 − x)/2 + lastApproximation

Check the value against that obtained by using the library method `Sqrt`.

12.10 Mathematical calculator
Write a program that acts as a mathematical calculator. It provides buttons with which to enter numbers, which are displayed like the display on a desk calculator. Buttons are also provided to carry out standard mathematical calculations like sine, cosine, natural logarithm and square root.

12.11 Interest calculator
Rewrite the calculation part of the program given above in the text so as to use an `Integer` number (instead of a `Double`) to represent an amount of money (expressed in cents).

12.12 Graph drawer
Enhance the graph-drawing program in the program text so that it:

- draws the x- and y-axes;
- inputs the coefficients from text boxes instead of track bars (to give precision);
- inputs a horizontal and a vertical scaling (zoom) factor from track bars;
- draws a second graph of the same function, but with different coefficients;
- draws the graphs of some other functions. One way to do this would be to rewrite the method `TheFunction`.

12.13 Numerical integration
Write a program that calculates the integral of a function y using the 'trapezium rule'. The area under the graph of the function is divided into n equal strips of width d. Then the area under the curve (the integral) is approximately the sum of all the (small) trapeziums:

area ≅ $d(y_0 + 2y_1 + 2y_2 + \ldots + 2y_{n-1} + y_n)/2$

or:

area = (half the width of the strip) × (first + last + twice the sum of the others)

Use a function for which you know the answer, and experiment by using smaller and smaller values of d.

12.14 Mandelbrot set
The Mandelbrot set (Figure 12.3) is a famous and striking image produced by repeatedly evaluating a formula at each point in a two-dimensional space. Take a point, with coordinates x_{start} and y_{start}. Then repeatedly calculate new values of x and y from the old values using the formulae:

$x_{new} = x_{old}^2 - y_{old}^2 - x_{start}$
$y_{new} = 2x_{old}y_{old} - y_{start}$

The first values of x_{old} and y_{old} are x_{start} and y_{start}. For each iteration, calculate $r = \sqrt{x_{new}^2 + y_{new}^2}$. Repeat until r > 10 000 or 100 iterations, whichever comes first.

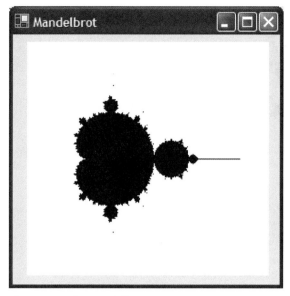

Figure 12.3 The Mandelbrot set.

If r is greater than 10 000, colour the pixel corresponding to this coordinate white, otherwise black.

Repeat for all points with x between −1.0 and +2.0 and y in the range −2.0 to +2.0.

As the iteration proceeds, starting from particular values of x_{start} and y_{start}, the value of r sometimes remains reasonably small (around 1.0). For other values of x_{start} and y_{start}, the value of r quickly becomes very large and tends to shoot off to infinity.

ANSWERS TO SELF-TEST QUESTIONS

12.1   `5E3`
         `-0.56E-6`

12.2   `0.12`
         `123,456.70`

12.3   `Const lightSpeed As Double = 299792458`

Data structures – list boxes and lists

This chapter explains:

- how to use the list box control;
- the idea of a list;
- how to add, insert and remove items from a list box;
- how to obtain the length of a list box;
- the idea of an index;
- how to carry out typical operations on a list box, such as lookup, addition and searching.

Introduction

A list box control displays a list of string items in a box. It provides a number of facilities, including the ability to select an item in a list by clicking on it, add items and delete items. The list box control is available along with the other controls on the toolbox and can be placed as usual on a form. We will use as an example a shopping list, building it up by adding items one by one. After some items have been added, the list box looks like Figure 13.1. Each item occupies a single line. If the complete list cannot be displayed in the available space, a scroll bar is automatically displayed. Later we will see how to delete items from the list.

List boxes provide a good introduction to using data structures because they provide a direct, visual representation of the information. This chapter explores using list boxes as data structures and it can be read and studied independently of the chapters on arrays.

Figure 13.1 A list box.

Lists

When we use a list box by dragging it on to the form from the toolbox, we are creating a new instance of the `ListBox` class. The `ListBox` class makes use of another class, called a `List`, to carry out its functions. A list box merely *displays* information on the form and handles mouse-click events, but a list actually *holds* the information displayed in a text box. So while a list box supports the events `Click` and `DoubleClick` and properties such as `SelectedItem`, a list provides methods to add and remove items from the list.

For example, if we create a list box named `Shopping`, then the property `Shopping.Items` is the list containing the information displayed in the list box:

```
Dim myList As List
myList = Shopping.Items
```

We can then use the properties and methods of lists with `myList`. For example, we can obtain a count of the number of items in the list (and in the list box) as follows:

```
Dim numberOfItems As Integer
numberOfItems = myList.Count
```

This series of statements can be written more concisely as follows:

```
Dim numberOfItems As Integer
numberOfItems = Shopping.Items.Count
```

in which we have chosen not to explicitly mention the list.

Adding items to a list

The example program shown in Figure 13.2 allows the user to add items to a list box. The following method responds to a button-click and places an item of shopping at the end of the list box.

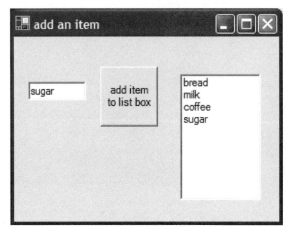

Figure 13.2 Adding items to a shopping list.

```
Private Sub Button1_Click(ByVal sender As System.Object, _
                  ByVal e As System.EventArgs) _
                  Handles Button1.Click
    Shopping.Items.Add(TextBox1.Text)
End Sub
```

In this example the name of the list box is `Shopping`. As we have seen, one of the properties of a list box is `Items` and this property represents the contents of the list box as an instance of the `List` class. This class in turn provides a number of methods, one of which is the `Add` method that allows items to be added to a list. Its parameter is the value to be added to the list. It must be a string.

Another way of placing items in a list box is to do it at design-time. Selecting the `Items` property of a list box throws up a new window in which items can be inserted into the list box.

● The length of a list

Next, here is a method that responds to a button-click and displays a message box containing the number of items currently in the list box.

```
Private Sub CountButton_Click(ByVal sender As System.Object, _
                  ByVal e As System.EventArgs) _
                  Handles CountButton.Click
    MessageBox.Show(CStr(Shopping.Items.Count))
End Sub
```

Again we see how the property `Items` of the list box named `Shopping` is used. In turn the property `Count` of the `List` class is used to obtain the number of items held in the list box.

0	bread
1	milk
2	coffee

Figure 13.3 Diagram of a list box showing the indexes.

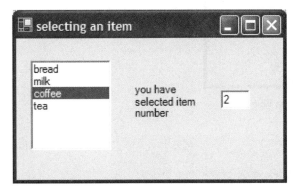

Figure 13.4 Selecting an item from a list box.

● Indices

A program refers to the items in a list box by an *index*. An index is an integer that says which item is being referred to. The first item has index value 0, the second 1, etc. We can visualize the above list box as a table as shown in Figure 13.3, with the index values alongside (but not actually stored with the data).

We now look at a program that emphasizes and demonstrates index values. The user clicks on an item in a list box and the program displays the equivalent index value in a text box (Figure 13.4). When the click event arrives, the following method is called to handle the event.

```
Private Sub Shopping_Click( _
            ByVal sender As System.Object, _
            ByVal e As System.EventArgs) _
            Handles Shopping.Click
    TextBox1.Text = CStr(Shopping.SelectedIndex)
End Sub
```

`SelectedIndex` is a list box property that provides the index value of the item clicked on (or −1 if nothing has been selected). Running this program emphasizes that the index values are not actually stored as part of a list box, but that the computer knows the values and they can be used as and when necessary. You also confirm, when you run this program, that the index values start at zero (not at 1).

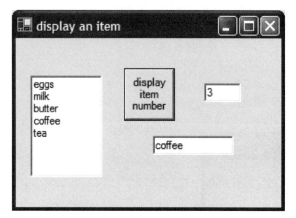

Figure 13.5 Displaying an item from a list box.

> **SELF-TEST QUESTION**
>
> **13.1** In Figure 13.4, what is the index value of the item bread?

Figure 13.5 shows a program that allows the user to display the item corresponding to a chosen index value. The code to handle the button-click is:

```
Private Sub Button1_Click(ByVal sender As System.Object, _
                ByVal e As System.EventArgs) _
                Handles Button1.Click
    Dim index As Integer

    index = CInt(IndexTextBox.Text)
    ValueTextBox.Text = CStr(Shopping.Items(index))
End Sub
```

The program extracts the value from the list box using the expression:

```
Shopping.Items(index)
```

In this expression, `Shopping` is the name of the list box. `Items` is the property of a list box that gives the contents of the list box, which is a list. Finally the index value is placed in brackets after the name of the list. Thus, for example:

```
Shopping.Items(2)
```

would give us the value in the list box at index value 2.

> **SELF-TEST QUESTION**
>
> **13.2** In Figure 13.5, what item is at index value 1?

Removing items from a list

We have seen how to add items to a list box. Now we consider removing information. The method `RemoveAt` of the class `List` removes the item at a particular index value. So if we have a list box `Shopping`, we can remove the item at index value 3 by:

    Shopping.Items.RemoveAt(3)

When this happens, the gap created is closed up.

Inserting items within a list

We have seen how to add items to the end of a list using the method `Add`. It is also possible to insert items within the body of a list, using method `Insert`. Given an existing list, we can for example do this:

    Shopping.Items.Insert(5, "tea")

The item formerly at index value 5 is moved down the list, along with any subsequent items.

Lookup

A table such as a list box is conveniently used for lookup. For example, we can construct a list box (Figure 13.6) that contains the names of the months, January to December. Then if someone gives us a month expressed as a number (1 to 12) we can use the table to convert the number to the equivalent text.

Figure 13.7 shows how the program looks to its user. We will make this list box invisible (by setting its `Visible` property to `False`), since there is no need for the user of the program to know about it.

When the program is designed, we enter the values January, February, March, etc., directly into the `Items` property of the list box.

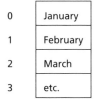

Figure 13.6 Diagram of a list box for converting integers to month names.

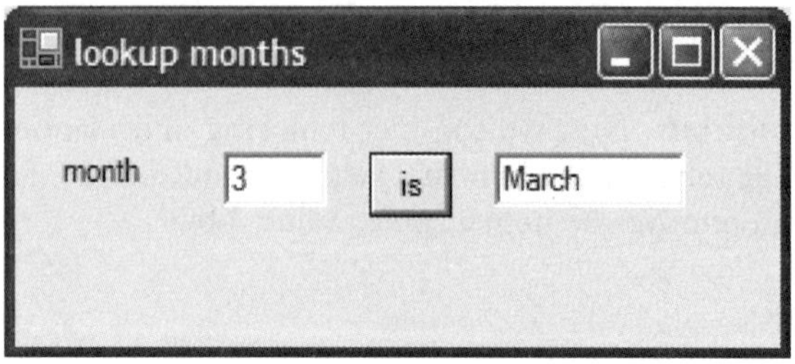

Figure 13.7 The month conversion program.

When the program runs, a number entered via a text box can be converted as follows:

```
Private Sub Button1_Click(ByVal sender As System.Object, _
                         ByVal e As System.EventArgs) _
                         Handles Button1.Click
    Dim monthNumber As Integer
    Dim monthName As String

    monthNumber = CInt(MonthNumberTextBox.Text)
    monthName = CStr(Months.Items(monthNumber - 1))
    MonthNameTextBox.Text = monthName
End Sub
```

The numbers representing a month run from 1 to 12, whereas index values start at 0. Therefore we need to subtract 1 from the month number, as shown, to convert it into an appropriate index. The `Items` property of a list box allows the program to access the value of an item in the list box named `Months`.

Using a lookup table as above is an alternative to writing a series of `If` statements to carry out the conversion, which has the following structure:

```
If monthNumber = 1 Then
    monthName = "January"
Else
    If monthNumber = 2 Then
        monthName = "February"
    End If
End If
```

Yet another alternative would be to use a `Select Case` statement. Employing `If` statements or a `Select Case` statement makes use of actions to carry out the conversion. In contrast, using a table (such as a list box) embodies the conversion information more neatly within the table.

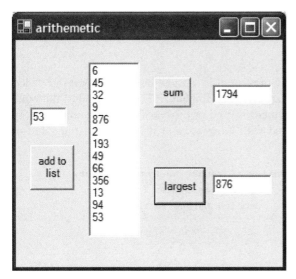

Figure 13.8 Arithmetic on a list box.

Arithmetic on a list box

We now look at a list box, named **Numbers**, that contains integer numbers and we will carry out arithmetic on the numbers. A list box always contains strings, but one kind of string is a string of digits – a number. Figure 13.8 shows a program that allows its user to enter numbers into a list box. Then one button causes the sum of the numbers to be displayed and another button causes the largest number to be displayed.

Here is the program to add together all the numbers in a list. A **For** statement is used to run through all the values of the index. Remember index values start at 0. The index of the last item in the list is equal to the length of the list −1. Each value in the list is added to a running total, called **sum**, which is initially made equal to 0. Finally the value is placed in a text box.

```
Private Sub SumButton_Click(ByVal sender As System.Object, _
                            ByVal e As System.EventArgs) _
                            Handles SumButton.Click
    Dim number As Integer
    Dim index As Integer
    Dim sum As Integer

    sum = 0

    For index = 0 To Numbers.Items.Count - 1
        number = CInt(Numbers.Items(index))
        sum = sum + number
```

```
        Next
        SumTextBox.Text = CStr(sum)
End Sub
```

Next we study a method to find the largest item in a list of numbers. A variable called `largest` is used to keep track of the largest value. Initially, it is made equal to the value at index 0 in the list box. A `For` statement is used to process all of the numbers in the list. Each item in the list is compared with `largest`, and if it is larger, the value of `largest` is updated.

```
Private Sub LargestButton_Click(ByVal sender As System.Object, _
                                ByVal e As System.EventArgs) _
                                Handles LargestButton.Click
    Dim number As Integer
    Dim index As Integer
    Dim largest As Integer

    largest = CInt(Numbers.Items(0))
    For index = 1 To Numbers.Items.Count - 1
        number = CInt(Numbers.Items(index))
        If number > largest Then
            largest = number
        End If
    Next
    LargestTextBox.Text = CStr(largest)
End Sub
```

> **SELF-TEST QUESTION**
>
> **13.3** Modify this method very simply so as to find the smallest item in the list.

These two sections of program illustrate a common feature of programs that manipulate lists: whenever you need to process every item in a list, a `For` statement is the appropriate tool. Clearly a loop is needed to examine repetitively each item in what might be a long list. The alternative structures for describing a loop are the `For` statement and the `While` statement. The `For` statement is preferable in this case because we know at the outset of the loop how many repetitions are necessary.

● For Each

Some `For` loops can be written more concisely using the `For Each` statement. For example, the above method to sum up the numbers in a list box can be written:

```
Private Sub SumButton_Click(ByVal sender As System.Object, _
                            ByVal e As System.EventArgs) _
                            Handles SumButton.Click
    Dim number As Integer
    Dim sum As Integer

    sum = 0

    For Each number As Integer In Numbers.Items
        sum = sum + CInt(number)
    Next
    SumTextBox.Text = CStr(sum)

End Sub
```

You will see that mention of the index values has vanished. Instead we simply mention the name of a variable (number in this case) that takes on each of the values in the list, one by one.

Although the For Each loop is very concise, it has some disadvantages:

1. the program cannot use any index values;
2. the program cannot change any of the values in the list.

● Searching

This next program carries out a search. It assumes that a list (for example, the shopping list) is already set up and that we want to search the list for some item. The user enters the desired item (for example sugar) into a text box as shown in Figure 13.9.

The program starts from the first item in the list and continues down the list one item at a time, trying to find the desired item. If it is not found, the index value

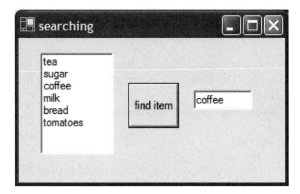

Figure 13.9 Searching a list box.

becomes equal to the size of the list, `length`, and the loop ends. If the item is found, the `Boolean` variable `found` is set to `True` and the loop terminates. A `While` statement is used rather than a `For` statement for controlling the loop, since we do not know in advance how many repetitions will be necessary.

```
Private Sub Button1_Click(ByVal sender As System.Object, _
                  ByVal e As System.EventArgs) _
                  Handles Button1.Click
    Dim length As Integer
    Dim index As Integer
    Dim found As Boolean
    Dim itemWanted As String
    length = Shopping.Items.Count

    itemWanted = TextBox1.Text

    found = False
    index = 0
    While (found = False) And (index < length)

        If CStr(Shopping.Items(index)) = itemWanted Then
            found = True
            MessageBox.Show("Item found")
        Else
            index = index + 1
        End If
    End While

End Sub
```

This is a classical serial search method.

Using a list – generics

All the examples we have seen so far use a list box. A list box uses a list to hold the strings. Now we look at using a list directly. The difference is that when you use a list, the contents are not displayed automatically.

Suppose we need to create a list to hold some strings. We do it like this:

```
Private myList As New List(Of String)
```

You will see that the name of the class of the objects that the list is to hold is placed in brackets after the keyword `of`. This feature goes by the name of *generics*. It simply means that we can create a list tailored to hold objects of a particular class.

Methods and properties of lists

Now that we have created a list to hold strings, we can add some items:

```
Private Sub AddButton_Click(ByVal sender As System.Object, _
                            ByVal e As System.EventArgs) _
                            Handles Button1.Click
    myList.Add("bread")
    myList.Add("milk")
    myList.Add("coffee")
End Sub
```

Note that a list automatically expands to accommodate however many items are added. It also contracts when items are removed.

If we need to display the contents of the list, we will need to write code to do it explicitly. We could display the above list in a list box as follows, by copying the string values, one by one:

```
Private Sub DisplayButton_Click(ByVal sender As System.Object, _
                                ByVal e As System.EventArgs) _
                                Handles Button1.Click
    Dim index As Integer
    For index = 0 To myList.Count - 1
        MyListBox.Items.Add(myList(index))
    Next
End Sub
```

Notice that the index value is enclosed in brackets after the list name.

This method can be written more concisely using the `For Each` statement:

```
Private Sub DisplayButton_Click(ByVal sender As System.Object, _
                                ByVal e As System.EventArgs) _
                                Handles Button1.Click
    For Each s As String In myList
        MyListBox.Items.Add(s)
    Next
End Sub
```

● Methods and properties of lists

Here are some of the most useful methods and properties that can be used with a list. Some of these we have met already.

Add

This method adds an object at the end of the list. For example:

```
myList.Add("bread")
```

The list expands.

Clear

`Clear` removes all elements from the list. For example:

```
myList.Clear
```

Contains

This method returns `True` if the specified object is within the list. Otherwise it returns `False`. For example:

```
Dim found As Boolean = myList.Contains("bread")
```

IndexOf

`IndexOf` returns the index of the first occurrence of the object in the list. For example:

```
Dim index As Integer = myList.IndexOf("bread")
```

Insert

This method inserts the object at the specified index. The other elements move down in order to create space. The list expands. For example:

```
myList.Insert(4, "tea")
```

RemoveAt

`RemoveAt` removes the object at the specified index. For example:

```
myList.RemoveAt(2)
```

The gap is removed and the list shrinks.

Remove

`Remove` removes the first occurrence of the specified object. For example:

```
myList.Remove("bread")
```

The gap is removed and the list shrinks.

The () notation

The bracket notation provides access to the value at the specified index, either to access it or to change it. For example:

```
Dim value As String = myList(3)
myList(4) = "bread"
```

Count

The `count` property gives the number of elements in the list, e.g.

```
Dim size As Integer = myList.Count
```

● Lists of objects

Thus far we have looked at lists that hold strings. However, we can also construct lists that hold any kind of object. In this book we have frequently used the example of a balloon class and balloon objects. We will create some balloon objects, add them to a list and then display them (Figure 13.10).

First, here is class `Balloon`, which contains a method to change the size of a balloon and to display a balloon:

```
Public Class Balloon
    Private x As Integer
    Private y As Integer
    Private diameter As Integer

    Public Sub New(ByVal initialX As Integer, _
                   ByVal initialY As Integer, _
                   ByVal initialDiameter As Integer)
        MyBase.New()
        x = initialX
        y = initialY
        diameter = initialDiameter
    End Sub

    Public Sub ChangeSize(ByVal change As Integer)
        diameter = diameter + change
    End Sub

    Public Sub Display(ByVal drawArea As Graphics, _
                       ByVal myPen As Pen)
        drawArea.DrawEllipse(myPen, x, y, diameter, diameter)
    End Sub

End Class
```

We can now create a list of balloons called `party` that is ready to hold objects of the class `Balloon` using the `Of` notation:

```
Private party As New List(Of Balloon)
```

Next we create some balloons and add them to the list as follows:

```
party.Add(New Balloon(10, 10, 50))
party.Add(New Balloon(50, 50, 100))
party.Add(New Balloon(100, 100, 200))
```

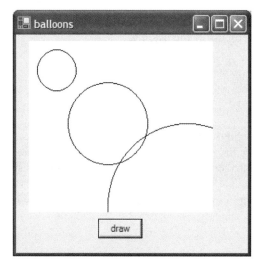

Figure 13.10 Display of balloons.

and display all the balloons in a picture box (Figure 13.10):

```
Private Sub DisplayBalloons()
    Dim myPen As Pen = New Pen(Color.Black)
    Dim drawArea As Graphics
    drawArea = PictureBox1.CreateGraphics()
    drawArea.Clear(Color.White)

    For Each b As Balloon In party
        b.Display(drawArea, myPen)
    Next
End Sub
```

Programming principles

List boxes are perhaps the simplest kind of data structure provided by Visual Basic. They enable a list of strings to be assembled, displayed and manipulated. A data structure is a group of data items that can be processed in a uniform manner. Because they can be made visible, list boxes are a good way of learning about data structures.

A list box employs a list object to store the information. Like a list box, a list expands and contracts as necessary. A data structure such as a list is set up in the main memory of the computer (not on backing storage) so that it exists only as long as the program runs. When the program terminates, the data structure is destroyed.

Lists are one of the classic structures in computing. One of the oldest and most venerated languages, LISP (short for List Processing), uses nothing but lists. A list is a sequence of items that can grow and shrink in length. Items can be added to the end of a list and removed from anywhere within the list. Also the values of items within a list can be changed. Thus a list is a flexible structure for representing a collection of items that are related in some way. Most types of data structure are invisible and, if required, a list box can be made invisible.

Another major type of data structure is the array (explained in Chapter 14). An array is a collection of similar data items, each distinguished by an index. Unlike a list box, an array is invisible and when items need to be displayed, the programmer must write explicit instructions to do it. Furthermore, although items can be inserted and removed from the body of a list box, arrays do not support these facilities.

In circumstances where all the items in a list box need processing, the natural control structure is a `For` loop.

The task of finding the largest item in a list of numbers is a classic problem in programming. This is also true of the search method.

Programming pitfalls

A common error is to think that index values start at 1. (They start at 0.)

New language elements

`For Each` provides a convenient and concise way of looping through all the values of a data structure such as a list.

The generics facility allows us to specify the class of objects that a list will contain. This is done using the keyword `of`. For example:

```
Private party As New List(Of Balloon)
```

Summary

- A list box is a GUI box that contains a list of strings.
- Each item in a list box is uniquely identified by an integer, called an *index*. Index values are not stored. Index values always start at 0.
- A program can add items to the end of a list box, remove an item, change an item or insert an item anywhere within a list box.
- A list box employs a list (`List`) object to store the information in the list. It is the list object that supports the methods to add and remove items from a list box.
- A list holds a collection of data values or objects. Such a list grows or shrinks according to how much data it contains.
- Each item in a list is uniquely identified by an integer, an index.

- When a list is created, the programmer states what kind of objects it will contain.
- A set of methods is provided to act on a list. They include `Add`, `Clear`, `Contains`, `IndexOf`, `Insert`, `RemoveAt`, `Remove`.
- Generics allow the programmer to specify the type of items that a list holds.

EXERCISES

13.1 Write a program in which an item selected in a list box (by clicking on it) is immediately deleted. Alternatively, provide a 'delete' button to delete the item that is currently selected.

13.2 Alter the program so that items in the list box are automatically always sorted into alphabetical order. (To accomplish this, investigate the properties of list box.)

13.3 Add a button that causes the list box to be emptied, using the method `Clear`.

13.4 Alter the program so that an item in the list box can be replaced by some other text. For example, 'milk' is replaced by 'sugar'. Provide a button marked 'replace' that carries out this action. The new text is to be entered into a text box.

13.5 Write a program that allows items to be inserted or removed from any position within a list box, using suitable buttons.

13.6 Improve the search method so that it displays a message whether or not the required item is found in the list box.

ANSWERS TO SELF-TEST QUESTIONS

13.1 0

13.2 milk

13.3 Change the greater-than sign to a less-than sign.

Arrays

This chapter explains:

- how to declare an array;
- how to use an index;
- how to obtain the size of an array;
- how to use `ReDim`;
- how to pass arrays as parameters;
- how to initialize an array;
- how to carry out typical operations such as lookup and searching;
- how to create arrays of objects.

● Introduction

So far in this book, we have described data items (variables) that are individual and isolated. For example:

```
Dim count, sum As Integer
Dim name As String
```

These live on their own, performing useful roles in programs as counters, sums or whatever. We can think of these variables as places in memory that have individual names attached to them.

In contrast, we very often in life deal with data that is not isolated, but grouped together into a collection of information. Sometimes the information is in tables. Examples are a train timetable, a telephone directory or a bank statement. In programming, these things are called data structures. The information in a table is related in some way to the other information within the table. One of the simplest types of data structure in programming is an array. An array can be regarded simply as a table, with a single row of information. (Alternatively you can visualize a table as a single column of information.) This could be a table of numbers, a table of strings or a table of anything.

In this chapter we will look at arrays of numbers, arrays of strings and arrays of other objects, such as graphical objects.

Here is an array of numbers:

| 23 | 54 | 96 | 13 | 7 | 32 |

which might represent the ages of a group of people at a party. And here is a table of words, which holds the names of the members of a band:

| John | Paul | George | Ringo |

In VB, a table like this is called an array. In programming, an item in an array is known as an *element* and we refer to an element by its position in the array, called the *index*. (In the world of programming, the term *component* is sometimes used instead of element, and the term *subscript* instead of index.) To us humans, the name John is in the first position in this table, but in VB the first position in an array is called the zeroth position. Successive positions in an array are the zeroth, first, second, third, etc. Thus the string Ringo is in the third position in the above array. The position of an element in an array is called the index. We can therefore picture an array, together with its indices, like this:

array: | John | Paul | George | Ringo |
indices: 0   1   2   3

Remember that the indices are not held in the computer's memory – only the data. The indices are the way that we locate information in an array.

Here is another array, this time containing numbers. The indices for the array are also shown:

array: | 23 | 54 | 96 | 13 | 7 | 32 |
indices: 0   1   2   3   4   5

In a program (as in real life) we typically have to carry out the following operations on arrays:

- Create the array – say how long it is and what sort of things it will contain.
- Put some values in the array (for example, enter some numbers into a personal telephone directory).
- Display the contents of the array on the screen (an array is held in the computer's memory and it is therefore invisible).
- Search the array to find some value (for example, searching the train timetable to find a train at a convenient time).
- Add up the contents of the array (for example, working out how much a customer spent at the supermarket).

During this chapter we shall see how to carry out these actions one by one and build up to doing all these things in a complete program. We shall start by looking at arrays of numbers. Our plan is to develop a program with the screen layout shown later in Figure 14.1 (see p. 248). An array holds the data on the rainfall for the seven days in a week (Monday to Sunday.) The user of the program can change the value of any individual data item in the array. The largest of the numbers in the array is to be displayed.

● Creating an array

In VB, an array is declared just like any other variable, usually either at the top of a class or at the top of a method. The programmer gives the array a name, like this:

```
Dim ages(5) As Integer
Dim band(3) As String
```

The variable named `ages` is now ready to hold an array of integers. As with any other variable, it is usual (and a good idea) to choose a name for the array that describes clearly what it is going to be used for. The name is the name for the complete array – the complete collection of data. The rules for choosing the name of an array are the same as for choosing any other variable name in VB. The number in brackets after the array name is the value of the largest index.

- The array called `ages` is big enough to contain six numbers, with indices going from 0 to 5.
- The array called `band` is big enough to contain four strings. The indices go from 0 to 3.

> **SELF-TEST QUESTION**
>
> 14.1 Declare an array to hold data for the rainfall for each of the seven days of the week.

● Indices

The way that a program refers to an individual item in an array is to specify an index value (sometimes called a subscript). Thus `ages(3)` refers to the element in the array with index 3 – the value 12 in this case. Similarly, `band(2)` contains the string `George`. Remember that indices start at 0, so an array of length 4 has indices that go from 0 to 3. Therefore a reference to `band(4)` is an error. The program will stop and an error message will be displayed.

In summary, index values:

- start at zero;
- are integers;
- go up to the value specified when the array is declared.

Sometimes, as we shall see, it is useful to use a variable value as an index. In such cases, it is usual to use `Integer` variables as indices.

We can input a value for an element of an array using a text box:

```
ages(2) = CInt(TextBox1.Text)
band(3) = TextBox2.Text
```

and similarly output values:

```
TextBox3.Text = "the first age is " & CStr(ages(0))
TextBox4.Text = "the 4th band member is " & band(3)
```

This latter example shows how careful you have to be with array indices.

You can change the values of individual elements of an array with assignments statements, like this:

```
ages(3) = 99
band(2) = "Mike"
```

In all these program fragments, we are referring to individual elements in an array by specifying the value of a index.

> **SELF-TEST QUESTION**
>
> **14.2** Given the declaration:
>
> ```
> Dim table(2) As Integer
> ```
>
> how long is the array and what is the valid range of indices?

Very often we want to refer to the *n*th element in an array, where *n* is a variable. This is how the power of arrays really comes into its own. Suppose, for example, we want to add up all the numbers in an array (of numbers). Let us suppose that we have an array with seven elements that hold the number of computers sold in a shop during each day in a week:

```
Dim sale(6) As Integer
```

We will insert values into the array with assignment statements. Suppose that on Monday (day 0), 13 computers are sold:

```
sale(0) = 13
```

and so on for the other days

```
sale(1) = 8
sale(2) = 22
sale(3) = 17
sale(4) = 24
sale(5) = 15
sale(6) = 23
```

Next we want to find the total sales for the week. The clumsy way to add up the sales would be to write:

```
sum = sale(0) + sale(1) + sale(2) + sale(3) + sale(4) + sale(5) _
    + sale(6)
```

which is quite correct, but does not exploit the regularity of an array. The alternative is to use a For loop. A variable called, say, dayNumber is used to hold the value of the index representing the day of the week. The index is made initially equal to 0 and then incremented each time the loop is repeated:

```
Dim sum As Integer
Dim dayNumber As Integer

sum = 0
For dayNumber = 0 To 6
    sum = sum + sale(dayNumber)
Next
```

Each time the loop is repeated, the next value in the array is added to the total. This program fragment is actually no shorter than what it replaces. But it would be considerably shorter if the array had 1000 items to add up! The other advantage is that the code explicitly shows that it is performing a systematic operation on an array.

Indices are the one place in programming when it is permissible (sometimes) to use a name that is a little cryptic. In the above program fragment, however, using the name dayNumber as the index is clear and relates strongly to the problem being solved.

> **SELF-TEST QUESTION**
>
> **14.3** What does the following program fragment do?
>
> ```
>         Dim table(9) As Integer
>         Dim index As Integer
>         For index = 0 To 10
>             table(index) = index
>         Next
> ```

● The length of an array

A running program can always find out how long an array is. For example if we have an array declared like this:

```
Dim table(9) As Integer
```

we can access its length by making use of the function UBound (short for upper bound) like this:

```
Dim length As Integer
length = UBound(table)
```

`UBound` means the largest valid index (9 in this case). We shall see that this facility is very useful.

Once you have created an array, its length is fixed. Arrays are not made of elastic – an array will not expand as necessary to hold information – but an array can be rebuilt to a different size. This is accomplished using the `ReDim` statement. For example, suppose we have an array:

```
Dim table(19) As Integer
```

Then we can change its size when the program runs by:

```
ReDim table(39)
```

We can even declare an array with no size, then specify its size later. For example:

```
Dim table() As Integer
ReDim table(24)
```

Doing a `ReDim` destroys the data in the array. But it can be preserved using `Preserve` as follows:

```
ReDim Preserve table(24)
```

When you design a new program, you need to consider how big any array should be. This is sometimes obvious from the nature of the problem. For example, if the data relates to the days of the week, then you know that the array needs seven elements. On some occasions, the size of the array needs to be flexible, and this is where `ReDim` comes in useful. However, there are other types of data structure (such as an array list) that expand and contract bit by bit as needed.

● Passing arrays as parameters

As we have seen in earlier chapters of this book, methods are very important in programming. An important aspect of using methods is passing information as parameters and returning a value. We now explain how to pass and return arrays.

Suppose we want to write a method whose job it is to calculate the sum of the elements in an array of integers. Being perceptive programmers, we want the method to be general-purpose, so that it will cope with arrays of any length. But that is OK because the method can easily find out the length of the array. So the parameter to be passed to the method is simply the array and the result to be returned to the user of the method is a number, the sum of the values.

A sample call of the method looks like this:

```
Dim table(23) As Integer
Dim total As Integer

total = Sum(table)
```

The method itself is:

```
Private Function Sum(ByVal array() As Integer) As Integer
    Dim total As Integer
    Dim index As Integer
    total = 0
    For index = 0 To UBound(array)
        total = total + array(index)
    Next
    Return total
End Function
```

Notice that in the header for the method the parameter is declared as an array, with brackets. But there is no parameter that spells out how long the array actually is. The method finds out the value of the largest index using the method UBound. Because it will accept an array of any length, this method is general purpose and potentially very useful. This is highly preferable to a special-purpose method that will only work when the array is, say, eight elements long.

> **SELF-TEST QUESTION**
>
> **14.4** Write a method that displays an array of integers, one per line, in a multiline text box. The single parameter to the method is the array.

● The For Each statement

It is very common to use For statements in conjunction with arrays. But on those occasions that the program needs to process every item in an array, there is a neat way of doing it using the For Each statement. We can rewrite the above method to calculate the sum of the integers in an array, as follows:

```
Private Function Sum(ByVal array() As Integer) As Integer
    Dim total As Integer
    total = 0
    For Each n As Integer In array
        total = total + n
    Next
    Return total
End Function
```

You will see that it is much neater and shorter. The For statement can be read as 'for each integer n in the array'. The loop is repeated for all the elements of the array. At each repetition, the variable n holds the value of the element in the array.

The type declared as part of the `For` statement (`Integer` in this example) must match with the type that the array holds. The variable (`n` in this example) can have any name, just like any other variable.

There are three things to remember when you are contemplating using a `For Each` statement:

- You can only use the `For Each` statement when you need to process all the items in an array.
- Inside the loop, the index value is not available.
- You cannot change the value of an array element using the `For Each`.

For these reasons you will see that only a small number of the programs in this chapter use `For Each`.

● Using constants

In a program with several arrays, there are declarations of the arrays and almost certainly lots of `For` loops. The arrays, together with their lengths, will be passed around the program as parameters. There is plenty of scope for confusion, particularly if two different arrays have the same length.

Suppose, for example, we are writing a program to analyse marks that students obtain in assignments. Suppose there are 10 students. We want one array to hold the average mark for each student:

```
Dim studentMark(9) As Integer
```

By coincidence, there are also 10 courses. We also want a second array to hold the average mark for each course:

```
Dim courseMark(9) As Integer
```

The problem is that, wherever we see the number 9 in the program, we do not know whether it is the number of students minus 1 or it is the number of courses minus 1. As things stand, of course, it does not matter – because they are the same! But suppose we needed to alter the program so that it deals with 20 students. We would very much like to change every occurrence of the number 9 to the number 19 using the replace function within the Integrated Development Environment. But because the arrays are the same length, this would cause great damage to the program.

One way to clarify such a program is to declare the lengths of the arrays as constants, and then to use the constants in `for` loops like this:

```
Const students As Integer = 19
Const courses As Integer = 24
```

Then we can use the constants as follows:

```
Dim studentMark(students) As Integer
Dim courseMark(courses) As Integer
```

```
Dim index As Integer
For index = 0 To students
    ' body of loop
Next
```

We can now make changes to the program with complete confidence, simply by changing a single number in the constant declaration.

> **SELF-TEST QUESTION**
>
> 14.5 Write the code to place zeroes in every element of the array `courseMark`.

Initializing an array

Initializing means giving a variable an initial or starting value. If you write this:

```
Dim table(9) As Integer
```

then an array is set up in memory and the array contains zeroes. When the programmer does not explicitly give initial values, the compiler inserts default values. These are zeroes for numbers, "" for strings and `Nothing` for objects.

A common way of explicitly initializing an array is to do it when the array is declared. The required initial values are enclosed in curly brackets and separated by commas. But the size of the array must not be given in its usual place. The following initialization:

```
Dim ages() As Integer = {23, 54, 96, 13, 7, 32}
```

is equivalent to:

```
Dim ages(5) As Integer
ages(0) = 23
ages(1) = 54
ages(2) = 96
ages(3) = 13
ages(4) = 7
ages(5) = 32
```

Here is another example, initializing an array of strings:

```
Dim band() As String = {"John", "Paul", "George", "Ringo"}
```

Another way to initialize an array is to use a loop as we saw earlier, like this:

```
Dim table(25) As Integer
Dim index As Integer
For index = 0 To UBound(table)
    table(index) = 0
Next
```

248 • Chapter 14/Arrays

If the program needs periodically to reset the array back to its initial values, then the way to do it is by using the `For` loop as shown above.

> **SELF-TEST QUESTION**
>
> **14.6** Declare an array called `numbers` of 5 integers and fill it with the numbers 1 to 5 as part of the declaration.

• A sample program

Now we will combine all the things we have explained into a program to input some numbers, put them in an array and display them. The screen is shown in Figure 14.1. The data displayed represents the rainfall for the seven days in a week (Monday to Sunday). The user of the program enters values into a text box to say which index value and a text box to provide the rainfall value for that day. The largest of the rainfall values is displayed.

First, the array is declared at the top of the form class. It has its values initialized to a selection of values.

```
Private rain() As Integer = {7, 8, 7, 4, 3, 8, 1}
```

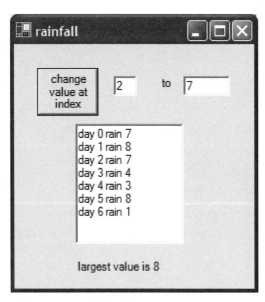

Figure 14.1 The display from the rainfall program.

Next the code to display the array values in a multiline text box:

```
Private Sub Display()
    Dim daynumber As Integer
    RainfallTextBox.Clear()
    For daynumber = 0 To 6
        RainfallTextBox.AppendText("day " & CStr(daynumber) _
                            & " rain " & CStr(rain(daynumber)) _
                            & NewLine)
    Next
End Sub
```

Next we look at the code to place a new value in an element of the array. The index value is in one text box; the actual value of the data in another. Finally the method `Display` is called to display the updated value, and `Largest` is called to display the largest value.

```
Private Sub NewValue()
    Dim index As Integer
    Dim data As Integer
    index = CInt(IndexTextBox.Text)
    data = CInt(ValueTextBox.Text)
    rain(index) = data
    Display()
    Largest()
End Sub
```

We now look at the code to calculate the largest rainfall value. The approach used is to start by assuming that the first item is the largest. Then we look at the remainder of the elements in turn, comparing them with this largest value. If we find a value that is larger than the one we have already got, we update our largest value. This is a classic approach.

```
Private Sub Largest()
    Dim highest As Integer
    Dim index As Integer
    highest = rain(0)
    For index = 0 To 6
        If highest < rain(index) Then
            highest = rain(index)
        End If
    Next
    LargestLabel.Text = "largest value is " & CStr(highest)
End Sub
```

You will see that it is very common to use the `For` statement in conjunction with arrays. They go together like a horse and carriage, in the words of the song. It is, of course, because a `For` loop makes the maximum use of the uniformity of arrays.

> **SELF-TEST QUESTION**
>
> **14.7** Write a method to calculate and display the total rainfall for the week.

● Lookup

Part of the power of arrays is that you can look up something very easily and quickly. In the rainfall program, we can extract the value of Tuesday's rainfall simply by referring to `rain(1)`. The same is true of any information that can be referred to by an integer index. For example, if we have a table showing the average height of people according to age, we can index the table using an age (25 in this example):

```
Dim height(99) As Double

Dim myHeight As Double
myHeight = height(25)
```

Similarly, if we have numbered the days of the week as 0 to 6, we can convert a number to a text string like this:

```
Dim dayNumber As Integer
Dim dayName As String
Dim name() As String = _
    {"Monday", "Tuesday", "Wednesday", "Thursday", _
     "Friday", "Saturday", "Sunday"}

dayName = name(dayNumber)
```

This could be accomplished in another way, using a `Select` statement, which is slightly longer and probably more cumbersome.

Using an array to look up something is extremely useful, simple and exploits the power of arrays.

> **SELF-TEST QUESTION**
>
> **14.8** Rewrite the above conversion using a `Select` statement.

● Searching

Another way of accessing information in an array is to search for it. This is what humans do in a telephone directory or a dictionary. The example we will consider is a telephone directory (Figure 14.2).

We will set up two arrays, one to hold names and one to hold the equivalent telephone numbers:

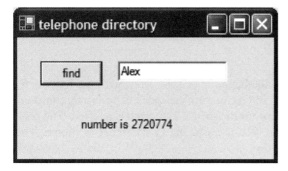

Figure 14.2 The telephone directory.

```
Private names(20) As String
Private numbers(20) As String
```

Now that the arrays have been created, we can place some data in them:

```
names(0) = "Alex"
numbers(0) = "2720774"

names(1) = "Megan"
numbers(1) = "5678554"

names(2) = "END"
```

A simple and effective way to search the directory is to start at the beginning and go from one entry to the next until we find the name that we are looking for. However, the name we seek might not be in the directory, and we must cater for that situation arising. So the search continues until either we find what we are looking for or we get to the end of the entries. We could check that we have got to the end of the array, but a more convenient approach is to put a special entry into the array to signify the end of the useful data. This end marker will consist of an entry with the name END.

Now we can write the loop to search for a desired telephone number.

```
Private Sub Find()
    Dim index As Integer
    Dim wanted As String

    wanted = TextBox1.Text
    index = 0
    Do Until names(index) = wanted _
             Or _
             names(index) = "END"
        index = index + 1
    Loop
    If names(index) = wanted Then
        Label1.Text = "number is " & numbers(index)
```

```
        Else
            Label1.Text = "name not found"
        End If
    End Sub
```

This is called a *serial* search. It starts at the beginning of the array, with the index zero, and continues searching item-by-item, adding one to the index. The search continues until either the wanted item is found or until the special name END is reached. The most convenient way of controlling this loop is to use a Do Until statement as shown. This repeats until the condition is True.

This type of search makes no assumptions about the order of the items in the table – they can be in any order. Other search techniques exploit the ordering of items in tables, such as alphabetical ordering. These techniques are beyond the scope of this book.

Information like telephone numbers is normally stored in a file, rather than an array, because data held in a file is more permanent. Usually the file is searched for the required information rather than an array. Alternatively, the file is input into memory, held in an array and searched as shown above.

● Arrays of objects

Arrays can hold anything – integers, floating-point numbers, strings, buttons, track bars, any object in the library, or any object that the programmer constructs. The only constraint is that all the objects in an array must be of the same type. We will create an array of balloon objects (Figure 14.3). We introduced the balloon object earlier in this book.

A balloon object (really just a circle) has a size and a position on the screen. Methods are provided as part of the object to move it, change its size and display it. Here is the class:

```
Public Class Balloon
    Private x As Integer
    Private y As Integer
    Private diameter As Integer

    Public Sub New(ByVal initialX As Integer, _
                   ByVal initialY As Integer, _
                   ByVal initialDiameter As Integer)
        MyBase.New()
        x = initialX
        y = initialY
        diameter = initialDiameter
    End Sub

    Public Sub ChangeSize(ByVal change As Integer)
        diameter = diameter + change
    End Sub
```

Arrays of objects ● 253

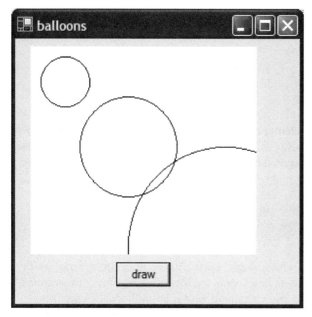

Figure 14.3 Drawing an array of balloons.

```
    Public Sub Display(ByVal drawArea As Graphics, _
                      ByVal myPen As Pen)
        drawArea.DrawEllipse(myPen, x, y, diameter, diameter)
    End Sub

End Class
```

We can now create an array of balloons:

```
Private party(10) As Balloon
```

But this only creates the array, ready to hold balloons. We now need to create some balloons as follows:

```
party(0) = New Balloon(10, 10, 50)
party(1) = New Balloon(50, 50, 100)
party(2) = New Balloon(100, 100, 200)
```

and display all the balloons:

```
Private Sub DisplayBalloons()
    Dim b As Integer
    drawArea.Clear(Color.White)
    For b = 0 To 2
        party(b).Display(drawArea, myPen)
    Next
End Sub
```

The advantage of storing the balloon objects in an array is that we can do something with them all in convenient way. For example, we can change the size of all the balloons at once:

```
For b = 0 To 2
    party(b).ChangeSize(20)
Next
```

Finally, we have said that all the elements in an array must be of the same type. There is an exception: if you declare an array of objects of the class `Object`, then you can place different types of objects in the array. This is because `Object` is the superclass of every other class.

Programming principles

- An array is a collection of data with a single name. All the items in an array are of the same type. Individual elements in an array are identified by means of an index, an integer. So if for example an array is named `table`, an individual element is referred to as `table(2)`, where 2 is the index. You can similarly refer to an element of an array using a integer variable as an index, like `table(index)`. It is this facility that makes arrays powerful.
- Once created, an array has a length and normally this length stays fixed. But the length can be changed as the program executes using `ReDim`, although this would be carried out at strategic times, rather than frequently.
- Arrays can hold data of any type – for example `Integer`, `Double`, `Boolean`, `Button`, `TextBox`. (But in any one array the data must all be of the same type.)
- The array is the oldest and most widely used data structure. Arrays are compact and are accessed very quickly using support from the computer's instructions.
- It is common to use the `For` loop in conjunction with arrays.

Programming pitfalls

A common error in VB is to confuse the length of an array with the range of valid indices. For example, the array:

```
Dim table(9) As Integer
```

has 10 elements. The valid range of indices for this array is 0 to 9. Reference to `table(10)` is a reference to an element of the array that simply does not exist. Luckily the VB system checks for violations like this as the program is running and will issue an error message.

Here is a common example of how to do things wrongly:

```
Dim table(9) As Integer
Dim index As Integer
For index = 0 To 10     'warning, erroneous
    table(index) = 0
Next
```

This will place a zero in all of the elements of the array `table`, but then go on to try to place a zero in whatever data item happens to be immediately after the array in the computer's memory. The program then fails with an '`IndexOutOfRange`' message. It is always worthwhile carefully checking the condition for terminating a `For` loop used with an array.

Students sometimes have difficulty in visualizing where an array is. An array is held in main memory; it is invisible; it only has a life while the program is running.

Grammar spot

An array with 21 elements is declared like this:

```
Dim table(20) As Double
```

To refer to an element of an array, the index is written in brackets, as in:

```
table(3) = 12.34
```

Summary

- An array is a collection of data. It is given a name by the programmer. All the items in an array must be of the same type (e.g. all `Integer`).
- An array is declared, along with other variables, like this:

    ```
    Dim harry(24) As Integer
    ```

    in which 24 is the value of the largest index. The array has 25 elements.
- An individual element in an array is referred to by an integer index, for example:

    ```
    harry(12) = 45
    ```

- Indices have values that start from zero and go up to the largest index value.

EXERCISES

Games

14.1 Nim The human plays against the computer. At the start of the game there are three piles of matches. In each pile there is a random number of matches in the range 1 to 20. The three piles are displayed throughout the game. A random choice determines who goes first. Players take it in turns to remove as many matches as they like from any one pile, but only from one pile. A player must remove at least one match. The winner is the player who makes the other player take the last match. Make the computer play randomly, that is, it chooses a pile randomly and then a number of matches randomly from those available.

14.2 **Safe combination** Set up an array to contain the six digits that open a safe. Ask the user to input six digits one-by-one from buttons labelled with the digits 0 to 9, and check whether they are correct. When a digit is entered, tell the user whether it is correct or not and give them three tries before making them start from the beginning again.

14.3 **Pontoon (vingt-et-un)** Write a program to play this card game. The computer acts as the dealer. The dealer first deals you two playing cards. These are random cards. (In the real game, the dealer has an enormous hand of cards, comprising several shuffled packs.) Your aim is to get a score higher than the dealer's, without going beyond 21 (vingt-et-un). Ace counts either as 1 or 11. At any time, you can say 'twist', which means that you want another card, or 'stick', which means you are content with what you have. You may also have gone 'bust', which means you have more than 21. When you finally stick or bust, it is the dealer's turn to deal cards for him- or herself. The dealer's aim is to get a bigger score than you, without going bust. But the dealer does not know your score and so gambles on what you might have.

Provide buttons to start a new game, twist and stick. Display both sets of cards that are dealt.

Basic operations on arrays

14.4 **Rain data** Complete the program to handle rainfall data by including the following operations:

- Add up the values and display the total.
- Find the largest value, the smallest value and display them.
- Find the index of the largest value.

14.5 **String array** Write a program that uses an array of 10 strings. Write methods that carry out each of the following operations:

- Input values from the keyboard via a text box.
- Display the values. (You can now observe that they have been entered correctly into your array.)
- Input a word from a text box and search to see whether it is present in the array. Display a message to say whether it is present in the array or not.

14.6 **Bar chart** Bar charts are useful for data like rainfall or changes in house prices. Write a method that displays a bar chart of the data that is passed to it as an array.

The array holds a number of values, such as the rainfall on each of the seven days of the week. The library method `FillRectangle` can be used to draw individual bars.

14.7 **Pie chart** Pie charts show the proportions of quantities and are therefore useful for data like personal budgets or company budgets. Write a method that displays a pie chart of the data that is passed to it as an array. The array holds the amounts spent on, for example, travel, food, housing, etc. Investigate the `FillPie` method.

14.8 **Graph drawer** Write a method to draw a graph of a data given as an array of x-coordinates and an array of corresponding y-coordinates. It has the heading:

```
Private Sub DrawGraph(ByVal x() As Double, ByVal y() As Double)
```

The method draws straight lines from one point to another. It also draws the axes.

Statistics

14.9 Write a program that inputs a series of integers into an array. The numbers are in the range 0 to 100.
Calculate and display:

- the largest number;
- the smallest number;
- the sum of the numbers;
- the mean of the numbers.

Display a histogram (bar chart) that shows how many numbers are in the ranges 0 to 9, 10 to 19, etc.

Random numbers

14.10 Check to see that the random number generator class (Chapter 6) works correctly. Set it up to provide random numbers in the range 1 to 100. Then call the method 100 times, placing the frequencies in an array as in the last exercise. Finally, display the frequency histogram, again as in the last exercise. Random numbers should be random, so the histogram should have bars of approximately equal height.

Words

14.11 **Word perm** Write a program that inputs four words and then displays all possible permutations of the words. So, for example, if the words mad, dog, bites and man are entered, then the following are output:

man bites mad dog
mad man bites dog
mad bites man dog
etc.

(Not all of the sentences will make sense!)

Information processing – searching

14.12 Dictionary Set up an array to contain pairs of equivalent English and Spanish words. Then input an English word, look up its Spanish equivalent and display it. Make sure you check to see whether the word is in the dictionary. Then add the facility to translate in the opposite direction, using the same data.

14.13 Library Each member of a library has a unique user code, an integer. When someone wants to borrow a book, a check is made that the user code is valid.
   Write a program that searches a table of user codes to find a particular code. The program should display a message saying that the code is either valid or invalid.

14.14 Telephone directory Enhance the telephone directory program given above within the chapter so that new names and numbers can be added to the directory. Then add the facility to remove a name and number.

Information processing – sorting

14.15 Sorting Write a program that inputs a series of numbers, sorts them into ascending numerical order and displays them.
   This program is not the easiest to write. There are very many approaches to sorting – in fact there are whole books on the subject. One approach is as follows.
   Find the smallest number in the array. Swap it with the first item in the array. Now the first item in the array is in the right place. Leave this first item alone and repeat the operation on the remainder of the array (everything except the first item). Repeat, carrying out this operation on a smaller and smaller array until the complete array is in order.

Arrays of objects

14.16 Balloons Extend the program that maintains an array of balloons. Add functionality to:

- blow up all the balloons by a random factor;
- move all the balloons by the same amount.

14.17 Telephone directory Write a program to create and maintain a telephone directory. Each element in the array is an object of the class `Entry`:

```
Public Class Entry
    Private name As String
    Private number As String

    ' properties to access the name and the number
End Class
```

Complete the class `Entry`. Then create the array:

```
Private directory(1000) As Entry
```

and place data into it like this:

```
directory(0).Name = "Douglas Bell"
directory(0).Number = "01 0114 253 3103"
```

Provide a GUI to enter data into the directory. Provide a search facility so that if a name is entered into a text box, the corresponding telephone number is displayed.

14.18 Playing cards This is an example that might be part of a game using playing cards. Each card is described by the class:

```
Public Class Card
    Private rank As Integer
    Private suit As String

    ' properties to access the rank and the suit
End Class
```

Complete the class `Card`. Then create an array that holds a complete deck of cards:

```
Private deck(51) As Card
```

Initialize the deck using a `For` loop to run through the four suits and a nested `For` loop to run through the different card ranks.

ANSWERS TO SELF-TEST QUESTIONS

14.1 `Dim rainfall(6) As Integer`

14.2 The array is 3 elements long. Valid indices are 0 to 2.

14.3 The program fragment places the numbers 0 to 10 in the array. But it attempts to access a non-existent element with index value 10. So the program will fail.

14.4
```
Private Sub Display(ByVal array() As Integer)
    Dim index As Integer
    TextBox.Clear()
    For index = 0 To UBound(array)
        TextBox.AppendText(CStr(array(index)) & NewLine)
    Next
End Sub
```

14.5
```
Dim index as Integer
For index = 0 To courses
    courseMark(index) = 0
Next
```

14.6 `Dim numbers() As Integer = {1, 2, 3, 4, 5}`

14.7
```
Private Sub WeekTotal()
    Dim total As Integer = 0
    Dim index As Integer
    For index = 0 To 6
        total = total + rain(index)
    Next
    TotalLabel.Text = "total is " & CStr(total)
End Sub
```

14.8
```
Select Case dayNumber
    Case 0
        dayName = "Monday"
    Case 1
        dayName = "Tuesday"
    Case 2
        dayName = "Wednesday"
    Case 3
        dayName = "Thursday"
    Case 4
        dayName = "Friday"
    Case 5
        dayName = "Saturday"
    Case 6
        dayName = "Sunday"
End Select
```

Arrays – two-dimensional

This chapter explains:

- how to declare a two-dimensional array;
- how indices are used with two-dimensional arrays;
- how to obtain the size of a two-dimensional array;
- how to use `ReDim`;
- how to pass two-dimensional arrays as parameters;
- how to initialize a two-dimensional array.

● Introduction

Two-dimensional arrays, or tables, are very common in everyday life:

- a chessboard;
- a train timetable;
- a spreadsheet.

In the last chapter, we looked at one-dimensional arrays. VB provides a natural extension of one-dimensional arrays to two dimensions. So, for example, the declaration:

```
Dim sales(3, 6) As Integer
```

declares a two-dimensional array of integers. It holds figures for the sales of computers at each of four shops on each of the seven days in a week (Figure 15.1). The array is called `sales`. We can think of it as having four rows and seven columns. Each row represents a week at a particular shop. Each column represents a single day at each of the four shops. The indices for the rows go from 0 to 3. The indices for the columns go from 0 to 6. Column 0 is Monday, column 1 is Tuesday, etc.

262 ● Chapter 15/Arrays – two-dimensional

		column numbers (days)						
		0	1	2	3	4	5	6
row numbers (shops)	0	22	49	4	93	0	12	32
	1	3	8	67	51	5	3	63
	2	14	8	23	14	5	23	16
	3	54	0	76	31	4	3	99

Figure 15.1 A two-dimensional array.

> **SELF-TEST QUESTION**
>
> **15.1** Which column represents Saturday? How many computers were sold on Thursday at shop 3? Which row and column number is this?

● **Declaring an array**

An array is declared along with other variables, either at the top of the class or at the top of a method. The programmer gives the array a name, like this:

```
Dim sales(3, 6) As Integer
Dim temps(9, 23) As Double
```

When you declare an array, you say what the greatest value of the row and column index values are. The array called `sales` has four rows – one for each of four shops. It has seven columns – one for each day in the week. The array contains sales figures for each of four shops for each day of the week. The array called `temps` holds information about the temperatures in each of 10 ovens, each hour during a 24-hour period.

As with any other variable, it is usual (and a good idea) to choose a name for the array that describes clearly what it is to be used for. The name is the name for the complete array – the complete collection of data.

> **SELF-TEST QUESTION**
>
> **15.2** Declare an array to represent an 8 x 8 chessboard. Each position in the array is to hold a string.

Indices

A program refers to an individual item in a two-dimensional array by specifying the values of two integer indices (sometimes called subscripts). Thus `sales(3, 2)` refers to the element in the array with row 3 and column 2, meaning shop number 3 and the day number 2 (Wednesday). Similarly, `chessBoard(2, 7)` might contain the string 'pawn'.

We can input a value for an element of an array like this:

```
sales(2, 3) = CInt(TextBox1.Text)
chessBoard(3, 4) = TextBox1.Text
```

and similarly display the values of the elements of an array using text boxes.

We can change the values with assignment statements, like this:

```
sales(3, 2) = 99
chessBoard(2, 7) = "knight"   ' place a knight on a square
```

In all these program fragments, we are referring to individual elements in an array by specifying the values of the indices that identify the particular element that we are interested in.

Often we want to refer to an element in an array by specifying *variables* for each of the two indices. This is the way in which the power of arrays can be exploited. Suppose, for example, we want to add up all the numbers in an array of numbers that holds data on sales of computers in four shops over a period of seven days:

```
Dim sales(3, 6) As Integer
```

The clumsy way to add up the sales would be to write:

```
sum = _
      sales(0, 0) + sales(0, 1) + sales(0, 2) + sales(0, 3) _
          + sales(0, 4) + sales(0, 5) + sales(0, 6) _
    + sales(1, 0) + sales(1, 1) + sales(1, 2) _
          + sales(1, 3) + sales(1, 4) + sales(1, 5) + sales(1, 6) _
    + etc
```

which is longwinded, difficult to understand, prone to error – but correct. However, it does not exploit the regularity of an array. The alternative would be to use a `For` loop. Variables are used to hold the values of the indices. Each index is made initially equal to 0 and then incremented each time the loop is repeated:

```
Dim sales(3, 6) As Integer
Dim sum As Integer

Dim shop As Integer
Dim dayNumber As Integer
```

```
sum = 0
For shop = 0 To 3
    For dayNumber = 0 To 6
        sum = sum + sales(shop, dayNumber)
    Next
Next
```

which is considerably shorter and much neater than if we had written out all the sums in explicit detail.

> **SELF-TEST QUESTION**
>
> **15.3** Write statements to place the text 'empty' on each square of the chessboard.

The size of an array

Once created like this:

```
Dim info(19, 39) As Double
```

an array has a fixed size that can expand or contract but only if it is done explicitly using a `ReDim` command. However, only the last (second) dimension can be changed – the first is fixed. The optional word `Preserve` causes the values of the array to be preserved when the size is changed. For example:

```
ReDim Preserve info(19,49)
```

converts the array into one with the same number of rows, but with a maximum column index value of 49. The data is preserved.

The largest index value of an array can always be obtained using the method `UBound`. For the above array:

```
Dim largestRowIndex As Integer
largestRowIndex = UBound(info, 1)
```

has the value 19 and

```
Dim largestColumnIndex As Integer
largestColumnIndex = UBound(info, 2)
```

has the value 49.

> **SELF-TEST QUESTION**
>
> **15.4** What is the value of `UBound(chessBoard, 1)`?

Passing arrays as parameters

Suppose we want to write a function whose job it is to calculate the sum of the elements in an array of integers. We want the method to be general-purpose, able to deal with arrays of any size. So we will pass the name of the array to the method as the parameter and the result to be returned to the user of the method is a number – the sum of the values.

A call of the method looks like this:

```
Dim sales(23, 11) As Integer
Dim total As Integer
total = Sum(sales)
```

The method itself is:

```
Private Function Sum(ByVal array(,) As Integer) As Integer
    Dim total As Integer
    Dim row, col As Integer
    total = 0
    For row = 0 To UBound(array, 1)
        For col = 0 To UBound(array, 2)
            total = total + array(row, Col)
        Next
    Next
    Return total
End Function
```

Constants

In a program with several arrays, there is plenty of scope for confusion, particularly if two different arrays have the same length. For example, in the program to analyse the sales figures of computers at a number of shops over a number of days, we used a two-dimensional array to hold the figures. Each column represents a day. The rows are the data for each shop. Now suppose that, by coincidence, there are seven shops. The array is:

```
Dim sales(6, 6) As Integer
```

The problem is that, wherever we see the number 6 in the program, we do not know whether it is the number of shops or it is the number of days. As things stand, of course, it doesn't matter – because they are the same! But suppose we needed to alter the program so that it deals with eight shops. We would very much like to change every occurrence of the number 6 to the number 7 using the editor. This is impossibly dangerous because the lengths are the same.

An excellent way to clarify such a program is to declare the maximum values of the index values as constants, like this:

```
Const dayMaximum As Integer = 6
Const shopMaximum As Integer = 6
```

and then declare the array as:

```
Dim sales(shopMaximum, dayMaximum) As Integer
```

Now if the number of shops changes, we can make the corresponding change to the program with confidence, simply by changing one number in the constant declaration. We can also write `For` loops that make use of the constants:

```
For index = 0 To shopMaximum
    ' body of loop
Next
```

● Initializing an array

Initializing means giving a variable an initial or starting value. If you write this:

```
Dim table(9, 9) As Integer
```

then space for the array is set up in memory and the array contains zeroes. The compiler assigns initial values to arrays that are not explicitly initialized. If the array consists of numbers, it assigns zeroes. If the array consists of strings it assigns the value *""*. If the array consists of objects, it assigns the value `Nothing` to all the elements of the array.

One way to explicitly initialize an array is to use nested loops, like this:

```
Dim row, col as Integer
For row = 0 To 9
    For col = 0 To 9
        table(row, col) = 99
    Next
Next
```

Another way of initializing an array is to declare it like this:

```
Dim table(,) As Integer = _
    {{1, 0, 1}, _
     {0, 1, 0}}
```

Note the use of curly brackets and commas. This both creates an array with two rows and three columns and gives it initial values. When this form of initialization is used, the size of the array must *not* appear in the brackets. The initialization is carried out once, when the array is created. If the program changes the value of an element in the array, the value will not change back to its original value – not until the program is run again.

If the program needs periodically to reset the array back to its initial values, then the way to do it is with the `For` loops as shown above.

> **SELF-TEST QUESTION**
>
> **15.5** Write the declaration of a 3 x 3 array of strings in such a way that the array is filled with the words one, two, three, etc.

A sample program

This program maintains a two-dimensional array of integers. These represent the rainfall over seven days at each of three locations. The screen is shown in Figure 15.2. The array is displayed in a multiline text box with an initial assortment of values. The user can change a value in the array by specifying its index values and the new value of the data.

First we declare the array:

```
Dim rainData(, ) As Integer = _
    {{10, 7, 3, 28, 5, 6, 3}, _
     {12, 3, 5, 7, 12, 5, 8}, _
     { 8, 5, 2, 1, 1, 4, 7}}
```

To display all the data:

```
Private Sub Display()
    Dim location As Integer
    Dim dayNumber As Integer
```

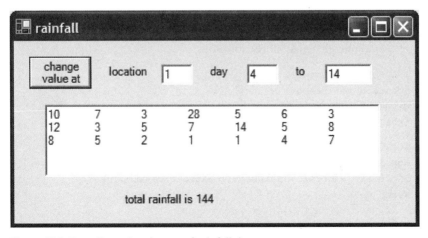

Figure 15.2 Two-dimensional array of rainfall data.

```
    TextBox1.Clear()
    For location = 0 To 2
        For dayNumber = 0 To 6
            TextBox1.AppendText(CStr(rainData(location, dayNumber)) _
                                                & Tab)
        Next
        TextBox1.AppendText(NewLine)
    Next
End Sub
```

The inner `For` loop deals with the different days, while the outer `For` loop deals with the different locations. The method uses the property `Tab`, which is in a library together with `NewLine` and can be used as shown provided that the following `Imports` statement is present at the head of the program:

```
Imports Microsoft.VisualBasic.ControlChars
```

To change an element in the array, the day number, location number and new data value are extracted from their text boxes:

```
Private Sub ChangeValue()
    Dim dataValue As Integer
    Dim dayNumber As Integer
    Dim location As Integer

    dayNumber = CInt(DayTextBox.Text)
    location = CInt(LocationTextBox.Text)
    dataValue = CInt(ValueTextBox.Text)
    rainData(location, dayNumber) = dataValue

    Display()
    CalculateTotal()
End Sub
```

To calculate the total rainfall across all the locations:

```
Private Sub CalculateTotal()
    Dim location As Integer
    Dim dayNumber As Integer
    Dim total As Integer = 0

    For location = 0 To 2
        For dayNumber = 0 To 6
            total = total + RainData(location, dayNumber)
        Next
    Next
    Label1.Text = "total rainfall is " & total
End Sub
```

When you run this program, be careful to enter row numbers in the range 0 to 2, and column numbers in the range 0 to 6.

You will see again that it is very common to see nested `For` statements used with two-dimensional arrays, because they make the maximum use of the uniformity of arrays.

For Each statement

The `For Each` statement can make loops more concise. Here, for example, is a method given above to calculate the total rainfall:

```
Private Sub CalculateTotal()
    Dim total As Integer = 0

    For Each item As Integer In rainData
        total = total + item
    Next
    TotalLabel.Text = "total rainfall is " & total
End Sub
```

In this version, there is no explicit mention of index values. At each repetition, the value of the variable `item` takes on the next value from the array.

Programming principles

A two-dimensional array is a collection of data, with a single name (for example `rainData`). An array can be visualized as a two-dimensional table, with rows and columns. Suppose we want to represent the rainfall data for each of seven days at each of three places. We declare an array:

```
Dim rainData(6, 2) As Integer
```

Elements in such an array are distinguished by specifying two indices, which are integers, for example `rainData(4, 2)`. You can think of the first index as describing the row number and the second as describing the column number. When the array is created the greatest value of the index of the array is specified – six and two in this example. This means that this array has seven rows and three columns. Indices always start at 0. In this example the row indices go from 0 to 6 and the column indices from 0 to 2.

The elements of an array can be any type – `Integer`, `Double`, `String`, or any other object. But all the elements in an array must be of the same type – `Integer` in this example. The exception is when an array is declared to consist of `Object`. In this case such an array can accommodate any mix of objects.

It is common to use nested `For` loops in conjunction with two-dimensional arrays.

In this book we have explored both one-dimensional and two-dimensional arrays. VB provides for arrays with up to 60 dimensions, but dimensions above 3 are rarely used in practice.

Programming pitfalls

A common error in VB is to confuse the length of an array with the range of valid indices. For example, the array:

```
Dim table(10,5) As Integer
```

has 11 rows and 6 columns. The valid range of indices for the rows is 0 to 10. The valid range of indices for the columns is 0 to 5. Reference to `table(11, 6)` will give rise to the program stopping and an error message being displayed.

Summary

- A two-dimensional array is a collection of data in a table, with rows and columns.
- An array is given a name by the programmer.
- An array is declared, along with other variables, like this:

    ```
    Dim alice(24,30) As Integer
    ```

    in which 24 is the greatest index of the rows and 30 is the greatest index of the columns.
- An individual element of an array is referred to by integer indices, for example:

    ```
    alice(12, 3) = 45
    ```

EXERCISES

Basic operations on two-dimensional arrays

15.1 Data handler Write a program that uses a 4 x 7 array of numbers similar to the rainfall program (with output as shown in Figure 15.2). Extend the program to carry out the following methods:

- When a button is pressed marked 'sums', add up the values for each of the seven columns and add up all the values of each of the four rows and display them.
- When a button marked 'largest' is pressed, find the largest value in each row, the largest in each column and the largest value in the complete array.
- When a button marked 'scale' is pressed, multiply every number in the array by a number entered into a text box. (This could be used to convert from centimetres to inches.)

Statistical measures

15.2 Extend the rainfall program so that it provides a button to calculate the average rainfall per day for each location. So for example the average rainfall per day in location two might be 23.

Extend it further to provide a button to calculate the mean and standard deviation of the daily rainfall in any location. So for illustration, the mean rainfall in any location could be 19, with a standard deviation of 6.4.

Bar charts and pie charts

15.3 Extend the rainfall program so that the user can specify a row (a location). The information is then displayed as a bar chart.

Extend the program to display the information in a single row or a single column as a pie chart.

Mathematical operations

15.4 Transpose The transpose of an array is the technical term used to describe swapping the elements in an array across one of the diagonals. The numbers on the diagonal do not change. So if an array is:

1	2	3	4
5	6	7	8
9	10	11	12
13	14	15	16

then its transpose is:

1	5	9	13
2	6	10	14
3	7	11	15
4	8	12	16

Write a program to input the elements of an array in the same manner as the rainfall program. It transposes the array when a button is pressed, and displays it.

Games

15.5 Tic tac toe Tic tac toe (or noughts and crosses) is played on a 3 × 3 grid, which is initially empty. Each of two players goes in turn. One places a cross in a blank square the other places a nought in a blank square.

The winner is the person who gets a line of three noughts or three crosses. Thus a win for noughts might look like this:

o	x	o
x	o	
x		o

Games can end in a draw, where neither side has obtained a line.

Write a program to play the game. There is just one button to start a new game. The program shows the noughts and crosses graphically, each in its own picture box.

The human player specifies a move by clicking with the mouse on the picture box where the cross is to be placed. The other player is the computer, which plays as noughts and decides where to play on a random basis.

Artificial life

15.6 Cellular life An organism consists of single cells that are on (alive) or off (dead). Each generation of life consists of a single row of cells. Each generation of life (each row) of the organism depends on the previous one (just like real life). Time moves downwards, from top to bottom. Each row represents a generation. The lives look like this:

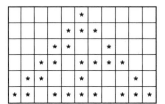

In the beginning, there is just one cell alive. Whether a cell is alive or dead depends on a combination of factors – whether or not it was alive in the last generation and whether or not its immediate neighbours were alive in the last generation. You can see that, even after only five generations, a pattern is emerging. These patterns are very subtle and mimic the patterns found in real living organisms. The rules are as follows.

A cell lives only if:

- it was dead, but only its left neighbour was alive;
- it was dead, but only its right neighbour was alive;
- it was alive, but its immediate neighbours were dead;
- it was alive, and only its right neighbour was alive.

So, for example, given the following generation:

- The first cell lives, because even though it was dead, its immediate right neighbour was alive.
- The second cell lives because only its immediate right neighbour was alive.
- The third living cell dies (through overcrowding, we surmise!).
- The fourth cell dies.
- The fifth cell lives because, although it was dead, its immediate left neighbour was alive.

So the new generation is:

Write a program that uses a two-dimensional array to chart the progress of the life form. Display the development on the screen as asterisks, as above. Provide a button that allows the user to go on to the next generation.

15.7 Conway's Game of Life In this life form, again, an organism consists of single cells that are on (alive) or off (dead). The organisms exist in a two-dimensional grid world, for example:

The rules governing this organism are:

- If a live cell has two or three neighbours, it will survive. Otherwise it will die of isolation or overcrowding.
- If an empty cell is surrounded by exactly three cells, then a new live cell will be born to fill the space.
- All births and deaths take place simultaneously.

Write a program to simulate this kind of life. The program should initially allow the user to click on the cells that are to be alive. Provide a button that allows the user to go on to the next generation and display it.

The program needs two arrays – one to represent the current state of life and another to represent the next generation. After each new generation is created, the roles of the two arrays are swapped.

ANSWERS TO SELF-TEST QUESTIONS

15.1 Column 5 is Saturday. 31 computers were sold at shop 3 on Thursday. This is row 3 and column 3.

15.2
```
Dim chessBoard(7, 7) As String
```

15.3
```
Dim chessBoard(7, 7) As String
Dim row, col As Integer

For row = 0 To 7
    For col = 0 To 7
        chessBoard(row, col) = "empty"
    Next
Next
```

15.4 The largest index is 7.

15.5
```
Dim numbers(,) As String = { _
                            {"one", "two", "three"}, _
                            {"four", "five", "six"}, _
                            {"seven", "eight", "nine"} _
                          }
```

String manipulation

This chapter explains:

- the string facilities you have seen so far;
- the main methods and properties of the `String` class.

● Introduction

Strings of characters are very important in software. All programming languages have facilities for primitive character manipulation, but VB has a particularly useful collection of methods. In this chapter, we will bring together the string features we have made use of up to now, and extend this by studying the set of string-processing methods.

Here are some situations in which strings are used:

- to display messages on the screen, which might involve placing text on labels;
- to input text from the user. This is often from a text box. In a console application, text might also be entered at a keyboard prompt;
- to store data in files. When we examine files in Chapter 18 we will see that the content of many types of file can be regarded as sequences of strings. Additionally, filenames and folder names are strings;
- for searching web pages;
- to hold text in memory for word-processors and editors.

● Using strings – a recap

Here, we bring together the string facilities that have been shown so far.

We can declare variables and provide an initial value, as in:

```
Dim x As String
Dim y As String = "USA"
```

We can assign one string to another, as in:

```
x = "England"
y = "France"
y = x
x = ""      ' a zero-length string
```

This illustrates that the length of a string can vary. Strictly, the old string is destroyed and it is replaced with a totally new value. The space that was occupied by the old value will be made available later for other variables to use.

We can use the `&` operator to concatenate strings, as in:

```
MessageBox.Show("I live in " & y)
```

A common feature of string processing is to begin with an initially empty string, and to join items onto it as the program runs. We might put:

```
x = x & "something"
```

which adds to the end of `x`. This is known as 'appending'.

We can compare strings, as in:

```
If x = "France" Then
    'do something
End If
```

We can create arrays of strings (with indices starting from 0), as in:

```
Dim cities(10) As String
```

We can convert strings to numbers and vice versa, using `CDbl`, `CInt` and `CStr`. This is useful when we are presented with strings from a text box (or from a file, as we shall see later). For example, we may put:

```
Dim n As Integer = 3
x = CStr(n)
y = "123"
n = CInt(y)
```

If a string cannot be converted to a number, an *exception* is produced. An exception can be intercepted and dealt with, and this is covered in Chapter 17. There is also the `IsNumeric` function, described below.

This much we have seen. Now we will look at the detail of strings and the available methods.

String indexing

Each character in a string has an index number, starting from zero. It is easy to confuse the length of a string with the maximum index value. Look at the following diagram, which shows the string `possible`:

String: | p | o | s | s | i | b | l | e |
Indices: 0   1   2   3   4   5   6   7

As you can see, the maximum index value is `7`, and the length of the string (the number of characters it contains) is `8`.

The characters within strings

Strings can contain any characters we wish, but when creating string values between quotes, there are a number of special cases. Here are the main ones:

- We might require a " character within quotes. To do this, we use two quotes to stand for a single one, as in:

    ```
    TextBox1.Text = "The word ""Object"""
    ```

    which displays:

    ```
    The word "Object"
    ```

- We might require end-of-line markers within a string. To do this, we use the constant `NewLine` with its required import, as in:

    ```
    Imports Microsoft.VisualBasic.ControlChars
    ...
    Dim s As String = "Tom" & NewLine & "Jerry"
    ```

Comparing strings

Often, we need to place strings in alphabetical order, which involves being able to determine whether one string precedes another. A VB project can be set up to use two types of ordering, and here we will use the traditional binary ordering. Behind the scenes, each character has a numeric code. Imagine `a` as the lowest, then `b`, etc. Following `z`, we have `A`, `B`, etc. Strings are compared starting at the leftmost character. Here are some examples:

ant is before bee
and is before ant
an is before and
ANT is before BEE

ant is before INSECT
insect is before INSECT

We can use the relational operators (=, >, <=, etc.) to compare two strings. We can interpret < as meaning 'before' and > as meaning 'after'. Thus we might put:

```
Dim name As String = "John"
Dim name2 As String = "Jean"
If name > name2 Then
...
```

in which the comparison is true.

The String class methods and properties

Here we shall look at the most useful methods of the String class. In order for you to use them, we have provided a framework:

```
Private Sub Button1_Click( _
                ByVal sender As System.Object, _
                ByVal e As System.EventArgs) _
                Handles Button1.Click

    Dim string1 As String
    Dim string2 As String
    Dim resultString As String
    Dim n, m As Integer
    Dim words() As String

    'place example code here:

    'end of example
End Sub
```

and its screenshot is in Figure 16.1. The program provides you with two text boxes (String1Box and String2Box) and a label (ResultLabel) to display any answers. In the following, you can paste example sections into the space indicated by the line:

```
' place example code here:
```

Amending strings

Here we look at methods which change a string. Behind the scenes, these methods create a new string rather than changing the original string.

ToLower

The ToLower method converts any upper-case letters in a string into lower-case letters, as in:

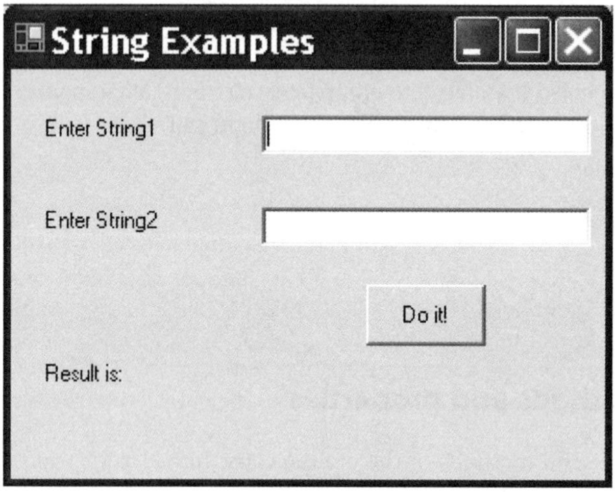

Chapter 16/String manipulation

Figure 16.1 Screenshot of framework for string examples.

```
string1 = "Version 1.1"
resultString = string1.ToLower()
```

which puts `"version 1.1"` in `resultString`. You can experiment with this by using the following lines of code:

```
'code example:
string1 = String1Box.Text
ResultLabel.Text = string1.ToLower()
```

ToUpper

The `ToUpper` method does a similar operation as `ToLower`, but changes any lower-case letters into upper-case equivalents. For example:

```
string1 = "Basic"
resultString = string1.ToUpper()
```

would set `resultString` to `"BASIC"`.

Trim

The `Trim` method removes spaces from both ends of a string. If we put:

```
string1 = "   Center   "
resultString = string1.Trim()
```

then `resultString` becomes `"Center"`. Here is some code to exercise `Trim`:

```
'code example:
string1 = String1Box.Text
ResultLabel.Text = string1.Trim()
```

Insert

This method lets us insert characters into a string at a specified position, as in:

```
string1 = "Visual programming"
resultString = string1.Insert(7, "Basic ")
```

The result is *"Visual Basic programming"*. Here we inserted a string at character number 7 (*"p"*). The characters from *"p"* onwards are shifted right to make room. Here is some code to use:

```
'code example:
MessageBox.Show("Enter the string to insert, and " & _
                "position to put it")
string1 = String1Box.Text
n = CInt(String2Box.Text)
string2 = "A string to insert into ..."
ResultLabel.Text = string2.Insert(n, string1)
```

Remove

This method removes a given number of characters at a given position, as in:

```
string1 = "Deadline"
resultString = string1.Remove(1, 4)
```

The order of arguments is, first, the starting position, followed by the number to remove. The result is *"Dine"*, because 4 characters, starting at position 1 (the character *"e"*) have been removed. Here is some code to use:

```
'code example:
MessageBox.Show("Enter the start position, and " & _
                "the number of characters to remove")
m = CInt(String1Box.Text)
n = CInt(String2Box.Text)
string1 = "An example string to remove from ..."
ResultLabel.Text = string1.Remove(m, n)
```

● Examining strings

These methods and properties allow us to examine a string – for example, to extract a section of it. A section of a string is often called a substring.

Length

The `Length` property provides the number of characters in a string, as in:

```
string1 = "VB Programming"
resultString = CStr(string1.Length)
```

Here, `n` is set to `14`.

Substring

The `Substring` method copies a specified part of a string. We provide the starting position, and the number of characters to be copied. For example:

```
string1 = "position"
resultString = string1.Substring(2, 3)
```

We have selected from `s` (which is at index `2`) for 3 characters, hence the result is `sit`. The value of `string1` is unchanged.

Here is the code for the example program, which displays its input with the first and last characters removed.

```
'code example:
MessageBox.Show("Enter the start position, and " & _
                "the number of characters to copy")
m = CInt(String1Box.Text)
n = CInt(String2Box.Text)
string1 = "An example string to take a substring from"
ResultLabel.Text = string1.Substring(m, n)
```

A common use is to fetch a single character from a string, as in:

```
n = 3
string1 = string2.Substring(n)
```

Varying `n` in a loop allows us to extract each character in turn.

> **SELF-TEST QUESTION**
>
> **16.1** Explain the effect of the following code:
>
> ```
> Dim word As String = "possible"
> Dim s As String = word.Substring(1, word.Length-2)
> ```

IndexOf

This method determines whether a substring is contained within a string. We can also provide an offset, specifying where the search is to start. For example:

```
string1 = "mississippi!"
n = string1.IndexOf("is")
```

sets n to 1, showing the position of the first `is`. (Recall that the first position of a string is numbered 0.)

However, if we put:

```
string1 = "mississippi!"
n = string1.IndexOf("is", 3)
```

then n becomes 4, as the first occurrence is ignored. If the string is not found, −1 is returned.

Here is some code for the example program, which reports on whether a string contains a substring.

```
'code example:
MessageBox.Show("Enter main string, then substring")
string1 = String1Box.Text
string2 = String2Box.Text
If string1.IndexOf(string2) = -1 Then
    ResultLabel.Text = "not found!"
Else
    ResultLabel.Text = "found"
End If
```

IsNumeric

Strictly, `IsNumeric` is a function, not part of the `string` class, but it is useful, and we cover it here for convenience. It returns a Boolean value indicating if its string argument is a valid number. Here is an example:

```
If IsNumeric(TextBox1.Text) = False Then
    MessageBox.Show("Error in number")
Else
    n = CInt(TextBox1.Text)
End If
```

Split

Here we are concerned with breaking a string up into sections. There is a method named `Split` in the `string` class, but it is not as simple to use as the `split` function. Here is an example of the latter:

```
Dim words() As String
string1 = "Guitar, bass , drums"
words = Split(string1, ",")
For n = 0 To UBound(words)
    words(n) = words(n).Trim()
Next
```

Note that we do not use `split` with a 'dot'. It is not a method of the `string` class. It is a function, and in fact existed in previous (non-object-oriented) versions of VB. We supply it with a string to split, and a string containing a separator character. Here, a comma is used as a separator between the three items, but we have made the data more realistic by adding extra spaces. The `split` function returns an array of strings set to the appropriate size (which we don't know in advance of course). In the above example, you will see that the array of strings has been declared without a size, which is unusual, but is allowed. Later, we use it to hold the result from `split`, and at this point we can use the `UBound` function to control a loop which processes each item in turn. Here, the processing involves trimming the extra spaces. Prior to trimming, the array values are:

```
"Guitar"
"   bass "
" drums"
```

After trimming, we have:

```
"Guitar"
"bass"
"drums"
```

LastIndexOf

This method is similar in concept to `IndexOf`, but returns the position of the rightmost occurrence of a substring. The value −1 is returned if no match is found. Here is an example:

```
string1 = "\directory\file"
n = string1.LastIndexOf("\")
```

The value 10 is returned.

StartsWith

This method is used to find out if a string starts with a particular substring. It avoids the added complexity of using the `Length` property. The method returns a Boolean value. For example:

```
string1 = "http://path/page.html"
startsResult = string1.StartsWith("http")
```

would set `startsResult` to true.

Here is some code for the example program, which determines whether a substring is present at the start of another string:

```
'code example:
MessageBox.Show("Enter main string, and string " & _
                " to find at start")
```

```
string1 = String1Box.Text
string2 = String2Box.Text
If string1.StartsWith(string2) Then
    ResultLabel.Text = "Found at start!"
Else
    ResultLabel.Text = "Not found at start"
End If
```

EndsWith

This method is used to find out if a string ends with a particular substring. Yes, you could use a combination of other methods to accomplish this, but the provided method is less error-prone. The method returns a Boolean value. For example:

```
string1 = "http://path/page.html"
endsResult = string1.EndsWith("html")
```

would set `endsResult` to true.

Here is some code for the example program, which determines whether a substring is present at the end of another string:

```
'code example:
MessageBox.Show("Enter main string, and string " & _
                " to find at end")
string1 = String1Box.Text
string2 = String2Box.Text
If string1.EndsWith(string2) Then
    ResultLabel.Text = "Found at end!"
Else
    ResultLabel.Text = "Not found at end"
End If
```

● An example of string processing

Here we will look at the creation of a string processing method which performs a commonly required task – to examine a string, replacing every occurrence of a given substring by another substring (of potentially different length). Note that the `string` class has a `Replace` method, but it can only replace a single character. Closer to home, there is a `Replace` function (not a member of the `string` class) which does what we require. However, it is instructive to look at the programming of such a method. We shall name it `Change` to avoid any conflict with the existing `Replace` function.

Here is an example of changing substrings. If we have the string:

```
"to be or not to be"
```

and we replace every occurrence of *"be"* with *"eat"*, we will create:

```
"to eat or not to eat"
```

The basic process is to use `IndexOf` to determine the position of a substring – *"be"* here. We then form a new string made up of the left part of the string, the right part, and the replacement string in the centre. We have:

```
"to " & "eat" & " or not to be"
```

The process must then be repeated until there are no more occurrences of *"be"*. There are three problem cases:

- The user of `Change` asks us to replace a value of *""*. We could regard any string as being preceded by an infinite number of such empty strings! Our approach here is to simply return the unchanged original string.
- The replacement string contains the string to be replaced. For example, we might try to change *"be"* to *"beat"*. To prevent an infinite number of replacements taking place, we ensure that we only consider substrings in the right-hand part of the string. We use the variable `startSearch` to keep track of the start of the right-hand part of the string.
- The replacement string combined with the original string produces the string to be replaced. For example, when we replace `bc` with `c` in `abbcd`, we get `abcd`. The solution to the previous case also handles this possibility.

The full code is:

```
Private Function Change(ByVal original As String, _
                        ByVal fromText As String, _
                        ByVal toText As String) As String
    Dim leftBit, rightBit As String
    Dim startSearch As Integer = 0
    Dim place As Integer = original.IndexOf(fromText)

    If fromText.Length <> 0 Then
        While place = startSearch
            leftBit = original.Substring(0, place)
            rightBit = original.Substring( _
                place + fromText.Length, _
                original.Length - place - fromText.Length)
            MessageBox.Show(leftBit)
            MessageBox.Show(rightBit)

            original = leftBit & toText & rightBit
            startSearch = leftBit.Length + toText.Length
            place = original.IndexOf(fromText)
        End While
    End If
```

```
        Return original
End Function
```

Here is how we might use our method:

```
Dim original As String = "to be or not to be"
Dim changed As String = Change(original, "be", "eat")
```

Now we will incorporate it into a program.

● Case study – Ask Frasier

In 1970, Joseph Weizenbaum wrote a program known as ELIZA to simulate a particular style of psychiatrist. It was a simple program, in the sense that it made little attempt to understand the sense of the input that users (patients) typed. For example, if the patient entered:

```
I am feeling sad
```

then ELIZA might respond with:

```
you are feeling sad - why?
```

Similarly, if the patient typed:

```
I am feeling VB
```

then ELIZA might respond with:

```
You are feeling VB - why?
```

Here we present an even more simplified version, which we will call Ask Frasier, after the US sitcom character. Basically, we will write a method named `GetReply`, which has a question as its argument, and which returns a reply. The input string comes from a textbox, and the reply is displayed in a label. Figure 16.2 shows a screenshot, and here is the code:

```
Private Sub Button1_Click( _
                ByVal sender As System.Object, _
                ByVal e As System.EventArgs) _
                Handles Button1.Click
    ReplyLabel.Text = getReply(QuestionBox.Text)
End Sub

Private Function getReply(ByVal question As String) _
                                    As String
    Dim randomNumber As Random = New Random()
    Dim variation As Integer
    Dim reply As String
```

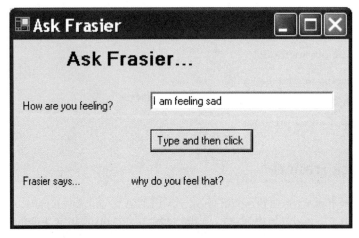

Figure 16.2 Screenshot of the Ask Frasier program.

```
    question = " " & question & " "
    variation = randomNumber.Next(0, 2)
    If variation = 0 Then
        reply = transform(question)
    ElseIf variation = 1 Then
        reply = "why do you feel that?"
    Else
        reply = "Please be frank!"
    End If
    Return reply
End Function

Private Function transform(ByVal question As String) _
                          As String
    Dim tempReply As String
    If question.IndexOf(" I ") >= 0 Then
        tempReply = Change(question, " I ", " you ")
        tempReply = Change(tempReply, " am ", " are ")
        Return Change(tempReply, " my ", " your ") & _
                                          "-why?"
    ElseIf question.IndexOf(" no ") >= 0 Then
        Return "'no'? - that is negative! Please explain."
    Else
        Return "'" & question & "' -Please explain."
    End If
End Function
```

Note that we must paste in the code for our `Change` method.

To make the responses seem more human, we add an element of randomness:

```
variation = randomNumber.Next(0, 2)
If variation = 0 Then
    reply = transform(question)
ElseIf variation = 1 Then
    reply = "why do you feel that?"
Else
    reply = "Please be frank!"
End If
```

The random integer provides three cases. In two of them, we produce a standard reply, but in the other case, we transform the question, by e.g. replacing every " I " with " you ". We add extra spaces at the start and end of the question to assist in detecting whole words. Note that the program has no knowledge of English meanings or grammar. To add this would involve a major programming effort.

Programming principles

- A string contains a sequence of characters.
- Strings can be operated on by methods, and with the relational operators.

Programming pitfalls

- Strings are objects, and the `string` class provides methods and properties. The correct usage for its methods is, for example:

    ```
    n = string1.IndexOf("/")
    ```

    rather than:

    ```
    n = IndexOf(string1)
    ```

- The exceptions to this are `Length`, which is a property and has no brackets, and `Split` and `IsNumeric`, which are functions, not part of the class `string`.

Grammar spot

The `string` class methods require us to provide a string to be operated on, as in:

```
Dim s As String = "demo"
n = s.Length
```

Note that we can supply a literal string, or a method call which returns a string, as in:

```
n = "another demo".Length
n = s.Substring(0, 2).Length ' length of "de"
```

New language elements

The use of "" within quoted strings, to stand for a single quote.

New IDE facilities

No new IDE facilities are introduced in this chapter.

Summary

- Instances of the class `string` contain a sequence of characters. The first character is at position 0.
- `string` instances can be declared and created by e.g.:

    ```
    Dim s As String
    Dim name As String = "Mike"
    ```

- The most useful facilities for string manipulation are:
    the use of relational operators(`>`, etc.) to determine the order of strings.

    ### Amending strings
    ```
    ToUpper
    ToLower
    Trim
    Insert
    Remove
    ```

    ### Examining strings
    ```
    Length
    Substring
    IndexOf
    LastIndexOf
    StartsWith
    EndsWith
    IsNumeric
    Split
    ```

    ### Conversion
    ```
    CStr
    CInt
    CDbl
    ```

EXERCISES

16.1 Write a program which inputs two strings from text boxes, and which joins them together. Show the resulting string and its length in labels.

16.2 Write a program which inputs one string and determines whether or not it is a palindrome. A palindrome reads the same backwards and forwards, so 'abba' is a palindrome. Assume that the string contains no spaces or punctuation.

16.3 Write a program to input a string which can be an `Integer` or a `Double` number in a textbox. Display the type of the number. Assume that a `Double` contains a decimal point.

16.4 Modify the Ask Frasier program to make it more human, by adding more variation to the replies.

16.5 Write a program which allows input of the form:

```
123 + 45
6783 - 5
```

(i.e. two integers with + or - between them, and with spaces separating items) and which displays the result of the calculation.

16.6 Extend Exercise 16.5 so that input of the form:

```
12 + 345 − 44 − 23 − 57 + 2345
```

can be handled. Assume that the user will make no errors.
(Hint: the pattern of such input is an initial number, followed by any number of operator/number pairs. Your program should handle the initial number, then loop to handle the following pairs.)

16.7 Extend Exercise 16.5 so that input can take two forms:

```
setm 2 426
12 + m2
```

The `setm` instruction is followed by two numbers. The first one refers to a memory store numbered from 0 to 9, and the second one is a number which is to be stored in the memory. Calculations can now be done using integers as earlier, and also memory names. (Hint: use an integer array to represent the memory.) Extend your program so that the following forms are processed:

```
m3 = 12 + m5 − 328 − m7
display m3
```

16.8 Write a program which inputs a suggested email address, and reports on whether it should be allowed or not. The address must be of the form:

```
somename@some.address
```

It must not contain spaces or other punctuation. Finally, extend the program so it rejects addresses which have special words in them, such as 'webmaster', 'government', etc. These special words are to be set up in a list box by the user.

ANSWER TO SELF-TEST QUESTION

16.1 We extract everything but the first and last character, so s becomes `"ossibl"`.

Exceptions

This chapter explains:

- what an exception is;
- why exceptions are useful;
- the VB exception facilities.

● Introduction

The term 'exception' is used in VB to convey the idea that something has gone wrong: in common terms, an error has occurred. It is an 'exceptional circumstance'. Note that we mean exceptional in the sense of unusual, rather than wonderful! As you will be aware from your use of computers, there are a variety of circumstances in which software can go wrong, but good-quality software should cope with predictable errors in a satisfactory way. For example, here are some awkward situations involving a typical word-processor, with possible (sometimes unsatisfactory) outcomes:

- The system invites you to type a font size as a number, but you type a name. The system could quit and return you to the operating system, or it could ignore your input and leave the font size as it was, or it could display a helpful message and invite you to try again.
- You attempt to open a file which cannot be found on disk. The responses could be similar to the previous case.
- You attempt to print a file, but your printer is out of paper. Again, this can be predicted, and software can be written to take sensible actions. However, this depends on the printer making its current state available to the software. In actual printers, the software can examine various status bits which indicate out-of-paper, on/offline, paper misfeed, etc.

> **SELF-TEST QUESTION**
>
> 17.1 In the above cases, decide on the best course of action that the word-processor should take.

Let us look at why we need some form of error notification, and how it might be provided.

When we build software and hardware systems, much of it comes as pre-packaged items, e.g. circuit boards, VB classes and methods. To simplify the design process it is essential to regard these items as encapsulated; we don't want to be bothered with how they work internally, but it is vital that the components which we use provide some indication of error situations. The software can then be written to detect such notification and to take alternative action. But what action to take? This is the difficult bit!

Complex systems consist of a hierarchy of methods (i.e. methods call other methods and so on.) Some exceptions can be handled locally in the method in which they occur, but some more serious cases may need to be passed upstairs to higher-level methods. It depends on the nature of the error. In short, there are different categories of error, which may need to be handled in different places.

Here is an analogy which illustrates this. Imagine an organization. The managing director starts things happening by giving his managers instructions. In turn, they might instruct programmers and technicians. But things can go wrong. Here are two cases:

- A printer runs out of paper. Normally, the technician handles it. In the rare case that the organization is out of paper, a manager might need to be informed.
- A technician trips over a cable and breaks a leg. Exceptions in this category (which might result in legal action etc.) should be handled by the managing director.

The analogy is that each person doing a job is a method. The job was initiated by someone superior to them. When errors occur, there really needs to be a plan in place saying who handles a particular type of error. The exception facilities of VB allow us to set this up.

Returning now to software. As we said, things go wrong. But do we need a special facility for errors? Surely our `If` statement will do? We could imagine code of this form:

```
If something wrong Then
    handle the problem
Else
    handle the normal situation
End If
```

Here we have used a mixture of English and VB to convey the main point. However, if we have a series of method calls, any of which could go wrong, the logic becomes complex, and can swamp out the normal case. The initially simple sequence of:

```
MethodA()
MethodB()
MethodC()
```

would become

```
MethodA()
If MethodA went wrong Then
    handle the MethodA problem
Else
    MethodB()
    If MethodB went wrong Then
        handle the MethodB problem
    Else
        MethodC()
        If MethodC went wrong Then
            handle the MethodC problem
        End If
    End If
End If
```

The error cases (which we hope won't happen very often) dominate the logic, and this complexity can make programmers shy away from taking them on. In fact, we will see that the VB exception facilities allow us to stick to the coding for the normal case, and to handle exceptions in a separate area of the program.

> **SELF-TEST QUESTION**
>
> **17.2** How could a method return a value which stated whether it worked or not? What if the method returned a value as part of its normal task (i.e. it was a function)?

● The jargon of exceptions

Exceptions are created by being *thrown*, and are detected elsewhere by being *caught*. VB has `Throw`, `Try` and `Catch` keywords to carry out these tasks. Initially, we will look at the simplest case of catching an exception thrown by a library class.

● A `Try-Catch` example

Here we present a simple program which lets the user enter a `Double` number representing the side of a square into a text box. The area of the square is then displayed, or an error message, as in:

A Try-Catch example

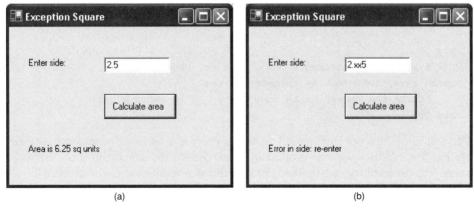

Figure 17.1 The Exception Square program: (a) correct data; (b) incorrect data detected.

```
Area is: 6.25
```

or

```
Error in side: re-enter
```

We shall look at the new features introduced in this particular program, then move on to general cases. Figures 17.1(a) and (b) show a run with correct input and a run involving an exception. Here is the code:

```
Private Sub Button1_Click(ByVal sender As System.Object, _
                ByVal e As System.EventArgs) _
                Handles Button1.Click
    Dim side As Double
    Try
        side = Double.Parse(TextBox1.Text)
        Label1.Text = "Area is " & CStr(side * side) _
                        & " sq units"
    Catch exceptionObject As FormatException
        Label1.Text = "Error in side: re-enter"
    End Try
End Sub
```

As a relatively minor point, note that in earlier chapters we made use of `CInt` and `CDbl` to convert a string of characters into a number, but here we have adopted a more object-oriented approach. In fact, `CDbl` is not a method of a class: behind the scenes, it makes use of a shared method in the `Double` class, called `Parse`. If we consult the documentation on the method, we find that an exception of the class `FormatException` is thrown by `Parse` if we supply a string argument containing characters that cannot be converted. (Incidentally, `Integer.Parse` is used to convert strings to integers).

However, the main feature of the example is the introduction of a new statement, which is basically a control structure. It takes the form:

```
Try
    a series of statements . . . (the try block)
Catch exceptionObject As FormatException
    handle the exception in some way . . . (a catch block)
End Try
```

The concept is that we instruct VB to try to execute a block of statements (the `Try` block). If it executes without producing an exception, the statements after the word `Catch` (the `Catch` block) are ignored, and execution continues after the `End Try`.

However, if an exception is produced due to some error in the `Try` block, the `Try` block stops executing, and we can specify that the `Catch` block executes by stating the class of exception that we wish to catch. In our example, we consulted the library documentation for `Double.Parse`, and found that an exception of class `FormatException` will be produced, i.e. thrown. If another kind of exception occurs, our catch will not be executed, and VB will attempt to find a catch elsewhere in our program which specifies this exception type. We will describe this process in more detail below.

Let us look at the catch block in more detail. In our example, we have:

```
Catch exceptionObject As FormatException
    Label1.Text = "Error in side: re-enter"
```

The line containing `Catch` is rather like the declaration of a method with one argument. We chose to name the argument `exceptionObject`. When the `FormatException` is thrown, VB sees that this particular catch can accept an argument of type `FormatException`. VB deposits an object of type `FormatException` in `exceptionObject`. We don't make use of this object in our example, but it can be used to find out more about the exception.

After the `Catch` block executes, execution continues beneath the `Catch` block. In many cases, because methods deal with one particular task which cannot sensibly continue after an exception related to that task, it is common to return from the method, as in:

```
Private Sub Method1()
    Try
        some code
    Catch exceptionObject As SomeExceptionClass
        handle it
    End Try
End Sub
```

In our example program, this is just what is required: the exception handler displays an error message and ends. The user can then enter a new number into the text box.

```
System.FormatException: The input string was not in a correct format.
   at System.Number.ParseDouble(String s, NumberStyles style,
NumberFormatInfo info)
   at System.Double. Parse(String s, NumberStyles style,
NumberFormatInfo info)
   at System.Double.Parse(String s)
   at ExceptionInserts.Form1.Button5_Click(Object sender,
     EventArgs e) in C:\mike\homePearVB\vbProjects\Exception Square\
     Exception Square.vb:line 139
```

Figure 17.2 Sample result from `ToString` with an `Exception` object.

Using the exception object

When we catch an exception, we already know that something has gone wrong, but additional information comes with the exception object. We can use the `Message` property and the `ToString` method, as in:

```
Catch exceptionObject As FormatException
    MessageBox.Show(exceptionObject.Message)
    MessageBox.Show(exceptionObject.ToString())
```

- The `Message` property provides a short string containing a descriptive error message. In this example, the message string is:

    ```
    The input string is not in a correct format.
    ```

- The `ToString` method returns a string containing several lines. The first line is the message as above, and the other lines in the string are a *stack trace*. It starts in the method where the exception occurs, then works backwards through the methods that were called leading up to the exception. It terminates when a matching `Catch` is found. Many of these lines will be related to methods within the VB system and libraries, but among them you will find information relating to your code. The key item is the line number within your program. It is here that the exception directly originated, or indirectly originated by calling a method which produced an exception. It is here where you should begin to study your code to find the reason for the exception. Figure 17.2 shows the output from `ToString`, with line `139` as the source of the error.

Classifying exceptions

Here we will explore the varieties of exception classes that are provided in the VB library. Basically, the library provides us with a list of exception class names, but if there

```
Exception
    SystemException
        ArithmeticException
            DivideByZeroException
            OverFlowException
        CoreException
            IndexOutOfRangeException
        FormatException
        NullReferenceException
    IOException
        EndOfStreamException
        FileNotFoundException
```

Figure 17.3 A selection of exception classes.

is no suitably named exception we can also create our own. We will not cover the process of inventing new exceptions, trusting that you will be able to find a suitably named existing one.

Inheritance is used to classify errors into different types. There are a large number of pre-defined exception classes, and Figure 17.3 shows a small selection of particularly useful ones.

Here is how to interpret the figure. All exceptions inherit from the `Exception` class – one such class is the `IOException` class, which itself is further subclassed, in the sense that `EndOfStreamException` and `FileNotFoundException` also inherit from `IOException`. As the indentation of the names increases, the exceptions become more specific. The reason for this classification system is that we can choose to catch a single exception type (such as `EndOfStreamException`) or a whole set of exceptions (such as `IOException`).

> **SELF-TEST QUESTION**
>
> **17.3** From Figure 17.3, what is the relationship between the `FormatException` class and the `IOException` class?

In Figure 17.3 we showed some common exceptions (and we will use some of these when we examine files, in Chapter 18). But there are many more exception classes. Moreover, merely knowing the names of the exceptions is not the whole story: we need to consider the source of an exception. For each method you use, refer to its documentation. This tells you what it does, what arguments it needs, any exceptions that it might throw, and what classes they belong to.

> **SELF-TEST QUESTION**
>
> 17.4 What would be the consequences for the programmer if exceptions were not classified – i.e. the exception structure was just a list of names?

● Multiple `Catch` blocks

Our squaring example only used one `Catch` block. However, it is possible to use several `Catch` blocks with one `Try`. If you do, the rule is that the more specific catch must come first, followed by the more general cases. In the following, we divide 100 by a number entered in a text box. We decided to catch the divide-by-zero exception, then catch any format exceptions, then any remaining system exceptions. The three `Catch` blocks must be in the order as shown.

```
Private Sub Button3_Click(ByVal sender As System.Object, _
                ByVal e As System.EventArgs) _
                Handles Button3.Click
    Dim bottom As Integer
    Dim top As Integer = 100
    Try
        bottom = Integer.Parse(TextBox1.Text)
        MessageBox.Show( _
            "Dividing into 100 gives " & CStr(top \ bottom))
    Catch exceptionObject As DivideByZeroException
        MessageBox.Show("Error - zero:re-enter data")
    Catch exceptionObject As FormatException
        MessageBox.Show("Error in number: re-enter")
    Catch exceptionObject As SystemException
        MessageBox.Show(exceptionObject.ToString())
    End Try
End Sub
```

Note that if we reversed the order of the last two catches, then a `FormatException` could never be singled out, because it would be encompassed by the `SystemException` class.

● The search for a catcher

So far, our examples have shown exceptions being produced and handled in the button-click method. But we might choose to handle the exception elsewhere. Here is a re-coding of our example:

```vb
Private Sub Button4_Click(ByVal sender As System.Object, _
                    ByVal e As System.EventArgs) _
                    Handles Button4.Click
    MessageBox.Show( _
        "This program squares the number in the Text Box . . .")
    Try
        DoCalc()
    Catch exceptionObject As FormatException
        MessageBox.Show("Error: please re-enter")
    End Try
End Sub

Private Sub DoCalc()
    Dim number As Double
    number = Double.Parse(TextBox1.Text)
    MessageBox.Show("val is" & CStr(number * number))
End Sub
```

The mechanism that is operating is as follows. When an exception happens, VB searches in the current method (`DoCalc` here) for a `Catch` block that matches exactly, or that matches a superclass of the exception. If the currently executing method does not provide one, VB abandons its execution, and looks in the method which called the method producing the exception (here, this is the button-click event method). In our example, it finds an appropriate catch here, and executes it. If a matching catch was not found, then the process repeats, looking in the caller of the button-click method. Here we are in the realms of VB system code, but the process is the same. Eventually, the top-most level of code is reached, and the program terminates, displaying a message box. Often this is undesirable – the point of exceptions is to keep the program running when possible.

Note that we do not need to group all our `Catch` blocks together in one method. The following code shows one exception being caught in `DoCalc`, and any others being caught in the button-click method.

```vb
Private Sub Button1_Click( _
                    ByVal sender As System.Object, _
                    ByVal e As System.EventArgs) _
                    Handles Button1.Click
    MessageBox.Show( _
      "This program squares the number in the Text Box . . .")
    Try
        DoCalc()
    Catch exceptionObject As Exception
        MessageBox.Show("Exception thrown from DoCalc()")
    End Try
End Sub
```

```
Private Sub DoCalc()
    Dim number As Double
    Try
        number = Double.Parse(TextBox1.Text)
        MessageBox.Show("Square is" & CStr(number * number))
    Catch exceptionObject As FormatException
        MessageBox.Show("Incorrect number: re-enter")
    End Try
End Sub
```

Here is a more general description of the mechanism. Assume that in a particular run of a program, `Method1` calls `Method2`, which in its turn calls `Method3`. (We do need to state that this is a particular run of a program, because the pattern of execution of methods might depend on data that the user enters.) Anyway, this run produces an exception in `Method3`. The process is:

- The execution of `Method3` is abandoned.
- If there is a matching `Catch` block in `Method3`, it is used and, eventually, execution of the method resumes after the `End Try`. Bear in mind that a `Catch` block matches if it specifies the particular exception, or a superclass of the exception.
  If, on the other hand, `Method3` does not have a matching `Catch` block, VB looks 'upward', in the method which called `Method3` (`Method2` here). If a matching `Catch` block is found, it is executed, and execution continues beneath the `End Try`.
- If `Method2` does not contain a matching catch, then its calling method (`Method1`) is examined. This process of looking backwards through the calls is termed 'propagating' the exception. If no catcher is found, the program eventually terminates, displaying details of the exception.

● Throwing – an introduction

Here we will code a method which throws an exception. The task of the method is to convert a string containing either *"ten"*, *"hundred"* or *"thousand"* to its equivalent integer. To make this method useful in a range of situations, we will throw an exception. This allows the caller of the method to decide on the action to take. We will opt to throw an instance of the `FormatException` class. Here is the code:

```
Private Sub Button6_Click(ByVal sender As System.Object, _
                ByVal e As System.EventArgs) _
                Handles Button6.Click
    MessageBox.Show(CStr(WordToNumber("hXndred")))
End Sub

Private Function WordToNumber(ByVal word As String) _
                    As Integer
    Dim result As Integer = 0
```

```
        If word = "ten" Then
            result = 10
        ElseIf word = "hundred" Then
            result = 100
        ElseIf word = "thousand" Then
            result = 1000
        Else
            Throw New FormatException _
                            ("Wrong input: WordToNumber")
        End If
        Return result
    End Function
```

The `Throw` statement is often executed as the result of an `If`: it creates a new instance of the specified exception class, and initiates a search for a matching catch. When creating a new exception, it is possible to provide an alternative message string, which the catcher can obtain by using the `Message` property.

● Handling – some possibilities

Approaches to handling depend on the nature of the exceptions and on the nature of the program they occur in. We will look at two exceptions:

- the `FormatException`;
- the `IndexOutOfRangeException`.

We made use of `FormatException` in our squaring program and adopted the handling approach of displaying an error message, asking the user to try again. This is possible (and sensible) here because the data comes directly from the user, who is interacting with the program. However, if the reason for the error was incorrect data in a database (perhaps a list of exam marks) we might not wish to offer the user a chance to try again. Instead, we might display a message suggesting that the user contacts the creator of the database, and then terminate the program.

Let us look at possibilities for `IndexOutOfRangeException`. It might come from code such as:

```
Dim a(9) As Integer
Dim n As Integer
For n = 0 To 10
    a(n) = 25
Next
```

This is different. Catching it is fine, but then what? The problem was not caused by user input. The `For` produces a loop from `0` to `10` inclusive, and thus attempts to access `a(10)`: we should have made the loop run from `0` to `9`. This is a programming mistake, which should really have been found at the testing stage. It needs fixing by debugging and re-compiling.

So, is it worth catching `IndexOutOfRangeException` and also `ArithmeticException` cases, which could originate from the misuse of commonplace facilities such as arrays and division? One approach is to ignore them. The search for a catcher will fail, and a message will appear on the screen. The program needs debugging and further testing should be performed.

Finally

The full `Try` statement has an additional facility, namely `Finally`. Here is an example in a mixture of English and VB. Assume that the task falls into two parts: the main task, followed by some termination code that must be performed whether or not an exception happens in the main calculation. Without `Finally`, we would code this as:

```
Try
    main task
    termination code
Catch exceptionObject As FormatException
    display an error message
    termination code
End Try
```

The use of `Finally` helps us to avoid duplicating the termination code, which we require to be performed in every situation, as in:

```
Try
    main task
Catch exceptionObject As FormatException
    display an error message
Finally
    termination code
End Try
```

Code that is placed in the `Finally` section will always be performed, whether or not an exception occurs. The `Finally` code will even be performed if our `Catch` does not match the exception, or if the `Try` block executes a `Return` or throws an exception itself.

Programming principles

- When writing general-purpose methods (where their future use might be unknown) you should throw exceptions, rather than terminating the program or concealing a possible error.

- An exception changes the order in which statements are obeyed, hence it is a form of control structure. But exceptions should not be used for normal cases. For example, if the user is entering a series of names, and will type `"END"` at the end of the list, then this is not an error. It should be handled by a `While` or `If`, rather than treating it as an exception.

Programming pitfalls

- Allowing an exception to be thrown from a method, when it can sensibly be handled locally.
- Attempting to catch and process exceptions such as `ArithmeticException` and `IndexOutOfRangeException`. In most cases, there is little that can be done. Catching such errors can conceal them, when instead the programmer needs to know about them.

Grammar spot

- The basic try-catch structure is:

```
Try
     a series of statements
Catch exceptionObject As SomeExceptionClass
     handle the exception
End Try
```

- A `Finally` section can precede the `End Try`.
- An exception can be thrown by:

```
Throw New SomeExceptionClass("error message")
```

New language elements

- `Try` and `End Try`
- `Catch`
- `Finally`
- `Throw`
- the exception hierarchy.

New IDE facilities

There are no new IDE facilities in this chapter.

Summary

- An exception is an unusual situation.
- Exceptions are instances of classes, created by `New`.
- `Try` blocks are used to surround code which could throw an exception.
- A `Catch` block can pick up one exception type or a class containing several exceptions.
- The inheritance tree of the class `Exception` (Figure 17.2) shows you the main exceptions you will have to deal with and which class they are in.
- Exceptions within the `SystemException` class are difficult to fix up, and in many cases can be intentionally ignored.

EXERCISES

17.1 Write a program which provides two textboxes for the input of integer values `a` and `b`. Display the result of `a\b` and `b\a`. (Recall that `\` performs integer division.) Incorporate exception handling for zero and non-numeric input text box values.

17.2 Write a method which solves quadratic equations. Normally, there are two real roots. The method call should take the form:

```
Solve(a, b, c, root1, root2)
```

where the roots are passed back through reference parameters. The formulae to calculate the roots are:

```
root1 = (-b+Math.Sqrt(b*b-4*a*c))/(2*a)
root2 = (b-Math.Sqrt(b*b-4*a*c))/(2*a)
```

In the case when the discriminant `b*b-4*a*c` is negative, throw an `ArithmeticException` with a suitable message. Write a calling method which catches your exception.

17.3 If you know the length of the three sides of a triangle, the area can be calculated by:

```
area = Math.Sqrt(s * (s - a) * (s - b) * (s - c))
```

where

```
s = (a+b+c)/2
```

Write a method for calculating and returning the area. Make it throw a suitable exception (with a message) message when the three lengths cannot form a triangle. Write a calling method which catches your exception.

17.4 Write a program which inputs three strings from three text boxes, representing day number, month number and year. For example, the strings "23", "5", "2007" represent the 23rd of May 2007. Produce a suitable error message if an item is non-numeric, missing completely or specifies an impossible date. Ignore leap years.

17.5 Write a program which calculates compound interest. The user inputs the initial amount (`i`), the interest rate per year (`r`) as a percentage value (a `Double`), and the number of years to run (`n`). Display the final amount (`f`). Provide full error-checking on input data. Here is the formula:

$$f = \left[1 + \frac{r}{100} \right]^n$$

ANSWERS TO SELF-TEST QUESTIONS

17.1 In the first two cases, quitting the program would be a poor course of action. A more useful response is to display some sort of error indication, and allow the user either to have another go or to abandon the selection of the item. In the third case, the complication is that the printer may run out of paper part-way through a print. The user needs to be informed of this, and may be provided with options to abandon the print request or, assuming that paper has been loaded, continue printing from a particular page.

17.2 If the method was not a function, it would be possible to use `Return` to pass back a `Boolean` value. The method would now be called like a function, as in:

```
Dim error As Boolean
error = DoTask()
```

However, if a value is already being returned, a reference parameter would have to be used, as in:

```
Dim error As Boolean
biggestValue = Bigger(44, 55, error)
If error = True Then
    ... etc.
```

Either approach is inconvenient.

17.3 `FormatException` inherits from `SystemException` (which in its turn inherits from `Exception`). `IOException` inherits from `Exception`. There is no relationship between the two classes apart from the fact that they inherit from `Exception`, as do all the exception classes.

17.4 Catching an exception which had never been inherited from would be as before. But consider the case of catching every exception. We would need a huge list of catches.

Files

This chapter explains:

- what a text file is;
- how to read and write data to files;
- how to manipulate folder paths and names.

● Introduction

You have already made use of files, in the sense of having used the IDE to create files containing VB programs, and having used Windows to view a hierarchical structure of folders (directories). In this chapter, we will look at the nature of the information you may choose to store in files, and how you can write programs to manipulate files.

Initially, let us clarify the difference between RAM (random-access memory) and file storage devices (e.g. disks, hard disk drives and CD-ROMs). Storage capacity is measured in bytes in all these cases. There are several major differences between RAM and file storage:

- RAM is used to store programs as they execute. They are copied from a file storage device immediately before execution.
- The time to access an item in RAM is much faster.
- The cost of RAM is higher (megabyte for megabyte).
- Data in RAM is temporary: it is erased when power is switched off. File storage devices can hold data permanently.

The capacity of file storage devices is higher. CD-ROMs have a capacity of around 740 Mbyte (megabytes) and DVD (Digital Versatile Disks) have a capacity of 4.7 Gbyte (gigabyte, 1024 Mbyte). Both CD-ROM and DVD have writable versions. Typical hard drives can hold around 300 Gbyte, and USB memory sticks can hold around 2 Gbyte. However, technology is evolving rapidly – the race is to create cheap fast, small storage devices that modern computer software requires, especially in the area of high-quality moving images and sound.

● The essentials of streams

Streams let us access a file as a sequence of items. The term 'stream' is used, in the sense of a stream of data flowing in or out of the program. Let us introduce the jargon, which is similar in most programming languages. If we wish to process the data in an existing file, we must:

1. Open the file.
2. Read (input) the data item-by-item into variables.
3. Close the file when we have finished with it.

To transfer some data from variables into a file, we must:

1. Open the file.
2. Output (write) our items in the required sequence.
3. Close the file when we have finished with it.

Note that, when reading from a file, all we can do is read the next item in the file. If for example, we only needed to examine the last item in a file, we would have to code a loop to read each preceding item in turn, until the required item is reached. For many tasks, it is convenient to visualize a text file as a series of lines, each made up of a number of characters. Each line is terminated by an end-of-line marker, consisting of either the line-feed character, or the carriage-return character, or both of these. Your response to this might be to say 'I just hit Enter at the end of a line!'. Behind the scenes, Windows software will put a line-feed character and a carriage-return character at the end of each line. Most of this intricacy is hidden by VB.

As well as files containing lines of text, VB can also manipulate files containing binary data, such as images. However, such data is usually arranged in a more complicated format within files.

We shall make use of the VB classes that allow us to access a file line-by-line, as text strings. This is particularly useful, because many applications (such as word-processors, text editors and spreadsheets) can read and write such files.

● The `StreamReader` and `StreamWriter` classes

To read and write lines of text, we will use:

- The `ReadLine` method of `StreamReader`. This reads a whole line of text into a string, excluding the end-of-line marker. (If we need to split the line into separate parts, we can use the `Split` function described in Chapter 16.)

- The `StreamWriter` class. This has two main methods: `Write` and `WriteLine`. They both write a string to a file, but `WriteLine` adds the end-of-line marker after the string. We can also use `WriteLine` with no string argument, where an end-of-line marker is written to the file.
- The `OpenText` and `CreateText` methods of the `File` class. These are shared methods, and provide us with a new instance of a text stream. A selection of other methods and properties of the `File` class is covered later in this chapter.

The file classes are in the `System.IO` namespace. This is not automatically imported, so we must put:

```
Imports System.IO
```

at the very top of all our file-processing programs.

File output

The File Output program opens a file and writes three lines to it. The user interface only consists of a single button, so is not shown. Here is the code:

```
Private Sub Button1_Click( _
                ByVal sender As System.Object, _
                ByVal e As System.EventArgs) _
                Handles Button1.Click
    ' write some lines of text to the file
    Dim outputStream As StreamWriter = _
                File.CreateText("c:\myfile.txt")
    outputStream.WriteLine("This file will")
    outputStream.WriteLine("contain 3")
    outputStream.WriteLine("lines of text.")
    outputStream.Close()
End Sub
```

First we create and open the file:

```
Dim outputStream As StreamWriter = _
                File.CreatText("c:\myfile.txt")
```

Here, we make use of the shared method `CreateText` from the `File` class. This creates a new `StreamReader` object for us, and opens the file. Note that there are two items which refer to the file:

- There is a string which specifies the file name that the operating system uses when it displays folders: `"c:\myfile.txt"`. Alter this path if you wish to create the file in a different place. If you omit the folder name and just use `myfile.txt`, then the file will be created in a folder named `bin`, which is a sub-folder of your current VB project.

- There is a variable which we chose to name as `outputStream`. It is an instance of the class `StreamWriter`, which provides us with the `WriteLine` method. The use of `CreateText` associates `outputStream` with the file `"c:\myfile.txt"`.

To actually write a line of text to the file, we use `WriteLine`, as in:

```
outputStream.WriteLine("This file will")
```

If the data we wish to place in the file is typed in by the user – perhaps in a text box – we would put:

```
outputStream.WriteLine(TextBox1.Text)
```

If the file existed already, its original contents will be erased, and replaced by the three lines.

Finally, we close the file:

```
outputStream.Close()
```

This ensures that any data in transit is actually placed in the file, and also allows the file to be reopened for reading or writing.

In summary, our file output process was:

- to open the file `"c:\myfile.txt"`;
- to output (write) some strings to the file;
- to close the file.

> **SELF-TEST QUESTION**
>
> **18.1** Explain what the following code does:
>
> ```
>         Dim lines, stars As Integer
>         Dim fileName As String = "c:\pattern.txt"
>         Dim streamOut As StreamWriter = _
>             File.CreateText(fileName)
>         For lines = 1 To 10
>             For stars = 1 To lines
>                 streamOut.Write("*")
>             Next
>             streamOut.WriteLine()
>         Next
>         streamOut.Close()
> ```

● File input

Here we examine the program named File Input, which opens a file, inputs its contents and displays it in a text box. The program makes use of `NewLine` when placing a string

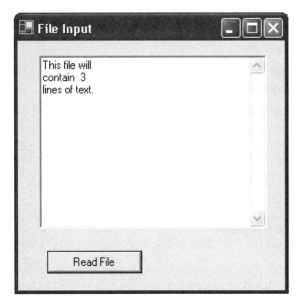

Figure 18.1 Screenshot of the File Input program.

in the text box. This requires an additional import, so the first two lines of the program are:

```
Imports System.IO
Imports Microsoft.VisualBasic.ControlChars
```

The screenshot (taken after the button was clicked) is given in Figure 18.1. Here is the code:

```
Private Sub Button1_Click( _
                ByVal sender As System.Object, _
                ByVal e As System.EventArgs) _
                Handles Button1.Click
    'read the file line-by-line
    Dim inputStream As StreamReader = _
                File.OpenText("c:\myfile.txt")
    Dim line As String
    line = inputStream.ReadLine()
    While line <> Nothing
        TextBox1.AppendText(line & NewLine)
        line = inputStream.ReadLine()
    End While
    inputStream.Close()
End Sub
```

The code is contained in the method `Button1_Click`. The file we choose to input is the one that was created by the previous File Output program, containing three lines of text.

First, we create a stream to access the file:

```
Dim inputStream As StreamReader = _
                File.OpenText("c:\myfile.txt")
```

(If the file we specify cannot be found, an exception will be produced. For now, we ignore this possibility, but discuss it later in this chapter.)

Then we use `ReadLine` to input the series of lines in the file, appending each one to our text box. There is one crucial point here: we don't know how many lines are in the file, so we set up a loop which terminates when there is nothing more to read:

```
line = inputStream.ReadLine()
While line <> Nothing
    TextBox1.AppendText(line & NewLine)
    line = inputStream.ReadLine()
End While
```

When `ReadLine` runs out of lines to read, it returns `Nothing`, and this is assigned to `line`. `Nothing` is a keyword in VB, indicating that the object does not exist.

Note that we have used `ReadLine` twice. The first `ReadLine` prior to the loop is needed so that the first time `While` tests `line`, it has a value.

Each line is placed at the end of any existing text already in the text box, by using `Append`. Because `ReadLine` does not provide us with the end-of-line characters, we need to use `NewLine`. If we omitted this, the text box would contain one long line, with no breaks.

Reading a file line-by-line allows us to process each line individually (as we do in the File Search program below). Alternatively, it might be more appropriate to read the whole file into one long string, complete with end-of-line markers. In this case, VB provides us with a method named `ReadToEnd`, which we use for the text editor program shown later.

In summary, the program:

1. opens a file;
2. inputs lines from the file and appends them to the text box, as long as the end of the file is not reached;
3. closes the file.

> **SELF-TEST QUESTIONS**
>
> **18.2** The following code is meant to display the length of each line in a file. Explain any problems.
>
> ```
> Dim fileName As String = "c:\tempvb7.txt"
> Dim stream As StreamReader = File.OpenText(fileName)
> Dim line As String
> ```

```
        line = stream.ReadLine()
        While line <> Nothing
            line = stream.ReadLine()
            TextBox1.AppendText("length: " & line.Length & ",")
        End While
        stream.Close()
```

18.3 Explain any problems in this code:

```
        Dim fileName As String = "c:\tempvb7.txt"
        Dim stream As StreamReader = File.OpenText(fileName)
        Dim line As String
        line = stream.ReadLine()
        While line <> Nothing
            TextBox1.AppendText(line)
        End While
        stream.Close()
```

File searching

Searching a file for an item that meets some specified criteria is a classic task. Here we will construct a program which searches a file of exam marks, which takes the form:

```
J.Doe, 43, 67
D.Bell, 87, 99
M.Parr, 54, 32
J.Hendrix, 67, 43
etc...
```

We might create this file by writing and running a VB program, or with a text editor. Each line is split into three areas, separated by commas. However, we will allow for extra spaces. In data processing, such areas are known as fields. The program will allow us to enter a filename, and to enter a student name, which we assume is unique. If the names are not unique, we would have to introduce an extra field to hold a unique identification number for each person. The program will search the file, and display the marks for our chosen student. The code we need to add to our previous file input example is a `While` which terminates when the end of the file is encountered or when the required name is found. We will use the `Split` function to separate the three fields.

Because there are two ways that the loop can terminate, we introduce an additional variable, `found`, to indicate whether the item was found or not. Note that we expect that the item will sometimes not be found – it is not regarded as an error, and we code this with `If` rather than using exceptions.

The informal English structure of the search is:

Figure 18.2 Screenshot of File Search program.

```
found = False
While (more lines to read) And found = False
    read line
    split line into three fields
    If first field matches name Then
          found = True
          display rest of fields in labels
    End If
End While
If Not found
    display a warning
End If
```

We have provided a search button, which causes the file to be opened and searched. The user can select any file for searching. Figure 18.2 shows the screenshot, and here is the code.

```
Private Sub Button1_Click( _
              ByVal sender As System.Object, _
              ByVal e As System.EventArgs) _
              Handles Button1.Click
    Dim line As String
    Dim words(3) As String
    Dim found As Boolean = False
    Dim inputStream As StreamReader
```

```
        'clear any previous results
        Result1Box.Text = ""
        Result2Box.Text = ""

        If FileNameBox.Text = "" Then
            MessageBox.Show("Error: missing file name!")
        ElseIf StudentNameBox.Text = "" Then
            MessageBox.Show("Error: missing student name!")
        Else
            inputStream = File.OpenText(FileNameBox.Text)
            line = inputStream.ReadLine()
            While (line <> Nothing) And found = False
                words = Split(line, ",")
                If Trim(words(0)) = StudentNameBox.Text Then
                    Result1Box.Text = Trim(words(1))
                    Result2Box.Text = Trim(words(2))
                    found = True
                Else
                    line = inputStream.ReadLine()
                End If
            End While
            If Not found Then
                MessageBox.Show(StudentNameBox.Text & " not found")
            End If
            inputStream.Close()
        End If
End Sub
```

> **SELF-TEST QUESTIONS**
>
> **18.4** Amend the search program so that the searching is done in a case-insensitive way (i.e. so that john matches john, John and JOHN).
>
> **18.5** Explain the problem that would arise if we re-coded our search loop with or, as in:
>
> ```
> While (line <> Nothing) Or found = False
> ```

Files and exceptions

File input–output is a major source of exceptions. For example, the file name supplied by the user might be incorrect, the disk might be full, or the user might remove a CD-ROM while reading is in progress. We can minimize the effects of incorrectly entered file names by using file dialogs (covered later), which let the user browse folders and click on file names, rather than typing the names into text boxes. But exceptions will still occur. In Chapter 17 we covered exceptions, and here we examine exceptions as they relate to files.

A number of exceptions can be thrown when we access files. Here is a selection:

- The `File.OpenText` method can throw a number of exceptions. We shall single out `FileNotFoundException` in particular.
- The `ReadLine` method of class `StreamReader` and the `WriteLine` method of class `StreamWriter` can throw an `IOException`, along with other classes of exceptions.

Here is another version of the search program, with exception-handling:

```
Private Sub Button2_Click( _
               ByVal sender As System.Object, _
               ByVal e As System.EventArgs) _
               Handles Button2.Click
    'search the file - with exception-handling
    Dim line As String
    Dim words(3) As String
    Dim found As Boolean = False
    Dim inputStream As StreamReader

    'clear any previous results
    Result1Box.Text = ""
    Result2Box.Text = ""

    If FileNameBox.Text = "" Then
        MessageBox.Show("Error: missing file name!")
    ElseIf StudentNameBox.Text = "" Then
        MessageBox.Show("Error: missing student name!")
    Else
        Try
            inputStream = File.OpenText(FileNameBox.Text)
            line = inputStream.ReadLine()
            While (line <> Nothing) And found = False
                words = Split(line, ",")
                If Trim(words(0)) = StudentNameBox.Text Then
                    Result1Box.Text = Trim(words(1))
                    Result2Box.Text = Trim(words(2))
                    found = True
                Else
                    line = inputStream.ReadLine()
                End If
            End While
            If Not found Then
                MessageBox.Show(StudentNameBox.Text _
                        & " not found")
            End If
```

```
            inputStream.Close()
        Catch problem As FileNotFoundException
            MessageBox.Show("Error - file not found: " _
                        & FileNameBox.Text _
                        & ". Re-enter name.")

        Catch problem As Exception
            MessageBox.Show("Error concerning file: " _
                        & FileNameBox.Text _
                        & ". " & problem.message())
        End Try
    End If
End Sub
```

We have singled out `FileNotFoundException` as the most likely exception, and have produced a specific error message. Other exceptions might occur, but they cannot be neatly classified – so we choose to catch them all in one place, by referring to the class `Exception`.

Message boxes and dialogs

Sometimes we need to bring the user's attention to a vital decision or piece of information. Merely displaying some text in a label is not enough. VB provides a range of overloaded message box methods to provide configured dialogs. In addition, there are specific dialogs to request file names from the user, which we review later. Here are the message box methods:

```
MessageBox.Show(message)
MessageBox.Show(message, title)
MessageBox.Show(message, title, buttons)
MessageBox.Show(message, title, buttons, icon)
```

The arguments are as follows:

- the message is positioned in the centre of the message box;
- the title argument goes at the top of the message box;
- the buttons argument is a constant, specifying any buttons we need. For example we might require yes/no buttons;
- the icon argument specifies a symbol, such as a large exclamation mark or question mark.

The `Show` method also returns a code which we can examine to find out which button was clicked. There is a set of `DialogResult` constants which we can use for comparison. Figures 18.3 and 18.4 show some examples, which show a warning message and a question.

316 ● Chapter 18/Files

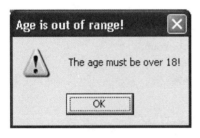

Figure 18.3 Warning with a message box.   **Figure 18.4** Question with a message box.

Here is the code. Note the style of calling the function method within an `If`, which accomplishes the dual role of displaying the message box and testing the result. When you run the code, you will see that the user cannot return to the form which displayed the message. First, the message box must be closed one way or another. The message box is described as *modal*.

```
'warning
MessageBox.Show("The age must be over 18!", _
                "Age is out of range!", _
                MessageBoxButtons.OK, _
                MessageBoxIcon.Exclamation)

'question
If MessageBox.Show("Do you want to buy this?", _
                "CD Purchase", _
                MessageBoxButtons.YesNo, _
                MessageBoxIcon.Question) _
    = DialogResult.Yes Then
    MessageBox.Show("user clicked Yes")
Else
    MessageBox.Show("user clicked No")
End If
```

> **SELF-TEST QUESTION**
>
> **18.6** Write code to display a message box which asks the question
>
> Is Paris the capital of France?
>
> Display suitable responses to the user's replies.

● Using file dialogs

When a user needs to open a file using a word-processor or editor, they will make use of a file dialog window, which allows them to browse directories and to click on a

Using file dialogs ● 317

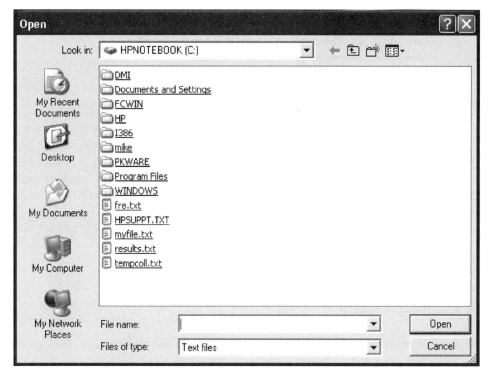

Figure 18.5 An `OpenFileDialog` in action.

selected file. Often, an application makes this available via a drop-down file menu at the top left of a window.

In VB, we are provided with the `OpenFileDialog` and `SaveFileDialog` classes. Figure 18.5 shows the appearance of an open dialog. The steps to follow when programming the file dialogs are:

- We select the dialog from the **Dialogs** section of the toolbox, and place it on the form. It moves to the component tray, because it does not reside on the form. The first dialog we create will be named `OpenFileDialog1`.
- We set its properties as required – at design-time if we know them. One of the most useful properties is its `InitialDirectory`, which is a string containing a directory path.
- We display the dialog using its `ShowDialog` method, which also returns a result to the program. The result indicates how the user closed the dialog, e.g. by clicking the **Open** or the **Cancel** button. The `DialogResult` class contains a list of conveniently named constants we can use.
- We make use of the `FileName` property, which provides us with a string containing the name of the selected file.

Here is some VB code which creates an `OpenFileDialog`:

```
If SaveFileDialog1.ShowDialog() = DialogResult.OK Then
    MessageBox.Show(OpenFileDialog1.FileName)
End If
```

We set its `InitialDirectory` property to the `c:\` directory.

We then use `ShowDialog` in an `If` statement. This compares the number returned from `ShowDialog` to the constant `DialogResult.OK`. (Using constants provided by VB is less error-prone than using the numbers themselves.) In this context, 'OK' means that the 'Open' button was clicked. If the user closed the dialog by shutting it down or by cancelling, we take no action. The process of using a `SaveFileDialog` is virtually identical. The following text editor program shows the dialogs incorporated with a menu containing 'Save', 'Open', and 'Save As' options.

When you have understood the operation of file dialogs, it is recommended that you use them rather than using a text box for file name input. They are slightly more difficult to program, but are much more resistant to file name errors.

● Creating a menu

Many applications provide a vast range of facilities, with the consequence that allocating a button to initiate each facility is impractical: too much valuable screen space would be consumed. The menu is one solution to the space problem. It occupies very little space, and its options only become visible when the menu is clicked.

In VB, we can create a menu at the top of a form by selecting **MenuStrip** from the **Menus & Toolbars** section of the toolbox and placing it on a form. (VB then opens the **component** tray, and places the menu there). Initially we are asked if the menu is to be a **MenuItem**, a **ComboBox**, or a **TextBox**. Choose **MenuItem**. Once this is done, some 'Type Here' prompts appear, as in Figure 18.6. These allow us to set the text that appears on the menus.

- We can create a new menu item by typing underneath the existing menu, or
- We can create a heading for a new list of menu items by typing at the right of the existing menu name.

We have created a menu named 'File', and have added the items 'Open . . .', 'Save', 'Save As . . .' and 'Exit'. There is a Windows convention of using a file menu at the left of the form, and of using '. . .' to indicate that further choices will appear. When a menu item has been created, we can change its name at design-time by clicking on it with the right mouse button, and selecting its name via the properties window. Here is the code for a program named Text Editor, and the screenshot is shown in Figure 18.7.

We renamed the menu items to `OpenMenu`, `SaveMenu`, `SaveAsMenu` and `ExitMenu`. VB creates event-handling methods based on these names.

Creating a menu ● 319

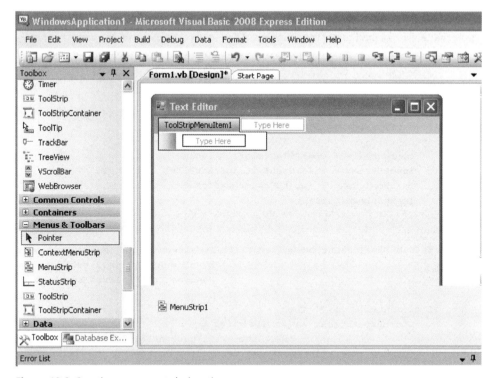

Figure 18.6 Creating a menu at design-time.

Figure 18.7 Screenshot of the Text Editor program.

```vb
        Private currentFile As String = "" 'instance variable
        Private Sub OpenToolStripMenuItem_Click(ByVal sender As System.Object, _
                                        ByVal e As System.EventArgs) _
                                        Handles OpenToolStripMenuItem. _
                                        Click
            Dim inputStream As StreamReader
            OpenFileDialog1.InitialDirectory = "c:\"
            If OpenFileDialog1.ShowDialog() = _
                                DialogResult.OK Then
                currentFile = OpenFileDialog1.FileName
                inputStream = File.OpenText(currentFile)
                TextBox1.Text = inputStream.ReadToEnd()
                inputStream.Close()
            End If
        End Sub
        Private Sub SaveToolStripMenuItem_Click(ByVal sender As System.Object, _
                                        ByVal e As System.EventArgs) _
                                        Handles SaveToolStripMenuItem. _
                                        Click
            If currentFile <> "" Then
                Dim outputStream As StreamWriter = _
                            File.CreateText(currentFile)
                outputStream.Write(TextBox1.Text)
                outputStream.Close()
            End If
        End Sub
        Private Sub SaveAsToolStripMenuItem_Click(ByVal sender As System.Object, _
                                        ByVal e As System.EventArgs) _
                                        Handles SaveAsToolStripMenuItem. _
                                        Click
            Dim outputStream As StreamWriter
            SaveFileDialog1.InitialDirectory = "c:\"
            If SaveFileDialog1.ShowDialog() = _
                DialogResult.OK Then
                currentFile = SaveFileDialog1.FileName
                outputStream = File.CreateText(currentFile)
                outputStream.Write(TextBox1.Text)
                outputStream.Close()
            End If
        End Sub
        Private Sub ExitToolStripMenuItem_Click(ByVal sender As System.Object, _
                                        ByVal e As System.EventArgs) _
                                        Handles ExitToolStripMenuItem. _
                                        Click
            End 'quit immediately
        End Sub
```

The menu usage is quite straightforward, in the sense that VB provides the event method headers; all we need to do is add a text box and some file access. Here are some points on the program.

- Most of the form area is usable by the text box, as can be seen from its screenshot.
- The properties of the text box have been set to provide both horizontal and vertical scroll bars. The multiline property is also set to true.
- When the user requests the opening of a file, we set the file dialog to start at the c:\ folder.
- To actually read the file, we make use of the `ReadToEnd` method of the `StreamReader` class. This reads all of the file (from the current position) into one string, which will contain end-of-line markers as well as the visible text. We can store this complete string in the text box by:

  ```
  TextBox1.Text = inputStream.ReadToEnd()
  ```

- In a similar manner, we can write the whole of the text box to a file with one instruction:

  ```
  outputStream.Write(TextBox1.Text)
  ```

- The variable `currentFile` is declared outside the methods as an instance variable, because several methods make use of it.
- For consistency with other Windows applications, we have provided an exit on our menu. The VB statement `End` causes the program to terminate immediately.

The text editor program shows the power of VB's components and programming environment:

- Creating the menu was simply a matter of entering the options and amending their names.
- The file dialogs provide familiar file access.
- The multiline text box allows text to be edited. The right mouse button also provides access to the clipboard for cut-and-paste facilities.

> **SELF-TEST QUESTION**
>
> **18.7** In the Text Editor program, saving the file results in the previous version being overwritten. This is how most editors and word-processors work. Modify its behaviour by providing a dialog which asks the user if the user really wants to do a save.

The `Directory` class

This class provides facilities to manipulate complete files and directories (folders). It is not concerned with accessing the data within files. You can make use of the `Directory`

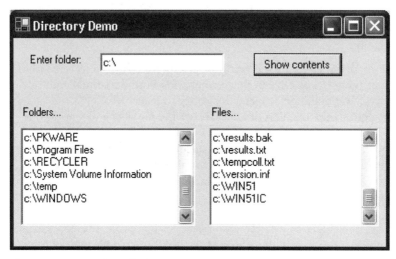

Figure 18.8 Screenshot of Directory Demo program.

class without making use of stream I/O, in the sense that you might wish to manipulate file names rather than the contents of the files. Figure 18.8 shows the screenshot of a program which displays directories and files within a selected directory, and we examine its code below.

First, some terminology. As you know, operating systems provide a hierarchical structure, with a path to a file of the form:

```
c:\data\exams.txt
```

This is a Windows-style path, with \ used as a separator. The terminology is that:

- the whole item is a path;
- the extension is `txt`;
- the directory path is `c:\data`;
- the file name in the path is `exams.txt`;
- if a program refers to a file without providing a directory (e.g. simply `exams.txt`), then the file is assumed to be in the same directory as the program is stored in and executed from.

Now we will provide details of some selected methods of the `Directory` class. They are shared: they provide useful methods for operating on strings that contain file paths.

`GetFiles`

This method operates on a string containing a directory path. It returns an array of strings containing all the file names within the specified directory. The following program (Directory Demo) shows it in action.

Sometimes we might need to check on the type of a file before opening it. Here is an example which checks if a file name ends in .txt. In Windows, capitals can also be used, so we convert the file name to upper-case before testing it. The EndsWith string method is convenient:

```
Dim fileName As String = "c:\tests\demo.txt"
If fileName.ToUpper().EndsWith(".TXT") Then
    MessageBox.Show("a text file")
End If
```

GetDirectories

This method operates on a string containing a directory name. It returns an array of strings containing the names of all the directories within the specified directory.

```
Dim dirs() As String = Directory.GetDirectories("c:\")
```

The following program shows it in action. Note that this method does not work through a directory tree to the very bottom. It only goes one level deep. Repeated calls of GetFiles are needed to progress deeper.

Here is a program, named Directory Demo, with its screenshot in Figure 18.8. The user can enter a directory name, and the program displays the name of every file and every directory in the chosen directory.

```
Private Sub Button1_Click(ByVal sender As System.Object _
            , ByVal e As System.EventArgs) _
            Handles Button1.Click

    Dim files() As String = _
                Directory.GetFiles(FileNameBox.Text)
    Dim count As Integer
    For count = 0 To UBound(files)
        FilesBox.AppendText(files(count) & NewLine)
    Next
    'display all directory names
    Dim dirs() As String = _
                Directory.GetDirectories(FileNameBox.Text)
    For count = 0 To UBound(dirs)
        FolderBox.AppendText(dirs(count) & NewLine)
    Next
End Sub
```

Once we have filled our arrays, we can use the UBound function to control a loop which looks at each element in turn.

Programming principles

- Programs use streams to read and write data to files.
- We use files to preserve data after the run of the program, or for passing data to other programs.

Programming pitfalls

- Forgetting to put any required importing details at the very top of the code. We used:

    ```
    Imports System.IO
    Imports Microsoft.VisualBasic.ControlChars
    ```

    The latter provides us with `NewLine` for use in text boxes.

Grammar spot

- We declare and create file streams by, e.g.:

    ```
    Dim inputStream As StreamReader = _
                File.OpenText("c:\myfile.txt")
    Dim outputStream As StreamWriter = _
                File.CreateText("c:\myfile.txt")
    ```

- We can read a file line-by-line with:

    ```
    Dim line As String
    line = inputStream.ReadLine()
    While line <> Nothing
        ' process the line . . .
        line = inputStream.ReadLine()
    End While
    ```

    or we can read the whole file at once with the `ReadToEnd` method.
- We close streams by, e.g.:

    ```
    outStream.Close();
    ```

New language elements

We have introduced these classes:

- `File`
- `Directory`

- `StreamReader` and `StreamWriter`
- `FileNotFoundException`
- `SaveFileDialog` and `OpenFileDialog`

New IDE facilities

- We can place a main menu on a form, and handle menu item clicks via a method that VB generates.
- We can place file dialogs onto a form. (They move to the component tray.) We can manipulate their properties at design-time and run-time.

Summary

- Files are opened, then written to (or read from), and finally closed.
- The `Directory` class allows you to access the contents of a directory. Its methods allow you to access the names of its sub-directories and its files.

EXERCISES

18.1 Write a program which puts your name and address in a file named `address.txt`. Use an editor to check that the file has the expected contents.

18.2 Write a program to count the number of lines in a file. Ensure that it works for an empty file (producing a value of zero).

18.3 Write a program which examines each line of a file to see if it contains a particular string. Append each of those lines to a multiline text box, preceded by the file name. Use another text box to hold the string to search for.

18.4 Write a program which reads two files line-by-line, and compares them for equality. It should display a message stating that the files are either equal or not equal. Obtain the file names by displaying two file dialogs.

18.5 Write a program which replaces one string with another in each line of a file, writing the new version to another file. Use two text boxes for the 'from' and 'to' strings. You could use the `Change` method created in Chapter 16.

18.6 This question involves writing two programs, which assist in extracting parts of files and inserting the parts into other files. For example, you might use them to insert code examples in an essay, or to insert standard headings at the start of a file.

- Write a program which reads a file line-by-line, copying those lines between special markers to an output file. Here is an example of an input file:

```
            Though most blues guitar players
            are right-handed, (or left-handed
            players who re-strung their guitars,
            such as Jimi Hendrix), two left-handed
            players have made their mark:
            EXTRACTTO:king.txt
            Albert King, whose style involves
            long bent notes, played slowly.
            ENDEXTRACT
            EXTRACTTO:rush.txt
            Otis Rush, who is a highly-rated
            songwriter and singer.
            ENDEXTRACT
            However, such an approach restricts
            the player to simple chord fingerings.
```

The lines between the first extract are to be copied to the file `king.txt`, and the second extract is to be copied to `rush.txt`.

- Write a program which copies one file line-by-line to another file. Any 'insert' instructions cause the specified file to be inserted in the input file. Here is an example:

```
            List Of Players:
            INSERTFROM:king.txt
            INSERTFROM:rush.txt
```

Assume that the files are as above, with no errors in the use of the special insert/extract lines.

18.7 Write a program which calculates the total number of lines stored in all the text files in a specified folder.

18.8 Write a program which examines each `txt` file in a selected folder for lines containing a particular string. Any such lines are to be appended to a multiline text box, preceded by their file name. Use a text box to allow the user to enter the string to find.

18.9 Write a program which appends the first 10 lines of every `.txt` file in a selected folder to a multiline text box, preceded by the file's name. If the file contains less than 10 lines, every line is to be displayed.

ANSWERS TO SELF-TEST QUESTIONS

18.1 It creates a file containing the following text:

```
      *
      **
      ***
        etc
```

If we omitted to use `WriteLine`, all the stars would appear on one long line.

18.2 When `Nothing` is returned at the end of the file, its length is displayed, resulting in a value of zero. We need to reverse the order of the two statements within the loop, so that the use of `ReadLine` is immediately followed by going up to the start of the loop and the test for end-of-file.

18.3 The program loops forever (or at least until the text box becomes full), because there is no `ReadLine` in the middle of the loop.

18.4 We can convert each item to e.g. upper case, as in:

```
If Trim(words(0)).ToUpper() = studentName.Text.ToUpper() Then
    etc.
```

18.5 A `While` loop repeats until the complete condition becomes false. Assume that we have two conditions that are initially true, with an `Or` between them. One condition becoming false does not make the whole condition false, because the other condition is still true.

On the other hand, if we connect the two conditions with `And`, one condition changing to false makes the overall condition false. It is correct to use `And` in our search. In our incorrect `Or` example, if the data is not found, there is no way out of the loop, because both conditions can never become false. The program loops forever.

18.6 We provide a question-mark icon and yes/no buttons, as in:

```
If MessageBox.Show("Is Paris the capital of France?", _
                  "Quiz", _
                  MessageBoxButtons.YesNo, _
                  MessageBoxIcon.Question) _
        = DialogResult.Yes Then
    MessageBox.Show("Yes - correct!")
Else
    MessageBox.Show("Sorry... wrong.")
End If
```

18.7 We add this code to the save menu event:

```
If MessageBox.Show("Do you really want to save?", _
                  "Text Editor", _
                  MessageBoxButtons.YesNo, _
                  MessageBoxIcon.Question) _
        = DialogResult.Yes Then
    MessageBox.Show("user clicked Yes")
    'code to save the text box in the file...
End If
```

Console programs

This chapter explains:

- how to create a console application;
- console input–output;
- The processing of command-line arguments;
- running programs from the command prompt;
- scripting with batch files.

Introduction

The user interface has changed enormously in power (and complexity) since the early days of computers. In the 1960s, a common device for interaction was the teletype (or operator's console) which was basically an electrical typewriter with a roll of paper for displaying text. All you could do was to type a line of text, which the program could interpret as a command or as data.

It might seem strange in this time of mice, high-resolution screens and voice input, that a style of interaction involving lines of text can be useful, but this is the case! Some types of program do not have a major interactive element. Here are some examples:

- A program which calculates the amount of free space on a disk drive. All the user needs to do is state the drive. Such a program might also be run automatically, perhaps when files are deleted.
- A program which prints a list of company employees. This list does not change very often. All we need to do is run the program.
- A program which is one part of a larger task, running without human intervention.

Such an approach is called 'scripting' or 'batch' programming. For example, when you boot up an operating system, a script (a file containing instructions which execute programs) is run.

A first console program

We shall create a small program which asks you for your name, then displays it. The steps to create a project are almost identical to creating a GUI program, except that we select 'Console Application' for the project type. Name the project `Hello`. The IDE will then display the following code:

```
Module Module1
    Sub Main()
    End Sub
End Module
```

We then modify the program so that it looks like:

```
Module Module1
    Sub Main()
        Dim name As String
        Console.WriteLine("Please enter your name:")
        name = Console.ReadLine()
        Console.WriteLine("Hi there " & name)
        Dim wait As String = Console.ReadLine()
    End Sub

End Module
```

Finally, use **Save As**, choosing the name `Hello.vb`. Run the program, and enter your name. Note the result, then press the **Enter** key to end the program. Figure 19.1 shows a screenshot of the program. Here is an explanation of the program.

- The program is contained within a *module*, which is similar in nature to a class, but without any inheritance possibilities.
- When the program is executed, the method named `Main` is called automatically. It starts things off.
- The `Console` class is imported automatically, and provides similar methods to those we used to access files. We have:
  - `WriteLine`, which writes a string to the screen, followed by an end-of-line. `Write` is similar, but does not add the end-of-line.
  - `ReadLine` inputs a complete line of text from the keyboard, as a string. The end-of-line marker is not stored in the string.
- When console applications terminate, their window closes automatically. As you will see, this is what we require in many cases, but for our first program it

```
┌ C:\mike\vbbook\vb1proj\Hello\bin\Hello.exe                              _ □ x ┐
│ Please enter your name:                                                       │
│ Bill                                                                          │
│ Hi there Bill                                                                 │
│                                                                               │
```

Figure 19.1 Running the Hello console application.

is inconvenient, because we can't see the output. To prevent the window closing, we have inserted an extra line:

```
Dim wait As String = Console.ReadLine()
```

We placed this immediately above the **End Sub**. Its effect is to wait for the user to enter another line of text – we can simply enter a blank line by pressing the enter key. You might use this line in the early stages of creating and debugging a console application, then remove it in the finished version.

- This particular project was named Hello, and we named the VB file after it. The project name need not match the VB file name, but it was suitable in this case. The IDE will create the executable version in the file:

    ```
    \Hello\bin\Debug\Hello.exe
    ```

    i.e. within the **bin\Debug** directory of our project. The name **bin** is short for 'binary'.
    The name of the executable file **Hello.exe** was derived from the name of the VB file.

● The command prompt: cd and dir

You are familiar with clicking on folder icons to navigate through folders, but when running console applications, it is sometimes necessary to use keyboard commands for the same tasks. Instructions are entered at the *command prompt*, which can be accessed in several ways:

- On Windows, use Windows Explorer to browse to the required folder. Right-click on the folder and select **Open Command Window Here**.
- On some earlier Windows systems, you might have to go via the **Start** menu, working through: **Start | All Programs | Accessories | Command Prompt**.

(Though details vary slightly depending on your version of Windows. Sometimes you do not need to look as far as the **Accessories** menu. On some versions of Windows, it might be described as MS-DOS.)

When you run the command prompt, a black window appears where you can type commands. To navigate through directories, we use the `dir` (directory) and the `cd` (change directory) commands. They have lots of options, but we will present the minimum you need. Note that these commands use the older terminology of 'directory' rather than 'folder'. They mean the same thing.

The `dir` command

When you run the command prompt, a line is shown, of the form:

```
C:\TEMP>
```

This shows that you are on the `c:` drive, in the directory `TEMP`. Typing `dir` shows us the names of all the directories and files in the current directory, as in Figure 19.2. Directories are indicated by `DIR` in angle brackets. To restrict the list to directories only, type:

```
dir /ad
```

The command is followed by a space, and capitals or lower-case letters can be used. This command is useful to remind you about directory names as you navigate.

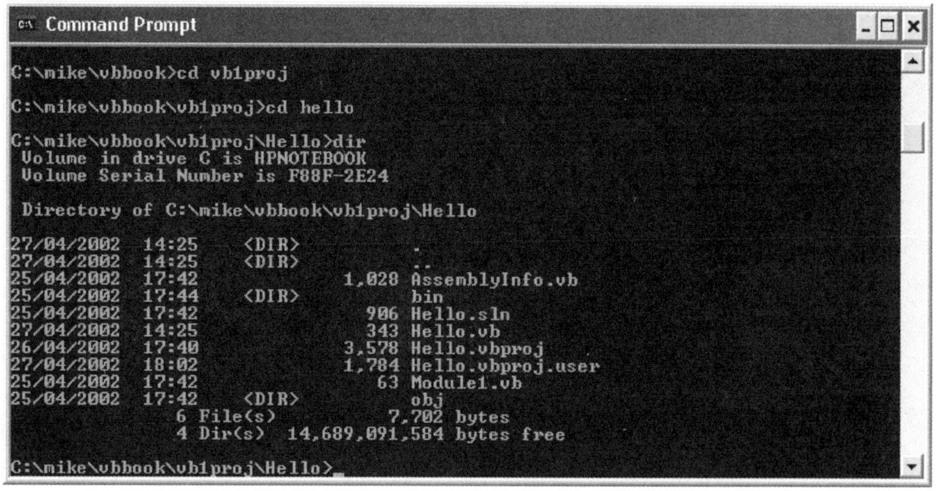

Figure 19.2 Using the `dir` command.

The `cd` command

This command is used to move between directories. Here are some examples. Note that `..` is used to stand for the directory above the current one.

```
cd mydir            change to the mydir sub-directory
cd ..               move up a level
cd ..\data          move up, then into the data directory
```

Note that the prompt changes. Use this to check that your command worked properly. Finally, to move to another drive, we type its letter, in the form:

```
d:                  move to the d: drive
```

> **SELF-TEST QUESTION**
>
> **19.1** Find out how to run the command prompt window on your computer. Experiment with the `dir` and `cd` commands. Navigate to a VB project directory, and find the `exe` file within the `bin\Debug` directory.

Ways of running programs

There are a number of ways to initiate the running of VB programs under Windows. Here are some of them:

- You can run a program from the IDE. This is used when creating and debugging programs.
- You can run a program by double-clicking on its name in Windows Explorer. For example, the above `Hello` program was saved as `Hello.vb`, and it can also be run by looking in the `bin\Debug` folder of its project folder and double-clicking on `Hello.exe`. Remember that its window will close automatically.
- You can run a program by typing its name at the command prompt. For example, to run our `Hello` program, we open the command prompt window in the project's `bin\Debug` directory, and then enter the name of the `exe` file, as in:

    ```
    Hello.exe
    ```

    Figure 19.3 shows the command prompt window, after the program has been run. Note that the window does not close, and we could type another command.

    If you want to run the program while you are in another directory, you can enter the full path to the `exe` file. For example, if your project directory was stored at the top level of the `c:` drive, you would type:

    ```
    c:\Hello\bin\Debug\Hello.exe
    ```

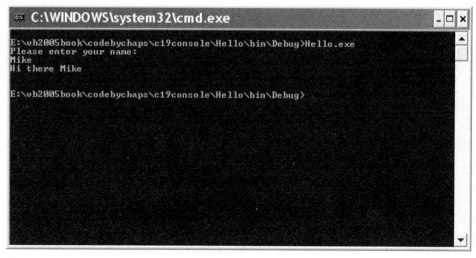

Figure 19.3 Running Hello from the command prompt.

- You can also run a program in a 'batch' manner. Here is an example, which you can run by following these steps:

  - Use a text editor, such as **NotePad** in the **Accessories** folder, to create a file named `hi.bat`, and put these two lines of text in it:

    ```
    Hello.exe
    Hello.exe
    ```

    Save the file in the `bin\Debug` directory of your project.
  - Run the `bat` file by double-clicking on `hi.bat` in Windows Explorer. Observe that your name is requested twice.

  As you have just seen, a batch file contains instructions to run a series of programs. Here we chose to run the same program twice. We shall discuss this approach in more detail later.

Classes in console applications

For small programs, you might choose to use a few methods, as in:

```
Module Module1

    Sub Main()
        MethodA()
    End Sub
```

```
        Private Sub MethodA()
            ...code for method
        End Sub

End Module
```

For larger programs, you might wish to incorporate library classes. This can be done by placing the appropriate `Imports` at the top of the file.

You might also wish to create new classes. As with GUI programs, you can put the classes in separate files, or in the same file.

● Command-line arguments

When we run console applications, we often need to supply starting details for items such as file names to use. The program could use `ReadLine` to input such items – and this is a good approach in some cases. However, later we will see programs which operate without user interaction but which still need some form of initialization. This is where command-line arguments come into use.

Here is an example: we will write a program called **Pick** which searches through a specified file, picking out and displaying every line containing a specified string. Here is the code:

```
Imports System.IO
Module Module1

    Sub Main(ByVal args() As String)
        Dim line As String
        Dim fileName As String = args(0)
        Dim wanted As String = args(1)
        Dim inputStream As StreamReader = _
                      File.OpenText(fileName)

        line = inputStream.ReadLine()
        While line <> Nothing
            If line.IndexOf(wanted) >= 0 Then
                Console.WriteLine(line)
            End If
            line = inputStream.ReadLine()
        End While
        inputStream.Close()
    End Sub

End Module
```

The program reads each line in turn from a specified file (as we explained in Chapter 18), and uses the `IndexOf` method from the `string` class to see if the required string exists anywhere within the line. If this is the case, we display the line on the screen.

Note that the program needs to get values for the strings `fileName` and `wanted`. Eventually we will use these in the conventional way via the command prompt window, but for debugging and testing, the IDE allows us to set up these values. Here is how:

1. In the IDE, create a Console Application project named **Pick**, and enter the above VB code. Save the code in the file `Pick.vb`.
2. Now we will set up the command-line arguments. From the menus, choose **Project | Properties . . .** , then click on **Debug**.
3. In the **Command line arguments** area, enter the following:

   ```
   demo.txt "lines"
   ```

   then click **OK**. The strings for the arguments are separated by a space or spaces. You can use quotes around an argument if you wish, and this is essential if an argument itself contains spaces. Incidentally, if the file to be examined is stored elsewhere, you can use its full path when you specify the program arguments.
4. Create a file to work with, called `demo.txt`, containing these lines:

   ```
   These lines are
   a test of the Pick program.
   It finds and displays lines
   containing a specified sub-string.
   ```

   To follow this example exactly, ensure that the file is stored in the `bin\Debug` directory within the **Pick** project directory.

When you run the program, its output will appear in a black window, and the window will close. To see the output, place the following line just above the `End Sub`, as we did in the Hello program:

```
Dim wait As String = Console.ReadLine()
```

Run the program again. You will see two lines shown below, each of which contains the string `lines`:

```
These lines are
It finds and displays lines
```

Press the 'enter' key to end the program.

When we run a console application, our `Sub Main` method is called by the run-time system. We do not call it ourselves. Any command-line arguments that we provide are passed into the method as an array of strings, which we chose to name as `args`. Before being placed in this array, some processing is done for us:

- The arguments are split up. A space or spaces separates one from another.
- Any spaces within quotes are not treated as a separator. For example, in our Pick program, we may have file paths containing spaces, or we may wish to find a string containing spaces. In these cases, we must set up the arguments with

quotes surrounding them. The quotes are removed from the argument before it is passed to `Sub Main`.
- The first argument is placed in position 0 of our array, not in position 1.

We can make use of the `UBound` function to find out how many arguments the user supplied and reject any errors.

> **SELF-TEST QUESTIONS**
>
> **19.2** Amend the **Pick** program so that it checks the number of supplied arguments. If there are not two arguments, the program should display an error message and terminate.
>
> **19.3** Modify the **Pick** program so that lower-case and upper-case versions of the required string are found.

Scripting and output redirection

Here we will examine some of the facilities that Windows systems offer for scripting, and actually do some scripting with our **Pick** program. Scripting covers a variety of techniques. Here we will regard a script as a file containing instructions for running a series of programs. They are known as batch files, and have the `.bat` extension. Their use promotes a 'building brick' approach, where we create new software by connecting existing software together, rather than coding from scratch.

Output redirection lets us control the destination of output text from a program. Recall our previous programs. We used `Console.WriteLine` to send text to the screen. However, sometimes we wish to place the results in a file. Here is an example: we need to place the output from **Pick** into a file, so we can use it elsewhere. This can be done by opening a command prompt window, then using the `cd` command to move into the `bin\Debug` directory of the **Pick** project. Type the following:

```
Pick.exe demo.txt "lines" > results.txt
```

The use of > causes the text that would have appeared on the screen to be redirected to the file `results.txt` in the `bin\Debug` directory. If this file existed already, it is overwritten. If it did not exist, it is created.

We chose to put spaces around the > for ease of reading, though this is not essential.

Another matter of preference is the use of capitals. The command-line software is based on MS-DOS, an early Microsoft operating system. When you type file names and paths, these get converted to upper-case internally, so the same effect is obtained from either of these lines:

```
PICK.EXE DEMO.TXT "lines"
Pick.exe demo.txt "lines"
pick.exe demo.txt "lines"
```

Here is another example: we wish to find every line containing the word `Dim` in a VB program. Moreover, we wish to add these lines to the existing `results.txt` file from above. We type:

```
Pick.exe SomeProg.vb "Dim" >> results.txt
```

The `>>` symbol means 'append', and its action is very much like `>`, except that text is placed at the end of an existing file, rather than replacing the file.

Input redirection is also possible, using `<`, but this requires a different technique for reading the data into the program. In our examples, we will always read from files rather than use input redirection.

The benefit of output redirection is that changing the destination of the data is simple: we don't need to rewrite the program, or click through a file dialog. The program becomes more flexible.

> **SELF-TEST QUESTIONS**
>
> **19.4** If we opened a command prompt window, moved into the `bin` directory of the `Hello` project, and typed:
>
> ```
> Hello.exe > temp.txt
> ```
>
> what would we expect to see on the screen and in the file `temp.txt`?
>
> **19.5** Here are two cases where we use **Pick**. The first use is with `>`:
>
> ```
> Pick.exe testfile.txt "Visual Basic" > out.txt
> Pick.exe testfile.txt "Visual Basic" > out.txt
> ```
>
> The second is with `>>`:
>
> ```
> Pick.exe testfile.txt "Visual Basic" >> out.txt
> Pick.exe testfile.txt "Visual Basic" >> out.txt
> ```
>
> How does the use of `>` or `>>` affect the contents of the file `out.txt`?

Scripting and batch files

Before the days of personal computers, punched cards were used. The programmer had to prepare a 'batch' of cards containing the program, and instructions on how to run the program. This concept of a sequence of instructions has its modern equivalent in the `bat` file. We can prepare a file containing instructions to run a number of programs; each program runs without user interaction.

Here is an example: as part of the documentation for a large VB program (here named `Big.vb`), we wish to create a file containing the header of every `Sub` and `Function` method. This requires **Pick** to be used twice. We can do this by:

1. Creating a file named (for example) `getsubs.bat` within the `bin\Debug` directory of the **Pick** project, containing:

```
Pick.exe Big.vb "Sub" > subs.txt
Pick.exe Big.vb "Function" >> subs.txt
```

2. Executing the file `getsubs.bat`. This can be done in several ways, as we saw earlier. We could double-click on its name in Windows Explorer, or type its name at the command prompt. In either case, this would initiate the execution of the instructions within the file.

The first use of **Pick** puts all the lines containing `Sub` into the file `subs.txt`, and the second use appends any lines containing the string `Function` to the end of the same file. The instructions to run **Pick** are obeyed in top-to-bottom order, working down the batch file.

> **SELF-TEST QUESTION**
>
> 19.6 Assume that we are given a large VB program, and we wish to find every line which contains an `If` referring to a variable `sum`. For example, we want lines such as:
>
> ```
> If sum = 0 Then
> If a = sum Then
> ```
>
> Prepare a batch file, which uses **Pick** to perform the task. Hint: use a temporary file named, for example, `temp.txt`.

Programming principles

- Not all programs warrant a GUI.
- I/O redirection can make programs more flexible.
- A batch file solution can prevent the need to write new software.

Programming pitfalls

- Forgetting to put a call to `ReadLine` when you wish to observe output on the screen.
- Accessing command-line arguments from position `1` in the string array. In fact, the items begin at position `0`.

Grammar spot

There is no new VB grammar in this chapter.

New language elements

- The `Console` class, and the methods `ReadLine`, `WriteLine`, `Write`.
- The `Module` for console applications.

New IDE facilities

- There is an option to create a console application.
- Command-line arguments can be set within the IDE, for debugging and testing.

Summary

- Console applications can display lines of text on the screen, and can read lines of text that the user types.
- They can access command-line arguments.
- They can be run in a variety of ways.
- Their output can be redirected to a file with > and >>.
- Batch files can contain instructions to execute programs.

EXERCISES

19.1 Write a console application which asks the user to enter an integer. The doubled value should be calculated and displayed. (Assume the user will not make any input errors.)

19.2 Write a console application which inputs a series of exam marks (one at a time) from the user. The program should display the sum of all the marks. The marks are all zero or above, and a negative number is used to end the sequence of marks. (Use a `While` loop.)

19.3 Write a console application which displays the first line of a file. The file name should be specified as a command-line argument. Check that the correct result appears on the screen, then run it with output redirection to place the output in a file.

19.4 Write a console application which counts the number of lines in a file, and displays the result.

19.5 It has been suggested that the complexity of a program can be measured by counting the number of decisions and loops it has. Ideally, we wish to avoid creating programs that are unduly complex. With the aid of our **Pick** program and your solution from Exercise 19.4, create a batch file which adds up the number of If, While, For and Select statements in a VB file, and displays this single number. (Do not write any new VB code.)

19.6 Write a console application which reads a file line-by-line and displays it on the screen. However, lines containing a particular sub-string are not to be displayed. The program has two command-line arguments: the file name, and the sub-string. The latter can be enclosed in quotes if it contains spaces. Use this program to provide a 'collapsed' version of a VB program by omitting every line containing eight spaces. (This will cause the inner nested code to be ignored, but the outer lines such as Imports, Class and Private to be displayed.)

19.7 Write a console application which replaces one string with another throughout a file. The program has three arguments: the file name, the string to be replaced, and the string to replace it with. Read the whole file at once into a string, and make use of the Change method used in Chapter 16. Redirect the output to a new file.

19.8 Write a program named Multirep, which does multiple string replacements in a file. The arguments for the program are the input file name and the name of a file containing pairs of lines specifying from/to replacements. Here is an example. We wish to replace every Mr with Mrs and every him with her in the file data.txt. We run the program by typing:

```
Multirep data.txt changes.txt > out.txt
```

The file changes.txt contains:

```
Mr
Mrs
him
her
```

If you know another programming language, investigate the use of Multirep in converting a VB program into that language.

ANSWERS TO SELF-TEST QUESTIONS

19.1 A small amount of practice is needed. Remember to look at the prompt to see the current directory, and type dir to check on the exact spelling of directory names.

19.2 We add an If to the code, and also ensure that we don't access any arguments before we have checked that they exist, as in:

```
        Dim line As String
        Dim fileName As String
        Dim wanted As String
        If UBound(args) = 1 Then
            fileName = args(0)
            wanted = args(1)
            Dim inputStream As StreamReader = _
                    File.OpenText(fileName)
            line = inputStream.ReadLine()
            While line <> Nothing
                If line.IndexOf(wanted) >= 0 Then
                    Console.WriteLine(line)
                End If
                line = inputStream.ReadLine()
            End While
            inputStream.Close()
        Else
            Console.WriteLine("Error: 2 arguments needed for Pick")
        End If
```

19.3 We convert both strings to upper-case before comparing, as in:

```
        If line.ToUpper().IndexOf(wanted.ToUpper()) >= 0 Then
```

19.4 The text from `Write` and `WriteLine` does not appear on the screen, so we have to guess that we must enter our name. In the file, we see:

```
        Please enter your name: Hi there Bill
```

19.5 In the `>` case, the file will contain only the lines with the required string in them. The second use of `>` overwrites any previous contents.

In the `>>` case, the file contains the same lines duplicated. In addition, if the output file is not empty to start with, its original contents will still be there.

19.6 The first execution of **Pick** should pick out every `If` line. These lines should then be used as input to another run of **Pick**, which picks out the lines containing sum. Here is the code, which you might place in a file named `ifsum.bat`:

```
        Pick.exe Big.vb "If" > temp.txt
        Pick.exe temp.txt "sum" > out.txt
```

The selected lines have been redirected to a file named `out.txt`.

Object-oriented design

This chapter explains:
- how to identify the classes that are needed in a program;
- how to distinguish between composition and inheritance;
- some guidelines for class design.

● Introduction

You probably wouldn't start to design a bridge by thinking about the size of the rivets. You would first make major decisions – like whether the bridge is cantilever or suspension. You wouldn't begin to design a building by thinking about the colour of the carpets. You would make major decisions first – like how many floors there are to be and where the elevators should be.

With a small program, design is not really needed – you can simply create the user interface and then go on to write the VB statements. But with a large program, it is widely recognized that the programmer should start with the major decisions rather than the detail. The programmer should do design, do it first and do it well. Decisions about detail – like the exact format of a number, or the position of a button – should be postponed. All the stages of programming are crucial, of course, but some are more crucial than others.

When you start out writing programs, you usually spend a lot of time in trial and error. This is often great fun and very creative. Sometimes you spend some time wrestling with the programming language. It takes some time to learn good practice and to recognize bad practice. It takes even longer to adopt an effective design approach to programming. The fun remains, the creativity remains, but the nuisance parts of programming are reduced.

Identifying objects, methods and properties

The design process takes as its input the specification of what the program is to do. The end product of the design process is a description of the classes, properties and methods that the program will employ.

This chapter explains how to use one mainstream approach to designing object-oriented programs. We shall use the simple example of the balloon program to illustrate how to do design. We will also introduce a more complex design example.

The design problem

We have seen that an object-oriented program consists of a collection of objects. The problem when starting to develop a new program is to identify suitable objects. We know that once we have identified the objects, we will reap all the benefits of object-oriented programming (OOP). But the fundamental problem of OOP is how to identify the objects. This is what a design method offers: an approach, a series of steps to identifying the objects. It is just like any other kind of design – you need a method. Knowing the principles of OOP is not enough. By analogy, knowing the laws of physics doesn't mean you can design a space shuttle; you also have to carry out some design.

One of the principles used in the design of object-oriented programs is to simulate real-world situations as objects. You build a software model of things in the real world. Here are some examples:

- If we are developing an office automation system, we set out to simulate users, mail, shared documents, files.
- In a factory automation system, we set out to simulate the different machines, queues of work, orders and deliveries.

The approach is to identify the objects in the problem to be addressed and to model them as objects in the program.

Abstraction plays a role in this process. We only need to model relevant parts for the problem to be solved, and we can ignore any irrelevant detail. If we model a balloon, we need to represent its position, its size and its colour. But we need not model the material from which it is made. If we are creating a personnel records system, we will probably model names, addresses and job descriptions but not hobbies and preferred music styles.

Identifying objects, methods and properties

One good way to carry out object-oriented design (OOD) is to examine the software specification to extract information about the objects, properties and methods. The approach to identifying objects and methods is:

344 • Chapter 20/Object-oriented design

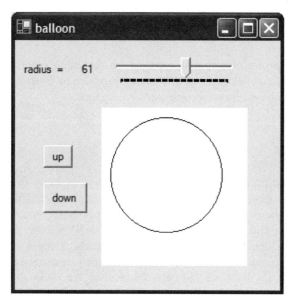

Figure 20.1 The balloon program.

1. look for nouns (things) in the specification – these are the objects;
2. look for verbs (doing words) in the specification – these are the methods.

Here, for example, is the specification for the simple balloon program:

> Write a program to represent a balloon and manipulate the balloon via a GUI. The balloon is displayed as a circle in a picture box. Using buttons, the position of the balloon can be changed by moving it a fixed distance up or down. Using a track bar, the radius of the balloon can be altered. The radius is displayed in a label.

The form is shown in Figure 20.1.

We look for verbs and nouns in the specification. In the above specification, we can see the following nouns:

> GUI, picture box, button, track bar, label, balloon, position, distance, radius

The GUI provides the user interface to the program. It consists of buttons, a track bar, a label and a picture box. The GUI is represented by an object that is an instance of the class `Form1`. The button, track bar, label and picture box objects are available as classes in the VB library.

The GUI object:

1. creates the buttons, track bar, label and picture box on the screen;
2. handles the events from mouse-clicks on the buttons and track bar;

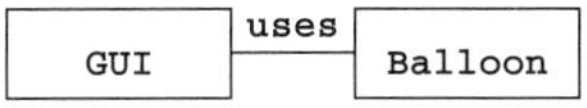

Identifying objects, methods and properties ● 345

```
     uses
GUI ────── Balloon
```

Figure 20.2 Class diagram showing the two main classes in the balloon program.

3. creates any other objects that are needed, such as the balloon object;
4. calls the methods and uses the properties of the balloon object.

The next major object is the balloon. It makes use of information to represent its position (*x*- and *y*-coordinates), the distance it moves and its radius. One option would be to create completely distinct full-blown objects to represent these items. But it is simpler to represent them simply as `Integer` variables.

This completes the identification of the objects within the program. We now generalize the objects and design classes corresponding to each object. Thus we need classes `GUI`, `Label`, `Balloon`, etc.

We now extract the verbs from the specification. They are effectively:

`ChangeRadius, MoveUp, MoveDown, DisplayBalloon, DisplayRadius`

We must create corresponding methods within the program we are designing. But we need to decide which object they apply to – the GUI object or the balloon object. It seems reasonable that the verbs `MoveUp`, `MoveDown` and `DisplayBalloon` are methods associated with the balloon object.

Now we turn our attention to the verbs `ChangeRadius` and `DisplayRadius`. We have already decided that the value of the radius is implemented as an `Integer` variable within the Balloon object. However, the GUI object needs access to this value to display it in the label. It also needs to change the value in response to changes in the value of the track bar. Thus the class `Balloon` needs to provide access to the value of the radius, and this can be accomplished either:

1. using methods (named `GetRadius` and `SetRadius`); or
2. using a property (named `Radius`).

Either approach is equally valid. We choose the second option.

To sum up, our design for this program consists of two non-library classes, `GUI` and `Balloon`, shown in the UML class diagram (Figure 20.2). Class `GUI` uses class `Balloon` by making calls on its methods and using its property.

We can now document each class by means of more detailed class diagrams. Each box describes a single class. It has four compartments, providing information on:

1. the class name;
2. a list of instance variables;
3. a list of methods;
4. a list of properties.

First, here is the description of the class `GUI`:

```
Class GUI

Instance variables

UpButton As Button
DownButton As Button
TrackBar1 As TrackBar
Label1 As Label
PictureBox1 As PictureBox

Methods

UpButton_Click
DownButton_Click
TrackBar1_Scroll
```

Next, here is the class diagram for the `Balloon` class:

```
Class Balloon

Instance variables

xCoordinate As Integer
yCoordinate As Integer
theRadius As Integer
distance As Integer

Methods

MoveUp
MoveDown
Display

Properties

Radius As Integer
```

The design of this program is now complete. Design ends at the stage where all the classes, objects, properties and methods are specified. Design is not concerned with writing (coding) the VB statements that make up these classes, properties and methods. However, it is natural for the reader to be curious about the code, so here is the code for the class `GUI`:

At the head of the form class is the instance variable:

```
Private theBalloon As Balloon
```

Within method New of the form is the creation of the Balloon object:

```
theBalloon = New Balloon()
```

Then we have the event handlers:

```
Private Sub DownButton_Click(ByVal sender As System.Object, _
                    ByVal e As System.EventArgs) _
                    Handles DownButton.Click
    theBalloon.MoveDown()
    Draw()
End Sub

Private Sub UpButton_Click(ByVal sender As System.Object, _
                    ByVal e As System.EventArgs) _
                    Handles UpButton.Click
    theBalloon.MoveUp()
    Draw()
End Sub

Private Sub TrackBar1_Scroll(ByVal sender As System.Object, _
                    ByVal e As System.EventArgs) _
                    Handles TrackBar1.Scroll
    theBalloon.Radius = TrackBar1.Value
    Draw()
End Sub
```

And a useful method:

```
Private Sub Draw()
    RadiusLabel.Text = CStr(theBalloon.Radius)
    theBalloon.Display(PictureBox1)
End Sub
```

This example is a simple one, with just two non-library objects. Nonetheless, it illustrates how to extract objects, methods and properties from a specification. We will look at a more complex example in a moment.

To summarize, the design method for identifying objects and methods is:

1. look for nouns in the specification – these are objects (or sometimes simple variables);
2. look for verbs in the specification – these are methods.

Once the objects have been identified, it is a simple step to generalize them by converting them into classes.

348 ● Chapter 20/Object-oriented design

Note that, although this program has been designed as two main classes, it could alternatively be designed as a single class. However, the design we have shown makes much more explicit use of the objects present in the specification of the program. The design also separates the GUI part of the program from the balloon itself. This is a widely recommended program structure in which the presentation code and the model logic (sometimes termed the domain logic) are separated. It means that each part of the program is easier to modify. For example, it allows the GUI to be changed independently of the coding of the `Balloon` class.

> **SELF-TEST QUESTION**
>
> **20.1** Code the method `MoveDown` within class `Balloon`.

● **Case study in design**

Here is the specification for a larger program:

Cyberspace invader

Cyberspace invader is a game. A picture box (Figure 20.3) displays a defender and an alien. The alien moves sideways. When it hits a wall, it reverses its direction. The alien periodically launches a bomb that moves vertically downwards. There is only one

Figure 20.3 The cyberspace invader game.

bomb in existence at any one time. If a bomb hits the defender, the defender loses. The defender moves left or right according to mouse movements. When the mouse is clicked, the defender fires a laser that moves upwards. There is only one laser in existence at a given time. When a laser hits the alien, the defender wins.

Remember that the major steps in design are:

1. Identify objects by searching for nouns in the specification.
2. Identify methods by searching for adjectives in the specification.

Scanning through the specification, we find the following nouns. As we might expect, some of these nouns are mentioned more than once.

   game, picture box, defender, alien, wall, bomb, mouse, laser

These nouns correspond to potential objects, and therefore classes within the program. So we translate these nouns into the names of classes in the model. The noun game becomes class Game. The noun picture box translates into the PictureBox class, available in the library. The nouns defender and alien translate into the classes Defender and Alien respectively. The noun wall need not be implemented as a class because it can be simply accommodated as a detail within the class Alien. The noun bomb translates into class Bomb. The noun mouse need not be a class because mouse-click events can be simply handled by the Game class. Finally we need a class Laser. Thus we arrive at the following list of non-library classes:

   Game, Defender, Alien, Laser, Bomb

as shown in the class diagram (Figure 20.4).

We have not yet quite completed our search for objects in the program. In order that collisions can be detected, objects need to know where other objects are and how big they are. Therefore, implicit in the specification are the ideas of the position and size of each object – the *x*- and *y*-coordinates, height and width of each object. Although these are potentially objects, they can instead be simply implemented as Integer variables within classes Defender, Alien, Laser and Bomb. These could either be accessed via methods or properties. But we choose to use properties named X, Y, Height and Width.

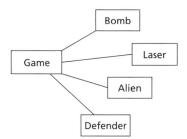

Figure 20.4 The non-library classes involved in the game program.

We now scan the specification again, this time looking for verbs that we can attach to the above list of objects. We see:

```
display, move, hit, launch, click, fire, win, lose
```

Again, some of these words are mentioned more than once. For example, both the aliens and the `defender` move. Also all the objects in the game need to be displayed.

One object that we have so far ignored in the design is a timer from the VB library that is set to click at small regular time intervals, in order to implement the animation. Whenever the timer ticks, the objects are moved, the picture box is cleared and all the objects are displayed.

We now allocate methods to classes, and the specification helps us to do this.

Now we can document each class as a UML class diagram that shows for each class its instance variables, its methods and properties. We start with class `Game`:

```
Class Game

Instance variables

aPictureBox As PictureBox
AnimationTimer As Timer
BombTimer As Timer

Methods

aPictureBox_MouseMove
AnimationTimer_Tick
BombTimer_Tick
aPictureBox.Click
```

Here, for the curious, is the code for this class. It begins with the instance declarations:

```
Private paper As Graphics
Private theDefender As Defender
Private theLaser As Laser
Private theBomb As Bomb
Private theAlien As Alien
```

Within the form's method `New`:

```
paper = aPictureBox.CreateGraphics()
theDefender = New Defender(defenderImage)
theAlien = New Alien(alienImage)
theBomb = New Bomb(bombImage)
theLaser = New Laser(laserImage)
```

Then the event handler methods and other methods:

```
Private Sub BombTimer_Tick(ByVal sender As System.Object, _
              ByVal e As System.EventArgs) _
              Handles BombTimer.Tick
    theBomb.Launch(theAlien.X, theAlien.Y)
End Sub

Private Sub AnimationTimer_Tick(ByVal sender As System.Object, _
              ByVal e As System.EventArgs) _
              Handles AnimationTimer.Tick
    MoveAll()
    DrawAll()
    CheckHits()
End Sub

Private Sub EndGame(ByVal winner As String)
    AnimationTimer.Enabled = False
    BombTimer.Enabled = False
    MessageBox.Show("game over - " & winner & " wins")
End Sub

Private Sub aPictureBox_MouseMove(ByVal sender As Object, _
              ByVal e As System.Windows.Forms.MouseEventArgs) _
              Handles PictureBox1.MouseMove
    theDefender.Move(e.X - theDefender.Width \ 2)
    DrawAll()
End Sub

Private Sub DrawAll()
    paper.Clear(Color.White)
    theDefender.Draw(paper)
    theAlien.Draw(paper)
    theLaser.Draw(paper)
    theBomb.Draw(paper)
End Sub

Private Sub aPictureBox_Click(ByVal sender As Object, _
                ByVal e As System.EventArgs)
    ' create a new laser at the top middle of the defender image
    Dim initialX As Integer = theDefender.X + theDefender.Width \ 2
    Dim initialY As Integer = theDefender.Y
    theLaser.Fire(initialX, initialY)
End Sub
```

Next we consider the defender object. It has a position within the picture box and a size. In response to a mouse movement, it moves. It can be displayed. Therefore its specification is:

```
Class Defender

Instance variables

xCoordinate As Integer
yCoordinate As Integer
height As Integer
width As Integer

Methods

Move
Display

Properties

X As Integer
Y As Integer
Height As Integer
Width As Integer
```

Next we design the `Alien` class. The alien has a position and a size. Whenever the clock ticks, it moves. Its direction and speed is controlled by the step size that is used when it moves. It can be created and displayed.

```
Class Alien

Instance variables

xCoordinate As Integer
yCoordinate As Integer
height As Integer
width As Integer
xStep As Integer

Methods
New
Move
Display

Properties

X As Integer
Y As Integer
Height As Integer
Width As Integer
```

Next we consider a laser object. A laser has a position and a size. It is created, moves, is fired and is displayed.

```
Class Laser

Instance variables
xCoordinate As Integer
yCoordinate As Integer
height As Integer
width As Integer
yStep AS Integer

Methods
New
Move
Display
Fire

Properties
X As Integer
Y As Integer
Height As Integer
Width As Integer
```

Finally, a bomb is very similar to a laser. One difference is that a bomb moves downwards, whereas a laser moves upwards. Another difference is that we need to check whether a bomb hits the defender, whereas a laser hits the alien.

> **SELF-TEST QUESTION**
>
> **20.2** Write the class diagram for the Bomb class.

We now have the full list of classes, and the methods and properties associated with each object – we have modelled the game and designed a structure for the program.

● Looking for reuse

The next act of design is to check to make sure that we are not reinventing the wheel. One of the main aims of OOP is to promote reuse of software components. Check whether

- what you need might be in one of the libraries;
- you may have written a class last month that is what you need;
- you may be able to generalize some of the classes you have designed for your program into a more general class that you can inherit from.

We see in the Cyberspace invader program that we can make good use of GUI components such as the picture box, available in the VB library. Another library component that is useful is a timer.

If you find an existing class that is similar to what you need, think about using inheritance to customize it to do what you want. We looked at how to write the code to achieve inheritance in Chapter 11. We next examine an approach to exploring the relationships between classes using the 'is-a' and 'has-a' tests.

Composition or inheritance?

Once we have identified the classes within a program, the next step is to consider the relationships between the classes. The classes that make up a program collaborate with each other to achieve the required behaviour, but they use each other in different ways. An important objective in studying the classes is to identify any inheritance relationships between the classes. If we can find any such relationships, we can simplify and shorten the program, making good use of reuse.

There are two ways in which classes relate to each other:

1. *Composition.* An object creates an object from another class using **New**. An example is a form that creates a button.
2. *Inheritance.* One class inherits from another. An example is a class that extends the **Form** class (as most GUI programmes do).

An important task of design is to distinguish these two cases, so that inheritance can be successfully applied or avoided. One way of checking that we have correctly identified the appropriate relationships between classes is to use the 'is-a or has-a' test:

- The use of the phrase 'is-a' in the description of an object (or class) signifies that it is probably an inheritance relationship.
- The use of the phrase 'has-a' indicates that there is no inheritance relationship. Instead the relationship is composition. (An alternative phrase that has the same meaning is 'consists-of'.)

Let us look at an example to see how inheritance is identified. In the specification for a program to support the transactions in a bank, we find the following information:

> A bank account consists of a person's name, address, account number and current balance. There are two types of account – current and deposit. Borrowers have to give one week's notice to withdraw from a deposit account, but the account accrues interest.

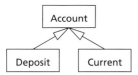

Figure 20.5 Class diagram for bank accounts.

Paraphrasing this specification, we could say 'a current account is a bank account' and 'a deposit account is a bank account'. We see the crucial words 'is a' and so recognize that bank account is the superclass of both deposit account and current account. Deposit account and current account are each subclasses of account. They will inherit some of the properties and methods from the superclass, for example, a property to access the address and a method to update the balance. Note the relationship between a bank account and a balance – a bank account 'has a' balance.

A class diagram (Figure 20.5) can be useful in describing the inheritance relationships between classes.

As another example, consider the description of a form: 'the form has a button and a text box'. This is a 'has a' relationship, which is not inheritance. The class representing the form simply declares and instantiates `Button` and `TextBox` objects and then uses them.

In the game program, several of the classes incorporate the same properties. These properties are: `x`, `y`, `Height` and `Width`, which represent the position and size of the graphical objects. We can remove these ingredients from each class and place them in a superclass called, say, `Sprite`. Sprite is a commonly used term for a moving object in games programming. The UML diagram for the `Sprite` class is:

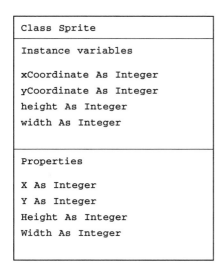

The VB code for the class `Sprite` is as follows:

```
Public Class Sprite

    Protected xValue, yValue, widthValue, heightValue As Integer

    Public ReadOnly Property X() As Integer
        Get
            Return xValue
        End Get
    End Property

    Public ReadOnly Property Y() As Integer
        Get
            Return yValue
        End Get
    End Property

    Public ReadOnly Property Width() As Integer
        Get
            Return widthValue
        End Get
    End Property

    Public ReadOnly Property Height() As Integer
        Get
            Return heightValue
        End Get
    End Property

End Class
```

The classes `Defender`, `Alien`, `Laser` and `Bomb` now inherit these properties from the superclass. Checking the validity of this design, we say 'each of the classes `Defender`, `Alien`, `Laser` and `Bomb` is a `Sprite`'. Figure 20.6 shows the class diagram.

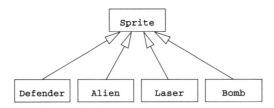

Figure 20.6 Class diagram for inherited components in the game.

Now that the design is complete, the code for class `Alien` is:

```
Public Class Alien
    Inherits Sprite

    Private stepSize As Integer
    Private alienImage As PictureBox
```

```
    Public Sub New(ByVal initialAlienImage As PictureBox)
        xValue = 100
        yValue = 50
        widthValue = 25
        heightvalue = 25
        alienImage = initialAlienImage
        stepSize = 1
    End Sub

    Public Sub Draw(ByVal paper As Graphics)
        Dim myImage As Image = alienImage.Image
        paper.DrawImage(myImage, xValue, yValue, Me.Width, Me.Height)
    End Sub

    Public Sub Move()
        If xValue > 250 Or xValue < 0 Then
            stepSize = -stepSize
        End If
        xValue = xValue + stepSize
    End Sub

End Class
```

The code for class Bomb is:

```
Public Class Bomb
    Inherits Sprite

    Private stepSize As Integer
    Private bombImage As PictureBox

    Public Sub New(ByVal initialBombImage As PictureBox)
        xValue = 100
        yValue = 50
        widthValue = 5
        heightValue = 5
        stepSize = 1
        bombImage = initialBombImage
    End Sub

    Public Sub Draw(ByVal paper As Graphics)
        Dim myImage As Image = bombImage.Image
        paper.DrawImage(myImage, xValue, yValue, Me.Width, Me.Height)
    End Sub

    Public Sub Launch(ByVal newX As Integer, ByVal newY As Integer)
        xValue = newX
        yValue = newY
    End Sub
```

```
Public Sub Move()
    yValue = yValue + stepSize
End Sub
```
```
End Class
```

To sum up, the two kinds of relationship between classes are as follows.

Relationship between classes	Test	VB code involves
Inheritance	is-a	`Inherits`
Composition	has-a or consists-of	`New`

> **SELF-TEST QUESTION**
>
> **20.3** Analyse the relationships between the following groups of classes (are they is-a or has-a):
>
> 1. house, door, roof, dwelling
> 2. person, man, woman
> 3. car, piston, gearbox, engine
> 4. vehicle, car, bus

● Guidelines for class design

Use of the design approach that we have described is not guaranteed to lead to the perfect design. It is always worthwhile checking the design of each class against the following guidelines.

Keep data private

Variables should always be declared as `Private` (or sometimes `Protected`), but never as `Public`. This maintains data hiding, one of the central principles of OOP. If data needs to be accessed or changed, do it via properties or methods provided as part of the class.

Initialize the data

Although VB automatically initializes instance variables (but not local variables) to particular values, it is good practice to initialize them explicitly, either within the data declaration itself or as part of a constructor method.

Avoid large classes

If a class is more than two pages of text, it is a candidate for consideration for division into two or smaller classes. But this should only be done if there are clearly obvious classes to be formed from the large one. It is counter-productive to split an elegant cohesive class into contrived and ugly classes.

Make the class, property and method names meaningful

This will make them easy to use and more appealing for reuse.

Do not contrive inheritance

In the game program discussed above, some of the objects move horizontally and some move vertically. So we might consider using classes `MovesVertically` and `MovesHorizontally` to exploit this situation. However it turns out that if we investigate these possibilities, no simplification is gained and so it is pointless.

Using inheritance when it is not really appropriate can lead to contrived classes, which are more complex and perhaps longer than they need be.

When using inheritance, put shared items in the superclass

In the example of the bank account discussed above, all those variables, methods and properties that are common to all bank accounts should be written as part of the super-class so that they can be shared by all the subclasses without duplication. Examples are the methods to update the address and to update the balance.

We also saw in the game program that we could identify identical properties in several of the classes, and thus create a superclass named `Sprite`. There are further promising common elements in the classes `Laser`, `Alien`, `Defender` and `Bomb`.

Use refactoring

After an initial design has been created, or when some coding has been carried out, a study of the design may reveal that some simplification is possible. This may mean moving some properties and methods to another class. It may mean creating new classes or amalgamating existing classes. This process is termed *refactoring*. We have already met a guideline for refactoring – place shared properties and methods in the superclass.

For example, in the game program, there is an obvious need to test whether objects are colliding. But there are several alternative places in the program where this collision detection can be carried out.

Refactoring recognizes that it is often not possible to create an initial design that is ideal. Instead the design sometimes evolves towards an optimal structure. This may involve changing the design after coding is under way. Thus development is not carried out in distinct stages.

Summary

The OO design task consists of identifying appropriate objects and classes. The steps in the approach to OO design advocated in this chapter are:

1. Study the specification and clarify it if necessary.

2. Derive objects, properties and methods from the specification, so that the design acts as a model of the application. The verbs are methods and the nouns are objects.

3. Generalize the objects into classes.

4. Check for reuse of library classes and other existing classes, using composition and inheritance as appropriate. 'Is-a' and 'has-a' analysis help check out whether inheritance or composition is appropriate.

5. Use guidelines to refine a design.

EXERCISES

20.1 Write the code for the class `Balloon` in the balloon program designed in this chapter (Figure 20.1).

20.2 Complete the development of the Cyberspace invader program.

20.3 A good design can be judged on how well it copes with modifications or enhancements. Consider the following enhancements to the Cyberspace invader program. Assess what changes are needed to the design and coding:

(a) multiple lasers and bombs;
(b) a row of aliens;
(c) a line of bunkers that protects the defender from bombs.

20.4 An alternative design for the Cyberspace invader program uses a class named `ScreenManager` that:

(a) maintains information about all the objects displayed on the screen;
(b) calls all the objects to display themselves;
(c) detects collisions between any pairs of objects on the screen.

Re-design the program so as to use this class.

20.5 Design the classes for a program with the following specification.
The program acts as a simple desk calculator (Figure 20.7) that acts on integer numbers. A text box acts as a display. The calculator has one button for each of the 10 digits, 0 to 9. It has a button to add and a button to subtract. It has a clear button, to clear the display, and an equals (=) button to get the answer.

Figure 20.7 The desk calculator.

When the clear button is pressed the display is set to zero and the (hidden) total is set to zero.

When a digit button is pressed, the digit is added to the right of those already in the display (if any).

When the + button is pressed, the number in the display is added to the total (and similar for the – button).

When the equals button is pressed, the value of the total is displayed.

ANSWERS TO SELF-TEST QUESTIONS

20.1
```
Public Sub MoveDown()
    yCoordinate = yCoordinate + 10
End Sub
```

20.2

Class Bomb
Instance variables xCoordinate As Integer yCoordinate As Integer height As Integer width As Integer yStep AS Integer
Methods New Move Display Launch
Properties X As Integer Y As Integer Height As Integer Width As Integer

20.3
1. has-a
2. is-a
3. has-a
4. is-a

21

Program style

This chapter suggests style guidelines for:
- program layout;
- comments;
- constants;
- classes;
- nested `If` statements and loops;
- complex conditions;
- documentation.

Introduction

Programming is a highly creative and exciting activity. Programmers often get very absorbed in their work and regard the programs that they produce as being very much their personal creations. The stereotypical programmer (man or woman) wears jeans and a T-shirt. He or she drinks 20 cups of coffee in a day and stays up all night just for the fun of programming.

But the facts of programming life are often rather different. Most programming is done within commercial organizations. Most programs are worked on by several different people. Many organizations have standards manuals that detail what programs should look like.

When you write a program it is tempting to see it as your own individual creation. But most programs are read by several people. Others are: the people who take on your work when you get promoted or move to another project, the people who will test your program, and the generations of programmers who will look after your program, fixing bugs and making improvements long after you have got another job. So, making your program easy to read is a vital ingredient of programming.

Another aspect of good style is reusability. A program that exhibits style will contain classes that can be reused later in another program.

Though people's views on programming style often differ, one thing that they always agree on is that a style should be applied consistently throughout a program. If the style is inconsistent it makes the program hard to read (not to say annoying). It also creates a worry that the original programmer did not really care about the program and that there is something wrong with it. Throughout this book we have used one consistent style for the layout of programs.

Unless you are a hobbyist, it is important to know how to produce programs that have good style. We have endeavoured to write stylish programs that serve as good examples throughout this book.

Program layout

There is plenty of scope for creativity and individuality in coding a program. However, as we have seen, most programs are read by several people other than the original author. So good appearance is vital. We will now look at a set of style guidelines for VB programs. There is always controversy about guidelines like these. No doubt you, the reader, will disagree with some of them.

Names

The programmer gives names to variables, classes, properties and methods. There is plenty of scope for imagination because names can be as long as 255 characters, provided that they consist of letters, digits and underscore, and provided that the name starts with a letter.

The advice on names is to make them as meaningful as possible. This rules out cryptic names like `i`, `j`, `x`, `y`, which usually signify that the programmer has some background in mathematics (but not much imagination for creating meaningful names). But even short names can be appropriate on the right occasion. For example, we often use `x` and `y` in this book to describe the *x*- and *y*-coordinates of a point in a picture box.

It is often the case that you want to build a name from a number of words. Use capital letters to distinguish the words within the name – for example `WishYouWereHere`.

Most names start with a capital letter, but a few should start with lower case. The suggested convention is as follows:

Start with a capital:	Start with lower case:
keyword	parameter
class	local variable
method	instance variable
property	

The VB IDE gives default names to controls and these are OK as long as there is only one control of each type. But when there is more than one of a kind, for example several buttons or labels, we suggest replacing the default name with a distinctive name such as `CalculateButton`, `AgeTextBox`, `ResultLabel`.

Indentation

Indentation emphasizes program structure. While VB and its compiler do not need indentation, it assists us humans in understanding a program when selection and looping statements are indented appropriately. Fortunately the VB Integrated Development Environment automatically indents programs.

VB programs often contain long lines, which disappear off to the right of the window. To see the whole line at once, we need to break the line (with a space and underscore) at a suitable point. Though you can break a line anywhere, it is clearest to break it at, say, a comma, rather than in the middle of a word. The remainder of the line should then be indented to show the structure of the statement. Look at how we have indented the event-handling methods throughout this book to see this in action.

Blank lines

Blank lines are often used within a class to separate the variable declarations from the methods and properties, and one method or property from another. If there are a lot of variable declarations, different blocks of data can also be separated by blank lines.

Classes and files

You can hold all your classes in a single file, but it is probably better to place them in different files so that there is the maximum chance of them being reused. The IDE assists with this maintenance.

● Comments

There are two ways of putting comments into VB programs:

```
' this is a comment to the end of the line
REM this is a comment on a line by itself
```

There is always great controversy about comments in programs. Some people argue that 'the more the better'. However, sometimes you see code like this:

```
' display the hello message
TextBox1.Text = "hello"
```

in which the comment merely repeats the code, and is therefore superfluous.

Sometimes code is overwhelmed by suffocating comments which add little to the understanding of the code. It is like a Christmas tree that is overwhelmed with tinsel, baubles and lights – you can't see the tree for the decorations. There is another problem: some studies have shown that, where there are a lot of comments, the reader reads the comments and ignores the code. Thus, if the code is wrong, it will remain so.

Some people argue that comments are needed when the code is complex or difficult to understand in some way. This seems reasonable until you wonder why the code needs to be complex in the first place. Sometimes, perhaps, the code can be simplified so that it is easy to understand without comments. We give example of such situations below.

Some programmers like to place a comment at the start of every class and, perhaps, the start of a property or method in order to describe its overall purpose. Class, property and method names should, of course, try to describe what they do, so a comment may be redundant.

Our view is that perhaps comments should be used sparingly and judiciously. For example, a complex section of code may need an explanatory comment.

Using constants

Many programs have values that do not change while the program is running and don't change very often anyway. Examples are a tax rate, the age for voting, the threshold for paying tax and mathematical constants. VB provides the facility to declare data items as constants and give them a value. So, for these examples, we can write:

```
Const taxRate As Double = 17.5
Const votingAge As Integer = 18
Const taxThreshold As Integer = 5000
```

Variables like this with constant values can only be declared at the top of a class and not as local variables within a method.

Strings can also be given constant values (but arrays cannot):

```
Const ourPlanet As String = "Earth"
```

One benefit of using `Const` values is that the compiler will detect any attempt (no doubt by mistake!) to change the value of a constant. Thus, for example, given the declaration above:

```
votingAge = 17
```

will provoke an error message.

Another, more powerful, benefit is that a program that otherwise might be peppered with rather meaningless numbers, instead contains variables (which are constant) with clear, meaningful names. This enhances program clarity, with all its consequent benefits.

Suppose, for example, we need to alter a tax program to reflect a change in regulations. We have a nightmare task if the tax thresholds and tax rates are built into the program as numbers that appear as-and-when throughout the program. Suppose that the old tax threshold is $5000. We could use a text editor to search for all occurrences of

5000. The editor will dutifully tell us where all the occurrences are, but we are left unsure that this number has the same meaning everywhere. What if the number 4999 appears in the program? Is it the tax threshold minus 1? Or does it have some other completely unrelated meaning? The answer, of course, is to use constants, with good names, and to distinguish carefully between different data items.

Another common use for constants is to specify the sizes of any arrays used in a program, as in:

```
Const maxIndex As Integer = 10
```

and thereafter:

```
Dim myArray(maxIndex) As Integer
```

Finally, some people favour the style in which the names of constants are written in CAPITALS, so that they are distinctive.

Classes

Classes are an important building block of OO programs. Good design of classes helps to ensure that the program is clear and comprehensible. Chapter 20 on object-oriented design (OOD) explains an approach to design. OOD attempts to create classes that correspond to ideas in the problem being solved and these classes are usually present in the specification for the program. Thus a good design will be such that the classes are recognizable as being a model of the specification. As a by-product, the design will reflect the complexity of the problem and no more.

Classes are also the unit that facilitates reusability of software components. It is a class that is inherited, or extended. So it is important that classes have good style. Here are some guidelines.

Class size

If a class is longer than, say, two pages it may be too long and complex. Consider carefully dividing it into two or more classes, in such a way as to create viable new classes. It is damaging, however, to divide a coherent class into clumsy incoherent classes. A coherent class is one in which all the parts contribute towards a single idea.

Method size

It is possible to get into long and enjoyable arguments about how long a method should be.

One view is that a method should not be longer than the screen or a single page of listing (say 40 lines of text). That way, you do not have to scroll or turn a page to study it as a whole. You can thoroughly study the method in its entirety. It is not so long that you lose track of some parts of it.

Any method that is longer than half a page is a serious candidate for restructuring into smaller methods. However, it depends on what the method does – it may do a single cohesive task, and an attempt to split it up may introduce complications involving parameters and scope. Do not apply any length recommendation blindly.

Encapsulation

The idea of object-oriented design is to hide or encapsulate data, so that every interaction between classes take place via the properties and methods, rather than by direct access to data. A good class design has a minimum of `Public` variables.

Property and method names

We have already emphasized the importance of meaningful method and property names. When a method has the single role of obtaining some value, say the value of a salary, it is convention to call it `getSalary`. Similarly, if a method is to be provided to change the value of this same variable, then the conventional name is `setSalary`.

Field order

Fields are the variables, properties and methods declared within a class. What order should they appear in? There are both `Public` and `Private` fields to consider. The usual convention is to write them in the following order:

1. instance variables (`Public` and `Private`);
2. `Public` methods;
3. properties;
4. `Private` methods.

● Nested `If`s

Nesting means writing a statement within another statement, for example an `If` statement within an `If` statement or a `While` loop within a `For` loop (considered later). Sometimes a nested program is simple and clear. But generally, a high degree of nesting is considered to be bad style, and best avoided. Nesting is always avoidable by rewriting the program. Consider the problem of finding the largest of three numbers. Here is an initial program that uses nesting:

```
Dim a, b, c As Integer
Dim largest As Integer

If a > b Then
    If a > c Then
        largest = a
```

```
        Else
            largest = c
        End If
    Else
        If b > c Then
            largest = b
        Else
            largest = c
        End If
    End If
```

This is certainly a complicated-looking piece of program, and some people might have a little trouble understanding it. Arguably the complexity arises from the nesting of the If statements.

An alternative piece of program that avoids the nesting, but increases the complexity of the conditions, is:

```
If a >= b And a >= c Then
    largest = a
End If
If b >= a And b >= c Then
    largest = b
End If
If c >= a And c >= b Then
    largest = c
End If
```

which may be clearer to some people. But the best solution is probably the following, which uses ElseIf:

```
If a >= b And a >= c Then
    largest = a
ElseIf b >= a And b >= c Then
    largest = b
Else
    largest = c
End If
```

This is both more concise and shows the symmetry present in the problem.

We have examined three solutions to the same problem. The moral is that there is often more than one solution to a problem and each has its own strengths and weaknesses.

It can be difficult to read and understand nested programs. This example shows how a program that involves nested Ifs can be converted into a program without nesting and, in general, any nested program can be converted in a similar way. But nested If statements are not always bad, and there are occasions where nesting simply and clearly describes what needs to be done.

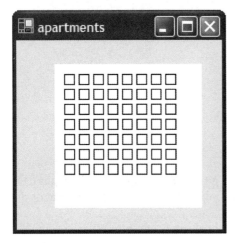

Figure 21.1 Display of a block of flats.

● Nested loops

We now look at nesting loops. Suppose we are writing a program that displays a pattern on the screen as in Figure 21.1, which is a crude graphic of a block of flats (apartments in North America).

The piece of program could look like this:

```
Private Sub DrawFlats(ByVal floors As Integer, _
                     ByVal flats As Integer)

    Dim xCoord, yCoord As Integer
    Dim floor, flat As Integer

    Dim paper As Graphics
    paper = PictureBox1.CreateGraphics()
    Dim myPen As Pen = New Pen(Color.Black)

    yCoord = 10
    For floor = 0 To floors
        xCoord = 10
        For flat = 0 To flats
            paper.DrawRectangle(myPen, xCoord, yCoord, 10, 10)
            xCoord = xCoord + 15
        Next
        yCoord = yCoord + 15
    Next
End Sub
```

in which one loop is nested within the other. This is not a particularly complex piece of code, but we can simplify it using another method:

```
    Private Sub DrawFlats2(ByVal floors As Integer, _
                          ByVal flats As Integer)
        Dim yCoord As Integer
        Dim floor As Integer

        yCoord = 10
        For floor = 0 To floors
            DrawFloor(yCoord, flats)
            yCoord = yCoord + 15
        Next
    End Sub

    Private Sub DrawFloor(ByVal yCoord As Integer, _
                          ByVal flats As Integer)
        Dim xCoord As Integer = 10
        Dim flat As Integer

        Dim paper As Graphics
        paper = .PictureBox1.CreateGraphics()
        Dim myPen As Pen = New Pen(Color.Black)

        For flat = 0 To flats
            paper.DrawRectangle(myPen, xCoord, yCoord, 10, 10)
            xCoord = xCoord + 15
        Next
    End Sub
```

By using an additional method we have eliminated the nesting. We have also expressed explicitly in the coding the fact that the block of flats consists of a number of floors. We have disentangled two problems into separate parts; this is sometimes known as problem decomposition. We have clarified the requirement that there is a change in the *y*-coordinate for each floor of the block. It is always possible to eliminate nested loops in this manner, and sometimes this results in a simplification of the program.

Research studies have shown that we humans find it difficult to understand programs that use nesting. One researcher has summed this up by saying 'Nesting is for the birds'. But nesting is not *always* bad. Take, for example, the coding to initialize a two-dimensional array:

```
Dim table(9, 9) As Integer
Dim row, col As Integer

For row = 0 To 9
    For col = 0 To 9
        table(row, col) = 0
    Next
Next
```

which is clear even with nesting.

Chapter 21/Program style

Complex conditions

Complexity in an `If`, `For`, `While` or `Do` statement can arise when the condition being tested involves one or more `And` and `Or`s. A complex condition can make a program very difficult to understand, debug and get right. As an example, we will look at a program that searches an array of numbers to find a desired number:

```
Const maxIndex As Integer = 99
Dim table(maxIndex) As Integer

Dim wanted As Integer
Dim index As Integer

wanted = CInt(InputTextBox.Text)

index = 0
While index < maxIndex And table(index) <> wanted
    index = index + 1
End While
If table(index) = wanted Then
    ResultTextBox.Text = "found"
Else
    ResultTextBox.Text = "not found"
End If
```

The problem with this program is that the condition in the `While` is complex. Even for an experienced programmer it can be difficult to check what has been written and to convince yourself that it is correct. There is an alternative; we will use a flag. It is simply an `Integer` variable, but its value at any time records the status of the search. There are three possible states that the search can be in.

- The program is still searching; the item is not yet found. This is also the initial state of the search. The flag has the value 0.
- The item has been found. The value is 1.
- The search has been completed but without finding the item. The value is 2.

Using this flag, called `state`, the program becomes:

```
Const maxIndex As Integer = 99
Dim table(maxIndex) As Integer

Dim wanted As Integer
Dim index As Integer

Dim state As Integer
Const stillSearching As Integer = 0
Const found As Integer = 1
Const notFound As Integer = 2
```

```
wanted = CInt(InputTextBox.Text)
index = 0
state = stillSearching
While state = stillSearching
    If wanted = table (index) Then
        state = found
    ElseIf index = maxIndex Then
        state = notFound
    End If
    index = index + 1
End While

If state = found Then
    ResultTextBox.Text = "found"
Else
    ResultTextBox.Text = "not found"
End If
```

What has been accomplished is that the various tests have been disentangled. The condition in the `While` loop is clear and simple. The other tests are separate and simple. The program overall is perhaps simpler. Yet another way to write a search program is given in Chapter 14 on one-dimensional arrays.

The moral is that it is often possible to write a piece of program in different ways and some solutions are simpler and clearer than others. Sometimes it is possible to avoid complexity in a condition by rewriting the program fragment with the use of a flag.

● Documentation

Documentation is the bugbear of the programmer – until, of course, you yourself are asked to sort out someone else's program! Commercial organizations usually try to encourage programmers to document their programs well. They tell the old and probably fictitious story about the programmer who had a program 95% complete, did no documentation and then got run over by a bus. The colleagues who remained allegedly had a terrible job trying to continue work on the program.

Program documentation typically consists of the following ingredients:

- the program specification;
- screen dumps;
- the source code, including appropriate comments;
- design information, for example, class diagrams;
- the test schedule;
- the test results;
- the modification history;
- the user manual.

If you ever get asked to take over someone's program, this is what you will need – but don't expect to get it!

Programmers generally find creating documentation a boring chore and tend to skimp on it. They generally leave it to the end of the project, when there is little time available. No wonder it is often not done or done poorly.

The only way to ease the pain is to do the documentation as you go along, mixing it in with the more interesting tasks of programming.

Programming pitfalls

Check whether there are any standards used in your organization before you start to code. You might be required to follow them. If you do want to stick to a plan for laying out the program, it's often better to do it from the start, rather than typing the program in roughly and changing it later.

Summary

- Program style is important to promote readability for debugging and maintenance.
- Guidelines for good program layout embrace good names, indentation, blank lines and comments.
- VB has a useful facility for making appropriate data items constant.
- Classes should have a clear cohesive purpose.
- Nested `If`s, loops and complex conditions should be used judiciously.
- Good documentation is always worthy.

EXERCISES

21.1 In a program to play a game of cards, the suit of a card is encoded as an integer (1 to 4). Consider a method to convert this integer into the appropriate string – 'hearts', 'clubs', etc. Write the method four ways:

(a) using nested `If` statements
(b) using distinct `If` statements
(c) using `ElseIf`
(d) using `Select Case`

Which solution is best and why?

21.2 Look at as many programs as you can (including your own) and review their styles. Are they good or bad? Why?

21.3 Discuss the issue of guidelines with colleagues or friends. Does style matter? If so what constitutes good style?

21.4 Devise a set of style guidelines for VB programs.

21.5 (Optional) Use your style guidelines for evermore.

Testing

This chapter explains:

- why exhaustive testing is not feasible;
- how to carry out functional testing;
- how to carry out structural testing;
- how to perform walkthroughs;
- how to carry out testing using single stepping;
- the role of formal verification;
- incremental development.

Introduction

Programs are complex and it is difficult to make them work correctly. Testing is the set of techniques used to attempt to verify that a program does work correctly. Put another way, testing attempts to reveal the existence of bugs. Once you realize that there is a bug, you then need to locate it using debugging (see Chapter 9). As we shall see, testing techniques cannot guarantee to expose all the bugs in a program and so most large programs have hidden bugs in them. Nonetheless testing is enormously important. This is evidenced by the fact that it can typically consume up to one half of the total time spent on developing a program. At Microsoft, for example, there are teams of programmers (who write programs) and separate teams of testers (who test programs). There are as many testers as programmers. Because it needs so much time and effort to test and debug programs, often a decision has to be made whether to continue the testing or whether to deliver the program in its current state to the customers or clients.

In academic circles, the task of trying to ensure that a program does what is expected is called *verification*. The aim is to *verify* that a program meets its specification.

In this chapter we will see how to carry out testing systematically, review different approaches to verification and see what their deficiencies are.

The techniques we will review are:

- black box or functional testing;
- white box or structural testing;
- reviews or walkthroughs;
- stepping through code with a debugger;
- formal methods.

A small program that consists only of a single class can usually be tested all at once. A larger program that involves two or more classes may be of such complexity that it must be tested in pieces. In VB the natural size for these pieces is the class and it is convenient to test a program class by class. This is called *unit testing*. When the complete program is brought together for testing the task is called *integration* or *system testing*.

We will also look at developing a program bit-by-bit, rather than as a complete program.

Program specifications

The starting point for any testing is the specification. Time is never wasted in studying and clarifying the specification. This may well necessitate going back to the client or the future user of the program. Take the following specification, for example:

> Write a program that inputs a series of numbers via a text box. The program calculates and displays the sum of the numbers.

On first reading, this specification may look simple and clear. But, even though it is so short, it contains pitfalls:

- Are the numbers integers or floating-point?
- What is the permissible range and precision of the numbers?
- Are negative numbers to be included in the sum?

These questions should be clarified before the programmer starts any programming. Indeed it is part of the job of programming to study the specification, discover any omissions or confusions, and gain agreement to a clear specification. After all, it is no use writing a brilliant program if it doesn't do what the client wanted.

Here now is a clearer version of the specification, which we will use as a case study in looking at testing methods:

> Write a program that inputs a series of integers via a text box. The integers are in the range 0 to 10 000. The program calculates and displays the sum of the numbers.

You can see that this specification is more precise – for example it stipulates the permissible range of input values.

> **SELF-TEST QUESTION**
>
> **22.1** Can you see any remaining deficiencies in the specification that need clarification?

● Exhaustive testing

One approach to testing would be to test a program with all possible data values as input. But consider even the simplest of programs: one that inputs a pair of integer numbers and displays their product. Exhaustive testing would mean that we select all possible values of the first number and all possible values for the second. And then we use all possible combinations of numbers. In VB, an `Integer` number has a huge range of possible values. All in all, the number of possible combinations of numbers is enormous. All the different values would have to be keyed in and the program run. The human time taken to assemble the test data would be years. Even the time that the computer needs would be days – fast as they are. Finally, checking that the computer had got the answers correct would drive someone mad with tedium.

Thus exhaustive testing – even for a small and simple program – is not feasible. It is important to recognize that perfect testing, for all but the smallest program, is impossible. Therefore we have to adopt some other approach.

● Black box (functional) testing

Knowing that exhaustive testing is infeasible, the *black box* approach to testing is to devise sample data that is representative of all possible data. Then we run the program, input the data and see what happens. This type of testing is termed black box testing because no knowledge of the workings of the program is used as part of the testing – we only consider inputs and outputs. The program is thought of as being invisibly enclosed within a black box. Black box testing is also known as functional testing because it uses only a knowledge of the function of the program (not how it works).

Ideally, testing proceeds by writing down the test data and the expected outcome of the test, before testing takes place. This is called a test specification or schedule. Then you run the program, input the data and examine the outputs for discrepancies between the predicted outcome and the actual outcome. Test data should also check out whether exceptions are handled by the program in accordance with its specification.

Consider a program that decides whether a person can vote, depending on their age (Figure 22.1). The minimum voting age is 18.

We know that we cannot realistically test this program with all possible values, but instead we need some typical values. This approach to devising test data for black box testing is to use *equivalence partitioning*. This means looking at the nature of the input data to identify common features. Such a common feature is called a partition. In the voting program, we recognize that the input data falls into two partitions:

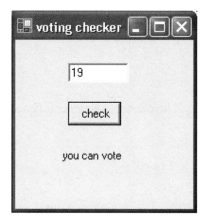

Figure 22.1 The voting checker program.

- the numbers less than 18;
- the numbers greater than or equal to 18.

This can be diagrammed as follows:

0	17	18	infinity

There are two partitions, one including the age range 0 to 17 and the other partition with numbers 18 to infinity. We then take the step of asserting that every number within a partition is equivalent to any other, for the purpose of testing this program. (Hence the term equivalence partitioning.) We now argue that the number 12 is equivalent to any other in the first partition and the number 21 is equivalent to any number in the second. So we devise two tests:

Test number	Data	Outcome
1	12	cannot vote
2	21	can vote

We have reasoned that we need two sets of test data to test this program. These two sets, together with a statement of the expected outcomes from testing, constitute a test specification. We run the program with the two sets of data and note any discrepancies between predicted and actual outcome.

Unfortunately we can see that these tests have not investigated the important distinction between someone aged 17 and someone aged 18. Anyone who has ever written a program knows that using `If` statements is error prone. So it is advisable to investigate this particular region of the data. This is the same as recognizing that data values at the edges of the partitions are worthy of inclusion into the testing. Therefore we create two additional tests:

Test number	Data	Outcome
3	17	cannot vote
4	18	can vote

In summary, the rules for selecting test data for black box testing using equivalence partitioning are:

1. Partition the input data values.
2. Select representative data from each partition (equivalent data).
3. Select data at the boundaries of partitions.

We have now selected the data for testing. In this program, there is a single input; there are four data values and therefore four tests. However, most programs process a number of inputs. Suppose we wish to test a program that displays the larger of two numbers, each in the range 0 to 10 000, entered into a pair of text boxes. If the values are equal, the program displays either value.

Each input is within a partition that runs from 0 to 10 000. We choose values at each end of the partitions and sample values somewhere in the middle:

First number:	0	54	10 000
Second number:	0	142	10 000

Now that we have selected representative values, we need to consider what combinations of values we should use. Exhaustive testing would mean using every possible combination of every possible data value – but this is, of course, infeasible. Instead, we use every combination of the representative values. So the tests are:

Test number	First number	Second number	Outcome
1	0	0	0
2	0	142	142
3	0	10 000	10 000
4	54	0	54
5	54	142	142
6	54	10 000	10 000
7	10 000	0	10 000
8	10 000	142	10 000
9	10 000	10 000	10 000

Thus the additional step in testing is to use every combination of the (limited) representative data values.

> **SELF-TEST QUESTION**
>
> **22.2** In a program to play the game of chess, the player specifies the destination for a move as a pair of indices, the row and column number. The program checks that the destination square is valid, that is, not outside the board. Devise black box test data to check that this part of the program is working correctly.

● White box (structural) testing

White box testing makes use of knowledge of how the program works – the structure of the program – as the basis for devising test data. In white box testing every statement in the program is executed at some time during the testing. This is equivalent to ensuring that every path (every sequence of instructions) through the program is executed at some time during testing. This testing should include any exception handling carried out by the program.

Here is the code for the voting checker program we are using as a case study:

```
Private Sub Button1_Click(ByVal sender As System.Object, _
                          ByVal e As System.EventArgs) _
                          Handles Button1.Click
    Dim age As Integer
    age = CInt(TextBox1.Text)
    If age >= 18 Then
        Label1.Text = "you can vote"
    Else
        Label1.Text = "you cannot vote"
    End If
End Sub
```

In this program, there are two paths (because the `If` has two branches) and therefore two sets of data will serve to ensure that all statements are executed at some time during the testing:

Test number	Data	Expected outcome
1	12	cannot vote
2	21	can vote

If we are cautious, we realize that errors in programming are often made within the conditions of `If` and `While` statements. So we add a further two tests to ensure that the `If` statement is working correctly:

Test number	Data	Expected outcome
3	17	cannot vote
4	18	can vote

Thus we need four sets of data to test this program in a white box fashion. This happens to be the same data that we devised for black box testing. But the reasoning that led to the two sets of data is different. Had the program been written differently, the white box test data would be different. Suppose, for example, the program used an array, named `table`, with one element for each age specifying whether someone of that age can vote. Then the program is simply the following statement to lookup eligibility:

```
Label1.Text = table(age)
```

and the white box testing data is different.

> **SELF-TEST QUESTIONS**
>
> **22.3** A program's function is to find the largest of three numbers. Devise white box test data for this section of program.
>
> The code is:
>
> ```
> Dim a, b, c As Integer
> Dim largest As Integer
>
> If a > b Then
>     If a > c
>         largest = a
>     Else
>         largest = c
>     End If
> Else
>     If b > c Then
>         largest = b
>     Else
>         largest = c
>     End If
> End If
> ```
>
> **22.4** In a program to play the game of chess, the player specifies the destination for a move as a pair of integer subscripts, the row and column number. The program checks that the destination square is valid, that is, not outside the board. Devise white box test data to check that this part of the program is working correctly.

The code for this part of the program is:

```
If (row > 8) Or (row < 1) Then
    MessageBox.Show("error")
End If
If (col > 8) Or (col < 1) Then
    MessageBox.Show("error")
End If
```

Inspections and walkthroughs

This is an approach that doesn't make use of a computer at all in trying to eradicate faults – it is called inspection or a walkthrough. In an inspection, someone simply studies the program listing (along with the specification) in order to try to see bugs. It works better if the person doing the inspecting is not the person who wrote the program. This is because people tend to be blind to their own errors. So get a friend or a colleague to inspect your program. It is extraordinary to witness how quickly someone else sees an error that has been defeating you for hours.

To inspect a program you need:

- the specification;
- the text of the program on paper.

In carrying out an inspection, one approach is to study it a method at a time. Some of the checks are fairly mechanical:

- variables initialized;
- loops correctly initialized and terminated;
- method calls have the correct parameters.

Further checking examines the logic of the program. Pretend to execute the method as if you were a computer, avoiding following any method calls into other methods. (This is why a walkthrough is so-called.) Check that:

- the logic of the method achieves its desired purpose.

During inspection, you can check that:

- variable and method names are meaningful;
- the logic is clear and correct.

Although the prime goal of an inspection is not to check for style, a weakness in any of these areas may point to a bug.

The evidence from controlled experiments suggests that inspections are a very effective way of finding errors. In fact inspections are at least as good a way of identifying bugs as actually running the program (doing testing).

Stepping through code

The debugger within the VB IDE (Chapter 9) allows you to step through a program, executing just one instruction at a time. This is called single stepping. Each time you execute an instruction you can see which path of execution has been taken. You can also see (or watch) the values of variables by placing the cursor over a variable name. It is rather like an automated structured walkthrough.

In this form of testing you concentrate on the variables and closely check their values as they are changed by the program, to verify that they have been changed correctly.

Whereas the debugger is usually used for debugging (locating a bug), in this technique it is used for testing (denying or confirming the existence of a bug).

Formal verification

Formal methods employ the precision and power of mathematics in attempting to verify that a program meets its specification. They then place emphasis on the precision of the specification, which must first be rewritten in a formal mathematical notation. One such specification language is called Z. Once the formal specification for a program has been written, there are two alternative approaches:

1. Write the program and then verify that it conforms to the specification. This requires considerable time and skill.
2. Derive the program from the specification by means of a series of transformations, each of which preserve the correctness of the product. This is currently the favoured approach.

Formal verification is very appealing because of its potential for rigorously verifying a program's correctness beyond all possible doubt. However, it must be remembered that these methods are carried out by fallible human beings who make mistakes. So they are not a cure-all.

Formal verification is still in its infancy and is not widely used in industry and commerce, except in a few safety-critical applications. Further discussion of this approach is beyond the scope of this book.

Incremental development

One approach to writing a program is to write the complete program, key it in and try to run it. The salient word here is 'try', because most programmers find that the friendly compiler will find lots of errors in their program. It can be very disheartening – particularly for novices – to see so many errors displayed by a program that was the result of so much effort. Once the compilation errors have been banished, the program will usually exhibit strange behaviours during the (sometimes lengthy) period of debugging and testing. If all the parts of a program are keyed in together for testing, it can be difficult to locate any errors. A useful technique for helping to avoid these frustrations is to do things bit by bit. Thus an alternative to big-bang development is piece-by-piece programming – usually called *incremental* programming. The steps are:

1. Design and construct the user interface (the form).
2. Write a small piece of the program.
3. Key it in, fix the syntax errors, run it and debug it.
4. Add a new small piece of the program.
5. Repeat from step 2 until the program is complete.

The trick is to identify which piece of program to start with and which order to do things in. The best approach is probably to start by writing the simplest of the event-handling methods. Then write any methods that are used by this first method. Then write another event-handling method, and so on.

Programming principles

There is no foolproof testing method that will ensure that a program is free of errors. The best approach would be to use a combination of testing methods – black box, white box and inspection – because they have been shown to find different errors. To use all three methods is, however, very time consuming. So you need to exercise considerable judgement and skill to decide what sort of testing to do and how much testing to do. A systematic approach is vital.

Incremental testing avoids looking for a needle in a haystack, since a newly discovered error is probably in the newly incorporated class.

Testing is a frustrating business, because we know that, however patient and systematic we are, we can never be sure that we have done enough. Testing requires massive patience, attention to detail and organization.

Writing a program is a constructive experience, but testing is destructive. It can be difficult to try to demolish an object of pride that it has taken hours to create – knowing that if an error is found, then further hours may be needed in order to rectify the problem. So it is all too easy to behave like an ostrich during testing, trying to avoid the problems.

Summary

- Testing is a technique that tries to establish that a program is free from errors.
- Testing cannot be exhaustive because there are too many cases.
- Black box testing uses only the specification to choose test data.
- White box testing uses a knowledge of how the program works in order to choose test data.

- Inspection simply means studying the program listing in order to find errors.
- Stepping through code using a debugger can be a valuable way of testing a program.
- Incremental development can avoid the complexities of developing large programs.

EXERCISES

22.1 Devise black box and white box test data to test the following program. The specification is:

> The program inputs integers using a text box and a button. The program displays the largest of the numbers entered so far.

Try not to look at the text of the program, given below, until you have completed the design of the black box data.

At class level, there is an instance variable declaration:

```
Private largest As Integer = 0
```

The event-handling code is:

```
Private Sub Button1_Click(ByVal sender As System.Object, _
                         ByVal e As System.EventArgs) _
                         Handles Button1.Click
    Dim number As Integer
    number = CInt(TextBox1.Text)
    If number > largest Then
        largest = number
    End If
    Label1.Text = "largest so far is " & CStr(largest)
End Sub
```

22.2 Devise black box and white box test data to test the following program. The specification is given below. Try not to look at the text of the program, also given below, until you have completed the design of the black box data.

> The program determines insurance premiums for a holiday, based upon the age and gender (male or female) of the client.

> For a female of age >= 18 and <= 30 the premium is $5.
> A female aged >= 31 pays $3.50.
> A male of age >= 18 and <= 35 pays $6.
> A male aged >= 36 pays $5.50.
> Any other ages or genders are an error, which is signalled as a premium of zero.

The code for this program is:

```
Public Function CalcPremium(ByVal age As Double, _
                            ByVal gender As String) As Double
    Dim premium As Double

    If gender = "female" Then
        If (age >= 18) And (age <= 30) Then
            premium = 5.0
        Else
            If age >= 31 Then
                premium = 3.50
            Else
                premium = 0
            End If
        End If
    Else
        If gender = "male" Then
            If (age >= 18) And (age <= 35) Then
                premium = 6.0
            Else
                If age >= 36 Then
                    premium = 5.5
                Else
                    premium = 0
                End If
            End If
        Else
            premium = 0
        End If
    End If

    Return premium
End Function
```

ANSWERS TO SELF-TEST QUESTIONS

22.1 The specification does not say what is to happen if an exception arises. There are several possibilities. The first situation is if the user enters data that is not a valid integer – for example a letter is entered instead of a digit. The next situation is if the user enters a number greater than 10 000. The final eventuality that might arise is if the sum of the numbers exceeds the size of number that can be accommodated by the computer. If integers are represented as `Integer` types in the program, this limit is huge, but it could arise.

22.2 A row number is in three partitions:

1. within the range 1 to 8;
2. less than 1;
3. greater than 8.

If we choose one representative value in each partition (say 3, –3 and 11 respectively) and a similar set of values for the column numbers (say 5, –2 and 34), the test data will be:

Test no.	Row	Column	Outcome
1	3	5	OK
2	–3	5	invalid
3	11	5	invalid
4	3	–2	invalid
5	–3	–2	invalid
6	11	–2	invalid
7	3	34	invalid
8	–3	34	invalid
9	11	34	invalid

We now consider that data near the boundary of the partitions is important and therefore add to the test data for each partition so that it becomes:

1. within the range 1 to 8 (say 3);
2. less than 1 (say –3);
3. greater than 8 (say 11);
4. boundary value 1;
5. boundary value 8;
6. boundary value 0;
7. boundary value 9;

which now gives many more combinations to use as test data.

22.3 There are four paths through the program, which can be exercised by the following test data:

Test no.	Outcome			
1	3	2	1	3
2	3	2	5	5
3	2	3	1	3
4	2	3	5	5

22.4 There are three paths through the program extract, including the path where neither of the conditions in the `If` statements are true. But each of the error messages can be triggered by two conditions. Suitable test data is therefore:

Test no.	Row	Column	Outcome
1	5	6	OK
2	0	4	invalid
3	9	4	invalid
4	5	9	invalid
5	5	0	invalid

Interfaces

This chapter explains:

- how to use interfaces in describing the structure of a program;
- how to use interfaces in ensuring the interoperability of the classes within a program;
- a comparison of interfaces with abstract classes.

● Introduction

VB provides a notation for describing the outward appearance of a class, called an *interface*. An interface is just like the description of a class but with the bodies of the properties and methods omitted. Do not confuse this use of the word interface with the same word in the term graphical user interface (GUI). Two uses for interfaces are:

- in design;
- to promote interoperability.

● Interfaces for design

The importance of design during the initial planning of a large program is often emphasized. This involves designing all the classes for the program. A specification of the class names, their properties and methods, written in English, is one way to document such a design. But it is also possible to write this description in VB. For example, the interface for the class `Balloon` is:

```
Public Interface BalloonInterface
      Sub ChangeSize(ByVal newDiameter As Integer)
      Property XCoord() As Integer
      Sub Display(ByVal drawArea As Graphics)
End Interface
```

Notice that the word `class` is omitted in an interface description. Notice also that methods and properties are not declared as `Public` (or anything else).

Only the property and method names and their parameters are described in an interface, while the bodies of the properties and methods are omitted. An interface describes a class, but does not say how the properties, methods and the data items are implemented. It thus describes only the services provided by the class – it represents the outward appearance of a class as seen by users of the class (or an object instantiated from it). By implication it also says what the person who implements the class must provide.

An interface can be compiled along with any other classes, but clearly cannot be executed. However, someone who is planning to *use* a class can compile the program along with the interface and thereby check that it is being used correctly. Anyone who has written a VB program knows that the compiler is extremely vigilant in finding errors that otherwise might cause mischievous problems when the program executes. So any checking that can be done at compile-time is most worthwhile.

A person who is implementing an interface can specify in the heading of the class that a particular interface is being implemented. Earlier, as an example, we wrote an interface describing the interface to a class `Balloon`. Now we write the class `Balloon` itself:

```
Public Class Balloon
     Implements BalloonInterface

     Private diameter, x, y As Integer

     Public Sub ChangeSize(ByVal newDiameter As Integer) _
            Implements BalloonInterface.ChangeSize
         diameter = newDiameter
     End Sub

     Public Property XCoord() As Integer _
            Implements BalloonInterface.XCoord
         Get
             Return x
         End Get
         Set(ByVal value As Integer)
             x = value
         End Set
     End Property
```

```
        Public Sub Display(ByVal drawArea As Graphics) _
            Implements BalloonInterface.Display
            Dim myPen As Pen = New Pen(Color.Black)
            drawArea.DrawEllipse(myPen, x, y, diameter, diameter)
        End Sub

    End Class
```

Notice that the class as a whole is described as implementing the `BalloonInterface` interface. Then each and every method and property is described as implementing the corresponding item from the interface. The compiler will then check that this class has been implemented to comply with the interface declaration – that is, it provides the properties and methods `ChangeSize`, `XCoord` and `Display`, together with their appropriate parameters. The rule is that if you implement an interface, you have to implement every property and method described in the interface.

Interfaces can also be used to describe an inheritance structure. For example, suppose we wanted to describe an interface for a `ColoredBalloon` type that is a subclass of the interface `Balloon` described above. We can write:

```
    Public Interface ColoredBalloonInterface
        Inherits BalloonInterface

        Sub SetColor(ByVal c As Color)

    End Interface
```

which inherits the interface `BalloonInterface` and states that the interface `ColoredBalloonInterface` has an additional method to set the colour of an object. We could similarly describe a whole tree structure of classes as interfaces, describing purely their outward appearance and their subclass–superclass relationships.

In summary, interfaces can be used to describe:

- the classes in a program;
- the inheritance structure in a program, the 'is-a' relationships.

What interfaces *cannot* describe are:

- the implementations of methods and properties (this is the whole point of interfaces);
- which classes use which other classes, the 'has-a' relationships (this needs some other notation).

To use interfaces in design, write the interfaces for all the classes in the program before beginning the coding of the implementation of the classes.

Interfaces become particularly useful in medium-sized and large programs that make use of more than a few classes. In large programs that involve teams of programmers, their use is almost vital as a way of facilitating communication amongst the team members. Interfaces complement class diagrams as the documentation of a program's design.

Interfaces and interoperability

Household appliances such as toasters and electric kettles come with a power cord with a plug on the end of it. The design of the plug is standard (throughout a country) and ensures that an appliance can be used anywhere (within the country). Thus the adoption of a common interface ensures interoperability. In VB, interfaces can be used in a similar fashion to ensure that objects exhibit a common interface. When such an object is passed around a program we can be sure that it supports all the properties and methods specified by the interface description.

As an example, we declare an interface named `Displayable`. Any class complying with this interface must include a method named `Display` which displays the object. The interface declaration is:

```
Public Interface Displayable
    Sub Display(ByVal drawArea As Graphics)
End Interface
```

Now we write a new class, named `Square`, which represents square graphical objects. We say in the header of the class that it `Implements Displayable`. We include within the body of the class the method `Display`:

```
Public Class Square
    Implements Displayable

    Private x, y, size As Integer

    Public Sub Display(ByVal drawArea As Graphics) _
        Implements Displayable.Display

        Dim myPen As Pen = New Pen(Color.Black)
        drawArea.DrawRectangle(myPen, x, y, size, size)
    End Sub

    ' other methods and properties of the class Square

End Class
```

As the heading states, this class (and any object created from it) conforms to the `Displayable` interface. It means that any object of this class can be passed around a program and, when necessary, we are confident that it can be displayed by calling its method `Display`.

Finally we mention that just as a TV has interfaces both to a power source and to a signal source, so in VB we can specify that a class implements a number of interfaces. So while a class can only inherit from one other class, it can implement any number of interfaces.

Programming principles

Interfaces and abstract classes are similar. Abstract classes are described in Chapter 11 on inheritance. The purpose of an abstract class is to describe as a superclass the common features of a group of classes, and is introduced by the keyword `MustInherit`. The differences between abstract classes and interfaces are as follows:

1. An abstract class often provides an implementation of some of the methods and properties. In contrast, an interface never describes any implementation.
2. A class can implement more than one interface, but only inherit from one abstract class.
3. An interface is used at compile-time to perform checking. By contrast, an abstract class implies inheritance, which involves linking the appropriate method or property at run-time.
4. An abstract class implies that its `MustOverride` methods and properties will be fleshed out by classes that extend it. Inheritance is expected. But an interface simply specifies the skeleton for a class, with no implication that it will be used for inheritance.

Programming pitfalls

Remember that:

- A class can only inherit from one other class, including an abstract class.
- A class can implement any number of interfaces.

New language elements

- `Interface` – the description of the external interface to a class which may not yet be written.
- `Implements` – used in the header of a class to specify that the class, property or method implements a named interface.

Summary

- Interfaces are used to describe the services provided by a class.
- Interfaces are useful for describing the structure of a program. This description can be checked by the VB compiler.
- Interfaces can be used to ensure that a class conforms to a particular interface. This supports interoperability.

EXERCISES

Interfaces as design descriptions

23.1 Write an interface to describe selected properties and methods of the `TextBox` class from the toolbox.

23.2 Write an interface to describe a class that represents bank accounts. The class is called `Account`. It has methods `Deposit` and `Withdraw`, and a property `CurrentBalance`. Decide on suitable parameters for the methods.

23.3 Write interfaces to describe the structure of a program that consists of a number of classes, such as the game program described in Chapter 20 on design.

Interfaces for interoperability

23.4 Write a class named `Circle` that describes circle objects and conforms to the `Displayable` interface given above.

Polymorphism

This chapter explains:

- how to use polymorphism;
- when to use polymorphism.

● Introduction

We introduce the idea of polymorphism with a simple example. Suppose we have two classes, named `Sphere` and `Bubble`. We can create an instance of `Sphere` and an instance of `Bubble` in the usual way:

```
Dim sphere1 As Sphere = New Sphere()
Dim bubble1 As Bubble = New Bubble()
```

Suppose that each class has a method named `Display`. Then we can display the two objects as follows:

```
sphere1.Display(paper)
bubble1.Display(paper)
```

and although these two calls look very similar, in each case the appropriate version of `Display` is called. There are two methods with the same name (`Display`), but they are different. The VB system makes sure that the correct one is selected. So when `Display` is called for the object `sphere1`, it is the method defined within the class `Sphere` that is called. When `Display` is called for the object `bubble1`, it is the method defined within the class `Bubble` that is called. This is the essence of polymorphism.

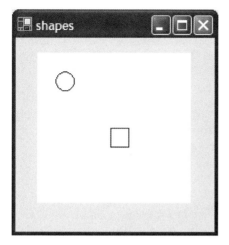

Figure 24.1 Display of the shapes using polymorphism.

● Polymorphism in action

In this chapter we use as an example a program that displays graphical – squares and circles – shapes on the screen (Figure 24.1). The program uses an abstract class named Shape, which describes all the shared attributes of these shapes, including where they are on the screen. (Abstract classes were explained in Chapter 11 on inheritance.)

```
Public MustInherit Class Shape

    Protected x As Integer, y As Integer
    Protected size As Integer = 20
    Protected myPen As Pen = New Pen(Color.Black)

    Public MustOverride Sub Display(ByVal drawArea As Graphics)

End Class
```

Each shape is described by its own class, a subclass of class Shape (Figure 24.2). For example:

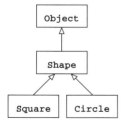

Figure 24.2 Class diagram for the shapes classes.

```
Public Class Circle
    Inherits Shape

    Sub New(ByVal initX As Integer, ByVal initY As Integer)
        x = initX
        y = initY
    End Sub

    Public Overrides Sub Display(ByVal drawArea As Graphics)
        drawArea.DrawEllipse(myPen, x, y, size, size)
    End Sub

End Class

Public Class Square
    Inherits Shape

    Sub New(ByVal initX As Integer, ByVal initY As Integer)
        x = initX
        y = initY
    End Sub

    Public Overrides Sub Display(ByVal drawArea As Graphics)
        drawArea.DrawRectangle(myPen, x, y, size, size)
    End Sub

End Class
```

Here is a program that illustrates using these classes. The program:

1. Creates two shapes, `circle1` and `square1`.
2. Creates a list named `group` in order to hold objects of the class `Shape`. A list, explained in Chapter 13, is a convenient data structure that expands or contracts to accommodate the required data.
3. Adds the two objects to `group`.
4. Displays the objects using a `For Each` loop.

The output from the program is shown in Figure 24.1.

```
Private Sub PictureBox1_Click(ByVal sender As System.Object, _
                              ByVal e As System.EventArgs) _
                              Handles PictureBox1.Click
    Dim paper As Graphics = PictureBox1.CreateGraphics()
    Dim circle1 As Circle = New Circle(20, 20)
    Dim square1 As Square = New Square(80, 80)
    Dim group As List(Of Shape) = New List(Of Shape)

    group.Add(circle1)
    group.Add(square1)
```

```
        For Each aShape As Shape In group
            aShape.Display(paper)
        Next
    End Sub
```

Polymorphism is in use here – the method `Display` is called on two occasions (within the `For` loop) with different results according to which object is in use. You can see that the two calls of `Display`:

```
    aShape.Display(paper)
```

give two different outputs. This is not necessarily what you might expect, but it is entirely correct. Two different outputs are displayed because the VB system automatically selects the version of `Display` associated with the class of the object (not the class of the variable that refers to it). The class of an object is determined when the object is created using `New`, and stays the same whatever happens to the object. Whatever you do to an object in a program, it always retains the properties it had when it was created. An object can be assigned to a variable of another class and passed around the program as a parameter, but it never loses its true identity. 'Once a square, always a square' might be an appropriate slogan.

When method `Display` is first called, the variable `aShape` contains the object `circle1` and so the version of `Display` in the class `Circle` is called. The corresponding thing happens with `square1`.

When you call a method (or use a property), polymorphism makes sure that the appropriate version of the method (or property) is automatically selected. Most of the time when you program in VB you are not aware that the VB system is selecting the correct method to call. It is automatic and invisible.

In the family analogy, you retain your identity and your relationship with your ancestors whether you get married, change your name, move to another country or whatever. This seems common sense, and indeed it is.

Polymorphism allows us to write a single statement such as:

```
    aShape.Display(paper)
```

instead of a series of `If` statements like this:

```
    If TypeOf aShape Is Square Then
        aShape.DisplaySquare(paper)
    End If
    If TypeOf aShape Is Circle Then
        aShape.DisplayCircle(paper)
    End If
```

which is more clumsy and long-winded. This uses a VB feature, `TypeOf`, to test whether an object belongs to a particular class. If there were a large number of shapes, there would be a correspondingly large number of `If` statements. This demonstrates how powerful and concise polymorphism is.

As we have seen in this small example, polymorphism often makes a segment of program smaller and neater through the elimination of a series of `If` statements. But this achievement is much more significant than it may seem. It means that a statement like:

```
aShape.Display(paper)
```

knows nothing about the possible variety of objects that may be used as the value of `aShape`. So information hiding (already present in large measure in an OO program) is extended. We can check this out by assessing how much we would need to change this program to accommodate some new type of shape (some additional subclass of `Shape`), say an ellipse. The answer is that we would not need to modify it at all. Thus polymorphism enhances modularity, reusability and maintainability.

Programming principles

Polymorphism represents the third major element of OOP. The complete set of three are:

1. Encapsulation – objects can be made highly modular.
2. Inheritance – desirable features in an existing class can be reused in other classes, without affecting the integrity of the original class.
3. Polymorphism – designing code that can easily manipulate objects of different classes. Differences between similar objects can be accommodated easily.

Novice programmers normally start out by using encapsulation, later move on to inheritance and subsequently use polymorphism.

The case study presented above uses a diversity of objects (shapes) that have common factors incorporated into a superclass. Now we know that the facility of inheritance helps describe the similarity of groups of objects in an economical fashion. The other side of the coin is using objects, and this is where polymorphism helps us to use objects in a concise uniform way. The diversity is handled not by a proliferation of `If` statements, but instead by a single method call:

```
aShape.Display(paper)
```

so making use of polymorphism to select the appropriate method. When this happens the version of the method `Display` that matches the actual object is selected. This can only be decided when the program is running, immediately before the method is called. This is termed *late binding, dynamic linking* or *delayed binding*. It is an essential feature of a language that supports polymorphism.

Polymorphism helps construct programs that are:

- concise (shorter than they might otherwise be);
- modular (unrelated parts are kept separate);
- easy to change and adapt (for example, introducing new objects).

In general, the approach to exploiting polymorphism within a particular program is as follows:

1. Use the same names for similar methods and properties.
2. Identify any similarities (common methods, properties and variables) between any objects or classes in the program.
3. Design a superclass that embodies the common features of the classes.
4. Design the subclasses that describe the distinctive features of each of the classes, whilst inheriting the common features from the superclass.
5. Identify any place in the program where the same operation must be applied to any of the similar objects. It may be tempting to use `If` statements at this location. Instead, this is the place to use polymorphism.
6. Make sure that the superclass contains an abstract method (or property) corresponding to every method (or property) that is to be used polymorphically.

Programming pitfalls

If you are exploiting polymorphism, and grouping a number of classes under a single superclass, you must ensure that the superclass describes all the methods and properties that will be used on any instance of the superclass. Sometimes this will require abstract methods and properties in the superclass that serve no purpose other than enabling the program to compile.

New language elements

The keyword `TypeOf` allows the program to test whether an object belongs to a particular class.

Summary

- The principles of polymorphism are:
  1. An object always retains the identity of the class from which it was created. (An object can never be converted into an object of another class.)
  2. When a method or property is used on an object, the appropriate method or property is automatically selected.
- Polymorphism enhances information hiding and reusability by helping to make pieces of code widely applicable.

EXERCISES

24.1 An abstract class `Animal` has constructor method `New`, a property `Weight`, and a function method `Says`. The `Weight` property represents the weight of the animal, an `Integer` value. `Says` returns a string, the noise that the animal makes. Class `Animal` has subclasses `Cow`, `Snake` and `Pig`. These subclasses have different implementations of `Says`, returning values "moo", "hiss" and "grunt" respectively. Write the class `Animal` and the three subclasses. Create objects `petCow`, `petSnake` and `petPig` respectively from the three classes and use their properties and methods. Display the information in a text box.

24.2 In the shapes program add a new shape – a straight line – to the collection of available shapes. Use the library method `DisplayLine` to actually draw a line object. Add code to create a line object, add it to the list of objects (in the list) and display it along with the other shapes.

24.3 Enhance the shapes program into a full-blown drawing package that allows shapes to be selected from a menu and placed at a desired location in a picture box. The user specifies the position with a mouse click.

24.4 A bank offers its customers two kinds of account – a regular account and a gold account. The two types of account provide some shared facilities but they also offer distinctive features. The common facilities are:

- recording name and address;
- opening an account with an initial balance;
- maintaining and displaying a record of the current balance;
- methods to deposit and withdraw an amount of money.

A regular account cannot be overdrawn. A gold account holder can overdraw indefinitely. A regular account has interest calculated as 5% per year of the amount. A gold account has interest at 6% per year, less a fixed charge of $100 per year.

Write a class that describes the common features and classes to describe regular and gold accounts.

Construct a program to use these classes by creating two bank accounts – one a regular account, and the other a gold account. Each is created with a person's name and some initial amount of money. Display the name, balance and interest of each account.

Databases

This chapter explains:

- the nature of simple databases and the SQL language;
- how SQL can be used with VB;
- the VB classes which provide database access.

● Introduction

This chapter is for those who are familiar with creating a relational database (for example via Microsoft Access) and who wish to manipulate the database with a VB program. They might wish to do this because:

- As one of its tasks, the VB program needs some form of data store, and a database is most suitable.
- The programmer wishes to take advantage of the power of VB and its classes to provide a more powerful interface to a database than a conventional standalone database product allows.

Though you are likely to be familiar with SQL (Standard Query Language), we provide a short introduction.

● The elements of a database

Though this book assumes that the reader can create relational databases (and can perform the prior analysis stages involving for example normalization), we will review the essential terminology.

Artists

Artist	Company	Sales
The Visuals	ABC Co	65.2
RadioStar	ABC Co	22.7
Mike Parr	Media Ltd	3.5
The Objects	Class UK	12.6
Assignment 182	Media Ltd	34.6
The Trees	United Co	3.72

Figure 25.1 The `Artists` table.

Here is an example of a database, which was created with Microsoft Access. It was stored in a file named `MusicSales.mdb`. It consists of two tables: the first was named `Artists`, and the second was named `Companies`. Incidentally, we could have created the database by writing VB code, but using Access is simpler. The file can be downloaded from our website.

Figure 25.1 shows the `Artists` table, involving recording artists, their management company and their music sales (in millions of dollars). Note that:

- The table is made up of a collection of similar *records*. In Figure 25.1 we have represented each record as a row.
- A record is made up of a number of *fields*. In Figure 25.1 we have three fields, named **Artist**, **Company** and **Sales**. Effectively, a field name is a column name.
- The assumption has been made that artist names are unique, so we used this as the primary key. However, if the table contained, for example, student names in a college, we would have to introduce a unique student ID number. For the above table, we set up the **Artist** field as the primary key when we created it, and this prohibits us from introducing other artists with the same name.

A database can consist of one or more such tables. Figure 25.2 shows the second table, named `Companies` (with `Company` set as the primary key for the table), which lists company names together with their location. The relationship between the tables is that

Companies

Company	Location
ABC Co	London
Media Ltd	Chicago
Class UK	Madrid
United Co	London

Figure 25.2 The `Companies` table.

the `Company` column of the `Artists` table is a foreign key of the `Company` column in the `Companies` table. This was specified when we designed the database.

The SQL language – introduction

SQL (Structured Query Language) was standardized in the mid-eighties, and since then has become the major language for database access. SQL statements can be used to retrieve and modify the contents of a database. Though it is possible to enter SQL statements manually, it is normal to present a simpler interface to the user. We shall do this in VB by building strings which contain SQL statements, and then sending the strings to the database. Thus, the SQL statements are hidden from the user.

Before we do this, here are some examples of the most useful SQL statements. In traditional use, SQL statements must be terminated with a semicolon, but this is not needed when we pass an individual statement to the ADO.NET classes.

The `select` statement

This is used to retrieve records from a database. We can specify criteria that a record must match. Here are some examples, using the database we introduced earlier. Here we use lower-case for SQL key words (such as `select` and `insert`), but capitals can also be used.

- `select Artist from Artists`
  This returns an item from every `Artist` field in the `Artists` table (i.e. the complete Artist column).
- `select * from Artists`
  This returns the items from *every* field in the `Artists` table. Effectively, it returns the complete table.
- `select * from Artists where Company = 'Media Ltd'`
  This returns only the records from `Artists` where the company is `Media Ltd`. We enclose strings in single quotes. Strings are case-sensitive, so use capitals where they were used in the original database.
- `select * from Artists where Sales > 20`
  This returns only those records with sales above 20. Note that there are no quotes around numbers. The available operators are:

  `>   <   >=   <=   <>   =`

  where `<>` means 'not equals'.
- `select * from Companies where Company = 'ABC Co'`
  This returns the single record from `Companies`, involving `ABC Co`.
- `select * from Artists order by Sales asc`
  The `order by` item can be added to any selection. We can use `asc` or `desc` to specify ascending or descending order. The above statement puts the records in ascending order of sales.

The `insert` statement

```
insert into Artists (Artist, Company, Sales)
                    values('The Regulars', 'ABC Co', 23.8)
```

inserts a new record with the specified values. We provide a bracketed list of column names, and a bracketed list of values. Note that we can choose to split a long statement into several lines to improve its readability.

The `delete` statement

```
delete from Artists where Artist = 'RadioStar'
delete from Artists where Company = 'ABC Co'
```

deletes the specified record(s).

The `update` statement

```
update Artists set Sales = 30.8 where Artist = 'RadioStar'
update Artists set Company = 'Class UK', Sales = 56.8
    where Artist = 'RadioStar'
```

updates the `RadioStar` record. The examples show, first, a single field being updated, then two fields. As with `delete`, it is possible to specify several records in the `where` item.

This concludes our SQL overview. There are more statements, and even those we illustrated have extensions. However, the above will suffice for the programs in this chapter.

● The VB database classes

Throughout its life, Microsoft has provided a series of approaches for database manipulation, including ODBC (Open DataBase Connectivity), and ADO (ActiveX Data Objects). The .NET framework now provides ADO.NET. It is termed an API (applications program interface) – a set of classes and their methods which provide access to a complex item. For example, the file classes such as `Directory` are a kind of API, in that they enable programs to access the Windows file system.

The ADO.NET classes we will use are:

```
OleDbConnection, OleDbCommand, OleDbDataAdapter, DataTable,
DataGridView, BindingNavigator and OleDbCommandBuilder.
```

The `OleDb` namespace contains many of these classes, and you will see this used when we declare instances.

You might wish to read this section whilst looking at the complete examples, whose screenshots are shown in Figures 25.3, 25.5 and 25.6.

The `OleDbConnection` class

This class deals with connecting to the database. We need to provide it with the 'connection string', which states the type of database (e.g. Oracle, Microsoft Access) and its location on disk. In our binding navigator example below, the VB system will do this initialization automatically, but in the other two examples, we do it manually.

The `OleDbDataAdapter` class

This class provides facilities for sending SQL statements to a database. This can involve transferring data from the database into `DataTable` objects held temporarily in RAM.

The class structure of `OleDbDataAdapter` is rather complicated: it has some properties (named `UpdateCommand`, `InsertCommand` and `DeleteCommand`) which in their turn are instances of another complex class named `OleDbCommand`. In its turn, this class has its own properties and methods (such as `CommandText`). The `Fill` method lets us place the results of a query in a data table. The last two examples in this chapter show you how to use the class.

The `DataTable` class

Instances can hold a single table in RAM. The data is presented to the programmer in row/column form, rather like a 2-dimensional array. Note that it provides no visual representation of a table. We can choose to fill a data table with an exact copy of a table in a database, or we can pick out the records we need. This is determined by the SQL string we send to the adapter.

We can access individual items of a data table by using the `Rows` property, followed by a row number and column number, as in:

```
Dim name As String
name = CStr(dataTable.Rows(0)(1))
```

Note that:

- rows and columns are numbered from 0 upwards;
- The data table holds instances of the class `Object`, so when we extract an item, we convert it to the appropriate type. (For example we convert an item to a `String` if it is to be displayed in a text box.)

To find out how many rows a data table currently contains, we use the `Count` property, as in:

```
Dim lastRowNumber As Integer
lastRowNumber = dataTable.Rows.Count - 1
```

Remember that the rows are numbered from 0 upwards. To empty a data table, we use the `Clear` method.

The row/column structure will be familiar to you from using arrays, and it is tempting to begin to write loops to search data tables. However, this is to be avoided. Try to do as much work as possible in SQL. This approach results in simpler code. The data grid view example shows the data table in use.

The `OleDbCommandBuilder` class

This class deals with generating a set of commands to update a database, based on changes that might have been made to a data table (perhaps via a data grid view user interface). The **Save** button in the second example (data grid view) shows it in use.

The `DataGridView` class

This visual control provides for the display of a `DataTable` in row/column format. It also allows the editing of existing data, and the insertion of new records at the bottom of the grid. Note that changes to the data are not automatically transferred to the database. We make use of an `OleDbCommandBuilder` to perform the updating.

We use the `DataSource` property to 'bind' a data grid view to a data table. From then on, any changes to the table are automatically displayed in the grid. The data grid view is in the **Data** section of the toolbox, and is positioned in the same way as other controls.

The `BindingNavigator` class

This visual control provides a toolbar (normally placed along the top of a form) with buttons to step forwards and backwards through a database. It can be found in the **Data** section of the toolbox. It can control the contents of (for example) text boxes which have been bound to a database. Example 1 shows this in use.

Adding a data connection to Visual Basic

The first stage in accessing an existing database from a program involves adding a data connection to the VB system. Before actually adding it, go through these steps:

1. Create a new project, then, without doing any coding, do **File | Save All**, choosing a suitable folder.
2. Using Windows Explorer, copy our supplied **MusicSales.mdb** into the folder which contains your project. In fact, the database can be stored anywhere, but this step ensures that if we move the program, the database moves with it.

At the end of these preliminary steps, we have a new project and a database file ready to be connected. If the database you are accessing is on a network drive, simply create a new project.

Adding a data connection – the detail

Before the program can use a database, we need to tell the VB system about it. We add a data connection:

1. Choose **View | Database Explorer**. If this is not visible use the **Server Explorer**.
2. In the database (or server) explorer panel, right-click on **Data Connections** and choose **Add Connection**.
3. An **Add Connection** window opens. For our provided database, ensure that the data source is set to
   Microsoft Access Database File. Click **Continue**.
4. Click **Browse** and choose the database file (e.g. MusicSales.mdb). Delete any existing text from the user name area and the password area.
5. Click **Test Connection**. You should see the message:

   ```
   Test connection succeeded
   ```

   If you don't see the message, check that the above steps have been done properly.
6. Finally, click **OK** to close the **Add Connection** window. You will see the added database in the **Database Explorer** panel.

Note:

- The VB system remembers any data connections that you add. For example, if you create another new project, the **Database Explorer** panel will show previous databases. You might need to expand **Data Connections** to see them. To allow a particular program to use a data connection, we make use of the Data Sources panel, described later.
- Databases have properties. In the **Database Explorer** panel, right-click on your database, choosing **Properties**. Its properties will be displayed at the bottom-right area of the screen, where the properties of controls are normally shown. Ensure that you can see the **Connection String** property. It looks something like:

  Provider=Microsoft.Jet . . . etc

  Later, you will need to copy and paste this text.

Example 1: creating a `BindingNavigator` program

Our first program will let us scroll backwards and forwards through the records of a database. Figure 25.3 shows the screen. We will not need to write code. Follow these steps:

1. Create a new project, and save it. If you need to, copy the database into your project folder.
2. Add a data connection to VB, as explained above. At the end of this process, the connection should be visible in the **Database Explorer** or the **Server Explorer**.
3. Look at the top right of the screen. You will see the **Solution Explorer** area. In fact, this area is composed of two tabs: **Solution Explorer** and **Data Sources**. Figure 25.4 shows this. Switch to the Data Sources panel, and click on the **Add New Data Source . . .** link.

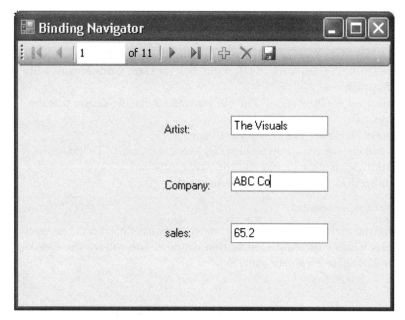

Figure 25.3 Example 1: the BindingNavigator program.

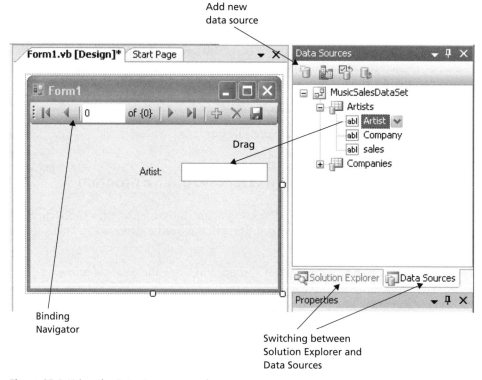

Figure 25.4 Using the Data Sources panel.

4. The **Data Source Configuration Wizard** runs. Choose **Database**, then **Next**.
5. The **Choose Your Data Connection** step appears. From the drop-down list of added connections, choose the one you want, then **Next**.
6. A long message appears, asking if you want to copy the file to your project, and modify the connection. We suggest choosing **No**.
(Selecting **No** ensures that any changes you make to the original database are really made, so if you delete all the records accidentally, you will have to get a fresh copy of it. However, it is clear to see that any code which changes the database is in fact working. If you choose **Yes**, your code operates on a *copy* of the database, and there is the possibility of confusion between the original version and VB's copy.)
7. A **Save Connection String** question appears. Just click **Next**.
8. A **Choose Your Database Objects** screen appears. Put a tick against **Tables** and click **Finish**.
9. The binding navigator can now make use of your database.

Look at Figure 25.4. It shows the data source panel when every table has been expanded by clicking the + alongside them.

Now comes the magic. We will create a program:

- In data sources, select **Artist** (not Artists) and drag it on to your form. Two things happen:
  - An empty text box and a label containing **Artist** are placed on the form. The text box is bound to the artist data in your database.
  - A binding navigator is placed across the top of the form. This happens when the first column name is dropped on to the form. This component controls the navigation of the bound controls, i.e. the data that is displayed in the text box.

- In addition, drag on **Company** and **sales**.
- Run the program – your screen should resemble Figure 25.3. Use the arrow controls to navigate through the data. You can also enter a record number.

As it stands the program lets you update the database, but validation of new records is not performed. To prevent updating, you could disable selected buttons within the navigator.

● Example 2: a `DataGridView` program

This program shows the data grid view in action. Figure 25.5 shows the screen. The user enters a sales figure, and an SQL query is constructed which fills a data table with records whose sales are equal to or above the entered value. A value of 0 will select every record. The data grid can be edited, and changes can be made permanent via a **Save** button. At the bottom of the form, we show the generated SQL select command that is used. Here is the code:

412 • Chapter 25/Databases

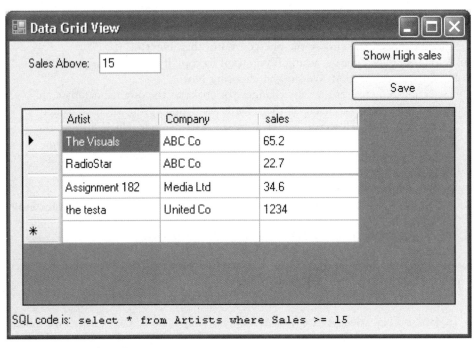

Figure 25.5 Example 2: the DataGridView program.

```
Public Class Form1
    Private dataTable As New DataTable()
    'set the 'connection string'
    Private dbInfo As String = _
    "Provider=Microsoft.Jet.OLEDB.4.0;Data Source=" _
        + "E:\bigdrive\vb2005book\codebychaps\" _
        + "database2005\dataGridnew\MusicSales.mdb"

    Private Sub HighSalesButton_Click( _
        ByVal sender As System.Object, _
        ByVal e As System.EventArgs) _
        Handles HighSalesButton.Click

        Dim command As String

        Try
            'make a command
            command = "select * from Artists where " _
                & "Sales >= " & SalesAboveBox.Text
            SQLLabel.Text = command

            'create an adapter, incorporating an SQL select
            Dim adapter As New OleDb.OleDbDataAdapter(command, dbInfo)
```

Example 2: a `DataGridView` program

```vb
            dataTable.Clear()
            'fill data table with results from sql select
            adapter.Fill(dataTable)
            DataGridView1.DataSource = dataTable
        Catch exceptionObject As Exception
            MessageBox.Show(exceptionObject.Message)
        End Try
    End Sub

    Private Sub SaveButton_Click( _
        ByVal sender As System.Object, _
        ByVal e As System.EventArgs) _
        Handles SaveButton.Click
        Try
            'create an adapter, selecting every artist
            Dim adapter As New OleDb.OleDbDataAdapter _
                ("select * from Artists", dbInfo)

            Dim commandbuilder As New _
                    OleDb.OleDbCommandBuilder(adapter)
            adapter.Update(dataTable)
        Catch exceptionObject As Exception
            MessageBox.Show(exceptionObject.Message)
        End Try
    End Sub
End Class
```

Note:

- To create the program, the first step is to add your database to the VB system. Follow the **Add Connection** instructions above. At the end of this step, you should be able to see the database name in the **Database Explorer** (or **Server Explorer**) panel.
- Now we need to find the connection string for the database. Right-click on the database in the **Database Explorer** and select **Properties**. The properties of the selected database are shown at the bottom right of the VB screen, where control properties are normally shown. For an Access database, the string is similar to:

    `Provider=Microsoft.Jet.OLEDB...etc`

    Copy this string with your mouse.
- You need to create an instance variable of type `string`, and initialize it to the connection string. We chose the name `dbInfo`. In our code, we have split the long connection string into shorter strings, and joined them. This is so you can see the whole thing on paper. There is no need to do this when you are working at the screen. Incidentally, if you move the database to another folder, repeat the **Add Connection** and **Add Data Source** tasks, and copy the new connection string.

- Place a data grid view on the form. It can be found in the data section of the toolbox.
- The data table is declared as an instance variable, because it is shared by both methods.
- The DataSource property of the grid is used to bind the data table. This means that when the table changes (via the Fill method) then the table is re-displayed in the grid automatically.
- The data grid can be altered by the user:
  - To update a record, type in the new values.
  - To insert a new record, type it at the bottom of the grid, alongside the *.
  - To delete a record, click the button at the left of the record. This highlights all the fields. Press the **delete** key on the keyboard to delete it. Any changes are not yet transferred to the file. You must use the **Save** command to do that.
  - To resize the columns, place the mouse between the buttons at the top of the columns, and drag.
  - To sort the records based on a particular column, click the button at the top of a column. Clicking again changes from ascending order to descending order.
- The program does not check for errors after each modification of the data grid. For example, if the user enters a company that does not already exist in the **Companies** table, then this error will only come to light when we click **Save**. Thus, exception-handling is essential at the saving stage.

> **SELF-TEST QUESTION**
>
> **25.1** How would you provide a **Show All Records** button for the user?

Example 3: SQL example

This program provides a form which allows the user to search, delete, insert and update records. Figure 25.6 shows the form, and here is the code:

```
Public Class Form1
    'set the 'connection string'
    Private dbInfo As String = _
    "Provider=Microsoft.Jet.OLEDB.4.0;Data Source=E:\" + _
    "bigdrive\VB2005book\codebychaps\database2005\MusicSales.mdb"

    Private Sub FindButton_Click( _
        ByVal sender As System.Object, _
        ByVal e As System.EventArgs) _
        Handles FindButton.Click

        Try
            Dim table As New DataTable()
            Dim command As String
```

Example 3: SQL example

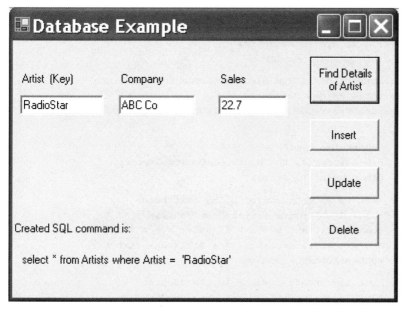

Figure 25.6 Example 3: the SQL Example program.

```
Dim recordCount As Integer
'set up an SQL query
command = "select * from Artists where " _
    & "Artist = " & " '" & ArtistBox.Text & "'"
'create an adapter, incorporating a select command
Dim adapter As New _
OleDb.OleDbDataAdapter(command, dbInfo)
SQLLabel.Text = command

'do the query
table.Clear()
recordCount = adapter.Fill(table)

'display any result
If recordCount <> 0 Then ' we have a result
    CompanyBox.Text = CStr(table.Rows(0)(1))
    SalesBox.Text = CStr(table.Rows(0)(2))
Else
    MessageBox.Show("Artist not found!!")
End If
Catch exceptionObject As Exception
    MessageBox.Show(exceptionObject.Message)
End Try
End Sub
```

```
Private Sub UpdateButton_Click( _
    ByVal sender As System.Object, _
    ByVal e As System.EventArgs) _
    Handles UpdateButton.Click

    Dim connection As New OleDb.OleDbConnection(dbInfo)
    Dim table As New DataTable
    Dim oleDbUpdateCommand = New OleDb.OleDbCommand()

    Try
        connection.Open()
        Dim adapter As New OleDb.OleDbDataAdapter()
        Dim command As String

        'set up an SQL update, using text boxes
        command = "update Artists set Company = '" & _
        CompanyBox.Text & "', " & "Sales = " & SalesBox.Text _
            & " where Artist = '" & ArtistBox.Text & "'"
        SQLLabel.Text = command

        'put the update command in the adapter
        oleDbUpdateCommand.Connection = connection
        oleDbUpdateCommand.CommandText = command
        adapter.UpdateCommand = oleDbUpdateCommand

        'do the update
        adapter.UpdateCommand.ExecuteNonQuery()
    Catch exceptionObject As Exception
        MessageBox.Show(exceptionObject.Message)
    Finally
        connection.Close()
    End Try
End Sub

Private Sub InsertButton_Click( _
    ByVal sender As System.Object, _
    ByVal e As System.EventArgs) _
    Handles InsertButton.Click

    Dim connection As New OleDb.OleDbConnection(dbInfo)
    Dim oleDbInsertCommand = New OleDb.OleDbCommand()
    Dim command As String
    Dim adapter As New OleDb.OleDbDataAdapter()

    Try
        connection.Open()
        'make an SQL insert command
        command = "insert into Artists" _
            & "(Artist, Company, Sales )" _
            & " values('" & ArtistBox.Text & "', '" _
            & CompanyBox.Text & "', " & SalesBox.Text & ")"
        SQLLabel.Text = command
```

```vbnet
            'put the insert command into the adapter
            oleDbInsertCommand.Connection = connection
            oleDbInsertCommand.CommandText = command
            adapter.InsertCommand = oleDbInsertCommand

            ' do the insert
            adapter.InsertCommand.ExecuteNonQuery()
        Catch exceptionObject As Exception
            MessageBox.Show(exceptionObject.Message)
        Finally
            connection.Close()
        End Try
    End Sub

    Private Sub DeleteButton_Click( _
        ByVal sender As System.Object, _
        ByVal e As System.EventArgs) _
        Handles DeleteButton.Click

        Dim connection As New OleDb.OleDbConnection(dbInfo)
        Dim command As String
        Dim oleDbDeleteCommand = New OleDb.OleDbCommand()
        Dim rowsAffected As Integer
        Dim adapter As New OleDb.OleDbDataAdapter()

        Try
            connection.Open()
            'make an SQL delete command
            command = "delete from Artists where Artist = '" _
                & ArtistBox.Text & "';"
            SQLLabel.Text = command

            'put the delete command into the adapter
            oleDbDeleteCommand.Connection = connection
            oleDbDeleteCommand.CommandText = command
            adapter.DeleteCommand = oleDbDeleteCommand

            'do the command
            rowsAffected = adapter.DeleteCommand.ExecuteNonQuery()
            If rowsAffected = 0 Then  'nothing was altered
                MessageBox.Show("Deletion not done.")
            Else
                MessageBox.Show("Deletion done.")
            End If
        Catch exceptionObject As Exception
            MessageBox.Show(exceptionObject.Message)
        Finally
            connection.Close()
        End Try
    End Sub
End Class
```

Here are some points on the program:

- The user interface is not error-proofed. For example, an insert can be attempted even if all the fields are empty. The omission is intentional, to avoid obscuring the database code.
- To create the program, follow the setting-up process as used for the data grid view example, then enter the code. The three text boxes have been renamed `ArtistBox`, `CompanyBox` and `SalesBox`.
- The code for inserting, deleting and updating is similar. It involves creating an instance of `OleDbCommand`, setting its properties (`Connection` and `CommandText`) and assigning it to the appropriate property of an adapter. Finally, `ExecuteNonQuery` actually carries out the command. It is important to follow the given coding sequence.
- Every time we create an SQL command, we display it in `SQLLabel` at the bottom of the form, before executing the command. The reason is that, although the VB compiler makes detailed checks on your VB coding, it does not check the contents of strings, and knows nothing about SQL. Thus, SQL statement errors are only detected at run-time, and it is useful to have a display of the SQL code. Many errors are simple mistakes with single quotes.
- It is essential to use exception-handling. In this program, we display the `Message` property, which provides an explanation of any errors. Examples of errors that might be caught are:

    – trying to add a new record using a company not in the Companies table;
    – trying to add a record with a non-numeric sales figure.

- When deleting, inserting and updating, we need to open and close the connection. We place the `Close` call within the `Finally` of the exception-handling code, so that it is performed whatever happens within the `Try`.

> **SELF-TEST QUESTION**
>
> 25.2 In the SQL example program, which text boxes need values when
>
>   (a) deleting a record?
>   (b) inserting a record?

Programming principles

This chapter has no new VB principles – we are using the power of the ADO classes.

Programming pitfalls

- It is very easy to make errors when creating SQL strings. Take care with single quotes and, when debugging, display the SQL command.
- When executing queries with `Fill`, you do not need to use `Open` and `Close`. In every other case they are needed.

Grammar spot

- The `Rows` property of a data table takes two bracketed integer expressions, and returns an `Object`. We convert it to our required type, as in:

   ```
   Dim n As Integer = CInt(table.Rows(3) (4))
   ```

New language elements

The classes:

```
OleDbConnection
OleDbCommand
OleDbDataAdapter
DataTable
BindingNavigator
DataGridView
OleDbCommandBuilder
```

New IDE facilities

The **Database Explorer** or the **Server Explorer** can be used to make a database known to the VB system. The **Data Sources** panel is used to allow a database to be used by a particular program.

Summary

- We have used the ADO.NET classes to access databases.
- A range of databases can be accessed, not only those created by Microsoft Access.
- The basic approach is to create and execute strings containing SQL statements.

EXERCISES

We have based these exercises on the **MusicSales.mdb** database, because you may not have facilities to create your own database. When you download it, we advise you to save a backup copy, in case you accidentally delete all the contents.

25.1 Write a program which allows the user to enter a company name, and which then displays the location of the company. Provide suitable error messages. Do not provide delete, insert and update facilities.

25.2 Write a program which displays the number of companies in the database.

25.3 Write a program which displays the highest sales figure, along with the name of the artist. (Reminder: SQL has an `order by` facility.)

25.4 Write a program which displays the **Artists** table in a data grid, in ascending order of sales.

25.5 Modify the SQL example program so that the insert operation first checks that the entered company exists in the **Companies** table. If it does not, ask the user if they wish to add a new company, and insert a new record into Companies if required.

ANSWERS TO SELF-TEST QUESTIONS

25.1 The coding for the button would be almost identical to the **Sales Above** button, but the SQL command can be simplified to:

```
command = "select * from Artists"
```

25.2 (a) The **Artist** field needs a value. In the program, any values in other text boxes are ignored. We could enforce this with an `If` as follows:

```
If ArtistBox.Text <> "" Then
    ...code to delete a record
End If
```

(b) All three text boxes need values.

Appendix A

Selected library components

This appendix lists selected VB library classes, with a summary of their important properties, methods and events. The chosen components are used throughout this book. They are presented in alphabetical order:

```
Button
Graphics
Label
List
ListBox
PictureBox
Random
TextBox
Timer
TrackBar
```

● Provided by all GUI classes

All GUI components (`Button`, `Label`, `ListBox`, `PictureBox`, `TextBox`, `TrackBar`) share some common properties as follows.

Properties

`Top`	*y*-coordinate of the top of the component.
`Left`	*x*-coordinate of the left-hand side of the component.
`Width`	Width of the component.
`Height`	Height of the component.

`Visible`	Whether the component is visible or not when the program is running. If `True`, the component is visible. If `False`, the component is invisible.
`Enabled`	Whether the component is available for use (`True`) or greyed out (`False`).

● Button

Properties

`Text`	The text displayed on the button.

Events

`Click`	Called when the user clicks on the button.

● Graphics

Constructor

Created from a picture box object using `CreateGraphics`. For example:

`Dim paper As Graphics = PictureBox1.CreateGraphics()`

Methods

`Clear`	Clear the graphics area and fill it with the colour provided as the parameter.
`DrawLine`	Draw a line. Parameters: `myPen As Pen, x, y, width, height`
`DrawEllipse`	Draw an ellipse. Parameters: `myPen As Pen, x, y, width, height`
`DrawImage`	Draw an image. Parameters: `myImage As Image, x, y, width, height`
`DrawRectangle`	Draw a rectangle. Parameters: `myPen As Pen, x, y, width, height`
`FillEllipse`	Draw a filled ellipse. Parameters: `myBrush As SolidBrush, x, y, width, height`
`FillRectangle`	Draw a filled rectangle. Parameters: `myBrush As SolidBrush, x, y, width, height`

● Label

Properties

Text	The text displayed in the label.
AutoSize	If `True`, the size is determined by the text being displayed. If `False`, the programmer can manipulate the size.

● List

Constructor

`List(Of ClassName)`	Creates a new array list. The class of the content is specified. For example: `Dim myList As List(Of Balloon) = New List(Of Balloon)`

Properties

Count	The number of items in the list.
Item	Get or set the element at the specified index.
()	Get or set the value at the specified index. For example: `Dim value As String = myList(3)`

Methods

Add	Add a new object to the list. The new item is added at the end of the list.
Clear	Remove all the elements from the list.
Contains	Returns `True` if the specified object is within the list, otherwise returns `False`.
IndexOf	Returns the index of the first occurrence of the specified object.
Insert	Insert a new object into the list at the index position specified. Any items are moved down to make space for the new item. Parameters: `index As Integer, newItem As ClassName`
RemoveAt	Return and remove the object at the specified index from the array list. Any remaining items are moved up to fill the gap created.
Remove	Remove the specified object from the list. If there is more than one occurrence, the first is removed.

ListBox

Properties

`SelectedIndex`	The index of the currently selected (highlighted) item in the list (or −1 if no item is currently selected).
`SelectedItem`	The string value of the item currently selected in the list box.
`Items`	A `List` object containing all the items in the list. See entry on `List` for available methods and properties.
`Sorted`	If `True`, ensures that the items in the list are automatically sorted and kept sorted even when new items are added.

Events

`Click`	Called when the user clicks on a list box item.
`DoubleClick`	Called when the user double-clicks on a list box item.

PictureBox

Properties

`Image`	The image in the picture box. Can either be set at design-time or at run-time using `FromFile`. For example: `PictureBox1.Image = Graphics.FromFile("fileName")` An image can be extracted from a picture box, then copied to another picture box or drawn within a `Graphics` area.

`MousePosition`	The current mouse coordinates. Example:
	`Dim x As Integer = PictureBox1.MousePosition.X`
	`Dim y As Integer = PictureBox1.MousePosition.Y`

Events

`Click`	Called when the user clicks on the picture.
`DoubleClick`	Called when the user double-clicks on the picture.
`MouseMove`	Called when the user moves the mouse.

Methods

`CreateGraphics`	Create a `Graphics` object.

Random

Constructor

Random
Example:
`Dim ran As Random = New Random()`

Methods

Next
Returns a random number in the range `lowValue` to `highValue` − 1. Parameters:
`lowValue As Integer, highValue As Integer`
The largest generated number will be `highValue - 1`

TextBox

Properties

Text	The text held in the text box.
Locked	Whether the text can be altered by the user.
MultiLine	Whether the box will accommodate more than one line.
ReadOnly	Whether the text box text can be changed by the user.
ScrollBars	Options for horizontal and vertical scroll bars.
BackColor	Colour of the background.
Font	Font style and size of the text.

Methods

AppendText
Append text at the end of the current text. Parameter:
`newText As String`

Clear
Empty the text box.

SetFocus
Move the cursor to the text box.

Timer

Properties

Enabled
Set to `True` to switch the timer on.

Interval
The frequency of `Tick` events in milliseconds (1/1000 seconds).

Events

Tick
Called when the timer ticks every `Interval` in milliseconds.

TrackBar

Properties

`Maximum`	Greatest value that the track bar can be set to by the user.
`Minimum`	Smallest value that the track bar can be set to by the user.
`Orientation`	Whether horizontal or vertical.
`Value`	Current value of the track bar.

Events

`Scroll`	Called when the track bar is moved.

Appendix B

Keywords

Certain words are already reserved by VB, so you can't use them for variable, class, method or property names.

AddHandler	AddressOf	Alias	And
AndAlso	As	Boolean	ByRef
Byte	ByVal	Call	Case
Catch	CBool	CByte	CChar
CDate	CDec	CDbl	Char
CInt	Class	CLng	CObj
Const	Continue	CSByte	CShort
CSng	CStr	CType	CUInt
CULng	CUShort	Date	Decimal
Declare	Default	Delegate	Dim
DirectCast	Do	Double	Each
Else	ElseIf	End	EndIf
Enum	Erase	Error	Event
Exit	False	Finally	For
Friend	Function	Get	GetType
Global	GoSub	GoTo	Handles
If	Implements	Imports	In
Inherits	Integer	Interface	Is
IsNot	Let	Lib	Like
Long	Loop	Me	Mod
Module	MustInherit	MustOverride	MyBase
MyClass	Namespace	Narrowing	New
Next	Not	Nothing	NotInheritable
NotOverridable	Object	Of	On
Operator	Option	Optional	Or
OrElse	Overloads	Overridable	Overrides
ParamArray	Partial	Private	Property
Protected	Public	RaiseEvent	ReadOnly
ReDim	REM	RemoveHandler	Resume
Return	SByte	Select	Set
Shadows	Shared	Short	Single
Static	Step	Stop	String
Structure	Sub	SyncLock	Then
Throw	To	True	Try
TryCast	TypeOf	Variant	Wend
UInteger	ULong	UShort	Using
When	While	Widening	With
WithEvents	WriteOnly		

Bibliography

This is intended for readers who want to follow up topics.

Refactoring, **Martin Fowler, Addison-Wesley, 1999.**
Chapter 20 on design mentions refactoring as a technique for rearranging the methods and properties in a design. This is the seminal book on refactoring. Better still it is easy to read. You can just dip into it to see useful techniques and insights.

Extreme Programming Explained 2nd Edn, **Kent Beck with Cynthia Andres, Addison-Wesley, 2005.**
In Chapter 22 on testing and in Chapter 20 on design, we explain briefly some approaches to program development. Lots of really good ideas about how to go about programming in a stress-free but effective way. Very readable.

UML Distilled 3nd Edn, **Martin Fowler with Kendall Scott, Addison-Wesley, 2004.**
UML is the mainstream notation for describing programs. We use the notation sparingly, as appropriate, throughout the book. One of the simpler books from the huge number of books on UML.

About Face 2.0, **Alan Cooper and Robert Reimann, Wiley, 2003.**
Alan Cooper is credited as the person who created the first Visual Basic system. This book contains his individual ideas on user interface design. Maybe it is not a book you would read from cover to cover, but his criticisms of some user interfaces and suggestions for better systems make illuminating reading. Unlike many of the user-interface textbooks, he focuses on Microsoft Windows systems.

Index

' (single-quote key) 36, 365
- (subtract) 45
(hash character) 208
& operator 48–50
* (multiply) 45
/ (division of doubles) 45
\ (division of integers) 45
^ (exponent) 45
{} (curly brackets) 234, 247, 266, 423
+ (add) 45
< (less than) 114, 142
< > (not equal to) 114, 142
<= (less than or equal to) 114, 142, 277
= (equals) 43, 114, 142, 277
> (greater than) 114, 142, 277
> (output redirection) 336
>= (greater than or equal to) 114, 142
» (append) 337
() (brackets) 45

abstract classes 200–1
  and polymorphism 397
abstract data type (ADT) 184, 185
abstraction in design process 343
accessibility 184
activity diagrams
  If statement 110–11
  If . . . Else statement 113
  For loop 139–40

  Select statement 123–4
  While loop 143
actual parameters 65
Add Connection 409, 413
Add method 224, 233, 423
ADO (ActiveX Data Objects) 406
ADO.NET classes 405, 406
alphabetical order of strings 276
And 115, 144
API (applications program interface) 406
AppendText method 425
arguments 30
  command-line in console programs 334–6
  and parameters 65–6
  passing 63–5
  passing by reference 77–8
arithmetic exceptions 164
arithmetic operators 45–7
array indices, errors in 164–5
array lists 223
arrays 237, 239–55
  constants, using 246–7
  creating 241
  indices 241–3
  initializing 247–8
  length 243–4
  lookup 250
  of objects 252–4
  passing as parameter 244–5

arrays (*continued*)
  ample program 248–9
  searching 250–2
  see also two-dimensional arrays
assignment statement 43
`AutoSize` property 423

`BackColor` property 17, 425
BASIC 1
batch files 336, 337–8
batch programming 329, 337–8
`BindingNavigator` class 408, 409–121
bitmaps 32
black box testing 378–80
blank lines 365
body of loop 137
`Boolean` 126–9
Boolean variables 126–9
breaking up long lines 19
breakpoints 159–60
bug 158
`Button` control 15–16
`ByRef` 65
`ByVal` 65

calculations 43–4, 206–18
  case studies 211–13
  constants 210
  exceptions 216–17
  graphs 213–16
  library functions and constants 209–10
  numbers, formatting 207–9
call 30
calling 63
case
  in command-line 331
  and program style 364
  in strings 277–8
`Case` 123
catching exceptions 297–9
`cd` command 332
`CDbl` 49, 54, 275
character 276
`CInt` 49, 52, 54, 275
clashes, name 70–1
`Class` 171, 186
class diagrams 169, 196, 204
  in object-oriented design 345–6, 349, 355, 356, 397

classes 183
  abstract 200–1
  in console programs 333–4
  designing 169–71
  in graphics 25–6
  large, in object-oriented design 359
  names, in object-oriented design 359
  size of 367
  and style 365, 367–8
  writing 168–87
class-level variables 92, 171
`Clear` method 234, 422, 423, 425
`Click` 422, 424
`Close` method 308
colours in graphics 32–3
command prompt 330–2
command-line arguments in console 334–6
comments
  adding 34–5
  and style 365–6
common errors 162–6
comparison operators 114
compilation 157–8
compilation errors 162–3
complex conditions 372–3
component 240
Component Tray 102
composition in object-oriented design 354–8
condition 129
conditions, complex 372–3
connection string 407
console programs 328–39
  batch files 337–8
  classes 333–4
  command prompt 330–2
  command-line arguments 334–6
  output redirection 336–7
  running programs 332–3
  scripting 329, 336–8
`Const` 210, 218
constants
  in arrays 246–7
  in calculations 210
  and style 366–7
  in two-dimensional arrays 265–6
constructor of form 93–5
constructor method 178
constructors 178
  and inheritance 198–9

Contains method 234, 423
control structures, combining 148–50
controls at design-time 13–14
conversions, errors in 163
converting between numbers 53–4
coordinate system for graphics 28–9
Count property 223, 224, 235, 423
CreateGraphics method 424
CreateText method 307
CStr 49, 52, 275

data connection, adding 408–9
data structures 222–38
  adding items 223–4
  arithmetic 229–30
  array lists 223
  indices 225–6
  inserting items 227
  list, length of 224
  lookup 227–8
  removing items 227
  searching 231–2
Database Explorer 409, 413
databases, elements of 403–5
DataGridView class 408, 411–14
DataTable class 407–8
debugger 159, 384
debugging 157–66, 384
  breakpoints in 159–60
  case study 161–2
  common errors 162–6
  compilation 157–8
  linking 158
  menu 161
  running 158–9
delayed binding 400
delete statement 406
design 169–71
  interfaces for 390–2
design-time, controls at 13–14
destruction of objects 181–2
development environment 7–22
DialogResult class 315, 317
dialogs 315–16
  file, using 316–18
Dim 42
dir command 331
Directory class 321–3, 325, 406
Display method 399

documentation 373–4
Do . . . Loop 145–6, 150, 151
Double 38, 39, 218
DoubleClick 424
double-quotes 49
DrawEllipse method 31, 422
DrawImage method 32, 422
DrawLine method 31, 422
DrawRectangle method 30, 31, 422
dynamic linking 400

E 210
editor facilities 18–19
element 240
ELIZA 285
Else 113, 124
ElseIf 118–22
Enabled property 422, 425
encapsulation 172
  polymorphism and 400
  and program style 368
End 63, 110, 118, 123, 142, 171, 175, 293, 329, 391, 392
EndOfStreamException class 296
EndsWith method 283
equivalence partitioning 378
Error List window 18
error notification 291
errors 18
  arithmetic exceptions 164
  array indices 164–5
  common 162–6
  compilation 162–3
  logic 165–6
  non-existent object, using 165–6
  run-time 163
event-handling methods 71
events 15–16
exception handling 300–1
exception object, using 295
exception throwing 299–300
exceptions 290–303
  arithmetic 164
  in calculations 216–17
  catcher, search for 297–9
  classifying 295–6
  definition 290
  and files 313–15
  jargon of 292

exceptions (*continued*)
    multiple `Catch` blocks 297
    in strings 275
    thrown and caught 292
    `Try-Catch` example 292–5
exhaustive testing 378
Explicit option 22, 158, 166
expressions, role of 54–5

`False` 126
field order 368
fields 404
`File` class 307
file storage devices 305
`FileName` property 317
`FileNotFoundException` class 296, 314
files 305–25
    `Directory` class 321–3
    and exceptions 313–15
    file dialogs 316–18
    input 308–10
    menus 318–21
    message boxes and dialogs 315–16
    output 307–8
    and program style 365
    searching 311–13
    streams 306–7
`FillEllipse` method 32, 422
`FillRectangle` method 31–2, 422
`Finally` 301
floating-point computing 38
`Font` property 425
`For` loop 137–40, 150, 151, 230–1, 237, 254, 255
`For Each` statement 230–1, 237, 245–6, 269
form 10, 11
form constructor 93–5
formal parameters 65
formal verification 384
`Format` method 208
`FormatException` 293, 294
formatting numbers 207–9
function methods 71–4, 85
functional testing 378–80

garbage collection 182
generics 232–3
`Get` 175, 187

`GetDirectories` method 323
`GetFiles` method 322–3
graphical user interfaces (GUIs) 13, 202, 390
    library components 421–6
graphics 25–36
    colours 32–3
    coordinate system 28–9
    drawing methods 30–2
    program, creating 27–8
    program explanation 29–30
`Graphics` class 29, 422
graphs 213–16

`Handles` 16
handling events 16
has-a relationship 354, 355, 358
`Height` property 421
help 21

IDE 7, 8
`If` statement 110–13
`If . . . Else` 112–13
`Image` 424
`Implements` 391–2, 394
imports 309
`Imports` 97–8, 105, 137, 232, 309
incremental development and testing 384–5
indentation 111
    and program style 365
indexing 225–6, 240
    strings 276
    in two-dimensional arrays 261, 263–4
`IndexOf` method 234, 280–1, 423
indices of arrays 241–3
    errors in 164–5
information hiding 172
inheritance 191–203
    and constructors 198–9
    in object-oriented design 354–8
    polymorphism and 400
    using 192–3
    workings of 197
`Inherits` 193, 203
`InitialDirectory` property 317
initializing data 94, 178, 247–8, 266–7
`InputBox` 53
`Insert` method 227, 234, 279, 406, 423

inspections in testing 383
instance of a class 184
instance variables 90–2, 171
integer 38
`Integer` 38, 39, 218
Integrated Development Environment (IDE) 7, 8
  debugger in 159
integration testing 377
`Interface` 391, 394
interfaces 390–4
  for design 390–2
  and interoperability 393
  limitations of 392
interoperability, interfaces and 393
`Interval` property 425
`IOException` class 296, 314
is-a relationship 354, 355, 358
`IsNumeric` function 281, 287
`Items` 223, 423
iteration 213

Kemeney, John 1
keywords 41, 427
Kurtz, Thomas 1

`Label` class 50
labels 50–2
`LastIndexof` method 282
late binding 400
layout and style 364–5
`Left` property 421
length
  of array 243–4
  of list 224
`Length` property 280, 287
library components 421–6
library functions and constants 209–10
linking 158
LISP 236
list boxes *see* lists and list boxes
`ListBox` class 424
lists and list boxes 223
  adding items 223–4
  arithmetic on 229–30
  generics 232–3
  inserting items into 227
  length of 224

  methods and properties 233–5, 423–4
  removing items 227
literals 207
local variables 40, 69
`Locked` property 425
logic errors 165–6
logical operators 115, 144
lookup
  in arrays 250
  in data structures 227–8
loops 136
  logical operators in 115, 144
  and program style 370–1

Mandelbrot Set 220–1
`Math` class 209
`Maximum` property 426
`Me` 81–2, 85, 187
menus, creating 318–21
message box 20, 315–16
`MessageBox` 20
methods 3–4, 15, 60–85
  and access to data 177
  building on 74–6
  calling 63
  event-handling 71
  first method 61–3
  function 71–4
  in graphics 25–6
  names, and program style 368
  names, in object-oriented design 359
  and new classes 194
  in object-oriented design 343–8
  passing arguments 63–5
  passing objects to 83
  private 179–80
  protected 193–4
  public 172
  `Shared` 182–3
  size of 367–8
  writing 61
Microsoft .NET 2
`Minimum` property 96, 426
Mod (modulo) 45
`Mod` operator 47–8
modal message box 316
module 329
module scope 92

`MouseMove` event 424
`MousePosition` property 424
`MultiLine` property 138, 425
multiple `Catch` blocks 297
multiple constructors 178–9
`MustInherit` 201, 203, 204, 394
`MustOverride` 201, 203, 394
`MyBase` 197, 203, 204

name clashes 70–1
names
    errors in 163
    and style 364–5
namespaces 97–8
nested `Ifs` and `ElseIfs` 118–22
    and program style 368–9
nesting
    `Ifs` and `ElseIfs` 118–22
    loops 146–8
    and style 368–71
`New` 26, 94, 105, 168, 185, 186, 187, 399
    in constructors 178
`NewLine` 137, 308, 324
`Next` method 101–2, 137, 425
non-existent object, using 165–6
`Not` 115–16, 144
`Nothing` 185, 187
`Nothing` keyword 310
nouns in object-oriented design 344
`NullReferenceException` 105
numbers
    converting between 53–4
    formatting 207–9

object-oriented design 342–60
    case study in design 348–53
    composition 354–8
    design problem 343
    guidelines for 358–9
    inheritance 354–8
    objects, methods, properties in 343–8
    reuse 353–4
object-oriented language xviii
object-oriented programming 183, 184
objects 4, 183
    arrays of 252–4
    destruction of 181–2
    in graphics 25–6

    lists of 235–6
    `Me` and 81–2
    in object-oriented design 343–8
    operations on 180–1
    passing to methods 83
    using 90–106
ODBC (Open Database Connectivity) 406
`OleDb` namespace 406
`OleDbCommandBuilder` class 407
`OleDbConnection` class 407
`OleDbDataAdapter` class 407
`OpenFileDialog` class 317
`OpenText` method 307
operators 43–4
Option Explicit 8, 158
Option Strict 8, 158
`Or` 115, 144
`Orientation` property 96, 426
output redirection 336–7
overflow 217
overloading 82–3, 195, 203
`Overridable` 192, 203
overriding 195–6, 203

parameters 30, 64
    and arguments 65–6
    passing arrays as 244–5
    passing two-dimensional arrays as 265
`Parse` method 293, 294
passing arguments 63–5
    by reference 77–8
passing objects to methods 83
`PI` 210
picture box 28
`PictureBox` class 424
pixels 28
polymorphism 396–401
    principles 400–1
    use of 397–400
`Preserve` 244, 264
primitive types 180
`Private` 92, 105, 171–2, 184, 186, 187, 204
private data in object-oriented design 358
private methods 179–80
private variables 171–2
program, defined 2–4
program text 15
programming language 3

project 9
  opening 17
properties 10, 13–14
  and access to data 174–7
  documenting settings 17–18
  in graphics 25–6
  as members of class 98
  names, and program style 368
  names, in object-oriented design 345
  and new classes 194
  in object-oriented design 343–8
  `Shared` 182–3
  of strings 277
`Property` 175, 186, 187
`Protected` 192, 193–4, 203, 204
`Public` 171, 172, 184, 186, 187, 204
public methods 172–3

RAM 305
`Random` class 99–102, 105, 425
`ReadLine` method 306, 310, 329, 338, 339
`ReadOnly` 176, 186, 187, 425
`ReadToEnd` method 310, 321
ready-made objects 4
records 404
`ReDim` 244, 264
refactoring 359
references 78–80
  passing arguments by 77–8
  `Swap` method 80–1
REM 365
`Remove` method 234, 279, 423
`RemoveAt` method 227, 234, 423
repetition 3, 136–52
`Return` 72, 85
reuse 201–2
  in object-oriented design 353–4
running 158–9
run-time 13
run-time errors 163

`SaveFileDialog` class 317
scope 69, 92
scope rules 184
scripting 329, 336–8
`Scroll` event 97, 426
`ScrollBars` property 425

searching
  arrays 250–2
  data structures 231–2
  files 311–13
`Select Case` 123
`Select` statement 122–5, 405
`SelectedIndex` property 225, 424
`SelectedIndexChanged` event 225, 424
`SelectedItem` property 424
selection 3, 109, 129
sequence 3, 34
`Set` 175, 187
`SetFocus` method 425
`Shared` methods and properties 182–3, 186, 187
`Show` 20
`ShowDialog` method 317
single inheritance 197, 203
single stepping 160–1
size
  of classes and methods 367–8
  of two-dimensional arrays 264
`Size` property 28
`Sorted` property 424
specification
  and program design 343
  and testing 377
`Split` method 281–2, 287, 311
SQL (Standard Query Language) 403, 405–6
  example program 414–18
`Sqrt` method 209
`Start` method 102
`StartsWith` method 282–3
stepping through code in testing 384
`Stop` method 102
`StreamReader` class 306–7
streams 306–7
`StreamWriter` class 306–7
Strict option 22, 158, 166
`String` class 277, 287
strings 48–50
  amending 277–9
  case study 285–7
  characters within 276
  comparing 276–7
  examining 279–83
  indexing 276
  manipulation of 274–88

strings (*continued*)
  methods and properties 277
  processing 283–5
  using 274–5
structural testing 381–2
style 363–74
  classes 367–8
  comments 365–6
  complex conditions 372–3
  constants 366–7
  documentation 373–4
  layout 364–5
  nesting 368–71
`Sub` 63, 85
subclass 193
subscript 240, 241
`SubString` method 280
superclass 193
  in object-oriented design 359
`Swap` method 80–1
system testing 377

`Tab` 137
tables 403–5
tabs 15
testing 158–9, 376–86
  exhaustive 378
  formal verification 384
  functional 378–80
  incremental development 384–5
  inspections 383
  program specification 377
  stepping through code 384
  structural 381–2
  walkthroughs 383
text boxes 50–2
`Text` property 15, 26, 50, 97, 422, 423, 425
`TextBox` class 50, 425
`Throw` statement 300
`Tick` event 425
`Tick` method 102
`Timer` class 102–4, 105, 425
`ToLower` method 277–8
toolbox 10
`Top` property 421
`ToUpper` method 278
`TrackBar` class 95–7, 105, 426
triangle method 66–9
`Trim` method 278–9

`True` 126
`Try-Catch` example 292–5, 302
two-dimensional arrays 261–70
  constants 265–6
  declaring 262
  indices 261, 263–4
  initializing 266–7
  passing as parameters 265
  size of 264

`UBound` 243, 264
Unified Modeling Language (UML) xix
unit testing 377
update statement 406
user interfaces 328

`Value` property 97, 426
variable names, errors in 163
variables 38–56
  arithmetic operators 45–7
  assignment 43
  Boolean 126–9
  declaring 40–3
  instance 90–2, 171
  local 40, 69
  `Mod` operator 47–8
  and new classes 194
  numbers 48–50
  private 171–2
  strings 48–50
VB code 15
verbs in object-oriented design 344
verification 376, 384
visibility 184
`Visible` property 126, 422
Visual Basic
  background to 1–5
  first program, creating 8–13
  installation and configuration 7–8

walkthroughs in testing 383
Watch window 160
Weizenbaum, Joseph 285
`While` loop 140–3, 150, 151, 311
white box testing 381–2
`Width` property 421
`Write` method 329, 339
`WriteLine` method 307, 308, 329, 339
`WriteOnly` 176, 186, 187

System Requirements:

Supported Architectures

- x86
- x64 (WOW)

Supported Operating Systems

- Windows XP Service Pack 2 or above
- Windows Server 2003 Service Pack 1 or above
- Windows Server 2003 R2 or above
- Windows Vista
- Windows Server 2008

Hardware Requirements

- Minimum: 1.6 GHz CPU, 192 MB RAM, 1024 × 768 display, 5400 RPM hard disk
- Recommended: 2.2 GHz or higher CPU, 384 MB or more RAM, 1280 × 1024 display, 7200 RPM or higher hard disk
- On Windows Vista: 2.4 GHz CPU, 768 MB RAM
- 1.3 GB of available disk space for the full installation

***Important note** Windows XP Home Edition is not supported for development of Web applications

This program was reproduced by Pearson Education under a special agreement with Microsoft Corporation. For this reason, Pearson Education is responsible for the product warranty. If your diskette is defective, please return it to Pearson Education who will arrange for its replacement. PLEASE DO NOT RETURN IT TO OR CONTACT MICROSOFT CORPORATION FOR SOFTWARE SUPPORT. This product is provided for free, and no support is provided by Pearson Education or Microsoft Corporation. To the extent of any inconsistencies between this statement and the end-user license agreement which accompanies the program, this statement shall govern.